REPRINTS OF ECONOMIC CLASSICS

A HISTORY OF THE
IRISH POOR LAW

Also Published In

REPRINTS OF ECONOMIC CLASSICS

By Sir George Nicholls

A HISTORY OF THE ENGLISH POOR LAW
3 VOLS., [1898]

A HISTORY OF THE SCOTCH POOR LAW [1856]

A
HISTORY

OF THE

IRISH POOR LAW

BY

SIR GEORGE NICHOLLS

[1856]

REPRINTS OF ECONOMIC CLASSICS

AUGUSTUS M. KELLEY · PUBLISHERS
NEW YORK · 1967

First Edition 1856

(London: John Murray, *Albemarle Street;*
Knight & Co., *90 Fleet Street*, 1856)

Reprinted 1967 by

AUGUSTUS M. KELLEY · PUBLISHERS

Library of Congress Catalogue Card Number

67 -28454

PRINTED IN THE UNITED STATES OF AMERICA
by SENTRY PRESS, NEW YORK, N. Y. 10019

A HISTORY

OF THE

IRISH POOR LAW,

IN CONNEXION WITH

THE CONDITION OF THE PEOPLE.

By SIR GEORGE NICHOLLS, K.C.B.,

LATE POOR LAW COMMISSIONER, AND SECRETARY TO THE POOR LAW BOARD.

"Let every man be occupied, and occupied in the highest employment of which his nature is capable, and die with the consciousness that he has done his best."—SYDNEY SMITH

LONDON:

JOHN MURRAY, ALBEMARLE STREET.

KNIGHT & Co., 90, FLEET STREET.

1856.

DEDICATION.

To the Ex-officio and Elected Members of the Boards of Guardians in Ireland, in the hope that it may be of use to them in the performance of their important Duties, this History of the Irish Poor Law is dedicated,

By their faithful servant,

THE AUTHOR.

November 1856.

PREFACE.

THE Irish Poor Law was in its origin no more than a branch or offshoot of the English law, but it is a measure of so much importance, and has so close a bearing upon the social well-being of the Irish people, that it seems to be entitled to a separate consideration. The severe trials moreover to which the law has been exposed, and the changes that have been made in its organization and executive, have given to it a new and distinctive character, on which account also a separate description of its progress and the incidents connected with it appears to be necessary. Hence therefore the intention which I at first entertained of combining the history of the Irish Poor Law with that of its English parent has been abandoned, and it is now published as a separate and independent work.

Notwithstanding the separate publication of the histories however, it must always be remembered that the English and the Irish laws are similar in principle, and identical in their objects. The end sought to be attained by each is, to relieve the community from the demoralization as well as from the danger consequent on the prevalence of extensive and unmitigated destitution, and to do this in such a way as shall have the least possible tendency to create the evil which it is sought to guard against. This is the legitimate object of a Poor Law, and the facts and reasonings on which such a law is founded, are not limited to Ireland or England or Scotland, but are in their nature

universal.   I hardly need say that this object is distinct
from charity, in the ordinary sense of the term, although
it is undoubtedly charity in its largest acceptation, embracing the whole community—It is in truth the charity
of the statesman and the philanthropist, seeking to secure
the largest amount of good for his fellow men, with
the smallest amount of accompanying evil.

The part that was assigned to me, first in the framing of the Irish Poor Law, and then in its introduction,
seems to render any apology for my undertaking to
write its history unnecessary.   Although failing health
and advancing years had compelled me to retire from
the public service, I thought that I might still be usefully
employed in recording the circumstances under which
the law was established, and the events attending its
administration ; and I am most thankful for having been
enabled to undertake the task, and for being permitted
to bring it to a conclusion.

It is true that for the last nine years I have not
been immediately connected with the Irish Poor Law,
but I have nevertheless continued to watch its progress
with the greatest solicitude, and have spared no pains
to obtain information as to its working.   I could indeed
hardly have failed to do this, after the part I had taken
in the framing of the measure, even without reference
to the heavy trials through which the Irish people have
passed, and which obtained for them universal sympathy and commiseration.   If such was the general
feeling with regard to Ireland in its season of trial, it
will readily be believed that mine could not have formed
an exception ; and in the authorship of the present
work, I may therefore I trust venture to claim credit,
not only on account of my connexion with the origin
and introduction of the law, but also for having attended to its subsequent progress, and acquired such a

knowledge of its operation and results as to warrant the undertaking.

A history of the Irish Poor Law, explaining its origin and the principles on which it was founded, together with an account of its progress and the effects of its application would, it might reasonably be supposed, afford information that must be generally useful—that it would be useful to the administrators of the law, can hardly admit of doubt. Such a history would place before them in a complete and regular series, all that it would be necessary for them to know, and all that ought to be borne in mind, in order that the examples of the past may prepare them for promptly dealing with the present, or for anticipating the future. The following work has been framed chiefly with this view; and I can only say that I have earnestly endeavoured to make it sufficient for the purpose, without any other wish or object than that it should prove useful in a cause to which during several years my best energies were devoted, and to the furtherance of which I could no longer contribute in any other way.

G. N.

November 1856.

CONTENTS

CHAPTER IV.

CHAPTER V.

CHAPTER VI.

HISTORY

OF

THE IRISH POOR LAW,

IN CONNEXION WITH

THE CONDITION OF THE PEOPLE.

CHAPTER I.

State of Ireland before the conquest — Its subjection by Henry II. — Spenser's
account of the state of the country — Plantation of Ulster — Progress of
population — Legislation previous to the accession of Anne — Dublin and
Cork Workhouse Acts — Hiring and wages — Apprenticeship — Provision
for foundling and deserted children — Licensed beggars — Arthur Young's
account of the state of Ireland.

AFTER Strongbow's expedition to Ireland in the year
1170, which was followed by that of Henry the Second
and the general submission of the chieftains of the several clans in 1172, the history of Ireland becomes closely
connected with and may be said to form a portion of
that of England. The accounts we have of the state of
the country anterior to Strongbow's invasion are vague
and uncertain, although there are grounds for believing
that some degree of civilization had prevailed, and that
intercourse with the East had been to some extent
maintained, at a very early period. It has been said
that "The Gauls or Celtes from the north-west parts of
Britain, and certain tribes from the north-west parts of
Spain peopled Ireland, either originally or by subduing
the Phœnician colonies which had been established
there;" and that the Irish, and their kinsmen the High-
landers of Scotland, are supposed to be "the remains of
a people who in ancient times had occupied not only

Britain, but a considerable part of Gaul and Spain." [a]
The Irish were no doubt commonly known by the
name of Scots, and the proximity of the two countries,
irrespective of all other considerations, renders the
identity of origin highly probable.

The Romans never extended their conquests to Ireland, and it was protected by its insular position from
the irruption of barbarians which burst upon the Roman
provinces in the fifth and sixth centuries, and caused
the dismemberment of the western empire. In that age,
we are told, " Irish missionaries taught the Anglo-
Saxons of the north, who also resorted to Ireland for
instruction." Lingard says that " when learning was
almost extinguished on the continent of Europe, a faint
light was emitted from the shores of Erin ; and that
strangers from Britain, from Gaul, and from Germany,
resorted to the Irish schools." It is probable however
that the light was partial as well as faint, and that the
Christian monasteries with their learned men which
constituted the " schools," existed in only a few places
in Ireland, each establishment forming as it were a
speck of civilization, like an oasis in the desert of barbarism. It is certain that the Irish of that day paid no
Peter's pence, and acknowledged no supremacy in the
see of Rome ; and there is reason to believe that the
Irish Church was derived rather from the Greek than
the Latin hierarchy. [b] Whatever glimmering of civilization prevailed in Ireland at this early period, must
have been damped and prevented from expanding " by

---

[a] See the 'Liber Munerum publicorum Hibernie,' the first and following
chapters on the Establishments of Ireland, supplementary to the History of
England, by Rowley Lascelles, of the Middle Temple, printed by authority in
1824. This work has been chiefly relied upon for historical reference. It bears
evidence of great research, and is on every account entitled to much weight in
the conflicting testimonies with regard to the early events of Irish history.

[b] See ' The Handbook of Architecture,' a recent publication in which the
ingenious author supports this conclusion by showing the similarity of the religious buildings erected in the East and in Ireland, which in both differ
materially from what is seen in Italy and the other countries of Europe.

the rude influence of the native institutions, and it was nearly if not quite extinguished by the irruptions of the Northmen, or Danes, who annually made incursions into Ireland from the middle of the eighth to the end of the tenth century." The ancient division of the country into the four provinces of Munster, Connaught, Leinster, and Ulster, which must be referred to this early period, seems to have been for ecclesiastical purposes. The division into counties, of which there are thirty-two, took place long after.

The Conqueror is said to have at one time entertained the project of bringing Ireland under subjection, but notwithstanding its proximity to England, and the obvious advantages that would result from uniting the two islands under one government, neither he nor his three immediate successors made any effort to accomplish this object. In the reign of Henry the Second however, a circumstance occurred which drew the attention of the English sovereign to the state of Ireland, and led to consequences most important to both countries. In the year 1169 Dermod, king of Leinster, who had been expelled by O'Connor, king of Connaught, sought the protection of Henry, who accepted the tendered allegiance, and permitted his subjects to assist the Irish chief. Earl Strigul (or Strongbow) took advantage of this permission, and in 1170 embarked for Ireland with a few armed retainers. He was followed two years afterwards by the king himself, with a considerable force. Henry was everywhere received as a conqueror, the Irish princes and chiefs submitting without opposition; and at a council assembled at Lismore, the laws of England are said to have been gratefully accepted by all, and established under the sanction of a solemn oath.

1172.
Subjection of Ireland by Henry II.

The chieftains who had however, so readily submitted to become Henry's vassals, as readily withdrew their allegiance on his quitting Ireland, which he was com-

pelled to do at the end of little more than six months,
in consequence of Becket's murder, and the rebellion of
his own sons.   Thenceforward for the long period of
400 years, the country was distracted by local dissensions and jealousies, and the conflicts of contending
chiefs.   Treachery and murder everywhere prevailed.
The sovereigns of England were too much occupied
with the crusades, and their French wars, to attend to
the state of Ireland; and although the English race
maintained itself in that country, it is said to have
become wilder and less civilized in each succeeding
generation.   " The first adventurers (we are told)
trampled down the original Irish; they were themselves
in their turn trampled down by the next adventurers;
these by subsequent ones; and so on in a continual
series, as if each race had forfeited all rights, or power
of acquiring and retaining any rights whatsoever, more
than a common robber or pirate."

Little was done towards establishing order and the
supremacy of law in Ireland, until Henry the Seventh,
after having put an end to civil strife in England, was
enabled to direct his attention to the state of that
country, where he was alike successful.   Henry the
Eighth assumed the title of king, instead of that of lord
of Ireland as used by his predecessors.   His efforts
to establish the Reformation in Ireland, were not so
successful as in England, where a great majority of the
nobility and the people were with him, but in Ireland
he had neither.   The power of the government moreover was there less, and might be opposed or disregarded with comparative impunity.   On the accession
of Mary in 1553, " so little had been done in advancing
the Reformation, that there was little to undo."   In
the reign of Elizabeth, however, the whole ecclesiastical
system was assimilated to that of England, and such
of the clergy as would not conform, were deprived of
their cures.   Throughout great part of Elizabeth's

reign, Ireland was kept in a state of disquiet by Spanish emissaries, the landing of Spanish troops, and the intrigues of Tyrone and other Irish chieftains; but the Spaniards were compelled to evacuate the country, Tyrone submitted, and before the close of her reign in 1603, peace had been everywhere restored.[c]

Our great poet Spenser has left us a description of the state of Ireland in the latter part of Elizabeth's reign. Both he and his friend Raleigh had obtained grants of land there, and Spenser had resided in Ireland for several years, and thus acquired a knowledge of the country, which he describes with all the fancy of a poet and the fervour of a patriot—" and sure (he says) it is a most beautiful and sweet country as any under heaven, being stored thro'out with many goodly rivers, replenished with all sorts of fish most abundantly, sprinkled with many very sweet islands and goodly lakes, like little inland seas, that will carry even shippes upon their waters; adorned with goodly woods even fit for building houses and ships, so commodiously, as that if some princes in the world had them, they would soon hope to be lords of all the seas, and ere long of all the world; also full of very good ports and havens opening upon England, as inviting us to come unto them, to see what excellent commodities that country can afford, besides the soyle itself most fertile, fit to yield all kinds of fruit that shall be committed thereunto. And lastly, the heavens most mild and temperate, though somewhat more moist in the parts towards the west."

After thus eulogising the country as most sweet and beautiful, Spenser describes the habits of the people, in less favourable colours certainly, but no doubt with equal truth—

" All the Irish almost (he says) boast themselves to

*1596.
Spenser's account of the state of Ireland.*

---

[c] In ten years Ireland is said to have cost Elizabeth the immense sum of 3,400,000*l.* See 'History of the English Poor Law,' vol. i. p. 205.

be gentlemen, no less than the Welsh; for if he can derive himself from the head of any sept (as most of them can, they are so expert by their bardes) then he holdeth himself a gentleman, and thereupon scorneth to worke, or use any hard labour, which he saith is the life of a peasant or churl; but henceforth becometh either an horseboy or a stocah (attendant) to some kerne, inuring himself to his weapon, and to the gentlemanly trade of stealing, as they count it. So that if a gentleman, or any wealthy man yeoman of them, have any children, the eldest of them perhaps shall be kept in some order, but all the rest shall shift for themselves and fall to this occupation. And moreover it is a common use among some of their gentlemen's sonnes, that so soon as they are able to use their weapons, they straight gather to themselves three or four straglers, or kearnes, with whom wandering up and down idly the country, taking only meate, he at last falleth unto some bad occasion that shall be offered, which being once made known, he is thenceforth counted a man of worth, in whom there is courage; whereupon there draw to him many other like loose young men, which stirring him up with encouragement, provoke him shortly to flat rebellion; and this happens not only sometimes in the sonnes of their gentlemen, but also of their noblemen, specially of them who have base sonnes; for they are not only not ashamed to acknowledge them, but also boast of them, and use them for such secret services as they themselves will not be seen in, as to plague their enemies, to spoil their neighbours, to oppress and crush some of their own too stubborn freeholders, which are not tractable to their wills."

Having thus given a general description of the country and the people, Spenser next adverts to circumstances connected with the landlord and tenant classes in particular, to the first of which classes it will be remembered he himself belonged—

" There is (he says) one general inconvenience which reigneth almost thro'out Ireland : that is, the lords of land and freeholders, doe not there use to set out their land in farme, or for terme of years, to their tenants, but only from year to year, and some during pleasure ; neither indeed will the Irish tenant or husbandman otherwise take his land than so long as he list himself. The reason hereof in the tenant is, for that the landlords there use most shamefully to racke their tenants, laying upon them coigny and livery at pleasure, and exacting of them (besides his covenants) what he pleaseth. So that the poor husbandman either dare not binde himself to him for longer terme, or thinketh by his continual liberty of change, to keep his landlord the rather in awe from wronging of him "—" The evils which cometh hereby are great, for by this means both the landlord thinketh that he hath his tenant more at command, to follow him into what action soever he shall enter, and also the tenant being left at his liberty, is fit for every occasion of change that shall be offered by time, and so much the more ready and willing is he to runne into the same, for that he hath no such state in any his houlding, no such building upon any farme, no such coste employed in fencing or husbanding the same, as might withhold him from any such wilfull course as his lord's cause, or his own lewde disposition may carry him unto "—" and this inconvenience may be reason enough to ground any ordinance for the good of the common wealth, against the private behoof or will of any landlord that shall refuse to graunt any such terme of estate unto his tenant, as may tende to the good of the whole realme."

It appears that Tipperary was at that time distinguished from the other counties, being the only county palatine in Ireland ; and of it and its peculiar privileges, and the consequences to which these gave rise, Spenser thus complains—" A county palatine is, in effect, to have a privilege to spoyle the enemy's borders adjoining. And surely so it is used at this day, as a privilege place of spoiles and stealthes; for the county of Tipperary, which is now the only county palatine in Ireland, is, by abuse of some bad ones, made a receptacle to rob the rest of the counties about it, by means of whose privileges none will follow their stealthes; so as it being situate in the very lap of all the land, is made now a border, which how inconvenient it is, let every man judge."

Spenser also describes several measures which he considered necessary for the repression of disorder and the protection of life and property. In this "enumeration of needful points to be attended to for the good of the common wealth," he first wishes "that order were taken for the cutting and opening of all places through woods, so that a wide way of the space of 100 yards might be laid open in every of them for the safety of travellers, which use often in such perilous places to be robbed and sometimes murdered. Next that bridges were built upon the rivers, and all the fords marred and spilt, so as none might pass any other way but by those bridges, and every bridge to have a gate and a gatehouse set thereon, whereof this good will come, that no night stealthes, which are commonly driven in by-ways, and by blind fordes unused of any but such like, shall not be conveyed out of one country into another, as they use, but they must pass by those bridges, where they may be easily tracked, or not suffered to pass. Also that in all straights and narrow passages, as between two boggs, or through any deep ford, or under any mountain side, there should be some little fortilage set, which should keep and command that straight. Moreover that all highways should be fenced and shut up on both sides, having only forty feet for passage, so as none shall be able to pass but through the highways, whereby thieves and night robbers might be more easily pursued and encountered where there shall be no other way to drive their stolen cattle. And further, that there shall be in sundry convenient places by the highways, towns appointed to be built, the which should be free burgesses and incorporate under bailiffs, to be by their inhabitants well and strongly intrenched, or otherwise fenced, with gates on each side to be shut nightly, like as there is in many places in the English pale, and all the ways about it to be strongly shut up, so as none should pass but through the towne ; and to some it were good that the privilege of a market were given, for there is nothing that doth sooner cause civility in any country than many market townes, by reason that people repairing often thither for their needs, will daily see and learn civil manners of the better sort." [d]

These extracts throw much light upon the social condition of Ireland at that time, and no apology can be necessary for giving them insertion here. It is impossible to doubt the writer's sincerity, or the truthfulness of his descriptions ; and it is no small advantage to have such a testimony to the state of things then existing in Ireland, which may be regarded as a kind of standard or starting-point for future comparison.

Shortly after Elizabeth's death, and the accession of James the First, an insurrection again broke out in the north of Ireland. It was soon put down however, but it led to upwards of 500,000 acres of land being escheated to the crown. This vast tract, situated in the six northern counties, on which, we are told, " only robbers and rebels had found shelter," now afforded James The plantation the opportunity for carrying into effect his of Ulster. favourite scheme of a plantation in Ireland. The natives were removed to other localities, and settlers from

---

[d] See Spenser's View of the State of Ireland, written in 1596, vol. viii. of his works, printed in octavo in 1805.

England and Scotland introduced; and thus Ulster shortly became the most civilized and best cultivated of the four provinces, instead of being the most wild and disorderly, as had previously been the case.

In the contest between Charles the First and the parliament, the Roman Catholics of Ireland adhered to the cause of the king; but their adherence to that cause was accompanied by the treacherous massacre of the Protestant settlers in 1641—an atrocity that gave rise to the bitterest feelings throughout England, and eventually led to the exacting of a stern and ruthless retribution. In 1649, six months after the death of Charles, Cromwell proceeded to Ireland, taking with him a considerable body of his disciplined veterans. He landed at Dublin in August, and shortly afterwards Drogheda and Wexford were stormed with great slaughter, upon which Cork, Kinsale, and other towns opened their gates; and in ten months the entire country was brought under subjection, with the exception of Limerick and Waterford, the reduction of which Cromwell left to his son-in-law Ireton, and re-embarked for England where his presence had become necessary. If Cromwell had remained longer in Ireland, it is probable that he would with his usual vigour have crushed the seeds of many existing evils, and laid the foundation for future quiet; but this was not permitted, and the elements of disorder remained, repressed and weakened it is true, but still ready to burst forth whenever circumstances should give vent to the explosion.

At the Revolution in 1688, when England adopted William the Third, the Irish Roman Catholics adhered to James; and it was not until after the battle of the Boyne, and the surrender of Limerick, that Ireland can be said to have been again entirely subject to the English crown. During the insurrections which took place in favour of the exiled family in 1715 and 1745, Ireland remained quiet. But in 1798 the triumph of democracy in France, together with the active interference of French agents, and the promises of assistance held out by them, led to the outbreak of a rebellion, in the progress of which great enormities were perpetrated; and which was not put down until after a great loss of life, and the destruction of much property. Although doubtless to be lamented on these accounts, the rebellion of 1798 was not however without its use, for it showed in the strongest light the defects of the existing system in Ireland, and thus helped to establish the legislative union of the two countries, which took place at the commencement of the present century, when the whole of the British islands were included under the designation of " *The United Kingdom of Great Britain and Ireland.*" Since the passing of the Act of Union in 1800, there is nothing distinctive requiring to be noticed with regard to Ireland, its interests being thenceforward merged in the general interests of the empire.

The following summary of the estimated population of Ireland at several periods is abstracted from the memoir of Mr. Shaw Mason, the officer appointed under the Act for taking the census of Ireland in 1821, as the same is given in the Appendix to Selections from the Lords' Journals, by Mr. Rowley Lascelles— *Progress of population in Ireland.*

1672 as estimated by Sir William Petty	1,320,000
1695 „ by Captain South (doubtful)	1,034,102
1712 „ by Thomas Dobbs Esq., founded on returns of the hearth-money collectors	2,099,094
1718 „ .. .. .: do.	2,169,048
1725 „ .. .. .. do.	2,317,374
1726 „ .. .. .. do.	2,309,106
1731 „ by the magistrates and clergy ..	2,010,221
1754 „ by returns from the hearth-money collectors	2,372,634
1767 „ .. .. .. do.	2,544,276
1777 „ .. .. .. do.	2,690,556
1785 „ .. .. .. do.	2,845,932
1788 „ by Gervais Parker Bushe Esq., one of the commissioners of revenue	4,040,000

1791	as estimated by returns from the hearth-money collectors		4,206,612
1792	„	by the Rev. Dr. Beaufort	4,088,226
1805	„	by Major Thomas Newenham	5,395,456
1813	„	founded on the incomplete census under the Act of 1812	5,395,856
1821	ascertained by the census of 1821		6,801,827
e 1831	do.	1831	7,767,401
e 1841	do.	1841	8,175,124
e 1851	do.	1851	6,522,386

With reference to the above summary, it may be remarked that a rapid increase in the population of a country, cannot always be taken as a proof of the increase of wealth and civilization, or of improvement in the social condition of the people. It is possible indeed that it may be productive of results the very reverse in these respects, when the increase unduly presses upon or outruns the ordinary means of subsistence, as it sometimes undoubtedly did in certain parts of Ireland. But on the whole, and making every allowance for adverse circumstances, the above table affords grounds for concluding, that subsequently to 1672, the productive powers of the country were receiving continually increased development, to meet the wants of a continually increasing population. Or we might perhaps go further back, and date the increase from the time when Cromwell, with a strong hand, enforced order and established the ascendancy of the law in Ireland. The decrease in the population which took place between 1841 and 1851, when the number was forced back below what it had been thirty years preceding, indicates a period of great trial and suffering. In the latter portion of this period, the country was assailed by famine and pestilence — a fearful visitation which will be noticed hereafter in its order of date, and of which it would be out of place to say more at present.

Until a comparatively recent period, there was no law

---

e These are taken from the census returns of the respective periods.

directly providing for the relief of the Irish poor. In this respect the legislation of Ireland differed from that of England and Scotland, in both of which countries we have seen that such a provision was early made. The difference in this respect, was probably at first owing to the disturbed and unsettled state of Ireland; and afterwards, when it was brought more thoroughly under subjection, the difference of race and religion with other unfavourable circumstances, united to prevent the growth of that orderly gradation of classes, and that sympathy between one class and another, which exist in every well-conditioned community, and of which a poor-law is a natural development.

Although there was no direct provision for the relief of the poor in Ireland, several Acts of the Irish parliament were more or less subsidiary to that object, whilst others were calculated to illustrate the progress of civilization, and the general condition of the country. Various institutions of a charitable character were likewise established; and it will be necessary to notice certain of these matters, before entering upon a consideration of the important measure of 1838. The legislative enactments have precedence in order of time, and to these we will now in the first instance direct our attention.[f]

As early as 1310, in the reign of Edward the Second, we find that in a parliament assembled at Kilkenny "it was agreed that none should keep idle people or kearn in time of peace, to live upon the poor of the country; but those which will have them shall keep them at their own charges, so that the free tenants and farmers be not charged with them." And 130 years afterwards, in the reign of Henry the Sixth, among the ordinances established by a parliament holden in Dublin, it was declared—" that

1310.
Edward II.

1440.
Henry VI.

---

[f] The citations hereafter made, are taken from ' The Statutes at Large, passed in the Parliament held in Ireland'—published by authority in thirteen volumes folio, in 1786.

divers of the English do maintain and succour sundry
thieves robbers and rebels, because that the same thieves
robbers and rebels do put them into their safeguard and
comrick, so that the king's faithful subjects dare not
pursue their right against such thieves robbers and
rebels, for fear of them which have taken them into
their safeguard and comrick "—wherefore it is ordained,
that such as do put themselves, and such as do grant
such safeguard and comrick, be adjudged traitors, and
suffer accordingly. And in the same reign, at
a certain great council held in Dublin (1450) it
was declared—" that thieves and evildoers increase in
great store, and from day to day do increase in malice
more than they have done heretofore, and do destroy
the commons with their thefts stealings and manslaught-
ers, and also do cause the land to fall into decay and
poverty and waste every day more and more "—wherefore it is ordained that it shall be lawful for every liege
man to kill or take notorious thieves, and thieves found
robbing spoiling or breaking houses—" and that every
man that kills or takes any such thieves, shall have one
penny of every plough and one farthing of every cottage
within the barony where the manslaughter is done, for
every thief."

1450.
Henry VI.

These enactments show that the state of the country
within the English pale, or that portion of it which was
subject to English rule, was then very similar to what
existed at the same periods in England and Scotland,
more prone to violence and disorder perhaps, and therefore somewhat more backward in civilization; but all
the leading characteristics are nearly identical. Beyond
the pale however a far worse state of things prevailed.
There violence and disorder ranged without control.
" The Irishry," as they were called, were continually
engaged in battleings and feuds among themselves, one
chief or one sept against another, or in making inroads
and committing robberies and murders within the pale,

which again led to retaliations; and thus a species of
domestic or border warfare alike injurious to all parties,
and a state of ferment and insecurity throughout the
country, were kept up and perpetuated.

A parliament held at Trim in 1447, laments—" that
the sons of husbandmen and labourers, which   1447.
in old time were wont to be labourers and   Henry VI.
travaylers upon the ground, as to hold ploughs, to ere
the ground, and travayl with all other instruments
belonging to husbandry, to manure the ground, and do
all other works lawful and honest according to their
state—and now they will be kearnes, evildoers, wasters,
idle men, and destructioners of the king's leige people"
—wherefore it is ordained that the sons of labourers and
travaillers of the ground, shall use the same labours and
travails that their fathers have done.   And ten   1457.
years afterwards, at a parliament held at Naas,   Henry VI.
it was ordained—" forasmuch as the sons of many men
from day to day do rob spoil and coygnye the king's
poor liege people, and masterfully take their goods
without any pity—that every man shall answer for
the offence and ill doing of his son, as he himself that
did the trespass and offence ought to do, saving the
punishment of death, which shall incur to the trespasser
himself." This last enactment, making the father
answerable for the acts of his son, was perhaps under
the circumstances of the period calculated to check
violence and disorder and may be so far regarded as
defensible.   But the same cannot be said of the former
enactment requiring the son to follow the same occupation as the father.   Yet such has been the practice
throughout a great part of Asia from the earliest period.
In the present instance, the enforcement of the practice
by special enactment, seems to imply that the demand
for agricultural labour was increasing in Ireland, either
through an increase of land under cultivation, or an
increased amount of labour applied to it; and either the

one or the other must be considered as indicative of improvement.

In the reign of Edward the Fourth (1465) an Act was passed ordaining and establishing " that in every English town of this land [g] that pass three houses holden by tenants, where no other president is, there be chosen by his neighbours or by the lord of the said town, one constable to be president and governor of the same town, in all things that pertaineth to the common rule thereof"—doubtless a useful provision, and calculated to aid the cause of order and good government. In the same reign, at a parliament held at Naas, (1472) it is recorded—" For that there is so great lack of money in this land, and also the grain are enhanced to a great price because of great lading from day to day used and continued within this realm, by the which great dearth is like to be of graines, without some remedy be ordeyned"—whereupon the premises considered it is enacted—" that no person or persons lade no grain out of the said land to no other parts without, if one peck of the said grains exceed the price of ten pence, upon pain of forfeiture of the said grain or the value thereof, and also the ship in which the said grains are laden."

1465. Edward IV.

1472. Edward IV.

The prohibition of export has always been clamoured for, and often resorted to whenever the price of corn becomes high, whether it be in Ireland, England, or elsewhere ; and this always moreover on the ground here set forth, that is, for the sake of the poor classes, or " for that there is so great lack of money in this land." All such prohibitions are however based on erroneous views of economical policy. By prohibiting export cultivation is discouraged, and so in the long run corn is made dearer rather than cheaper. It may moreover be remarked, that if grain be exported, it will be for the

---

[g] That is every town within the English pale.

purpose of obtaining a higher price than can be obtained at home, and the exporting country will thus be better enabled to go to another market for a supply, and will have the benefit of whatever profit may arise in the double interchange. With respect to grain therefore, as with respect to all other commodities, the true principle is that of non-interference—they will then each and all find their own level, and that in the way most beneficial to all parties interested, whether as producers or consumers, whether those who want or those who have to spare. But this great truth was not recognised at that day. Neither is it indeed universally so at present; for at this time (the end of 1855) there are clamourings for a prohibition of the export of corn, on account of the present high price.[h]

We are now arrived at the reign of Henry the Seventh, by whom order was established in Ireland, as it previously had been established in England. The first important measure towards the accomplishment of this object was the passing of Poynings' Act,[i] 10*th* *Henry* 7*th, cap.* 4, which directs that no parliament shall be holden in Ireland, until the Acts be first certified into England, and be thence returned with sanction of the king and council expressed under the great seal. This secured a harmony of action between the legislatures of the two countries, and was otherwise beneficial. But there were two other Acts passed in the same year, not less important for the peace and good government of the country than the preceding, and therefore requiring to be separately noticed.

1495.
Poynings'
Act.'
10 Hen. VII.
cap. 4.

---

[h] The average price of wheat in Mark-lane for the week ending on the 10th of November, was 83s. 8d. per qr. For the week ending on Nov. 15, 1851 the price per quarter was 36s. 4d.; and for the week ending Nov. 13, 1852 the price per quarter was 39s. 11d.

[i] So called after Sir Edward Poynings, who was lord deputy in Ireland during a great part of Henry's reign, and in the earlier part of that of his successor. The lord deputy is described as " the active scourge of all insurgents," and it was latterly said of him that " he might call all Ireland his own." See Liber Munerum, book ii. cap. 1. Mr. Lascelles gives 1494 as the year in which this Act was passed. In the Statutes at Large it bears the date of 1495.

The first of these Acts, *cap.* 6, directs that no citizen shall receive livery or wages of any lord or gentleman; and it further enacts " That no lord nor gentleman of the land shall retain by livery, wages, or promise, sign or token, by indenture, or otherwise, any person or persons, but only such as be, or shall be his officers, as baylifs, steward, learned counsel, receivors, and menial servants daily in household at the said lord's cost." And if any lord or gentleman retain any person contrary to this Act, both the retainer and he that is retained are to forfeit to the king twenty pounds of lawful money for every such offence.

1495.
10 Hen. VII.
cap. 6.

10 Hen. VII.
cap. 17.

The second Act, *cap.* 17, directs " that no peace nor war be made with any man without licence of the governor." It recites—" Forasmuch as diverse lords and great gentlemen of Ireland, useth daily to make several peace with the king's Irish enemies, and where the peace hath been taken and concluded by the lieutenants and their deputies for the time being with the aforesaid enemies, and for the universal weal of our said sovereign lord's true subjects, the said lords and gentlemen for singular lucor and for malice, have diverse and many seasons and without any authority of the lieutenant or deputy, entered into the countries of such Irish enemies as have standen under the protection of our sovereign lord, and the same countries have robbed, spoiled, hurt and destroyed, by reason whereof the said enemies have likewise entered into the English country, and the true English subjects have robbed, spoiled and brent in semblable wise"—wherefore it is ordained, that thenceforward " there be no peace nor war taken or had within the land, without the lieutenant or deputy's licence;" and whatsoever persons break the said peace, or rob or spoil contrary to this Act, as often as they so offend are to forfeit 100*l.* to the king, and be committed to ward until the same is paid.

We see from the above, that the Irish beyond the

pale were still regarded as enemies ; and to prevent as
far as possible the barbarous conflicts that were continually taking place between them and the people
within the pale, was doubtless one reason for passing
these Acts. But independently of this object, the general
policy of the two measures is abundantly obvious. They
amount, taken together, to no more than extending to
Ireland the principle observed by Henry in his government of England, namely, that of reducing the exorbitant power assumed by the great nobility and gentry,
and making them amenable to the general law, a thing
no less necessary in one country than in the other,
although widely differing in so many respects.

On the accession of Henry the Eighth, Irish legislation became more active, but we shall only
notice a few of the Acts. *The* 13*th Henry* 8*th*,
cap. 1, declares, that " many ill-disposed persons for
malice, evil will, and displeasure, do daily burn corn,
as well in ricks in the fields, as in villages and towns,
thinking that it is no felony, and that they should not
suffer death for so doing"—wherefore it is enacted, that
all wilful burning of ricks of corn in fields and in
towns, and burning of houses of and upon any of the
king's true subjects, be high treason, and that execution
be awarded against such evil-doers accordingly. Twelve
years afterwards another Act (the 25th Henry
8th, cap. 1) was passed against lezers of corn.
It recites—" That whereas many inconveniences within
this land ensueth by reason that many and diverse persons, labourers strong of body, as well men as women,
falleth to idleness, and will not labour for their living,
but have their sole respect to gathering and lezing of
corn in harvest-time, and refuse to take money for their
wages to rippe or binde corn, to the intent that the
poor earth-tillers should give them sheaves of corn for
their labour, by colour whereof they steal men's cornes,
as well by night as by day, to the great hindrance and

impoverishing of the poor earth-tillers; and also by
giving of said sheafes, the church is defrauded of the
tythe of the same."—Wherefore it is ordained, that
henceforth no persons " being strong of body to labour
for their living, shall gather or leze in any place in
harvest-time, except it be in their own fields; and that
no impotent persons gather or leze in any other place,
saving in the parish where their dwelling is; and that
no man give nor take any corn in harvest for ripping
nor binding," under penalty of the same being taken
from him and forfeited.

These Acts for the protection of the corn-grower
against waste in time of harvest, and against incen-
diarism when the corn is in the rick, are indications of
the advance of agriculture in Ireland. The titheowner
may have had some influence in the passing of the
latter Act; but taking the two together, it seems impossible to doubt that the occupation of the " poor
earth-tillers," as they are termed, was considered to be
important with regard to the general welfare, and
therefore deserving of special protection.

Three years after the last preceding Act, another was
1537.
28 Hen. VIII. passed (*The* 28*th Henry* 8*th, cap.* 15) in which
cap. 15. it is declared that the king, considering that
" there is nothing which doth more conteyne and keep
many of his subjects of this his land in a certain savage
and wilde kind and manner of living, than the diver-
sitie that is betwixt them in tongue, language, order
and habite, which by the eye deceiveth the multitude,
and persuadeth them that they should be as it were of
sundry sorts, or rather of sundry countries, where indeed they be wholly together one body "—wherefore it
is enacted, that no person shall wear hair on the head
or face nor any manner of clothing, mantle, coat, or
hood, after the Irish fashion, but in all things shall
conform to the habits and manners of the civil people
within the English pale. And it is further enacted,

that all persons of whatsoever degree or condition
" to the uttermost of their power cunning and knowledge shall use and speak commonly the English
tongue," and cause their children to do the same, " and
shall use and keep their houses and households as
near as ever they can, according to the English order."
Spiritual promotion is moreover directed to be given
only to such as can speak English; so that nothing
appears to have been omitted for bringing about the
desired assimilation of the native Irish with their
fellow-subjects of the English race.   Subsequent events
showed however that these efforts were not crowned with
success, and a long period elapsed before the Irish of the
western districts can be said to have at all assimilated to
English habits, or become amenable to English rule.

The regulation of wages by legislative enactment so
frequently adopted in England,[k] was likewise
attempted in Ireland, but apparently with no
better result; for we find *The 33rd Henry 8th, cap.* 9,
complaining, that " forasmuch as prices of victuals,
cloth, and other necessaries for labourers, servants at
husbandry, and artificers, yearly change, as well sometimes by reason of dearth and scarceness of corn and
victual as otherwise, so that hard it is to limit in certain
what wages servants at husbandry should take by the
year, and other artificers and labourers by the day, by
reason whereof they now ask and take unreasonable
wages within the land of Ireland"—wherefore it is
enacted that the justices of peace at a sessions to be
held yearly within a month after Easter and Michaelmas, " shall make proclamation by their discretion,
having respect to such prices as victuals cloth and
other necessaries then shall be at, how much every
mason, carpenter, sclantor, and every other artificer and
labourer shall take by the day, as well in harvest-season
as any other time of the year, with meat and drink,

margin: 1542.
33 Hen. VIII.
cap. 9.

---

[k] See ' History of the English Poor Law,' vol. i. pages 100 and 110.   11*th
Henry 7th, cap.* 2, and *6th Henry 8th, cap.* 3.

and how much without meat and drink, between both
the said seasons; and also at the Easter sessions, how
much every servant at husbandry shall take by the
year following, with meat and drink; and that every
of them shall obey such proclamation from time to
time, as a thing made by Act of parliament for a law
in that behalf," on pain of imprisonment.   By thus
empowering justices to vary the rate of wages according to the variations in the price of provisions and
clothing, the objection which exists to a permanent fixed
rate is no doubt so far obviated; but the great primary
objection to any interference with the natural range of
prices, and to subjecting them to other control than
that of supply and demand still remains, and is not
susceptible of any defence.   Thus much on the score of
principle.   But the passing of such a measure as the
above, is nevertheless a proof of the increasing demand
for labour, and of the advance of regular industrial
employment, which is always an important step in the
progress of civilization.

The last enactment of the present reign requiring to
be noticed, in connexion with our subject, is
The 33rd Henry 8th, cap. 15, entitled ' An Act
for Vagabonds.'   It recites—" forasmuch as at a parliament holden at London, it was enacted and ordeyned
how aged poor and impotent persons compelled to live
by alms should be ordered, and how vagabonds and
mighty strong beggars should be punished, which
Act (*22nd Henry 8th, cap.* 12) for divers causes, is
thought very meet and necessary to be enacted in
this land "—wherefore it is ordained and established,
" That the same Act, and all and every article provision and thing comprised in the same, be an Act and
statute to be continued and kept as a law within this
land of Ireland, according to the tenor and purport of
the same."   The English Act (*22nd Henry 8th, cap.* 12)
is then given at length, and stands in the statutes as
an Act of the Irish parliament, and is to be obeyed

1537.
33 Hen. VIII.
cap. 15.

accordingly. A full account of this statute will be
found in the ' History of the English Poor Law ' (vol.
i. page 115) to which the reader is referred. Whether
the Act was entirely suited to the backward state of
Ireland at that time, may admit of doubt; but there
can be no doubt that if enforced it was calculated to
bring about a better order of things by repressing
vagabondism, and making some provision for the relief
of the destitute. We have no means of knowing to
what extent the Act was enforced, or whether it was
enforced at all. It could hardly have been brought
into operation beyond the English pale, and even
within the pale the arm of the law was then feeble,
and its action uncertain ; so it is probable that like
many other measures intended for the benefit of Ireland, the present Act was permitted to lie dormant. It
remained in force however, as one of the Irish statutes,
until 1772, when it was repealed by the 11*th* and 12*th*
George 3*rd, cap.* 30.[1]

There are only two of the Acts passed by the Irish
parliament in Elizabeth's reign calling for   1569.
notice, and this rather as exhibiting the con-   11 Elizabeth, cap. 4.
dition of the country at that time, than as directly connected with our subject. The first of these is *The* 11*th*
Elizabeth, cap. 4, entitled ' An Act that five persons
of the best and eldest of every nation amongst the
Irishrie, shall bring in all the idle persons of their surname, to be justified by law.' It declares that her
Majesty's " most humble and obedient subjects have been
these many years past grieved with a generation of
vile and base conditioned people (bred and maintained
by coynie and liveries), the ancient enemies to the
prosperity of this realm, of which sort the lords and
captains of this land hath to raise and stirr up some to
be maintained as outlaws to annoy each other's rules,

----

[1] See post, p. 51.

and so serving the iniquitie of the time, hath not only
in attending those practices imbased their own particular estates, but also brought the whole public wealth of
their supposed rules to ruin and utter decay." For
remedy whereof, it is now ordained, " that five persons
of the best and eldest of everie stirpe or nation of the
Irishrie, and in the countries that be not as yet shire
grounds, and till they be shire ground, shall be bound
to bring in to be justified by law, all idle persons of
their surname which shall be hereafter charged with
any offence, or else satisfie of their own proper goods
the hurts by them committed to the parties grieved,
and also such fines as shall be assessed upon them for
their offences." The Act we see applies to parts of
the country beyond the pale, " which be not yet shire
grounds," where " the lords and captains of the land "
were in the habit of maintaining a number of base-con-
ditioned people in a state of outlawry to annoy each
other's rules, which practice it is said hath not only
injured their own estates, but also brought the whole
country under their supposed rule to ruin and utter
decay. The remedy for these evils now sought to be
applied, is by making five of the principal people of
each sept or nation of the " Irishrie " answerable for
the rest of the clan, and it seems likely that nothing
better could have been devised under the circumstances ; but the resorting to it is nevertheless an
indication of the lawlessness and insecurity which prevailed, and how imperfectly the country had yet been
brought under subjection.

The other Irish Act of Elizabeth's reign requiring
notice, is *The 12th Elizabeth, cap.* 1, entitled
'An Act for the erection of Free Schools.'
It commences by reciting—" Forasmuch as the greatest
number of the people of this realm hath of long time lived
in rude and barbarous states, not understanding that
Almighty God hath by his divine laws forbidden the

1570.
12 Elizabeth,
cap. 1.

manifold and heinous offences which they spare not daily and hourly to commit and perpetrate, nor that He hath by His Holy Scriptures commanded a due and humble obedience from the people to their princes and rulers, whose ignorance in these so high points touching their damnation proceedeth only of lack of good bringing up of the youth of this realm, either in public or private schools, where through good discipline they might be taught to avoid those loathsome and horrible errours " —Wherefore it is enacted that there shall be a free school established in every diocess of Ireland, and that the schoolmaster shall be an Englishman, " or of the English birth of this realm." The archbishops of Armagh and Dublin, and the bishops of Meath and Kildare and their successors, are to appoint the schoolmasters within their respective dioceses, and the lord deputy for the time being is to have the appointment in the other dioceses. The schoolhouses are to be built in the principal shire towns, at the cost and charge of the whole diocess, under direction of the ordinary, the vicars general, and the sheriff; and the lord deputy for the time being is " according to the quality and quantities of every diocess," to appoint a yearly salary for every schoolmaster, whereof the ordinary of every diocess is to bear the third part, and the parsons, vicars, prebendaries, and other ecclesiastical persons of the diocess, by an equal contribution, are to bear the other two parts. The whole charge of these free schools was therefore, we see, to be borne by the clergy, on whom their superintendence also devolved.

The Reformation had at this time been established in Ireland, and the clergy whom the state recognised were necessarily all Protestant. The desire for extending education as a means for improving and enlighten-- ing the people, was therefore to be expected from them; and it is not improbable this desire was accompanied, and perhaps strengthened, by a belief that education

would bring about the conversion of such of the people
as were not yet of their flock, but still adhered to the
church of Rome. That such were the motives of the
Protestant clergy in the prominent part taken by them
with regard to these free schools, and that the government and the proprietary classes generally were influenced by similar motives, can hardly admit of doubt.
The result turned out different however from what was
anticipated. The great bulk of the people remained in
ignorance, and devotedly attached to the old religion,
as it was and still is called; and thus a separation
sprung up between one class and another, between the
more English and Protestant class, and the more Irish
and Romanist class, which has been a fruitful source of
evil to each, and in spite of the countervailing efforts
which have of late years been made, can hardly be said
to have altogether disappeared even at the present
day. How strange it seems that religion, which ought,
and we must believe was designed to be, a bond of concord and union, should be perverted into an occasion for
hatred and strife!—Yet so it unhappily too often has
been, and in no country perhaps more than in Ireland.

　　Little was done in the way of legislation during the
reign of James the First, and only one of
the Acts of the Irish parliament in his reign
requires to be noticed, namely *The 11th and
12th James 1st, cap.* 5.—It is entitled ' An Act of
Repeal of divers Statutes concerning the natives of this
kingdom of Ireland.' The preamble declares, that
" in former times the natives of this realm of Irish
blood, were for the most part in continual hostility
with the English and with those that did descend of
the English, and therefore the said Irish were held and
accounted, and in divers statutes and records were
termed and called Irish enemies." But—" Forasmuch
as the cause of the said difference and of making the
said laws doth now cease, in that all the natives and

1612.
11 and 12
James I.
cap. 5.

inhabitants of this kingdom, without difference and distinction, are taken under his Majesty's gracious protection, and do now live under one law as dutiful subjects, by means whereof a perfect agreement is and ought to be settled betwixt them "—Wherefore it is enacted, " that all the said Acts and statutes, and every clause and sentence in them conteyned, shall for ever be utterly and thoroughly repealed, frustrated, annihilated, and made void to all intents and purposes." The passing of this Act manifests a change in public feeling, and was certainly a step in the right direction. To treat a people as enemies, is the sure way to make them such ; and that the native Irish had long been so treated, the records of the antecedent period abundantly prove. The present was therefore a healing measure. By abolishing the distinction of race, and bringing all alike under protection of the law, the Act was no doubt intended to pave the way for an entire amalgamation of the two people. National distinctions and national grievances are however not easily obliterated or forgotten ; time, intercourse, and the mutual interchange of good offices being necessary for effecting the one, or blotting out the remembrance of the other. And even after this has been accomplished, and a kind of oblivion of the past established, ancient feuds are too apt to be revived by the occurrence of some circumstance, trivial perhaps in itself, and race to be again put at enmity with race, class to be arrayed against class, and sect against sect. The history of Ireland abounds in examples of such revival of enmities, promoting discord and disorder, retarding improvement, and exercising a baneful influence on the character as well as on the condition of the people.

The Irish parliament was somewhat more active in the reign of Charles the First, than it had been in that of his predecessor, and four of its Acts, all passed in the same year, we will now

1634-5.
10 and 11
Charles 1.
cap. 4.

proceed to notice, the first of these being—*The* 10*th and* 11*th Charles* 1*st, cap.* 4—entitled ' An Act for the erecting of Houses of Correction, and for the punishment of Rogues Vagabonds sturdy Beggars and other lewd and idle persons'—For which purpose it is enacted, that before Michaelmas in the following year " there shall be built or otherwise provided within every county of Ireland, one or more fit and convenient house or houses of correction, with convenient backside thereunto adjoining, together with mills, working-cards, and other necessary implements, to set the said rogues and other idle and disordered persons on work; the same houses to be built or provided in some convenient place or town in every county, which houses shall be purchased conveyed or assured unto such person or persons as by the justices of peace, or the most part of them shall be thought fit, upon trust, to the intent the same shall be used and employed for the keeping correcting and setting to work of the said rogues, vagabonds, sturdy beggars, and other idle and disorderly persons." The justices are empowered to make orders from time to time, for raising money upon the inhabitants of the county for providing the said houses, and for the government and ordering thereof, and for setting to work such persons as shall be committed to the same; and also for the yearly payment of the governor and such others as they shall think necessary to be employed therein. The justices are moreover to appoint honest and fit persons to be governors of such houses,—which governors " shall have power and authority to set such rogues vagabonds idle and disorderly persons as shall be sent to the said houses, to work and labour (being able) for such time as they shall there continue, and to punish the said rogues &c. by putting fetters or gyves upon them, and by moderate whipping." And it is further ordered, that the said rogues and vagabonds during the time they remain in

such house of correction, " shall in no sort be chargeable to the country for any allowance, either at their
bringing in or going forth, or during the time of their
abode there, but shall have such and so much allowance
as they shall deserve by their own labour and work."

The justices at their quarter session of the peace are
required to assign to the governors of the said houses
a fitting salary, to be paid quarterly in advance by the
treasurer of the county, which if the treasurer neglect
to pay, the governor is empowered to levy upon him
by distress of his goods. And in order that more care
may be taken by the governors of such houses of correction, " when the country hath been at trouble and
charge to bring all such disorderly persons to their safe
keeping," it is directed that they shall at every quarter
session yield a true account to the justices of all persons
committed to their custody ; and if any of such persons
" shall be troublesome to the country by going abroad,
or otherwise shall escape away from the said house of
correction before they shall be from thence lawfully
delivered, the justices may impose such fines and
penalties upon the said governor as they shall think
fit." The justices are to meet at least twice a year for
the better execution of this statute, and are by warrant
to command the constables of every barony, town,
parish, village and hamlet within the county ("who
shall be assisted with sufficient men of the same places ")
to make a general privy search in one night for finding out and apprehending all rogues, vagabonds, wandering and idle persons, who are to be brought before
the justices to be examined of their wandering idle life,
and punished accordingly, or otherwise sent to the
house of correction and there set to labour and work.

And that there may be no doubt as to who are liable
to punishment under these provisions, it is enacted—
" that all persons calling themselves scholars going
about begging ; all idle persons going about in any

country either begging or using any subtle craft, or
Who are to be deemed rogues, vaga-bonds, and sturdy beggars. unlawful games or plays, or feigning themselves to have knowledge in physiognomy
palmistry or other like crafty science, or
pretending that they can tell destinies, for-
tunes, or such other like phantastical imaginations;
all persons that be or utter themselves to be proctors,
procurers, patent gatherers, or collectors for gaols
prisons or hospitals; all fencers, bear-wards, common
players of interludes and minstrels wandering abroad;
all jugglers, wandering persons, and common labourers being able in body, using loytering, and refusing
to work for such reasonable wages as is taxed and
commonly given, and not having living otherwise
to maintain themselves; all persons delivered out of
gaols that beg for their fees, or otherwise travaile
begging; all such as wander abroad, pretending loss
by fire or otherwise; all such as wandering pretend
themselves to be Egyptians, or wander in the habit
form or attire of counterfeit Egyptians—shall be taken
adjudged and deemed rogues vagabonds and sturdy
beggars, and shall sustain such punishments as are
appointed by the 33*rd Henry* 8*th, cap.* 15,[m] or be otherwise dealt withall by sending them to the house of correction in the county where they shall be found, as to
the justices shall be thought fit."

It appears moreover that many wilful people having
children, and being able to labour for the maintenance
of themselves and their families, " do nevertheless run
away out of their parishes, and leave their families upon
the parish"—Wherefore it is enacted that all such persons so running away, shall be taken and deemed to be
incorrigible rogues, and suffer accordingly — " and if
either such man or woman, being able to work, shall
threaten to run away and leave their families as afore-

---

[m] *Ante*, p. 22.

said, the same being proved by two sufficient witnesses
upon oath before two justices of peace, the person so
threatening shall by the said justices be sent to the
house of correction, there to be dealt with as a sturdy
and wandering rogue, unless he or she can put in sufficient sureties for the discharge of the parish." This
enactment, and the recital by which it is introduced and
justified, might be taken for a part of our late English
poor-law system, so exactly does it accord with what
was frequently practised in English parishes. Yet nothing like settlement, or a right to relief, or any organization for providing or affording relief, existed in Ireland. The great principle of parochial chargeability
for relief of the destitute embodied in the 43rd *of Elizabeth*, seems nevertheless to have been in some degree
recognised, and was probably to some extent operative
in Ireland, although without legal sanction ; for unless
such were the case, persons running away could not be
said to leave their families a charge upon the parish,
neither perhaps would their threatening to run away
be so stringently dealt with as we here find it to be.

The provisions of this Act are no doubt important,
and the Act itself taken as a whole, throws considerable
light upon the condition of Ireland at that time, and
shows that the state of society there was gradually approximating to that which prevailed in England. The
persons subjected to punishment as rogues and vagabonds, are identical with those described in the English
Act 22nd *Henry* 8*th, cap.* 12.[n] The provisions with respect to houses of correction, are similar to those directed
by the English Acts 18*th Elizabeth, cap.* 3,[n] and the 7*th
James* 1*st, cap.* 4 ;[n] and the privy search ordered to be
made for apprehending vagrants &c. is the same as in
the Act of James.[n] With such a similarity of enactments therefore, we can hardly doubt that there was a

---

[n] See ' History of the English Poor Law,' vol. i. pp. 115, 171, 233 and 234.

general similarity in the circumstances of the two countries, although those parts of Ireland which were latest brought under subjection, may still have been in a rude and backward state, as indeed it is known that they then were, and for a long time afterwards continued to be.

In proof of the backwardness of at least some parts of Ireland at that time, two Acts passed in the same year as the foregoing may be cited. The first is, *The 10th and 11th Charles 1st, cap. 15,* entitled ' An Act against ploughing by the Tail and pulling the Wool off living Sheep.' It declares that " in many places of this kingdom there hath been a long time used a barbarous custom of ploughing, harrowing, drawing and working with horses, mares, geldings, garrans, and colts, by the tail, whereby (besides the cruelty used to the beasts) the breed of horses is much impaired in this kingdom, to the great prejudice thereof; and also, that divers have and yet do use the like barbarous custom, of pulling off the wool yearly from living sheep ° instead of clipping or shearing of them " —Wherefore all such barbarities are prohibited, and it is enacted that whomsoever shall so act in either case in future, or procure the same to be done, shall be subject to fine and imprisonment. The other Act is the *10th and 11th Charles 1st, cap.* 17, entitled ' An Act to prevent the unprofitable custom of burning Corn in the Straw.' It recites—" Whereas there is in the remote parts of this kingdom of Ireland commonly a great dearth of cattle yearly, which for the most part happeneth by reason of the ill husbandrie and improvident care of the owners, that neither provide fodder nor stover for them in winter, nor houses to put them in extremitie of stormy cold weather, but a

1634–5.
10 and 11
Charles I.
cap. 15.

1634–5.
10 and 11
Charles I.
cap. 17.

° A parallel to the " pulling off the wool from living sheep," may even now be witnessed all over the west of Ireland, in the plucking off the feathers from the living geese, a process that must be attended with great pain, and under the cruel infliction of which many of the poor geese perish.

natural lazie disposition possessing them, will not build
barnes to house and thresh their corn in, nor houses to
keep their cattle from the violence of such weather ; but
the better to enable them to be flitting from their lands,
and to deceive his Majesty of such debts as they may be
owing, and their landlords of their rents, do for a great
part instead of threshing, burn their corn in the straw,
thereby consuming the straw which might relieve their
cattle in winter, and afford materials towards covering
or thatching their houses, and spoiling the corn, making
it black, loathsome and filthy "—for prevention of which
unprofitable and uncivil customs it is ordained, that no
person shall " by himself, wife, children, servants, or
tenants," burn or cause to be burned any corn or grain
in the straw, on pain of being imprisoned ten days for
the first offence, for the second offence one month, and
for the third offence to pay a fine of forty shillings and
be bound to good behaviour.

These Acts certainly indicate the existence of very
rude and barbarous practices in some parts of Ireland
— so rude indeed, that one finds some difficulty in
giving credence to them ; but that they did prevail,
there can be no reasonable doubt. To plough by the
tail, to strip the wool off sheep, and to burn corn in the
straw, are doubtless all indications of a lamentable state
of backwardness and barbarism ; but how far this backwardness was owing to " a natural lazie disposition " in
the Irish tenantry, or whether it was the " better to
enable them to be flitting from their lands to deceive
their landlords of their rents," as asserted above, or
occasioned by the oppressive conduct of the landlords,
as described by Spenser,[p] it is impossible to say with
certainty. Most likely all these causes were in operation, together with a general feeling of insecurity, a

[p] See ante, p. 7.

backward state of civilization, and a feeble and uncertain administration of the law.

Another cause of backwardness and disorder is indicated by the ' Act for the suppressing of Cosherers and idle Wanderers.' This Act (*the 10th and 11th Charles 1st, cap.* 16) commences with the following recital—" Whereas there are many young gentlemen of this kingdom that have little or nothing to live on of their own, and will not apply themselves to labour or other honest industrious courses to support themselves, but do live idly and inordinately, coshering upon the country, and sessing themselves their followers their horses and their greyhounds upon the poor inhabitants, sometimes exacting money from them to spare them and their tenants, and to go elsewhere to their eaught and edraugh, viz. supper and breakfast, and sometimes craving helps from them ; all which the poor people dare not deny them, sometimes for shame, but most commonly for fear of mischief to be done them so refusing, and therefore do bear it although unwillingly, and many times when they are scarce able so to do, and yet dare not complain for fear of the inconveniences aforesaid, and to that end do make cuts levies and plotments upon themselves to pay them, and give such entertainment and helps to the utter impoverishing and disabling of the poor inhabitants to pay their duties to the king, and their rents unto their landlords ; and by that lawless kind of life of these idle gentlemen and others, being commonly active young men, and such as seek to have many followers and dependants upon them, many other inconveniences are likely to arise, for they are apt upon the least occasion of disturbance or insurrection, to rifle and make booty of his Majesty's loyal subjects, and to be heads and leaders of outlaws and rebels, and in the mean time do and must sometimes support their excessive and expenceful drinking and gaming by secret stealths, or growing into debts often-

1634–5.
10 and 11
Charles I.
cap. 16.

times filch and stand upon their keeping, and are not
amenable to law "—wherefore for prevention of such
inconveniences it is enacted, that if any person or persons shall directly or indirectly follow any of the above
practices in future, the justices of assize are to cause
them to be apprehended and bound to good behaviour,
and imprisoned until good sureties for the same be
given.   These " cosherers " are apparently the same
class of persons described by Spenser as infesting the
country half a century before,[q] too proud to beg, too
idle to labour, and for the most part living by the
plunder and intimidation of the poor tenantry.   There
could hardly have been a greater obstruction to improvement, or a more certain incentive to violence and
disorder, than the conduct of these " cosherers and idle
wanderers" as above described.   They must have been
in every way a curse to the country, stirring up and
perpetuating whatever was pernicious oppressive and
demoralizing, and subverting whatever had a contrary
tendency.

We have now approached the period of what is
emphatically called " the great Rebellion," which was
followed by the Commonwealth, the Protectorate, and
the Restoration; and then, after an interval, by the
Revolution of 1688, which led to the establishment of
constitutional monarchy.   But in none of these periods,
although all highly interesting and important in an
historical point of view, do we find anything in Irish
legislation so immediately bearing upon our present
subject, as to call for citation or remark.

The first enactment in the order of time which it is
necessary to notice, is *The 2nd Anne, cap.* 19,
entitled—' An Act for erecting a Workhouse
in the city of Dublin, for employing and maintaining the poor thereof.'   The preamble declares, that

1703.
2 Anne,
cap. 19.
The Dublin
workhouse.

---

[q] Ante, p. 6.

" the necessities number and continual increase of the
poor within the city of Dublin and liberties thereto adjoining, are very great and exceeding burdensome for
want of workhouses to set them at work, and a sufficient
authority to compel them thereto : and whereas the
lord mayor, sheriffs, commons and citizens of Dublin
for the encouragement of so charitable and necessary a
work, are willing not only to appropriate a piece of
ground for a workhouse within the said city, but also
to endow the same with lands of inheritance of the
value of one hundred pounds per annum"—It is enacted,
that from and immediately after the 1st of May 1704,
there shall be a corporation to continue for ever within
the county of the city of Dublin, to be entitled the
governors and guardians of the poor, and to consist of
the chief governor (or lord lieutenant) the lord mayor,
the lord chancellor, the archbishop of Dublin, the
sheriffs, the justices of peace, the members of the corporation, and a great many others specially named, who
are to have perpetual succession, with all the usual
powers and privileges of a corporation. They are to
assemble on the first Thursday in every month, " for
relieving, regulating, and setting at work, all vagabonds and beggars which shall come within the city or
liberties," and are to provide such necessaries and
material as are needful for the same. They are likewise
empowered to apprehend all idle or poor people begging
or seeking relief, or who receive parish alms within the
city or liberties; and also to detain and keep in the
service of the said corporation until the age of sixteen,
any poor child or children found or taken up within
the said city or liberties above five years of age, and to
apprentice out such children to any honest persons,
being protestants, a male child until the age of twenty-
four, and a female child until the age of twenty-one.
The governors and directors are moreover empowered
to inflict reasonable punishment or correction, from

time to time, on all persons within the workhouse who shall not conform to the established regulations; and are to have the care of the poor of the said city and liberties of what age or kind soever they be, infants under the age of five years only excepted ; and in order thereto, are empowered " to examine, search, and see what poor persons are come into, inhabiting, or residing within the said city and liberties, or any part thereof, and to apprehend any idle vagrants and beggars, and to cause them to be set and kept at work in the said workhouse, for any time not exceeding seven years."

For the encouragement of such as shall become bene-factors to the foregoing " good design," it is enacted that a donor of fifty pounds and upwards shall be eligible for the office of governor and guardian ; and power is also given for granting licences for the keeping of hackney coaches not exceeding 150 in number, and for sedan-chairs not exceeding 80 in number, to ply for hire within the city and liberties, every licence so granted being charged with the sum of 5l., to be paid to the governors and guardians of the poor by way of fine, and forty shillings annually afterwards, so long as the said licence shall be continued. It is further enacted for the support of the poor in the said work-house, that a rate of 3d. in the pound be charged on every house within the city and liberties, to be levied in the same way as ministers' money ; but in case any surplus should remain after defraying the necessary charges of the workhouse, and the poor maintained and employed therein, a proportional abatement is to be made in this tax upon houses.

The above is the substance of this important Act, important, that is, as being the first in which a direct provision is made for the relief of poverty in Ireland. The Act is local, it is true, its operation being limited to the city and liberties of Dublin ; but it recognises the principle of taxing the public for the prevention of

vagrancy and begging, conjointly with the alternative
of relieving the destitute—a principle universal in itself,
and susceptible of universal application.   The endeavour
to effect these objects through the agency of workhouses, was very generally resorted to in England
about this time.   They had been recommended by Sir
Matthew Hale, and also by Mr. Locke in his Report on
the state of the poor, and the Bristol, Worcester, and
other workhouses were established with a like intent,[r]
although the employment of the inmates with a view
to profit, was no doubt at the same time regarded as a
collateral advantage.   The direction that the poor
children " found or taken up" should be apprenticed to
" honest persons being protestants," seems, as in the
case of the free schools already noticed,[s] to indicate a
desire in the framers of the measure to make it sub-
servient to the spread of the reformed religion ; but at
that time the property, and nearly all the industrious
occupations of the country were in the hands of protestants, so that with them alone was there likely to
be an eligible opportunity for apprenticing out the
children.   The direction to do so was therefore superfluous, but it indicates the dominant feeling of the
time.   The corporation was reconstituted and its powers
extended by *the 1st George 2nd, cap.* 27, in 1728, and
ultimately the workhouse became merged in the Dublin
Foundling Hospital ; but as it will hereafter be necessary
to revert to this point we need not dwell on it at present.

The Act passed in 1635, 'for the suppression of
cosherers and idle wanderers,' has already been
noticed.[t]   In 1707 another was passed (*the 6th
Anne, cap.* 11,) explaining and amending the former,
and entitled ' An Act for the more effectual suppressing
tories robbers and rapparees, and for preventing persons

1707.
6 Anne,
cap. 11.

---

[r] See ' History of the English Poor Law,' vol. i. pp. 302, 372, 373 and 385.
[s] Ante, p. 24.   [t] Ante, p. 34.

becoming tories or resorting to them.' It directs—
" that all loose idle vagrants, and such as pretend to be
Irish gentlemen, and will not work nor betake themselves to any honest trade or livelihood, but wander
about demanding victuals and coshering from house to
house among their fosterers followers and others, and
also loose persons of infamous lives and characters, upon
presentments of the grand juries at assizes and general
quarter sessions, and upon warrant of the justices, shall
be imprisoned until sent on board the fleet, or transported to some of her Majesties plantations in America,
whither the justices are empowered to send them, unless
sufficient security for their good behaviour be given.
Many persons are moreover said to make a trade of
obtaining robbery money from the country, pretending
to have been robbed, " whereas they never were robbed,
or were not robbed of near the value they allege, and
so get money on that account which they never lost"
—Wherefore it is directed that all persons pretending
to be robbed, shall not only give notice thereof to some
neighbouring justice, but likewise to the high constable,
who is forthwith to publish the same in all the market
towns of the barony.

There appears to have been another species of fraud
in connexion with this "robbery money," for "Robbery
the principal inhabitants, when applotments money."
were made for reimbursing the persons that had been
robbed, do it is said, " usually lay the whole burthen on
the poorer sort, that are least able to bear it, or least able
to resist or pursue the tories, and thereby they pay
little or nothing themselves, who ought to be charged
according to their abilities"—Wherefore the parties
aggrieved are authorised to appeal to the judges of
assize, who are empowered to examine into the case
upon oath, and to determine the same. We thus see
how apt a law, however good in itself, is to be perverted·
to a bad purpose. The making the county answerable

for reimbursing a person who had been plundered,
would seem calculated to array all the inhabitants on
the side of honesty and good order; but without preventing robbery, the law in this case appears to have
given rise to a fraudulent trafficking in " robbery
money," and to gross injustice in other respects. There
is no other Act of the Irish parliament in Anne's reign
requiring to be noticed, but there is one in that of her
successor which must not be passed over.

The 2nd George 1st, cap. 17, may be called a multitu-
dinous Act, as it comprises a great variety of
enactments, but such parts only will be noticed
as bear upon our subject. It is entitled 'An Act to
empower justices to determine disputes about servants'
wages &c.' and it recites—" Whereas several persons
do refuse or neglect to pay the wages due to servants,
artificers, and day labourers, and there being no remedy
whereby they can in a summary way, without much
charge or delay recover what is due for their service"
—it is therefore enacted for the more easy recovery of
the same, that any neighbouring justice of the peace
or chief magistrate may receive the complaint of any
such servant upon oath, and may summon the master or
mistress and determine the demand, which if not paid
within ten days as so determined, may be levied by
distress. " And forasmuch as several servants are
drunkards, idle or otherwise disorderly in their services,
or waste and purloin their master's goods, or lend the
same without their master's or mistress's consent or
knowledge, or depart their service within the time for
which they had obliged themselves to serve," it is
further enacted, that on complaint upon oath of any
master or mistress to such effect before any justice of
peace or chief magistrate, they are to hear and determine the same, and if the offence be duly proved, may
commit the offender for six hours to the stocks, or to
the house of correction with hard labour for any time

1715.
2 George I.
cap. 17.

not exceeding ten days. It is also enacted, that on the discharge or quitting service of any servant, the master or mistress shall give a certificate in writing to that effect, " and shall in the said discharge certify, if desired, or if the master or mistress shall think fit, the behaviour of such servant;" and no servant is in future to be hired without producing such discharge or certificate of character. These enactments appear alike calculated to benefit the master and the servant class, and if fairly administered could hardly fail of so doing. They show moreover that social organization in Ireland had attained a more stable and orderly form, that its gradations were more distinctly marked and better understood, and that the duties of each were more clearly defined. We no longer see any allusion to the " Irishry" as a separate race. All are brought within the pale of the law, or it may rather be said that the law and the pale have become conterminous.

By the 11*th section* of the Act provision is made for apprenticing helpless children. It commences with this preamble—" and whereas there are in almost every part of this kingdom great numbers of helpless children who are forced to beg their bread, and who will in all likelihood, if some proper care be not taken of their education, become hereafter not only unprofitable but dangerous to their country ; and whereas it is hoped that many of them may be entertained in comfortable services, and others may be bound out to and bred up in useful callings, if well-disposed persons could have any fair prospect of receiving hereafter by the labour of such poor children, any return suitable to the trouble and charges they must necessarily undergo in bringing them through that state of childhood"—Wherefore it is enacted, that the minister and churchwardens shall have power, with consent of a justice of peace, to bind out any child they find begging within their parish, or any other poor child with consent of the parents, to any honest and

11th section. Apprenticing of helpless children.

substantial protestant housekeeper or tradesman that
will entertain such child, until the age of 21, if as a
menial servant, or till the age of 24, if as an apprentice
to a trade. And to prevent abuse of power in masters
and mistresses towards such servants and apprentices,
it is further enacted that justices of peace may, on
complaint of ill usage or cruel treatment examine into
the case, and if the complaint appear groundless, may
order reasonable correction for the servant or apprentice complaining without cause ; but if immoderate
severity or cruel usage be fully proved against the
master or mistress, the justice is empowered to discharge
the servant or apprentice from their service, and to bind
him or her to some other master or mistress for the
remainder of the time. We here see that the power of
apprenticing out poor children conferred upon the
Dublin corporation of governors and guardians of the
poor,[u] is now extended to the minister and churchwardens of every parish in Ireland, accompanied by a
like condition as to the master's being a protestant. In
this respect only is there any material difference
between the present enactment, and *The 39th Elizabeth,
cap. 3,*[x] with regard to apprenticing poor children,
although better provision is now made for protecting
them against improper treatment subsequently.

In 1735 an Act was passed for establishing a workhouse at Cork, similar in its main provisions
to that which was passed for Dublin in 1703.[u]
The present Act (*The 9th George 2nd, cap.* 25) however
makes provision for rebuilding the cathedral church of
St. Finbarry, as well as "for erecting a workhouse in
the city of Cork for employing and maintaining the
poor, punishing vagabonds, and providing for and edu-
cating foundling children." With respect to the former
of these provisions, it is only necessary to remark, that
the money authorised to be raised by a coal-tax, was

1735.
9 George II.
cap. 25.

---

[u] Ante, p. 35.
[x] See 'History of the English Poor Law,' vol. i. p. 183.

directed to be applied during the first four years to the purposes of the cathedral; and we may therefore abstain from further noticing that point, and proceed at once to a consideration of the other provisions of the Act.

The 9*th George* 2*nd, cap.* 25, has the same preamble as the Dublin Act. It constitutes the bishop of Cork, and the mayor, recorder, aldermen, sheriffs, common councilmen, the common speaker, together with twenty-six other persons who are to be elected annually, a corporation and body politic, entitled the " Governors of the Workhouse of the City of Cork." They are to have a common seal, with all the usual powers, and may purchase and take for the uses of the corporation any lands or other hereditaments not exceeding the annual value of 2000*l.*   The ground for the workhouse is given by the city corporation, and in order to defray the expenses to be incurred in carrying the several provisions of the Act into effect; a duty of one shilling per ton is imposed on all coal and culm imported into Cork during the term of thirty-one years, to be paid to the governors of the workhouse.   Four general assemblies of the governors are to be held in every year, and they may from among themselves annually appoint fifteen to be assistants, any five of whom are to have full power to carry the regulations established by the governors into effect, and likewise to regulate the management of the gaol or house of correction.   The beadles and constables are authorised to seize all beggars and other idle vagabonds, found stroll- Strolling beggars and vagabonds to be seized. ing in or frequenting any of the streets or houses within the city and suburbs, and to carry them before one of the said assistants, who is empowered to commit them to the workhouse and hard labour until the next meeting of the governors, who may if they see cause confine such beggars or vagabonds in the workhouse for any term not longer than four years, and keep them to hard labour or otherwise as shall be thought fit. If disorderly, they may be committed to the house of correction.

The workhouse at Cork, like that established in Dublin, is thus we see primarily intended for the repression of mendicancy and vagabondism, and like that too it is further designed for the reception and maintenance of foundlings. The 17*th section* of the Act declares that "the exposed or foundling children left yearly on the several parishes in the city and suburbs of Cork are very numerous, and do frequently perish for want of due care and provision for them"—Wherefore it is enacted, that as soon as the workhouse shall be built, the governors shall receive from the churchwardens of the respective parishes all the exposed or foundling children that are then within the same, and likewise all such as may thereafter be found exposed or left to be maintained by any of the said parishes, "and shall take due care to have such children nursed, clad, and taught to read and write, and thoroughly instructed in the principles of the protestant religion." The male children are to be taught some trade or calling, and employed thereon within the workhouse until the age of 21, when they are to be discharged, and furnished with a certificate under the seal of the corporation, stating their having been so brought up and taught such trade in the workhouse, which certificate will entitle them to the freedom of the city of Cork, with all the privileges other freemen enjoy.

Section 17.
Foundling children.

If the number of male foundlings should become so great, that the fund appropriated to the maintenance of the workhouse proves insufficient for continuing them therein until they severally attain the age of 21 years, the governors or assistants are empowered to place out so many of the male children to such art trade or calling, or to the sea service, or to be household servants, for any term not exceeding seven years, as they shall judge necessary and expedient. The female

children are to be instructed in such proper trades and
employments, and disposed of at such ages and in such
manner, as the governors may deem advisable; and
in order to prevent the improper interference of the
parents of such deserted children, many of whom being
Roman catholics are said to strive to hinder their
children from being brought up protestants, the governors of the workhouses of Dublin and Cork are
empowered to exchange the children maintained therein,
whenever such interchange shall be agreed upon by
the respective governors. This appears the only material addition suggested by the experience obtained in
the thirty years between the passing of the two Acts,
and it strikingly illustrates the difficulty of dealing
with matters connected in any way with differences in
religion. Here are parents so wanting in natural
affection as to desert their own progeny, and leave
them to be cared for by their protestant fellow-subjects, and who yet make it a point of conscience to
hinder their children's being brought up in the religion
of their protectors. It would seem impossible to carry
unreasoning inconsistency further.

Foundling hospitals have, from a remote period,
existed on the continent of Europe, especially in Italy
and France. It appears to have been thought that by
providing a place where mothers might deposit their
illegitimate offspring in safety, the frequent recurrence
of child-murder would be prevented. But it may be
doubted whether the exemption from the consequences
of illicit intercourse, does not tend to relax moral
restraints, and to increase the number of illegitimate
children.

The double functions assigned to the Dublin workhouse, of dealing both with vagrants and foundling children, were deemed to be inconsistent,
and *The 11th and 12th George 3rd, cap.* 11, was
passed to remedy this defect, and in fact to

1771-2.
11 and 12
George III.
cap. 11.
Dublin
Foundling
Hospital.

reconstitute the entire establishment. All former Acts affecting it were accordingly repealed, and a new corporation appointed, comprising a long list of persons official and non-official, from the lord-lieutenant downwards, who are to be called "the Governors of the Foundling Hospital and Workhouse of the city of Dublin." The corporation is invested with large powers, and may for its own use and benefit purchase and hold any lands, tenements or hereditaments, not exceeding the annual value of 2,000*l.*, or any personal estate whatsoever; and may make such rules by-laws and other regulations, as the governors shall judge necessary and expedient for the good government of the institution. There are to be four quarterly meetings of the governors in the year, and as in the case of Cork the governors may appoint annually from among themselves fifteen or more "to be called the Court of Assistants," who are to assemble as often as they think proper for putting in execution the orders and regulations ordained by the governors, and are invested with authority to inspect and regulate the management of the institution, "and the children received therein or sent out to nurse therefrom."

And as "the reception of vagabonds and strolling beggars into the same house, or within the same walls with childen, will be manifestly injurious by the setting a bad example,"—it is enacted that no vagabond or strolling beggar shall be sent into the same house, or kept within the same walls with the children ; but when apprehended shall be sent to bridewell, or to such other place as the governors shall appoint, separate and apart from the said children, and be there maintained and set to work at the expense of the corporation, under such management and regulation as the governors shall prescribe, the produce of their labour to be applied in aid of the revenues of the institution. The governors and the court of assistants

Vagabonds and strolling beggars not to be admitted.

are empowered to inflict reasonable punishment or correction from time to time, on any vagabond beggar or poor person within the said bridewell, or other place of confinement; and each of the governors, and every justice of peace, may apprehend any poor persons begging or seeking relief, and all vagabonds and strolling beggars, within the city and liberties. The beadles, constables, and inhabitants generally, are moreover required to seize and take all such persons before one of the said governors, or one of the said justices, in order to their being committed to bridewell or other appointed place, until the next quarterly court of governors, who may confine the beggars and idle vagabonds so committed for any term not exceeding three years, " there to be kept to hard labour, or otherwise usefully employed, as they shall see cause and shall order and direct."

The entire separation of the vagrant classes from the foundling children being thus provided for, it Section 16. is then by the 16*th section* enacted—" that all Foundling children. and every poor child and children under the age of six years, who shall be found or taken up within the said city and liberties, or sent to the foundling hospital, shall be received and kept therein, or sent to nurse therefrom; and that all children presented for reception who appear to· be six years old, and not exceeding eight, shall be received if there be room, and the children appear to be sound in mind and body." The children are to be instructed in the principles of the protestant religion, and taught to read write and cast accounts, together with such other useful matters as " may tend to increase the fund for the support of the said house." The governors may, from time to time, place out as apprentices by proper indentures any of the said children to persons being protestants and following any trade or calling, or to seafaring men, or to gentlemen or housekeepers for servants, for any term not exceeding seven years.[y] The maintenance and education afforded to these poor children, and their being thus placed out as servants, or apprenticed to a trade, naturally made the institution attractive; and it is declared to be necessary "that some further funds should be provided, as it is found by experience that the numbers of children are of late years greatly increased, and the children are brought to the hospital from all parts of the kingdom, and from his Majesty's neighbouring dominions."

Accordingly, the governors are empowered for "the better support of the said Foundling Hospital and workhouse, and for the maintenance and education of the children and other purposes of the Act," to grant licences to persons keeping hackney coaches, stages, or other vehicles plying for hire, and to porters or messengers within the city or suburbs or seven miles thereof, —on conditions and at rates of charge prescribed in the Act; and also to charge and receive 6d. in the pound on the yearly rent of all houses within the city and liberties, or within two Irish miles of Dublin Castle, as the same is returned for the minister's money, or if not so returned, on the rents payable by tenants in possession. And whenever the number of children causes the expense to exceed the revenue provided by the Act, the governors are to cause notice thereof to be inserted in the Dublin Gazette, after which no child is to be again received until notice to that effect be in like manner given.

On comparing this with the original Act of 1703, and with the Cork Act of 1735, it will be seen that the chief difference is the entire separation of the vagabond or culpable class from the foundling children which is now directed, and the reason for which is distinctly

---

[y] This limitation was afterwards removed by the 25th George 3rd, cap. 48, which allowed of children being apprenticed for any term, provided it did not exceed the age of 21 for a male and 18 for a female.

stated. This was doubtless an advantage, and it led to
so many other improvements in the care and management of the children, that the numbers deserted and
pressed upon the institution went on continually increasing, and soon became excessive. It is indeed complained of in the present Act, before the separation it
directs was carried into full effect, and the influence we
are told even extended beyond the limits of Ireland.
To provide for the additional charges thus arising, the
area of the house-tax was extended, and its rate increased from 3d. to 6d. in the pound. No change is
made in the charge for licensing carriages, but the
number to be licensed was increased, hackney coaches
from 150 to 300, and sedan-chairs from 80 to 400,
which may be taken as proof of the increasing wealth
and population of Dublin, if not of the country generally. This Act was repeatedly amended; and even in
the following year, on the ground that " the number of
children of the age of six years and under, have of late
years increased so far beyond the expectation of the
governors," it is directed by the 13th and 14th George
3rd, cap. 17, that children of three years old and
upwards are not to be received, and that the house-tax
be raised from 6d. to 10d. in the pound for two years,
on houses of 10l. rental and upwards.

Nothing further need at present be said with respect
to the above statute. But two other Acts were
subsequently passed, one in the same year, and
the other in the year following which require
to be noticed.—The first is *The 11th and 12th
George 3rd, cap.* 15, ' for the relief of poor infants who
are or shall be deserted by their parents'—the other is
The 13th and 14th George 3rd, cap. 24, for amending the
same. The first-named Act commences with this recital—" Whereas poor infants are frequently deserted
by their parents, and left exposed to the inclemency of
the weather in the streets and other places in cities;

(margin:) 1772–74.
11 and 12
George III.
cap. 15.
13 and 14
George III.
cap. 24.

and whereas the inhabitants of several parishes in which children are so exposed refuse to raise money for the support of such children, by which many of them perish"—it is therefore enacted, that in every parish of every city (excepting Dublin and Cork) a vestry shall be held in the first week of June annually, at which three overseers are to be chosen, who shall take up and provide for the maintenance and education of all such children as shall be so deserted and exposed within their respective parishes. The sum of 5l. is allowed for the bringing up of each child, and the entire expense is to be equally borne by the inhabitants of the cities respectively. The overseers are to collect the sums assessed upon each inhabitant, and apply the money so collected to the maintenance and education of such deserted children within their respective parishes. This provision is, we see, limited to cities; but the other Act (13th and 14th George 3rd, cap. 24) makes the provision general throughout the country. After citing the former Act, it directs—" that in every parish in this kingdom (except in the cities of Dublin and Cork for which particular provision is made) a vestry shall be held annually, at such time and with such powers as the former Act prescribes;" and the overseers in such parishes are to " take up and provide for the maintenance and education of all such children as shall be deserted and exposed within their respective parishes at the age of twelve months or under;" and such sums of money as shall be necessary for the purpose, are to be " raised upon the respective parishes in the same manner and with such remedies as other parish cesses." If any parish refuses or neglects to raise the amount necessary, the next going judge of assize, upon complaint of the minister or curate thereof, may order such sum to be raised as he shall think fit, " so as the same do not exceed the sum of 5l. for each child;" and the money so directed to be raised is to be assessed and

levied in the manner and with the like remedies as the
presentments of grand juries, and is to be paid to the
minister or curate of such parish, and by him applied to
the purposes of the Act.

These Acts, taken together, make provision for the
support of exposed and deserted children of tender age
in every parish in Ireland, by means of a compulsory
assessment upon the inhabitants. This amounts in fact
to a limited relief of the poor, or a restricted kind of
poor-law, the children being in almost every instance
the offspring of parents too poor to rear and maintain
them, whence (as was the case in England) the parish
of necessity becomes responsible for the performance of
these duties, and stands *in loco parentis.* After thus
legislating for one class of the destitute, and recognis-
ing the principle of compulsory assessment, it seems
remarkable that nothing further should be done in the
way of establishing a regular system of relief for the
destitute of every class, especially as vestries were now
being organised, and overseers appointed in all the
parishes of Ireland. Perhaps an Act passed about the
same time, and to which we will now turn, may serve
to explain this omission, as it attempts to effect the
object circuitously and by indirect means, instead of
openly charging property for the relief of destitution.

The 11*th and* 12*th George* 3*rd, cap.* 30, is entitled
' An Act for Badging such Poor as shall be
found unable to support themselves by labour,   1771–2.
and otherwise providing for them, and for re-   11 and 12
George III.
cap. 30.
straining such as shall be found able to support themselves by labour or industry from begging.' It commences as follows—" Whereas strolling beggars are
very numerous in this kingdom, and whereas it is
equally necessary to give countenance and assistance to
those poor who shall be found disabled by old age or
infirmities to earn their living, as to restrain and punish
those who may be able to support themselves by labour

or industry, and yet may choose to live in idleness by begging ; and it is just to call upon the humane and affluent to contribute to the support of real objects of charity ; and whereas those purposes may be better effected by one law, than by many laws tending to the same purpose"—it is enacted that the 33*rd* *Henry* 8*th*, *cap.* 15,[z] and the 10*th and* 11*th* *Charles* 1*st*, *cap.* 4,[z] be repealed.

The Act then proceeds—" And whereas the good purposes intended by this Act are most likely to be promoted by creating corporations in every county at large, and in every county of a city or town in this kingdom, who may execute the powers and trusts hereinafter expressed "—it is enacted that such corporations be established accordingly, consisting in counties of the archbishop or bishop, the county members, and the justices of peace ; and in counties of a city or town, of the chief magistrate, sheriffs, recorder, members of parliament and justices of peace. Every such corporation is to be called " The President and Assistants instituted for the relief of the Poor, and for punishing Vagabonds and Sturdy Beggars," of the county, city, or town, as the case may be ; and is to have a common seal, and to hold meetings at which the bishop when present is to preside, and to make by-laws and appoint standing committees, and is likewise empowered to elect such other persons as shall be thought fit, including those who contribute any sum not less than 20*l.*, or subscribe annually not less than 3*l.*, to the charitable purposes of the corporation, to be members thereof respectively. The corporations are authorised to accept donations, and to take or purchase lands and tenements not exceeding 500*l.* annual value, and to hold leases for terms not exceeding 21 years, and may also take by grant or devise any quantity of land in a city or town not ex-

Corporations to be established in every county.

---

[z] Ante, pp. 22 and 28.

ceeding two roods, and in the open country not exceeding twenty acres, " for the sites of houses to be built for the reception of the helpless poor, and for keeping in restraint sturdy beggars and vagabonds."

The corporations, constituted as above, are empowered to grant badges to such of the helpless poor as have resided one year in their respective counties cities or towns, with a licence to beg within such limits for such time as may be thought fit; and are also empowered to appoint certain of the justices to grant badges and licences likewise—" specifying the names and places of birth and the character of the persons so licensed, and the causes as nearly as may be collected of their poverty, and whether reduced to that state by sickness or misfortune." *The poor to be badged and licensed to beg.*

The said corporation are moreover required as soon as they possess sufficient funds, to build hospitals to be called workhouses or houses of industry for the relief of the poor in their respective counties, " as plain, as durable, and at as moderate expense as may be;" which hospitals are to be divided into four parts, one for such poor helpless men, and one other for such poor helpless women as shall be judged worthy of admission, a third for the reception of men able to labour and committed as vagabonds or sturdy beggars, and the fourth for idle strolling and disorderly women committed to the hospital and found fit for labour. *Houses of industry or workhouses to be provided.*

Every man above the age of fifteen found begging without a licence, and not wearing a badge, is to be committed to the stocks for any time not exceeding three hours for the first offence, and six hours for every subsequent offence; and old persevering offenders may be indicted at the sessions, and if convicted are to suffer imprisonment not exceeding two months; after which if they again offend they may be publicly whipped, and be again imprisoned for four months, and so on continually for every subse- *Persons begging without a licence to be apprehended.*

quent offence. Every female found begging without a licence and badge, may be confined in any place appointed for that purpose, not exceeding three hours for the first offence, and for every subsequent offence not exceeding six hours; and every old and persevering offender is, as in the case of the men, to be proceeded against at the sessions; and in order that these directions may be carried into effect, the corporations are empowered to appoint " such and so many persons as they shall think fit, at reasonable salaries, to seize and arrest all such persons whom they shall find begging without such licence and badge, and carry them before the next justice, who may commit the party to the stocks or otherwise as aforesaid." Justices are moreover empowered on their own view, to cause such persons to be seized and dealt with as is above directed for every first and subsequent offence.

Whenever a poor person deemed worthy of having a licence to beg, has one or more children under

Poor children to be provided for. the age of ten years not apprenticed or otherwise provided for, the age and number of such children are to be inserted in the licence by the person applied to in such case, or he may " at his or their election take such and so many of them as he or they shall think fit from the parent, and convey such child or children to the committee of that county, city or town, and insert the names of the rest in the parents' licence." If any fatherless or deserted poor children under eight years of age are found strolling and begging, they are to be conveyed to the committee of the particular county city or town, to be placed in such charter school nursery as will receive them when under eight, and the rest are to be apprenticed. The committees are required to keep up a correspondence with the Protestant Charter Schools Society,[a] that they may be informed from time to time

---

[a] Ante, p. 25.

when there is accommodation for poor children, in order
" that all poor children may as much as possible be prevented from strolling, and may be put to trades or to
industry."

As soon as the houses of industry are provided and
furnished for the purpose, the corporations are to place
therein so many vagrants sturdy beggars and vagabonds, and so many helpless poor as their funds admit
of ; " and they are authorised and required to seize every
strolling vagrant capable of labour who hath no Strolling
place of abode, and who doth not live by his or vagabonds
her labour or industry, and every person above mitted.
the age of fifteen who shall beg publicly without a
licence or badge, and every strolling prostitute capable
of labour, and to commit the said persons to the divisions
allotted for them respectively in the said houses, and
there to keep them to hard labour, and compel them to
work, maintaining them properly," and inflicting reasonable punishment when necessary, for the periods named
in the Act, varying from two months to four years.

" In order to furnish some revenues for the said corporations at the outset," the grand juries are Money to be
required to present annually at every spring grand-jury
assizes in every county of a city or town, to be ments.
raised off the lands and houses equally and rateably, any
sum not less than 100*l.* nor more than 200*l.*, and in every
county at large any sum not less than 200*l.* nor more
than 400*l.*, to be assessed and collected as other county
taxes are, and paid to the corporations respectively,
without fee or deduction whatever, for the charitable
purposes of the Act. All rectors vicars and incumbents
of parishes are likewise required to permit such clergymen as the respective corporations may appoint, to preach
sermons in their churches annually, and to permit collections to be made for the objects contemplated by the
Act.

We here see that provision has been made, partly by

compulsory assessment, partly by voluntary contributions, and through the instrumentality of corporations specially appointed—for the badging
and licensing of the poor to beg—for providing hospitals
workhouses or houses of industry in every county at
large and county of a city or town—for separately con-
fining therein able-bodied vagabonds and disorderly
women who are to be kept to hard labour—and for the
maintenance therein of poor helpless men and women.
Authority is likewise given to seize any one found
begging without a badge or licence, and to send such
as are above fifteen to the house of industry for punishment, whilst the children are to be placed at school or
put out to trade or service. And finally, persons are
appointed at reasonable salaries to carry these enactments against unlicensed begging into effect.

In this Act therefore we have stringent provisions
against mendicancy, coupled with a conditional permission for practising it. The deserving poor are
permitted to beg, or if helpless are maintained; the
undeserving poor if they beg are punished : but the
distinction between the two is not defined, neither is
it perhaps possible so to define it as to guard against
continual deception and fraud. The punishment of
vagrancy in every shape prescribed by this Act, accords
with what we find in all the earlier Scottish and English statutes, and if due provision were at the same
time made for relieving the destitute poor, this would
be open to little objection; but the relief of poverty
is here proposed to be effected chiefly by means of an
organised system of begging, the helpless poor for whom
provision is made in the houses of industry, being evidently those only who are too infirm to travel about for
that purpose. By thus combining two objects of an
opposite nature, it is evident neither will be accomplished—vagrancy will not be put down, and poverty
will not be relieved. The providing for the establish-

ment of corporations in every county, with powers to
erect hospitals, houses of industry, or workhouses, and
to tax the property of the country for such purpose, was
no doubt an important advance in the legislation with
regard to the poor; but like many other Irish enactments the present does not appear to have been carried
into effect, except in a very few instances; and as a
general measure the Act may be said to have been
inoperative. It possessed however so much of a general
character, and seemed to hold out such a promise of
efficiency by consolidating the provisions of former Acts,
that it was for a time relied upon, and upwards of half
a century elapsed before anything further was attempted
for the relief of the poor in Ireland.

The foregoing is the last of the Acts of the Irish
parliament which we shall have occasion to notice, and
when the Union took place in 1800, the Imperial legislation superseded that which had been local.

On here closing the last volume of Irish statutes, it may
be convenient to give a short statement of the nature
and extent of the previous legislation connected with our
subject. Houses of industry and foundling hospitals,
supported partly by public rates, and partly by voluntary
contributions, were we have seen established at Dublin
and Cork, for the reception and bringing up of exposed
and deserted children, and the confinement of vagrants
—free schools were directed to be maintained in every
diocese, for educating the children of the poor—parishes
were required to support the children exposed and
deserted within their limits, and vestries were organised
and .overseers appointed to attend to this duty—hospitals, houses of industry or workhouses, were to be
provided in every county, and county of a city or town—
severe punishments were enacted against idle vagabonds
and vagrants ; whilst the deserving poor were to be
badged and licensed to beg, or if infirm and helpless
were to be maintained in the hospitals or houses of

industry, for the building and upholding of which however, reliance was chiefly placed on the charitable aid
of the humane and affluent, assessments for the purpose
being limited to 400*l.* in counties at large, and to 200*l.*
in counties of cities or towns.

It is evident that each of these measures partakes
more or less of the nature of a poor-law, but there is
one material deficiency pervading them all, that is, the
want of a certain and sufficient provision for carrying
them into effect.   In no instance is such a provision
made compulsory upon the public.   A portion only of
what is necessary for the purpose is so imposed, and
the remainder is sought to be obtained by voluntary
contributions, a combination always attended with uncertainty, and in most cases leading to an insufficiency
of the necessary means.   Even if the various provisions
were fully carried into effect and generally acted upon,
this would go far towards rendering them practically
inefficient ; but at that time in Ireland, it by no means
followed because an Act was passed that its provisions
would be enforced, and there is reason to believe that
in very few instances only were the provisions contained
in these Acts carried into operation.   The existence of
such provisions however, defective and for the most
part inoperative as they were, would nevertheless serve
as an answer to any person who might be desirous of
seeing an efficient system established for the relief of
the destitute ; and thus the semblance of such a system
may have prevented the establishing of one that would
have been real, which it only could be when founded upon
a general rate, as in the Act of Elizabeth.   No such
foundation was however, we see, here provided. Neither
parochial nor parental liability as recognised and enforced in England, was established by these Acts.
Even in the case of fatherless and deserted children, the
entire chargeability of the parish for any such child
was limited to 5*l.*, an amount surely insufficient for its

rearing and maintenance until it attained an age to support itself; so that here also reliance must have been placed on the co-operation of private charity, or else upon the child's being received into one of the found-ling hospitals, and the parish being thus relieved from further expense. In short, the training up and edu-cating poor children as protestants, and the repression of vagabondism, appear to be the objects chiefly sought to be attained in all these Acts of the Irish parliament; and to these objects the relief of the infirm and desti-tute poor, seems to be regarded as a matter altogether secondary and subordinate.

A short account of the state of Ireland at this time will be a fitting conclusion of the present chapter, as well as a useful preparative for what is to follow. The best authority we can refer to for furnishing such an account I believe to be Arthur Young,[b] who devoted three years from 1776 to 1778 inclusive, to a personal examination of the country, its agriculture, commerce, and the social condition of the people. I have had con-siderable opportunities of testing the accuracy of Arthur Young's statements, and making due allowance for the changes which must be presumed to have taken place during a period of some sixty years, they have appeared to me to exhibit the circumstances of the country about the time they were written with remarkable accuracy and perspicuity. Of these statements, the following is such a condensed summary as will, it is hoped, show the reader what were Arthur Young's views of the then condition of Ireland, more especially with regard to matters bearing upon our present subject.

In natural fertility, acre for acre, Ireland is said to be superior to England. It has no such tracts of uncul-

---

[b] See Arthur Young's Tour in Ireland in the years 1776–77–78 and brought down to 1779. 2 vols. 8vo. Published in 1780.

tivated mountain as are seen in the English northern

counties, and its lighter shallower and more rocky soil (chiefly of limestone) is nourished by and flourishes under a fall of rain, which if it took place in England, would render the stiff clay lands almost useless. There is no chalk, and little sand or clay in Ireland. The fertility of England may be said to be in great measure owing to the application of skill industry and capital, that of Ireland chiefly to the soil and climate ; whilst the bogs, which else would be waste, afford abundance of fuel. Notwithstanding the naturally superior fertility of Ireland however, the rent of land there as compared with England is in the proportion of two to five, or in other words, the land which lets in Ireland for two shillings, would in England let for five. It is considered that 5*l.* per acre expended over all Ireland (which would amount to about eighty-eight millions) " would not more than build, fence, plant, drain and improve that country to be upon a par in those respects with England ;" and that it would take above twenty millions more to put the farmers in the two countries upon an equal footing. Profit in all undertakings depends upon capital, and the deficiency of capital thus accounts for the inferiority of the Irish rents. Tillage is little understood, and the produce is very inferior ; " and were it not for potatoes, which necessarily prepare for corn, there would not be half of what we see at present." The practice of harrowing by the tail, and burning corn in the straw, was still seen at Castlebar and other places in the west, notwithstanding its being prohibited by statute.[c] The moisture of the climate is favourable to pasturage and the keeping of cattle was much followed, as it well suited the indolent habits of the people.

Considerable pains are taken to show that the system

---

[c] See 10*th and* 11*th Charles* 1*st, caps.* 15 *and* 17, ante page 32.

of middlemen which then prevailed, or persons holding
tracts of land intermediately between the head landlord
and the smaller occupiers, was injurious to both, and a
bar to improvement. It was defended on the ground of
its affording greater security for the rent. But Arthur
Young says that the smaller tenantry were found to be
the most punctual rent-payers; and he further observes,
" that at the last extremity it is the occupier's stock
which is the real security of the landlord,—it is that he
distrains, and finds abundantly more valuable than the
laced hat hounds and pistols of the gentleman jobber,
from whom he is more likely in such a case to receive
a ' message ' than a remittance." These " profit-
renters " are said to waste their time and their means
in horseracing and hunting, and to be the hardest
drinkers and most dissolute class of men in Ireland, as
well as the greatest oppressors of the poor tenantry,
whose condition is described as little better than the
cottars they employ.

Arthur Young declares, that—to be ignorant of the
condition of the labouring classes and the poor generally, is to be wanting in the first rudiments of political
knowledge, and he states that he made every endeavour
to obtain the best information on the subject, from persons in every class of life. According to some, the
poor were all starving. According to others, they were
in a very tolerable state of comfort.—Whilst a third
party, who looked with a jaundiced eye on British administration, pointed at their poverty and rags as proofs
of the cruel treatment of their country. When truth is
thus liable to be warped, an inquirer should, he remarks,
be slow to believe and assiduous to examine, and he in-
timates that such had universally been his practice.

The recompense for labour is the means of living.
In England the recompense is given in money, in Ireland for the most part in land or commodities. Generally speaking the labouring poor in Ireland are said to

have a fair bellyfull of potatoes, and the greater part of
the year they also have milk. If there are cabins on a
farm, the labourers reside in them. If there are none,
the farmer marks out the potato-gardens, and the
labourers raise their own cabins, the farmer often
assisting them with the roof and other matters. A
verbal contract is then made for the rent of the potato-
garden, and the keep of one or two cows, as the case
may be; after this the cottar works with the farmer at
the rate of the neighbourhood, " usually sixpence half-
penny a day, a tally being kept, half by each party,
and a notch cut for every day's labour." At the end
of six or twelve months they reckon, and the balance is
paid. Such it is said is the Irish cottar system, and it
does not differ materially from that which prevailed in
Scotland at a period somewhat anterior. Many cabins
are however seen by the road-side or built in the ditch,
the inhabitants of which have no potato-gardens—" a
wandering family will fix themselves under a dry bank,
and with a few sticks, furze, fern &c., make up a hovel
no better than a pigsty, support themselves how they
can by work begging and pilfering, and if the neighbourhood wants hands or takes no notice of them the
hovel grows into a cabin "—these people are not
cottars, but are paid in money for whatever work they
perform, and consequently have no potato-ground.

The food of the smaller tenantry the cottars and
labouring poor generally, was potatoes and milk, of
which for the most part they are said to have a sufficiency. The English labourer's solitary and sparing
meal of bread and cheese, is contrasted with " the
Irishman's potato-bowl placed on the floor, the whole
family upon their hams around it, devouring quantities
almost incredible, the beggar seating himself to it with
a hearty welcome, and the pig taking his share." It
must be admitted that the contrast is sufficiently
striking, and scenes such as here described were no

doubt then often witnessed in Ireland, and with some little modification may even occasionally be met with at the present day. This luxurious abundance was however by no means universal, as is evident by statements in other parts of the work, where many of the people are described as living very poorly, "sometimes having for three months together only potatoes and salt and water." There is said to be a marked difference between the habits of the people in the north, and those inhabiting the southern and western districts. In the latter, land is alone looked to for affording the means of subsistence. The former are manufacturers as well as farmers, each man holding from 5 to 10 acres of land, and sometimes more, on which he raises the usual crops of corn and potatoes, together with a certain quantity of flax, which is prepared and spun, and sometimes also wove by himself and his family. This double occupation is however not favourable to excellence or improvement in either. The farming was bad, and the people generally very poor. The practice of subdividing the land, until it is brought down to the smallest modicum that can support a family, prevailed in the north as in the other parts of Ireland at that time, and has not entirely disappeared at the present day.

The people are said to be everywhere very indifferently clothed. Shoes and stockings were rarely seen on the feet of women or children, and the men were very commonly without them. They appeared more solicitous to feed than to clothe their children, the reverse of which is the case in England, where, as has often been remarked, it is common to pinch the belly in order to clothe the back. Education as far as reading and writing goes was pretty general. " Hedge schools," as they are called, were everywhere met with, and it is remarked that they might as well be called *ditch* schools, many a ditch being seen full of scholars. This shows the people to have been desirous of instruction, another proof of which is, the fact of there being schools for men. " Dancing is so universal among them that there are everywhere itinerant dancing-masters, to whom the cottars pay sixpence a quarter for teaching their families." The people are said to be more cheerful and lively than the English, but lazy to an excess at work, although active at play; and their love of society is as remarkable as is their curiosity, which is declared to be insatiable. Their truthfulness is however not to be relied upon, and petty thefts and pilferings are very common. They are " hard drinkers and quarrelsome, yet civil submissive and obedient." Such is the summary of the Irish character at that time, as drawn by Arthur Young, and there is no reason to doubt its general accuracy.

With regard to other matters, an Irish cabin is de-scribed as being the most miserable-looking hovel that can well be imagined. It is generally built of mud, and consists of only one room. There is neither chimney nor window. The door lets in the light, and should let out the smoke, but that for the sake of the heat it is mostly preferred to keep it in, which injures the complexion of the women. The roof, consisting of turf straw potato-stalks or heath, has often a hole in it, and weeds sprouting from every part, giving it all the appearance of a weedy dunghill, upon which a pig or a goat is sometimes seen grazing. The furniture ac-corded with the cabin, often consisting only of a pot for boiling the potatoes, and one or two stools probably broken. A bed is not always seen, the family often lying upon straw, equally partaken of by the cow and the pig. Sometimes however the cabin and furniture were seen of a better description, but on inquiry it generally appeared that the improvement had taken place within the last ten years.

The readiness with which habitations are procured in Ireland, and the facility of obtaining food for a

family by means of the potato, are considered to be one
cause of the rapid increase of population which is shown
to have taken place towards the end of the 18th century.[d]
Marriage was, and indeed still is, more early and
more universal in Ireland than in England.   An un-
married farmer or cottar is there rarely seen, and even
the house-servants, men as well as women, are commonly married.   Yet notwithstanding the rapid increase of population, there was a continual emigration
from the ports of Derry and Belfast, several ships
being regularly engaged in this passenger trade as it
was called, conveying emigrants to the American
colonies.   These emigrants were however chiefly from
the northern counties, partly farmers partly weavers.
When the linen trade, the great staple of Ireland flourished, the passenger trade was low, and when the
former was low the latter flourished.   The emigrants
are said to have been chiefly protestants, the Roman
catholics at that time rarely quitting the country.

The towns were said to have very much increased
during the last twenty years.   " It may in truth be
said that Ireland has been newly built over within that
period, and in a manner far superior to what was the
case before."   Towns are the markets for the general
produce of the country, which they help to enrich, and
at the same time also to improve.   The rise of rents
is a natural consequence of the increase of towns; and
on an average throughout Ireland, the rents are said
to have doubled in the last twenty-five years.   The
entire rental of Ireland at that time is set down at
5,293,312*l.*, but Arthur Young considered it to be not
less than six millions.   The cost of living was on the
whole found to be nearly one-half less than in England.
All the articles of use and consumption were cheaper in
Ireland, and the taxes trifling in comparison.   There

---

[d] See table at pages 11 and 12 ante.

was no land-tax, no poor's-rate, no window-tax, no candle or soap tax, only half a wheel tax, no servants' tax; and a variety of other things heavily burthened in England, were free or not so heavily burthened in Ireland. The expenses of a family in Dublin and in London, are considered to be in the proportion of five to eight; but the Irish do however, it is added, nevertheless contrive to spend their incomes.

CHAPTER II.

Rebellion of 1798 — The Union — Acts of the Imperial Parliament: respecting
dispensaries, hospitals, and infirmaries — Examination of bogs — Fever
hospitals — Officers of health — Lunatic asylums — Employment of the
poor — Deserted children — Report of 1804 respecting the poor — Dublin
House of Industry and Foundling Hospital — Reports of 1819 and 1823
on the state of disease and condition of the labouring poor — Report of
1830 on the state of the poorer classes — Report of the Committee on
Education — Mr. Secretary Stanley's letter to the Duke of Leinster —
Board of National Education — First and second Reports of commissioners
for inquiring into the condition of the poorer classes — The author's
'Suggestions' — The commissioners' third Report — Reasons for and
against a voluntary system of relief — Mr. Bicheno's 'Remarks on the
Evidence' —Mr. G. C. Lewis's 'Remarks on the Third Report.'

THE commencement of the nineteenth century is me-
morable for the legislative Union of Great Britain and
Ireland. This measure, fraught with such important
benefits to both countries, was probably hastened by
what occurred in Ireland in 1798, when the partizans
of democracy, excited by the events of the French
Revolution, and stimulated by French emissaries and
promises of support, broke out into open rebel-   1798.
lion. The rebellion was however soon put   Rebellion.
down, although not without the sacrifice of many of
the ignorant misguided people who had been led on to
take a part in it; and the speech from the throne at
the opening of the session on the 20th of November
1798, announced that "the French troops which had
been landed for its support were compelled to surrender, and that the armaments destined for the same
purpose were, by the vigilance and activity of our
squadrons, captured or dispersed." On the 22nd of
January following, a royal message relative to a union
with Ireland was delivered to parliament, in which the
king expressed his persuasion, that the unremitting
industry with which the enemy persevered in their

avowed design of effecting the separation of Ireland
from this kingdom, cannot fail to engage the particular
attention of both houses, and he recommended them to
consider of the most effectual means of counteracting
and defeating such design.

In the debate which followed the delivery of the
royal message, Mr. Pitt observed—" Ireland
is subject to great and deplorable evils, which
have a deep root, for they lie in the situation
of the country itself—in the present character
manners and habits of its people—in their want of
intelligence—in the unavoidable separation between
certain classes—in the state of property—in its religious distinctions—in the rancour which bigotry en-
genders and superstition rears and cherishes." If such
circumstances combine to make a country wretched, the
remedy ought, he said, to be sought for in the institution of " an imperial legislature, standing aloof from
local party connexion, and sufficiently removed from
the influence of contending factions, to be the advocate
or champion of neither. A legislature which will
neither give way to the haughty pretensions of a few,
nor open the door to popular inroads, to clamour, or to
invasion of all sacred forms and regularities, under the
false and imposing colours of philosophical improvement in the art of government." This, he said,
" is the thing that is wanted in Ireland. Where is it
to be found ?—in that country or in this ?—certainly in
England ; and to neglect to establish such a legislature
when it is possible to do so, would be (he declared) an
improvidence which nothing could justify."

Much of the evil which Ireland then laboured under
arose, Mr. Pitt considered, from the condition of the
parliament of that country. " When there are two
independent parliaments in one empire," he observed,
" you have no security for a continuance of their harmony and cordial co-operation. We all have in our
mouths a sentence that every good Englishman and

1800.
Mr. Pitt's
speech on
proposing
the Union,
January 22.

good Irishman feels—we must stand or fall together, we should live and die together—but without such a measure as that which is about to be proposed, there can be no security for the continuance of that sentiment." And he concluded a long and powerful address, by saying, " I am bound to convey to this house every information which it may be in my power to give ; but however acceptable to the one or to the other side of the house, however acceptable or otherwise to those whom I respect on the other side the water, my sentiments upon this subject may be, my duty compels me to speak them freely. I see the case so plainly, and I feel it so strongly, that there is no circumstance of apparent or probable difficulty, no apprehension of popularity, no fear of toil or labour, that shall prevent me from using every exertion which remains in my power to accomplish the work that is now before us, and on which I am persuaded depend the internal tranquillity of Ireland, the interest of the British empire at large, and I hope I may add, the happiness of a great part of the habitable world." The address in answer to the Royal message was carried without a division.

On the 31st of January following, Mr. Pitt submitted to the house of commons certain resolutions declaratory of the principles on which it was proposed to establish the union between the two countries, and explained most fully the various circumstances connected with the measure. It was not merely in a general view, he said, that the question ought to be considered—" We ought to look to it with a view peculiarly to the permanent interest and security of Ireland. When that country was threatened with the double danger of hostile attacks by enemies without, and of treason within, from what quarter did she derive the means of her deliverance ?—From the naval force of Great Britain—from the voluntary exertions of her military of every description, not called for by law—and from her pecuniary resources—added

(margin note) 1800. Mr. Pitt's speech on submitting resolutions for the Union.

to the loyalty and energy of the inhabitants of Ireland itself, of which it is impossible to speak with too much praise, and which shows how well they deserve to be called the brethren of Britons." Great Britain has, he observed, always felt a common interest in the safety of Ireland; "but the common interest was never so obvious and urgent as when the common enemy made her attack upon Great Britain through the medium of Ireland, and when their attack upon Ireland went to deprive her of her connexion with Great Britain, and to substitute in its stead the new government of the French Republic. When that danger threatened Ireland, the purse of Great Britain was as open for the wants of Ireland as for the necessities of England."

Among the great defects of Ireland, Mr. Pitt remarked, " one of the most prominent is its want of industry and capital—How are those wants to be supplied, but by blending more closely with Ireland the industry and the capital of this country?"—The advantages which Ireland will derive from the proposed arrangement are, he said, " the protection she will secure to herself in the hour of danger, the most effectual means of increasing her commerce and improving her agriculture, the command of English capital, the infusion of English manners and English industry necessarily tending to ameliorate her condition, to accelerate the progress of internal civilization, and to terminate the feuds and dissensions which now distract the country, and which she does not possess within herself the power either to control or to extinguish." And he added, " while I state thus strongly the commercial advantages to the sister kingdom, I have no alarm lest I should excite any sentiment of jealousy here. I know that the inhabitants of Great Britain wish well to the prosperity of Ireland; that if the kingdoms are really and solidly united, they feel that to increase the commercial wealth of one country, is not to diminish that of the other, but to increase the strength and power of both." He then cited the example of the union with Scotland—" a union as much opposed, and by much the same arguments prejudices and misconceptions, as are urged at this moment ; creating too the same alarms, and provoking the same outrages as have lately taken place in Dublin." Yet the population of Edinburgh is said to have nearly doubled since the Union, a new city being added to the old ; whilst the population of Glasgow since the Union, has increased in the proportion of between five and six to one. The division in favour of the measure was 140 to 15.

On the 2nd of April 1800 Mr. Pitt presented a message from the king, expressing his Majesty's satis-faction at being enabled to communicate to the house, the joint address of the lords and commons of Ireland, containing the terms proposed by them for an entire union between the two kingdoms ; and he earnestly recommends the house to take all such further steps as may best tend to the speedy and complete execution of a work so happily begun, and so interesting to the security and happiness of his subjects, and to the gene-ral strength and prosperity of the British empire. The session terminated on the 29th of July, when the king in his speech from the throne congratulated both houses on the success of the steps taken for effecting the union of Great Britain and Ireland, emphatically adding— " This great measure on which my wishes have been long earnestly bent, I shall ever consider as the happiest event of my reign, being persuaded that nothing could so effectually contribute to extend to my Irish subjects, the full participation of the blessings derived from the British constitution, and to establish on the most solid foundation the strength prosperity and power of the whole empire." [a]

---

[a] See British Statute 39th and 40th Geo. 3rd, c. 67, and Irish Statute 40th Geo. 3rd, c. 38.

It would seem impossible, having regard to the circumstances of the times, to doubt the necessity for
such a union as was thus established, and perhaps
equally impossible to doubt or over-estimate the benefits
it was calculated to confer. But as in the case of Scotland a century previous, the Union was now denounced
as an act of injustice and degradation to Ireland, although it is difficult to see how the combining of the
two countries under one united government and common designation, thus adding to the security and general importance of both, could be an injustice or degradation to either. The author is able to remember the
circumstances of that period, the alarms, the forebod-
ings of evil, the fervid declamations of popular patriots,
who regardless of the benefits that would ensue to their
country, could only be induced to acquiesce in the
measure by some immediate benefit accruing to themselves. The Union has indeed continued down even to
the present day, to be declaimed against as a grievance
by certain parties in Ireland, whenever for factious or
sectarian objects it suited their purpose to do so; and
the blending and amalgamation of the two peoples
which was hoped for, and which was foretold and
relied upon as a certain consequence of the Union by
its great promoter, has therefore been less entire than
it otherwise would have been. Notwithstanding this
drawback however, the material resources of Ireland
have vastly increased, and its general condition been in
all respects greatly improved, since it has by the Union
become an integral portion of the British empire.

The first parliament of " the United Kingdom of
Great Britain and Ireland," assembled on the
22nd of January 1801, when the king, in his
opening speech, declared his confidence " that
their deliberations will be uniformly directed
to the great object of improving the benefits of
that happy union, which by the blessing of Providence,

1801.
First parlia-
ment of
"The United
Kingdom of
Great Britain
and Ireland."

has now been effected, and of promoting to the utmost the prosperity of every part of his dominions."

There were certain Acts passed subsequent to the Union which it will be requisite to notice, as they exhibit the views of the now united parliament in regard to Ireland and the relief of the Irish poor, and form also a necessary introduction to the more important measure which followed in 1838.

The first of these Acts is *The 41st George 3rd, cap.* 73, which directs the application of certain sums of money granted by parliament to the Dublin Society and the farming societies in Ireland—namely any sum not exceeding 4,500l. Irish currency to the Dublin Society, to be applied towards completing their repository in Hawkins Street, and the botanic garden at Glassnevin; and any sum not exceeding 2,000l. Irish currency, to be applied in promoting the purposes of the farming societies in Ireland for the current year. The Irish Society is an institution founded for the purpose of promoting improvements generally, and the farming societies are exceedingly valuable as promoting agricultural improvements in particular. The imperial parliament could hardly therefore have better shown its desire for the improvement of Ireland, than by thus so immediately after it assembled giving its aid and high sanction to these two societies.

1801.
41 Geo. III.
cap. 73.

After referring to the Irish Acts which provide for the establishment of infirmaries and hospitals, *The 45th Geo. 3rd, cap.* 111, recites—" and whereas the distance of many parts of each county from the infirmary therein established, does not allow the poor of those parts the advantages of immediate medical aid and advice which such infirmary was proposed to afford "—it is then enacted, that in all cases where the governors of the county infirmary shall certify to the grand jury of the county, that they have

1805.
45 Geo. III.
cap. 111.
Dispensaries.

actually received from private subscription or donation any sum since the preceding assize, for the purpose of establishing in any place a dispensary for furnishing medicine, and giving medical aid and relief to the poor therein—the grand jury are empowered to raise from the county at large a sum equal in amount to the sum or sums so received, to be applied by the said governors, together with the moneys so received, in providing medicines and medical or surgical aid and advice for the poor of such place and its neighbourhood, in such manner as the said governors shall deem most advisable. Every person subscribing not less than one guinea towards the establishment or maintenance of any local dispensary, or towards the county hospital or infirmary, is entitled to be a member of the body corporate thereof, " so far as relates to the management of and direction of such local dispensary." The dispensaries are perhaps the most extensively useful of all the medical institutions in Ireland, and this Act providing for their establishment, cannot therefore fail of being considered as of great importance, more especially as regards the rural population residing at a distance from towns, and who are consequently deprived of access to hospitals or infirmaries.

The 46*th Geo. 3rd, cap.* 95, is entitled—' An Act for the more effectually regulating and providing for the Relief of the Poor and the Management of Infirmaries and Hospitals.' It refers to the 11*th and* 12*th Geo. 3rd, cap.* 30, of the Irish parliament,[b] and directs—that in case it shall be made to appear to the satisfaction of the judge at the summer assize in any county, that the corporation instituted under that Act is properly conducted, and that on comparison of the expense incurred in the former year, it is expedient that a greater sum should be presented

1806.
46 Geo. III.
cap. 95.
Hospitals and
infirmaries.

---

[b] Ante, p. 51.

and levied, or that it is expedient to provide for the
expense of building the house of industry—the grand
jury in the county of a city or town may present and
levy a sum not less in the whole than 400*l*., nor more
than 500*l*., and in any county at large a sum not less
than 500*l*., nor more than 700*l*., to be applied to the
purposes directed by the said Act.   The limits of such
presentments are thus we see greatly enlarged from
what was prescribed by the Act of 1772 ; but the entire
amount permitted to be raised by assessment is still
small, showing that voluntary contribution was still
chiefly relied upon.   All infirmaries and hospitals are
moreover now required to make out returns annually,
showing in detail the amount of their funds and their
expenditure, and the lord lieutenant may order an
examination of their state and condition.   By an Act
in the following year another sum of 100*l*. was allowed
to be presented for a fever hospital, " whenever one
had been established."

' An Act to appoint Commissioners for two years, to
examine into the nature and extent of the several Bogs in Ireland &c.,' was passed in 1809,
commencing with this recital—" whereas there
are large tracts of undrained bog in Ireland, the draining
whereof is necessary for their being brought into a
state of tillage ; and whereas the adding their contents
to the lands already under cultivation, would not only
increase the agriculture of Ireland, but is highly expedient towards promoting a secure supply of flax
and hemp within the United Kingdom for the use of
the navy, and support of the linen manufacture "—it is
therefore enacted that the lord lieutenant may appoint
not exceeding nine persons, to be commissioners for ascertaining the extent of such bogs as exceed 500 acres,
and for inquiring into the practicability and best modes
of draining the same, and the expense of so doing,—
also as to the depth of bog soil, the nature of the strata

underneath, the nature and distance of the manure best fitted for their improvement &c.—" together with the opinion of the said commissioners as to such measures as they shall deem necessary or expedient for carrying into speedy effect the drainage cultivation and improvement of all such bogs, and the future increase of timber in Ireland, by providing for the plantation and preservation of trees in such parts thereof as shall be best fitted for the purpose ;" and it is further enacted that the commissioners shall act without a salary.

This inquiry could hardly fail to prove useful, by directing attention to a subject of very great importance, both in a general and a local point of view : but in this, as in most other instances, the result fell short of what was anticipated. The appointing of such a commission however, evidenced a strong desire on the part of the imperial legislature for the amelioration of Ireland. The term of the commission was afterwards extended for another two years by the 51*st* *George 3rd*, *cap.* 122 ; and four elaborate Reports, the 1st in June 1810, and the last in April 1814, accompanied by a large mass of evidence on all matters connected with the subject, are proofs of the commissioners' zeal and industry in discharging the duties assigned them. The subject was moreover again reported upon by a special committee in 1819, and valuable evidence was taken in reference to it, in connexion with the employment of the poor.

The 54*th* *George 3rd*, *cap.* 112—provides—" that

1814–18. 54 Geo. III. cap. 112, and 58 Geo. III. cap. 47. Fever hospitals. whenever any fever hospital has been or shall be established in any county, or county of a city or town, it shall be lawful for the grand jury at the spring or summer assize to present such sum or sums of money, not exceeding 250*l.*, as shall appear to be necessary for the support of such fever hospital, to be raised off the county at large, or the county of a city or town as the case may be ;" and

four years afterwards another Act on the same subject
was passed (*The* 58*th George* 3*rd, cap.* 47) entitled—' An
Act to establish Fever Hospitals, and make other regulations for relief of the suffering Poor, and for preventing the increase of Fevers in Ireland,' commencing with
this preamble—" Whereas fevers of an infectious nature
have for some time past greatly prevailed among the
poor in several parts of Ireland, whereby the health of
the whole country has been endangered, and it is expedient that hospitals should be established for the
relief of the sufferers in such cases, and that regulations
should be made to prevent, as effectually as possible,
the increase of infection ; and such good purposes are
most likely to be promoted by creating corporations in
every county at large, and every county of a city or
town"—it is therefore enacted that such corporations
shall be created accordingly, to consist in counties of
the bishop or archbishop of the diocess, the represen-
tatives in parliament, and the justices of peace for the
county ; and in the county of a city or town, to consist
of the chief magistrate, sheriffs, recorder, representa-
tives in parliament, and justices of peace, all for the
time being, and also donors of not less than 20*l*., or
contributors of one guinea annually—which corporation
is to be called " The President and Assistants of the
Fever Hospital of ——," and is to have perpetual succession &c., and to hold meetings and make by-laws &c.,
and purchase and hold lands not exceeding 500*l*. yearly
value, as they shall think fit.

The corporations are required to build or hire houses
for hospitals for relief of the poor who are ill of fever,
in the several counties or counties of cities or towns,
" as soon as they shall be possessed of funds sufficient
for this purpose, as plain, as durable, and at as moderate
expense as may be." The hospitals are to be divided
into two parts, one for poor helpless men, the other
for poor helpless women, and the corporations are to

appoint masters, physicians, surgeons, apothecaries, nurses, and other fit persons and servants to govern and take care of such hospitals and the patients therein. Grand juries are empowered to present sums, not exceeding double the amount of private donations and subscriptions to fever hospitals, whether the same be attached to any dispensary or not, and they may also present in like proportion for local dispensaries ; and whenever such presentments are certified by the clerk of the crown, the lord lieutenant may order an advance of money from the consolidated fund ; and on the appearance of fever in any town or district, he may also appoint a board of health, with powers " to direct that all streets, lanes and courts, and all houses and all rooms therein, and all yards gardens or places belonging to such houses, shall be cleansed and purified, and that all nuisances prejudicial to health shall be removed therefrom."

The powers of this Act were extended in the following year by *The 59th George 3rd, cap.* 41, which declares that—" it has become highly expedient to provide for and secure constant attention to the health and comforts of the inhabitants of Ireland," and authorizes the appointment of officers of health to carry the sanitary measures specified above into effect. The increase of fever indicated by the passing of these Acts, would seem to have been very marked about this time, and may possibly have been in part owing to the rapid increase of the population, and the consequent overcrowding in the dwellings of the poorer classes. The practice of subdividing their land among all the members of a family, may also have had some share in causing fevers, by reducing the means and lowering the general standard of living, as well in their dwellings as in their food clothing and ordinary mode of subsistence.

The 57th George 3rd, cap. 106, commences by de-

1819.
59 Geo. III. cap. 41.
Officers of health to be appointed.

claring it to be " expedient, that the distressed state of
the lunatic poor in Ireland should be provided
for ;" and it empowers the lord lieutenant to
direct, that any number of asylums for the
lunatic poor shall be established in such districts as he
shall deem expedient; "and that every such district
shall consist of the whole of two or more counties, or of
one or more county or counties, and one or more county
or counties of cities or towns, but shall not include part
only of any county, or county of a city or town ;" and
that all lunatic poor within any such district respectively, shall be maintained and taken care of in the
asylum belonging thereto ; and that every such asylum
shall be sufficient to contain such number of lunatic
poor, not being less than 100, nor more than 150 in
any one asylum, as shall seem expedient to the lord
lieutenant. The grand juries respectively are to present
such sum or sums of money as shall be requisite for
defraying the expenses of erecting and establishing
such asylums, and for maintaining the same, to such
amount and in such proportion as shall be directed
by the lord lieutenant; who is further empowered
to appoint such persons as he shall think fit, to
be governors and directors of every such asylum,
and also to nominate any persons not exceeding
eight to be commissioners for superintending directing and regulating such asylums — " provided that
all such governors directors and commissioners shall
act without salary fee reward or emolument whatsoever."

The necessity for attending to the state of the poor
generally, including the lunatic and insane poor, seems
now to have been strongly felt, and this feeling naturally led to the passing of the present Act. Lunacy is
said to be more prevalent in Ireland, than it is either in
England or Scotland, whilst the poverty of the people
caused it to be there, if possible, a greater affliction than

Marginal note: 1817. 57 Geo. III. cap. 106. Lunatic asylums.

elsewhere, and rendered greater care necessary for the protection of its hapless victims.

The year 1822 was a period of much distress in Ireland, and on the 24th of May *The 3rd George 4th, cap.* 3, entitled ' An Act for the employment of the Poor' was passed, empowering the lord lieutenant in certain cases to order advances to be made from the public treasury, in anticipation of but not exceeding the amount of grand-jury presentments actually made. This does not however appear to have been sufficient to meet the emergency, and on the 26th of July *The 3rd George 4th, cap.* 84, was passed, the preamble declaring that—" Whereas by reason of the distress that exists in many parts of Ireland, it is in many counties thereof impossible without great severity and great mischief to the country to levy and raise the sums heretofore presented by the grand juries of such counties, and which ought by law to be levied and raised on or within the said counties respectively; and whereas the roads and works and other objects and purposes for which many of the said sums have been presented, cannot be delayed without great injury to the persons interested therein, and the commencement of such works, by employing the poor, must tend to alleviate the existing distress "—it is therefore enacted that certain advances which had been provisionally made by the lord lieutenant should be confirmed, and that he may further order advances for public works to be applied according to such directions as he shall give in connexion therewith; and the respective grand juries on being certified of the sums so advanced, are to present the same, to be raised by not less than four nor more than twelve half-yearly instalments, according to the state of the country. Such advances are therefore loans at longer or shorter periods, for road-making or other public works, as a means of relieving the distress of the people, there

1822.

3 George IV. caps. 3 and 84.

Distress and extension of relief.

being then no other source whence relief could be derived.

In 1825 an Act was passed 'to amend the Laws respecting Deserted Children in Ireland.' After referring to previous Acts, which provide that the sum of 5*l.* sterling shall be leviable on any parish for the support of each deserted child found therein, it proceeds—" and whereas the sum of 5*l.* is now required to be paid previous to the reception of any such deserted child into the General Foundling Hospital of Dublin, transmitted from any such parish; and whereas no fund at present exists either to pay the expense of maintaining such deserted children in the parishes wherein found, or of transmitting them to the city of Dublin "—It is therefore enacted that it shall henceforward be lawful " for the several parishes in Ireland to raise and levy such additional sum as may be necessary for maintaining such deserted children as shall be found therein, until such children shall be admitted into the foundling hospital aforesaid, and for transmitting such children thither." But it is further provided that no greater sum than fifty shillings shall be raised in any one year for the support of any such deserted child, or for its transmission to the foundling hospital in Dublin. The city and liberties of Cork are exempted from the provisions of the Act, which is limited to two years. It will not fail to be observed that this Act gives a legislative sanction to the rating of a parish for the relief of a destitute class " found therein," and so far may be said to amount to a species of poor-law.

The foregoing are the only Acts requiring to be noticed, between the period of the Union and the passing of the Irish Poor Relief Act in 1838. They show the feeling of the legislature with regard to the state of Ireland, and seem to point to further measures as being necessary for amending its social defects.

1825.
6 George IV.
cap. 102.
Deserted
children.

But in the interval there were moreover several commissions appointed by the crown, and several committees of parliament, whose reports contain much valuable information as to the state of the country and the condition of the people at the respective periods ; and some of the more prominent of these we will now proceed to notice.

In 1804 a Report was made to the house of commons by a committee which had been specially appointed to make inquiry " respecting the poor in Ireland." The committee, after considering the several statutes, and examining such evidence as was laid before them, came to the resolution—" that the adoption of a general system of provision for the poor of Ireland, by way of parish rate, as in England, or in any similar manner, .would be highly injurious to the country, and would not produce any real or permanent advantage, even to the lower class of people who must be the objects of such support." The committee further resolved, " that the Acts directing the establishment of a house of industry in every county and county of a city or town, have not been complied with, nor any presentment made by grand juries to assist in the support of such establishments for relief of the aged and infirm poor, and the punishment of vagrants and sturdy beggars, except in the counties of Cork, Waterford, Limerick, and Clare, and in the cities of Cork, Waterford, and Limerick." But the committee remark, that the house of industry in Dublin is open to the admission of the poor from all parts of Ireland, which may have induced the other counties and cities to consider it sufficient, " and precluded the necessity of their making further provision for the poor." The futility of this excuse must be sufficiently apparent, and coupled with the resolution against any systematic provision for the relief of the poor " by way of parish rate," shows the kind

1804.
Report of
committee
of house of
commons
respecting
the poor in
Ireland.

of feeling which prevailed at the time in parliament on the subject. It appeared to the committee however, that the Acts directing the establishment of infirmaries or county hospitals, and granting a certain allowance from the Treasury for the salary to the surgeon or physician attending thereon, "have been carried into effect in almost all the counties;" whilst the provisions of the 57th George 3rd[b] " empowering grand juries to present the sums necessary for support of a ward for idiots and insane persons have not been complied with; and the committee consider that there is a great want of accommodation for idiotic and lunatic persons, and recommend the establishment of an asylum in each of the four provinces, to be erected and maintained either by grand-jury presentment or otherwise as may thereafter be determined." The very important objects which had been referred to the committee require however, they say, more deliberation than the advanced period of the session permitted, and they therefore recommend that the investigation should be resumed in the ensuing session; but it does not appear that this was done, although the Acts passed in the two following years with regard to dispensaries infirmaries and hospitals, may very possibly have had their origin in the inquiries instituted by this committee.

The notice taken of the Dublin house of industry in the above Report, as well as the real import- Dublin house ance of the institution, renders some account of industry. of it here necessary. The house of industry was established in 1772, by the 11th and 12th George 3rd, cap. 11,[c] under the provisions of which Act it was separated from the foundling hospital, of which it had before formed a part; and was thenceforward applied to the maintenance of such helpless men and helpless women as from age and infirmity were deemed fitting objects

---

[b] Ante, p. 79.   [c] Ante, p. 45.

for admission, for the confinement of men who were committed as vagabonds or sturdy beggars, and for the punishment of such idle strolling and disorderly women as the magistrates might commit thither. Considerable additions were made to the building, and after a time some changes and modifications took place in the management, which ultimately led to the house of industry being used for the reception of poor aged and infirm men and women, idiots and incurable lunatics removed from the Richmond Lunatic Asylum, the sick poor and persons labouring under acute chronic and surgical complaints, for whom appropriate hospitals had been provided, and lastly strolling beggars thither committed by the magistrates of police. From the year 1773 to 1776 inclusive, the house of industry was supported by subscriptions, donations, and charity sermons, and afterwards by annual parliamentary grants, voluntary contributions, the profits (so called) arising from the labour of the poor, and a small sum of interest accruing on certain legacies. The voluntary contributions became less after aid was obtained from parliament, and as might be expected, soon ceased altogether. In 1776 the parliamentary grant to the institution was 3,000*l.*—In 1786 it was 8,600*l.*—In 1796 it was 14,500*l.* —In 1806 it was 22,177*l.*—In 1814 it was 49,113*l.*—In 1820 it was 26,474*l.*, and in 1827 it was 23,000*l.*[d] At first the house of industry was managed and governed by the corporation for the relief of the poor in the county of the city of Dublin, under the provisions of the Act of 1772—afterwards by seven persons balloted for and appointed "acting governors of the house of industry," in conformity with the 39*th George 3rd, cap.* 38. In 1800 the number of governors was reduced to

---

[d] The grants were made annually, and these years are selected as indicating the average amount. The whole is abstracted from a return made to parliament in 1828, and from Warburton Whitlaw and Walsh's History of Dublin, published in 1818.

five, and in 1820 the management was vested in a
single governor, with a salary of 500*l.* a year. The
number of admissions in 1803 was 4,468, and the
average number in the house was 1,313. In 1807 the
admissions were 5,900, and the average number in the
house was 1862. In this latter year 271 of the admissions were by committal.

The foundling hospital originally formed part of
the house of industry, the joint establishments Dublin
being founded in 1704 under *the 2nd Anne, cap.* Foundling Hospital.
19.[e] They remained so united until 1772, when the
objects of the two institutions being deemed incompatible, they were as before stated placed under separate
and distinct government by *the 11th and 12th George
3rd, cap.* 11.[e] The object of the institution is thenceforward said to be " the preservation of the lives of
deserted or exposed infants, by their indiscriminate admission from all parts of Ireland ;[f] putting them out to
nurse in the country until they are of a proper age to
be drafted into the hospital, and educating them there
in such manner as to qualify them for being apprenticed to trades, or as servants, and thus rendering them
useful members of society."[g] Down to 1823 the institution was supported partly by a house-tax levied on
the citizens of Dublin and its liberties and suburbs,
amounting to between 7,000*l.* and 8,000*l.* annually,
and partly by parliamentary grants, and the rent of a
small property of 115*l.* per annum : but the citizens of
Dublin were then relieved from the house-tax, and the
sum of 5*l.* was required to be paid with every child on
its admission to the hospital, by the overseers or the
minister and churchwardens of the parish whence the
infant was sent, no child being admissible whose age

---

[e] Ante, pp. 35 and 45.
[f] " Every child presented at the gate, or placed in the cradle, was immediately received, and taken to the infant nursery by a person appointed for that
purpose." See Warburton Whitlaw and Walsh's History of Dublin.
[g] See Parliamentary Return No. 2, ordered to be printed 21st March 1828.

exceeded twelve months. The aggregate of these latter payments amounted to about 2,000*l*. annually, and the annual grants by parliament varied from 21,554*l*. in 1800, to 34,000*l*. in 1828. The number of admissions was 2,041 in 1800, 2,168 in 1806, and 2,359 in 1811, at which time the number of children remaining on the books of the institution was 6,498.

In 1819 a select committee of the commons of

1819.   which Sir John Newport was the chairman,

Report on the state of disease, and the condition of the labouring poor in Ireland.   was appointed to inquire into the state of disease, and also into the condition of the labouring poor in Ireland; and a `Report on each of these subjects was presented to the house in course of the session, of which Reports the following is an abstract.

With regard to the first point, although it is said not

On the prevalence of fever.   to be " the most essential or most difficult object of their investigation," the committee consider the prevalence of contagious fever in Ireland a calamitous indication of general distress ; and in order " to prevent the migration through the country of numerous bodies of mendicant poor, who pressed by want and seeking for relief, have fatally contributed to the general diffusion of disease," they recommend that magistrates, churchwardens, or other appointed officers " be empowered to remove out of their respective parishes any persons found begging or wandering as vagabonds therein, or to confine such persons to hard labour for twenty-four hours in any bridewell or other public place of confinement, or to adopt both measures as the case may require ; and also to cause the persons and clothes of such vagabond beggars to be washed and cleansed during the period of such confinement." The committee consider that the Act of last session (58*th George 3rd, cap.* 47)[h] " enacted under circum-

---

[h] Ante, p. 76.

stances of severe and calamitous visitation," has on the
whole been productive of good, and they think it of
infinite moment that there should be a systematic local
control established in all cities and great towns for the
removal of nuisances which generate and increase disease ; for which purpose they recommend that officers
of health should be annually elected by the house-
holders in places containing above 1,000 inhabitants,
with power to direct the cleansing of streets &c., the
removal of nuisances, the ventilation of houses, and the
doing of all things necessary for the health and preservation of the inhabitants ; and also that such country
parishes as think proper may do the same, and that
the expenses incurred in performance of these duties
should be levied as a parish rate, and the expenditure
accounted for as in the case of other parochial assessments.

The committee then express their intention of proceeding, " in further execution of their duty," to
inquire into the practicability of ameliorating the condition of the labouring poor, " by facilitating the
application of the funds of private individuals and
associations for their employment in useful and productive labour," by which alone the entire and permanent
removal of the malady can be expected, although it is,
they say, much mitigated in its severity, and more
circumscribed in its extent than heretofore.   The disease still however, it is observed, continues to press
heavily on the community, and by " the united testimonies of every competent inquirer is attributed to the
want of employment of the labouring classes, as a
primary and powerfully efficient cause."

On the second head of inquiry, the condition, or in
other words, the employment of the labouring
poor, the committee " find themselves in a
great measure controlled by the unquestionable
principle that legislative interference in the

1819.
On the
condition of
the labouring
poor.

operations of human industry is as much as possible to be avoided." There are however, they say, certain exceptions to such a rule, either when injurious impediments are to be removed, or where any branch of industry cannot at its commencement be carried on by individual exertion, on which occasions, it is considered, parliament may with advantage interpose its aid. The existence of general distress and the deficiency of employment were so notorious, that the committee deemed it unnecessary to encumber their Report with evidence on the subject. Their inquiries were particularly directed to agriculture and the fisheries, as being the two most important departments of labour, and as " those likewise to which the greatest extension may be given without hazarding reaction." They refer to the Report of the Commissioners on the Bogs of Ireland, which they consider " prove the immense amount of land easily reclaimable, and convertible to the production of grain almost without limit for exportation "—whilst, " the small extent to which the commissioners' recommendations have been acted upon, demonstrates lamentably that want of capital which in Ireland unnerves all effort for improvement." The institution of cõmmissioners of sewers, as in England, is then recommended, as is also the draining of the great bogs and marshes, and the making a legal provision for repayment of the necessary outlay. The formation of roads in the mountainous districts is likewise recommended, those districts not having, it is said, " their due share of the benefits of the grand-jury system."

The want of capital the committee consider is attributable to a variety of causes. Capital, they justly remark, " can accumulate only out of the savings of individuals ; and in Ireland there are few persons who conduct their operations on such a scale, as to admit of much surplus for accumulation." The manufacture which flourishes most is the linen-trade, and this is said to be "spread abroad amongst a population which at the same time cultivates the soil for their sustenance," a state of things incompatible with large savings. Whilst in agriculture, the tendency to the subdivision of farms, and the practice of throwing the expense of buildings and repairs on the tenants, prevent the accumulation of profit in the hands of the farmers, and its application to agricultural improvements. There are, it is said, two millions of acres of bog in Ireland, capable when reclaimed of growing corn; and the mountain districts comprise a million and half of acres at present nearly unproductive, but about one-half of which is suitable for agriculture, and the remainder for pasturage and planting. The reclamation and improvement of these bogs and mountain districts would, the committee observe, afford profitable employment to the people, and greatly increase the productive powers of the country; but for this capital is necessary, and in Ireland the capital is not to be found.

With regard to the fisheries, it is declared that "in whatever view they can be considered, whether as a source of national wealth, as a means of employing an overflowing population, or as a nursery of the best seamen," they are of the utmost importance; and the revision and simplification of the fishery laws, and the direct application of encouragement to the fishermen of the coast, whose actual condition is said to be miserable, the committee consider essential to any successful fishery in Ireland. The northern, western, and southern coasts, are said to afford every advantage for a bay or coast fishery, and to be admirably suited for a deep-sea cod-fishery of great importance; and after noticing what had been done in Scotland, where an improved system of fishery laws, and parliamentary encouragement wisely applied, had been eminently successful, the committee earnestly recommend "on every ground of policy as well as justice," that the precedent of Scotland should be applied to Ireland. The circumstances of the two countries are declared to be remarkably similar, " both being mountainous and uncultivated, and abounding with an unemployed population."

On this last point, the committee remark—" It is almost impossible in theory to estimate the mischiefs attendant on a redundant, a growing and unemployed population, converting that which ought to be the strength into the peril of the state." It is obvious, they say, that the tendency of such a population to general misery, and the boundless multiplication of human beings satisfied with the lowest condition of existence, must be rapid in proportion to the facility of procuring human sustenance; and it is declared—" that such a population, excessive in proportion to the market for labour, exists and is growing in Ireland, a fact that demands the most serious attention of the legislature, and makes it not merely a matter of humanity, but of state policy, to give every reasonable encouragement to industry in that quarter of the empire." The non-residence of a great portion of the proprietors, and their spending their incomes in England, is then adverted to, as being a circumstance which " enhances the claim of Ireland on the generous consideration of parliament."

No one better knew the state of Ireland than the chairman of this committee, the substance of whose Report is here given. We may therefore rely upon the correctness of the statement, that there was then, twenty years after the Union, a redundant, an increasing, and unemployed population in Ireland, subsisting on food obtained with peculiar facility, (the potato) and consequently " leading to the boundless multiplication of human beings satisfied with the lowest condition of existence." Yet the land was fertile, the sea-coasts abounded in fish, and the bogs and mountain districts solicited improvement. It will probably be said that there must be something wrong in the character, habits, or social position of a people, where such circumstances existed. The Report points to want of capital, and the non-residence of proprietors, as being the cause or causes of what was wrong; and no doubt both circumstances may have been influential in the matter. But capital we are told is the accumulation of savings, which are the fruits of industry, which again is nourished and supported by its own progeny; so that a want of industry may have lain at the root of the evil as regards the mass of the population, whilst the proprietors through absence, or want of sympathy with the other classes, probably failed in their duty of originating and urging forward improvement. With the proprietor class indeed, as with the others, the capital arising from savings and applicable to objects of improvement, was of slender amount; and the committee appear to rely more upon " the generous consideration of parliament," than upon native energy or resource, for supplying the deficiencies and remedying the evils of which they complain.

In 1823 another select committee[1] was appointed " to inquire into the condition of the labouring poor in Ireland, with a view to facilitate the application of the funds of private individuals and associations for their employment in useful and productive labour." The committee made their Report on the 16th of July, and after adverting to the course pursued in the former inquiry of 1819, they state that during the last year " a pressure of distress wholly unexampled was felt in Ireland, which directed the attention of government, of parliament, and of the British public, to the condition of the Irish peasantry, and led to the appropriation of large sums voted by the legislature, and subscriptions by individuals for the

1823. Report on the condition of the labouring poor.

---

[1] Mr. Spring Rice, now Lord Monteagle, was the chairman of this committee.

purpose of mitigating if not of averting, that famine and disease which had extended to so alarming a degree in many districts in Ireland." [k]

It appears that early in May of the preceding year, a public meeting was held in the city of London to raise subscriptions for the relief of the distress in Ireland, and a committee of gentlemen was appointed to superintend the distribution of the money subscribed. Considerable grants of public money were also made by parliament for the same purpose. The committee state that the distressed districts comprised one-half of the surface of Ireland, and there were grounds for believing that considerably more than one-half of the entire population of these districts depended upon charitable assistance for support. The sums distributed through the city of London committee amounted to nearly 300,000*l.*, which with the amount advanced by government furnished means for continuing the relief until the month of August, when the necessity for its further continuance seems to have ceased; and it is satisfactory, the committee observe, to find that the most lively feelings of gratitude have been excited by this benevolent interposition, " which it is to be hoped will tend to unite the two parts of the empire in the strong ties of sympathy and obligation."

In the districts where the distress chiefly prevailed, the potato constituted the principal food of the peasantry, and the potato crop had failed; but there was no deficiency in the other crops, and the prices of corn and oatmeal were moderate. Indeed the exports of grain from ports within the distressed districts, was considerable during the entire period of the distress: so that those districts, the committee observe, " presented the remarkable example of possessing a surplus of food, whilst the inhabitants were suffering from

---

[k] Ante, p. 80.

actual want." The calamity of 1822 may therefore be said to have proceeded less from want of food in the country, than from the people's want of the means to purchase it, " or in other words, from their want of profitable employment." In some districts where the potato failed, but where the population were engaged in the linen-trade, no individual so employed is said to have had occasion for relief; and the committee come to the conclusion that the late distress had chiefly arisen from the circumstance that the peasantry depended for subsistence upon the food raised by themselves. When the potato fails, they have not the means to purchase other food, and the potato is not only uncertain as a crop but it soon decays, so that the surplus of one year cannot be preserved to supply the deficiency in another.

The agents of government, and of the London contributors, as well as the local associations which had been formed, made a point on all occasions as far as possible, of affording the necessary assistance in return for labour; and the committee express their entire approbation of this principle. " Relief purely gratuitous (they observe) can seldom in any case be given without considerable risk and inconvenience; but in Ireland, where it is more peculiarly important to discourage habits of pauperism and indolence, and where it is the obvious policy to excite an independent spirit of industry, and to induce the peasantry to rely upon themselves and their own exertions for support, gratuitous relief can never be given without leading to most mischievous consequences." Any system of relief, it is remarked, which leads the peasantry to depend upon the interposition of others, rather than upon their own labour, however benevolently it may be intended, cannot fail to repress the spirit of independent exertion which is essentially necessary to the improvement of the condition of the labouring classes.

The condition of the people in the districts to which the evidence obtained by the committee chiefly applied, appears " to be wretched and calamitous to the greatest degree." A large portion of the peasantry in those districts, are described as living in a state of the utmost misery. Their cabins scarcely contain an article that can be called furniture. In some families there are no such things as bedclothes, the place of which is supplied by a little fern, and a quantity of straw thrown over it, upon which they sleep in their working clothes. The witnesses agreed in this description with regard to a large portion of the peasantry, and they agreed also in attributing the existence of this state of things to the want of employment. Yet the people are represented as being willing to labour, and we are told that they quit their homes at particular seasons in search of employment elsewhere, whilst the inhabitants of the coasts bordering on the Atlantic, carry on their backs the sand and seaweed many miles inland for the purpose of manure.

The committee are of opinion that the rapid increase of the population[1] is one immediate cause of the want of employment. The demand for labour, they say, has not kept pace with the continually increasing number of persons seeking employment. Another cause of the want of employment, they consider, arises from the effect produced on the gentry of the country by the fall of prices. The fixed payments to which many of the landlords are subjected, whether in the shape of head-rents or interest on incumbrances, bear a greater proportion to the whole income than they did during the war, and consequently the balance remaining in the hands of the resident gentry is diminished, a reduced employment follows, labourers are discharged, and the distress of the higher class is thus visited upon the lower.

---

[1] See table, ante pp. 11 and 12.

The want of capital was however in most instances assigned as the principal cause of the want of employment. This want was manifested in the wretched description of implements commonly in use. The ploughs, carts, harrows, were of the very rudest kind, and there appeared to be a deficiency even of these. The same want of capital has, it is said, led to the payment of wages, not in money, but by allowances in account, or as a set-off against the landlord's claims for rent, or presentments, or some other object, which is not only a hardship to the labourer, but tends to an increase of local burdens; and as it was " generally admitted that if the wages of labour were paid in money, the labour would be more cheaply purchased and more cheerfully and efficiently given," the committee express a hope " that a system of ready money payment may be introduced, so far at least as the public works of the country are concerned."

The encouragement of the fisheries, the erection of piers, the formation of harbours, and the opening of mountain roads, are all recommended, as is also the instruction of the peasantry in agriculture, by combining instruction in this branch, with the other instruction imparted in the various educational establishments throughout the country. In conclusion, the committee admit that danger attends all interferences with industrial pursuits, which prosper best when left to their own natural development; but they consider that the state of Ireland constitutes it an exception to the general rule, and that the aid of government in support of local effort is there absolutely necessary.

At the end of seven years, another select committee of the commons was appointed " to take into consideration the state of the poorer classes in Ireland, and the best means of improving their condition," [m] and their very elaborate and com- 1830.
Report of
select committee on the
state of the
poorer classes
in Ireland.

[m] Mr. Spring Rice (now Lord Monteagle) was also the chairman of this committee.

prehensive Report, (which was ordered to be printed on the 16th of July,) will require to be especially considered.

The committee commence their Report by declaring that they entertain a deep sense of the difficulty and importance of the question referred to them, and that they have felt it their duty to make most minute inquiries into the actual state and condition of the Irish poor, considered in all points of view, moral, political, physical and economical, in order to enable the house to form a correct opinion on the entire subject. The Report is arranged under three principal heads—1st, the state and condition of the poorer classes—2ndly, the laws which affect the poor, and the charitable institutions —3rdly, the remedial measures suggested; and each of these is again subdivided into several minor headings. It is not intended to adhere to these divisions in the following summary, but to select such portions only as immediately bear upon our subject, and as are calculated to show what was then the general state of the country and the condition of the people.

Regret is expressed by the committee at their being compelled to state " that a very considerable portion of the population is considered to be out of employment." The number is, they say, estimated differently—by some at one-fifth, by others at one-fourth ; and this want of demand for labour necessarily causes distress among the labouring classes, which combined with the consequences of an altered system of managing land, is said to produce " misery and suffering which no language can possibly describe, and which it is necessary to witness in order fully to estimate." Yet the price of labour is not considered to have materially fallen. By returns from the county treasurers, the rate of wages appears to average 10*d*. per day on presentment works throughout Ireland, and an extensive contractor thinks that there is a tendency in wages to increase rather than otherwise, notwith-

State of the country, and condition of the people.

standing that the labourers can now, he says, purchase
for 6s., what would formerly have cost them 12s.
These are seemingly contradictions, and there is much
more of the same kind of conflicting testimony given
in the Report, which can only be accounted for by the
fact, that the several parts of Ireland differ widely
from each other, and that what is true in one case is
not true in another.   This indeed appears to be the
view taken by the committee, for they say however
consolatory the favourable testimony may be, it would
lead to a false inference were it to induce a disbelief
in the existence of very great distress and misery in
Ireland.   " The population and the wealth of a
country may (they observe) both increase, and increase
rapidly; but if the former proceeds in a greater ratio
than the latter, an increase of distress among the poor
may be concurrent with an augmentation of national
wealth."   The state of the labouring classes must, it is
considered, mainly depend on the proportion existing
between the number of the people and the capital which
can be profitably employed in labour.   Of the truth of
these propositions, there can be no reasonable doubt;
neither can it well be doubted, that much of the distress and misery which were seen in Ireland, was owing
to a disturbance of this proportion, the population
having become greatly in excess of the capital necessary for and applicable to profitable employment.

The committee consider that it would be impossible
to form a correct estimate of the condition of the poorer
classes in Ireland, without first ascertaining the nature
of the relations which existed between landlord and
tenant,—" the connexion between the inheritor and the
occupier of the soil being one which must influence if
not control the whole system of society."   Great attention is accordingly bestowed on this part of the subject,
and much evidence was taken in reference to it.

Under the excitement of war prices, it is observed,

agriculture advanced with extreme rapidity. The demand for labour increased, and the population augmented in proportion. Land rose in value from year to year, and lessees realised large profit rents by subletting, one or more persons being frequently interposed between the owner and the occupier who was ultimately liable for the rent, both to the head landlord and the intermediate tenants. It became the practice in most cases, we are told, for the occupying tenant either to sublet, or to divide the land among the members of his family—in the former case a class of middlemen was created, which operated as a bar to improvement, and led to the paying or to the promise of paying higher rents—in the latter case the practice of subdividing led to consequences perhaps still more mischievous. When the farmer of 40 acres subdivided the land among his children, those children were led to do the same among theirs, until the farm of 40 acres was cut up into holdings of one two or three acres, each holding occupied by its particular owner, and yielding no more than was barely sufficient for his subsistence. " Now if the tenant of 40 acres had been prevented from subdividing his land, he would," as is observed by one of the witnesses,[n] " have provided for his children by sending them one into the army, another into the navy, and then left his holding to a third, and thus the farm would have been continued in its first state." The cultivation of the land so subdivided and cut up is moreover always of the very worst description. The crops are uncertain, the liabilities to scarcity greater, the cabins are most miserable, and the visitations of fever are more frequent. The soil itself becomes deteriorated by bad tillage, and not a bush nor a tree is left standing; whilst the ease with which a cabin is

[n] Dr. Doyle, the Roman catholic Bishop of Kildare and Leighlin, whose evidence is entitled to the utmost consideration on this and every other question connected with the state of Ireland.

reared, and the meal of potatoes provided, induces early marriages, and the land teems with an excessive population.

The above is not an overdrawn description of the consequences of subdividing land, but a change in management is said to have taken place soon after the peace, when the decline in the price of agricultural produce disabled many of the middlemen as well as the occupying tenants from paying their rents, and created much anxiety and alarm in the minds of the landlords. An apprehension was morever, we are told, generally felt that a pauper population would go on increasing, and the value of the land at the same time go on diminishing, until the entire produce would become insufficient to maintain the· people.   The proprietors sought to devise a remedy for this state of things, so as to prevent the occurrence of such an evil; and Dr. Doyle stated in his evidence, that they did apply remedies, the principle of which he fully approved; but he added " that he thought, and still thinks, that those remedies ought to have been accompanied by some provision for the poor."

The remedy or change in management here adverted to was the consolidating of farms, which it is said would lead to better husbandry, to a greater certainy of crop, to the providing farm-buildings and more comfortable habitations, and to an increase in the quantity and improvement in the quality of the produce.   These are all important considerations, and if the landlords and the tenants who continued in possession were alone to be regarded, the change would appear an unmixed good. But there is another class, the ejected tenants, whose condition, it is said, necessarily becomes most deplorable. " It would be impossible for language to convey an idea of the state of distress to which the ejected tenantry have been reduced, or of the disease, misery, and even vice, which they have propagated in the towns wherein they have settled; so that not only they who have been ejected have been rendered miserable, but they have carried with them and propagated that misery."

Such is the testimony of Dr. Doyle on this point, and although the committee express a hope that it may be regarded as descriptive of an extreme case, they yet have no doubt " that in making the change, in itself important and salutary, a most fearful extent of suffering must have been produced." The change was however, they say, unavoidable, and delay would have increased and aggravated the evil which followed in its train. Various suggestions were made with a view to carry the country through the period of change, and the severe trials by which it must be attended — " Emigration, the improvement of bogs and waste lands; the embankment and drainage of marsh lands; the prosecution of public works on a large scale; the education of the people not only in elementary knowledge, but in habits of industry; the encouragement of manufactures; the extension of the fisheries; and lastly, the introduction of a system of poor-laws, either on the English or Scotch principles, or so modified as to be adapted to the peculiar circumstances of Ireland," were all recommended, and on each of these questions, the committee say, valuable evidence had been taken and would be submitted to the house.

On the subject of vagrancy, after referring to the old laws against it which had fallen into desuetude, and which are recommended to be repealed, the committee quote *the 6th Anne, cap. 11,*[o] under which (as amended by the *9th George 2nd, cap. 6*) idle vagrants, or pretended Irish gentlemen, who will not work &c., may on the presentment of a grand jury be apprehended and transported for seven years. They likewise quote *The 11th and 12th George 3rd,*

Vagrancy.

---

[o] Ante, p. 38.

cap. 30,° for establishing houses of industry, and these statutes are said to be in full force. A table is also given, showing that on an average of eight years the number of commitments under the first-named statutes was 160 annually; and the committee observe, that " although it is necessary to continue penalties against vagrancy," they " cannot but think that a more constitutional and efficient system may be adopted, than one which allows the penalty of transportation to be inflicted upon the mere presentment of a grand jury, and this, not for an offence defined with precision, but under contingencies extremely vague and uncertain." In the opinion thus expressed by the committee, every one must concur.

With regard to the county infirmaries, of which there were thirty-one,[p] the committee, after County infirmaries. referring to the several Acts under which they were established,[q] state that during the last year relief had been given to 7,729 intern patients, besides other medical assistance ; and that the entire incomes amounted to 54,693*l.*, the whole derived from local subscriptions and grand-jury presentments, excepting 3,000*l.* (Irish currency) furnished by government. The committee recommend that the several statutes should be consolidated, and that the grand juries should be enabled to provide more than one infirmary in the larger counties, and that their presenting powers should be extended in order to guard against insufficiency in any case. An efficient audit of the accounts, and a duly authenticated Report half-yearly of all particulars connected with the hospitals, together with a regular inspection by the grand juries, are likewise recommended ;

° Ante, p. 51.

[p] There was an infirmary in every county excepting Waterford, where the peculiar provisions of a local Act had prevented one being erected.

[q] Namely 5th George 3rd, cap. 20 ; 45th George 3rd, cap. 111 ; and 47th George 3rd, cap. 50.

and with these alterations, the committee are of opinion that " the county infirmaries of Ireland may be considered as adequate to the purposes for which they were intended." There does not however, it is added, appear to be any reason for continuing the government grant of 3,000l. Aid from the public purse should, it is said, be reserved exclusively for loans and advances, " and for cases in which local funds are inadequate to the immediate discharge of a necessary duty."

The subject of fever and fever hospitals is next adverted to by the committee. " From the occasional failure of the potato crop, and the misery which then invariably ensues, the poor of Ireland are (it is said) peculiarly liable to fever, which has at various times spread with such violence, and to such an extent, as to require extraordinary aid, not only from private charity and local assessment, but from the public purse." Dublin had suffered most severely from this calamity, upwards of 60,000 persons having in one year passed through the fever hospitals of that city. In 1817 fever extensively prevailed in Ireland, and a board of health was constituted whose Report to government showed " that on a moderate calculation a million and a half of persons suffered from fever, of which number at least 65,000 had died." By *the* 58*th George* 3*rd, cap.* 47,[r] additional facilities were given for establishing fever hospitals, and provision was made for the appointment of local boards of health. By *the* 59*th George* 3*rd, cap.* 41, effect was given to the recommendations of the select committee of 1819,[s] and under these statutes fever hospitals have been established in most parts of Ireland. No county is said to be without one in Munster, and the county of Cork has four, and Tipperary eight; but many

Fever hospitals and dispensaries.

---

[r] Ante, p. 77.   [s] Ante, pp. 78 and 86.

counties in the provinces of Ulster and Connaught have omitted to provide fever hospitals, and the committee consider that if the grand juries persist in such omission, the providing of them should be made compulsory. With respect to dispensaries for the medical relief of the sick poor, these were sanctioned by *the 45th George 3rd, cap.* 111,[t] under which Act nearly 400 are said to have been established, "affording relief annually to upwards of half a million of persons." But some doubts appear to have arisen as to whether the presentments for their support were optional or otherwise, and the committee recommend that such doubts should be removed by making the presentment imperative, as was apparently the intention of the framers of the statute ; and for security against abuse, it is also recommended that a Report of all matters connected with the dispensary, should in each case be annually submitted to the grand jury making the presentment.

The provision for the lunatic poor is said to have been for a long time very defective in Ireland. Lunatic asylums. A hospital attached to the house of industry in Dublin, a large asylum at Cork, and cells connected with some of the county infirmaries, were all that existed for the safe custody and proper treatment of the insane poor. In 1810 a grant was made for the establishment of the Richmond Lunatic Asylum, with accommodation for 200 patients. In 1817 the subject was inquired into by a select committee,[u] in accordance with whose recommendation *the 57th George 3rd, cap.* 106,[x] was passed, empowering the lord lieutenant to fix certain districts within which lunatic asylums should be erected, the cost in the first instance to be advanced by government, but to be ultimately repaid by local

---

[t] Ante, p. 73.　The chapter is by mistake stated in the Report to be 91.
[u] Of this committee Mr. Vesey Fitzgerald was chairman.
[x] Ante, p. 79.

presentments, from which also the maintenance of the asylums is to be derived. " When these institutions are completed, which is easily practicable within three years, every county in Ireland will be provided with receptacles for their lunatic poor ; and if these shall not be found sufficient for incurable as well as curable cases, a ward or two may be attached to each at a moderate expense, and the exigency may be thus completely provided for." This quotation is given from the inspector's Report to the Irish government on the subject in 1830, and the committee express their satisfaction, that as regards " one of the most painful afflictions to which humanity is exposed, there has been provided within a few years, a system of relief for the Irish poor as extensive as can be wished, and as perfect and effectual as is to be found in any other country." Still however the cases of idiots and incurable lunatics are not separately provided for ; and the committee consider it important that curable and incurable cases should be kept distinct, and that space should not be appropriated to the safe custody of incurables, which would be more usefully employed in the treatment of cases where there was a probability of recovery. Every lunatic establishment in Ireland, whether public or private, is subject to the visitation of the inspectors of prisons, who report regularly upon the condition and management of these institutions.

After referring to the 11th and 12th Geo. 3rd, cap. 30,
Houses of   the 46th Geo. 3rd, cap. 95, and the 58th Geo.
industry.   3rd, cap. 47,[y] the Acts under which houses of industry are established and regulated, the committee state that the number of these institutions in Ireland does not exceed twelve " including the great establishment bearing that name in Dublin, which is supported exclusively by votes of parliament." There are eight

---

[y] Ante, pp. 51, 74, and 77.

in Munster, and three in Leinster, but none either in Ulster or Connaught. A proposition is said to have been made for extending houses of industry generally throughout the country, and for rendering their erection and support compulsory. But the committee are of opinion that " establishments of this description combining the two distinct purposes of punishment and relief, are not likely to be useful either as prisons or hospitals." They think that coercion is more likely to be effective when applied in houses of correction, than when applied in asylums intended for old age infirmity and destitution. They also think that the criminal ought to be separated from the distressed poor, and that these asylums should be reserved for particular descriptions of the latter class only—or in the words of Dr. Chalmers, for " cases of hopeless and irrecoverable disease, and all cases of misery the relief of which has no tendency to increase the number of cases requiring relief." To the poor who suffer from loss of sight or limbs, and the deaf and dumb, the house of industry judiciously managed, would they say " afford a suitable place of refuge." Such are the views of the committee with regard to houses of industry, and they do not materially differ from what prevailed in England a century previous with regard to the almshouses or old parish poorhouses then so common.

The number of voluntary charities in Ireland maintained by private benevolence, independently of any contribution from general or local taxation, *Voluntary charities.* is said to be very great, and they are stated to be most liberally supported. " Among them will be found schools, hospitals, Magdalen asylums, houses of refuge, orphan establishments, lying-in hospitals, societies for relief of the sick and indigent, mendicity associations, and charitable loans." Yet notwithstanding the existence of these multifarious institutions, and the active exercise of private benevolence, and the frequent collections by the clergy of all persuasions,[z] " the committee have not the satisfaction to hope that more is accomplished than the mitigation of distress." Societies for the suppression of mendicity have it is said been formed in many parts of Ireland, on a plan similar to those established in London, Bath, and other places in England. In Dublin the income of the Mendicity Society amounts to 7,000l., and the committee are informed " that although the voluntary contributions are scarcely sufficient to maintain the establishment, still on the whole, supporting the poor as they do, they have enough." When the funds are very low, a threat is held out either of applying to parliament for a power of compulsory assessment, or else that the poor people supported by the society will be discharged into the streets, " and by these means additional subscriptions are called in." Institutions of this kind, supported by private contributions, are said to be complained of as casting an unfair and unequal burden upon the benevolent, and it has been suggested that they should be supported or at least aided by local assessment : but this suggestion, the committee observe, involves the entire principle of a poor-law, a question on which at that advanced period of the session they are not prepared to enter. They however recommend it as a subject for future consideration and inquiry.

With regard to emigration, although in some districts Emigration. " there exists a population exceeding that for whose labour there is a profitable demand," the committee nevertheless consider emigration to the full as much an imperial as a provincial question. The cause of the great influx of Irish labourers into Great

---

[z] Dr. Doyle in his evidence before the committee, stated that the poor were almost exclusively supported by the middle classes; and that " although these form a class not over numerous, and subject to great pressure, still of the million and a half or two millions now expended to support the Irish poor, nearly the entire falls upon the farmers and the other industrious classes."

Britain is, they say, the higher rate of wages which prevails there, and emigration from Ireland would "diminish that inducement, and lessen the number of Irish labourers in the British market." It might seem therefore that the expense of such emigration should be defrayed out of the general funds of the empire. But the committee say they are not prepared to recommend any compulsory system of taxation for the purpose, "nor yet to discuss the probability of the repayment of advances made to colonial settlers." They have however no doubt that colonization might be carried on to a great extent, "if facilities were afforded by government to those Irish peasants who were disposed voluntarily to seek a settlement in the colonies, and who could by themselves or their landlords provide all the expense required for their passage and location." In districts where the population is in excess, it must be alike the interest of all, of the landlords, the tenants, and the labourers, that such excess should be removed; and the committee consider the most legitimate mode of effecting this to be—" that upon the actual deposit of a sum sufficient to cover the entire expense, the government should undertake the appropriation of that sum in the way most effectual for the purpose "—that is, for the conveyance of the emigrants to, and helping them to obtain a suitable location in, some British colony.

Amongst the various remedial measures suggested, the committee urge at great length the importance of an extension of public works, roadmaking, drainage, embankments &c., founded chiefly on the example of Scotland, and the benefits which there ensued from opening out the Highlands by the formation of roads and the construction of the Caledonian canal. The evidence given by Mr. Telford the eminent engineer in 1817, is cited and much relied upon in this particular, and certainly no higher authority on the subject could have been adduced. An emendation of the grand-jury and vestry laws is also recommended, together with several other matters of minor import.

In the present very comprehensive Report, as in all preceding Reports on the state of Ireland, whether by committees of parliament or Royal commissions, the necessity for education is adverted to as a matter of paramount importance. It is now moreover said, that " the entire body of the Roman catholic hierarchy have by petitions to both houses of parliament, entreated that the recommendations of the select committee of 1827,ᵃ should be adopted"—on which account, as well as on account of its intrinsic importance with regard to the question of education generally, that Report now requires to be noticed.

Education.

The Report of the select committee appointed in 1827 here referred to, was printed by order of the House of Commons on the 19th May 1,828.ᵃ The committee declare that they " have proceeded to consider the Reports on the state of education in Ireland, with a full sense of the import- ance of the subject, and of the peculiar difficulties with which it is encompassed." During several centuries, they observe, the necessity for providing the means of education in Ireland has been recognised. As early as the reign of Henry the Eighth the prevalence of crime was attributed to the ignorance of the people, " and educa- tion was relied upon as producing moral improvement, and supporting the institutions of civil policy." Various statutes were passed and charters granted, and endow- ments made, with a view to this object; and inquiries had likewise been at different times instituted with the same intent. Of the commissions appointed, the two latest are the most important, namely that issued in 1806, and which terminated in 1812, after making

1828.
Report of the Select Committee on Education in Ireland.

ᵃ The committee consisted of twenty-one members, and Sir John Newport was the chairman.

" fourteen Reports upon the schools of royal and private foundation, the charter schools, foundling hospital, and the parochial and diocesan schools ;" and that issued in 1824, which terminated in 1827, after making " nine Reports on the various establishments for education." But the interference of the State was not solely confined to regulation and inquiry. " Parliamentary grants have been at various times most liberally made for the purposes of education," and of these a list is given, amounting in the whole to 2,914,140*l*. The number of scholars receiving instruction in the existing schools in 1826, is stated to be 560,549, " leaving in all probability upwards of 150,000 without the means of education." Of the number of scholars returned, it is said that 394,732 are brought up in the common pay schools, 46,119 in schools supported exclusively by the Roman catholic priesthood and laity, 84,295 in various establishments of private charity, and 55,246 in schools maintained in whole or in part at the public expense.

In pursuing their investigations, the committee say " their sole object has been to consider the principle upon which it will be expedient hereafter to grant public money in aid of Irish education ;" and they prefer recording the conclusions at which they have arrived in the form of abstract propositions, instead of reasoning upon and discussing the merits of different modes of procedure in this respect. After the most anxious deliberation, they have, they say, adopted a series of resolutions on the subject, which are given at length, and in fact constitute the substance of their Report; and it is now proposed to select such portions of these resolutions as will enable the reader to see clearly what the views of the committee were. To give the whole is unnecessary, and would be inconvenient. The various Reports of committees and commissioners on Irish education are so voluminous, as to make it impossible to quote them at length, and the abstracts of the more important portions herein given will be sufficient for our purpose.

A passage from the Report of the commissioners in 1812[b] is cited, to the effect—" that no plan of education, however wisely and unexceptionably contrived in other respects, can be carried into effectual operation in Ireland, unless it be explicitly avowed, and clearly understood as its leading principle, that no attempt shall be made to influence or disturb the peculiar religious tenets of any sect or denomination of Christians." A passage from the Report of the commissioners in 1824 is likewise cited, to the effect—" that in a country where mutual divisions exist between different classes of the people, schools should be established for the purpose of giving to children of all religious persuasions, such useful instruction as they may severally be capable and desirous of receiving, without having any ground to apprehend any interference with their respective religious principles." Another passage of the same Report is also cited—" in favour of the expediency of devising a system of mutual education, from which suspicion should if possible be banished, and the causes of distrust and jealousy be effectually removed ; and under which the children may imbibe similar ideas, and form congenial habits, tending to diminish, not to increase, that distinctness of feeling now but too prevalent."

The committee of 1828 adopt these several propositions, and resolve—" that it is of the utmost importance to bring together children of different religious persuasions in Ireland, for the purpose of instructing them in the general subjects of moral and literary knowledge, and providing facilities for their religious instruction *separately*, when differences of creed render it impracticable for them to receive religious instruction together."

---

[b] This Report was signed by three bishops, the provost, and several other distinguished clerical and lay members of the established church.

And in accordance likewise with the recommendations of the commissioners of 1812 and 1824, the committee further resolve—" that considering the very large sums of public money annually voted for the encouragement of education in Ireland, as well as the extreme discretion required in adopting a new system of united education, without permitting any interference in the peculiar religious tenets of the scholars—it is indispensably necessary to establish a fixed authority acting under the control of the government and of the legislature, bound by strict and impartial rules, and subject to full responsibility for the foundation control and management of such public schools of general instruction, as are supported on the whole or in part at the public expense."

The committee likewise record their opinion, that the selection of teachers in the schools should be made without regard to religious distinction, and that their qualifications should be proved by instruction or examination in a model school, the teacher first producing a certificate of character from a clergyman of his own communion. And they further resolve—" that for the purpose of carrying into effect the combined literary, and the separate religious education of the scholars, the course of study for four days of the week should be exclusively moral and literary; and that of the two remaining days, the one should be appropriated solely to the separate religious instruction of the protestant children, the other for the separate religious instruction of the Roman catholic children—the religious instruction in each case being placed under the exclusive superintendence of the clergy of the respective communions." The committee moreover recommend that a board of education should be appointed, " all persons being eligible without reference to religious distinctions;" and they also recommend, that as a rule the children be required to pay such small sums as may be directed, " but that free scholars, being either orphans or the children of parents unable to afford payment, be received on the recommendation of the parochial clergy, and dissenting ministers, and persons subscribing to the schools, or having granted land for the site."

The conditions under which the committee consider that the parliamentary grants in aid of the establishment and support of schools in Ireland, should in future be made, are as follows—

" Not to exceed two-thirds of the sum required.
" The school-houses and site to be conveyed to the commissioners.
" The managers to undertake to conduct the school according to the prescribed rules.
" Gratuities to teachers according to regulations prescribed by the commissioners.
" Books for the *literary* instruction of the children to be furnished at half price, and for the *separate religious* instruction at prime cost.
" A model school for the education of teachers to be provided.
" A system of inspection to be established.
" Public aid to depend on private contributions, and adherence to the commissioners' rules."

In conclusion the committee observe, that it has been their object to discover a mode in which the combined education of protestant and Roman catholic children may be carried on, resting upon religious instruction, but free from the suspicion of proselytism.—They have endeavoured, they say, " to avoid any violation of the liberty of conscience, or any demands or sacrifices inconsistent with the religious faith of any denomination of Christians." They propose to leave to the clergy of each persuasion, the duty and the privilege of giving religious instruction to those who are committed to their care. And finally, they express an earnest hope that if adopted, their recommendations will satisfy moderate and rational men of all opinions.

There can be no doubt that the committee were entitled to avow the expectation here expressed. The perfect fairness and impartiality of what they proposed with regard to religious teaching, and the simplicity and moderation of their recommendations, fortified moreover as these substantially are by the Reports of the commissions of 1812 and 1824, seem to leave no room for cavil or objection on any side. Yet we do not find that any steps were specifically taken for carrying the committee's recommendations into effect until October 1831, when Mr. Stanley,[c] the then Secretary for Ireland, addressed a letter to the Duke of Leinster, stating that it had been determined to constitute a board for the superintendence of a system of national education in Ireland, and that it was proposed, with the duke's consent, to place him at its head. The motives for constituting the new board, and the powers intended to be conferred upon it, " and the objects which it is expected that it will bear in view and carry into effect," are all then very fully explained.

A preceding government, it is observed, imagined that they had found a superintending body acting upon the impartial and non-proselytising system recommended by the committee of 1812, and had intrusted the distribution of the national grants to the care of the Kildare-street Society.[d]   But, the letter proceeds—

1831.
Mr. Stanley's letter to the Duke of Leinster on the formation of the Board of National Education.

---

[c] Afterwards Lord Stanley, and now Earl of Derby.

[d] This society, originally founded in 1811 under the designation of "The Society for promoting the Education of the Poor in Ireland," was managed by gentlemen of various religious persuasions, on the principle of promoting the establishment and assisting in the support of schools, in which the appointment of governors and teachers, and the admission of scholars should be uninfluenced by religious distinctions, and in which the Bible and Testament, without note or comment should be read, excluding catechisms and books of religious controversy. In 1814-15 a grant of 6,980l. Irish currency, for the above objects, was made to this society, which removed its establishment to

" His Majesty's present government are of opinion
that no private society deriving a part, however small,
of their annual income from private sources, and only
made the channel of the munificence of the legislature,
without being subject to any direct responsibility, could
adequately and satisfactorily accomplish the end proposed ; and while they do full justice to the liberal views
with which that society was originally instituted, they
cannot but be sensible that one of its leading principles
was calculated to defeat its avowed objects, as experience
has subsequently proved that it has. The determination to enforce in all their schools the reading of the
Holy Scriptures without note or comment, was undoubtedly taken with the purest motives ; with the
wish at once to connect religious with moral and literary education, and at the same time not to run the
risk of wounding the peculiar feelings of any sect, by
catechetical instruction, or comments which might tend
to subjects of polemical controversy. But it seems to
have been overlooked, that the principles of the Roman
catholic church (to which, in any system intended for
general diffusion throughout Ireland, the bulk of the
pupils must necessarily belong) were totally at variance
with this principle ; and that the indiscriminate reading
of the Holy Scriptures without note or comment, by
children, must be peculiarly obnoxious to a church
which denies, even to adults, the right of unaided
private interpretation of the sacred volume, with respect
to articles of religious belief."

" Shortly after its institution, although the society
prospered and extended its operations under the fos-
tering care of the legislature, this vital defect began to
be noticed ; and the Roman catholic clergy began to

Kildare-street, and thence took the name of " The Kildare-street Society ;"
and annual grants were continued subsequently, varying from 10,000l. in 1821,
to 25,000l. in 1830, the number of pupils within that period increasing from
36,637 to 132,530.

exert themselves with energy and success against a system to which they were on principle opposed, and which they feared might lead in its results to proselytism, even although no such object were contemplated by its promoters. When this opposition arose, founded on such grounds, it soon became manifest that the system could not become one of national education."

" The commissioners of education in 1824-5, sensible of the defects of the system, and of the ground, as well as the strength of the objection taken, recommended the appointment of two teachers in every school, one protestant and the other Roman catholic, to superintend separately the religious education of the children; and they hoped to have been able to agree upon a selection from the Scriptures that might have been generally acquiesced in by both persuasions. But it was soon found that these schemes were impracticable; and, in 1828, a committee of the house of commons,[e] to which were referred the various Reports of the commissioners of education, recommended a system to be adopted, which should afford, if possible, a combined literary, and a separate religious education, and should be capable of being so far adapted to the views of the religious persuasions which prevail in Ireland, as to render it, in truth, a system of National education for the poorer classes of the community."

The letter next points out, that on the composition of the board will in a great degree depend the obtaining of public confidence, and the success of the measure; and it is then declared to be the intention of government—

" That the board should exercise a complete control over the various schools which may be erected under its auspices; or which having been already established,

---

[e] Ante, p. 108.

may hereafter place themselves under its management, and submit to its regulations. Subject to these, applications for aid will be admissible from Christians of all denominations; but as one of the main objects must be to unite in one system, children of different creeds, and as much must depend upon the co-operation of the resident clergy, the board will probably look with peculiar favour upon applications proceeding either from—

" 1st.—The protestant and Roman catholic clergy of the parish; or

" 2nd.—One of the clergymen, and a certain number of the parishioners professing the opposite creed; or

" 3rd.—Parishioners of both denominations.

" Where the application proceeds exclusively from protestants, or exclusively from Roman catholics, it will be proper for the board to make inquiry as to the circumstances which lead to the absence of any names of the persuasion which does not appear.

" The board will note all applications for aid, whether granted or refused, with the ground of the decision; and annually submit to parliament a Report of their proceedings.

" They will invariably require, as a condition not to be departed from, that local funds shall be raised, upon which any aid from the public will be dependent."

The letter then goes into a statement of various kinds of local aid to be required; the school-hours to be observed; and the time for religious instruction. After which, it proceeds—

" The board will exercise the most entire control over all books to be used in the schools, whether in the combined moral and literary, or separate religious instruction; none to be employed in the first except under the sanction of the board, nor in the latter, but with the approbation of those members of the board who are of the same religious persuasion with those for whose use they are intended. *Although it is not designed to exclude from the list of books for the combined instruction such portions of sacred history, or of religious or moral teaching as may be approved of by the board, it is to be understood that this is by no means intended to convey a perfect and sufficient religious education, or to supersede the necessity of separate religious instruction on the day set apart for the purpose.*"

The part here printed in italics is not in the copy of the letter published with the 1st *Report* of the Commissioners of National Education, but it is in a copy annexed to the 8th *Report*, and is believed to be the true one. The remainder of the letter relates to school arrangements and other proceedings of the board.

On the 6th of March 1832, a lengthened discussion on the government plan of education took place in the house of commons, in the course of which Mr. Stanley stated his views on the subject in answer to the objections raised by several members; and ended by saying, that " He was far from thinking the system now about to be carried into effect was perfect, but he believed that it was the most likely to unite the people of all religious persuasions in the education of their children, and produce those results which, the Scriptures said, were the fruits of the Christian religion—peace, meekness, gentleness and love." On the 23rd of July following, 37,500*l.* was voted " in aid of the funds to be appropriated to the new system of education," which thenceforward may be regarded as permanently established; and in 1844 the board was duly incorporated by royal charter.

*1832.
Discussion in parliament on the government plan of education.*

We now approach a period when public attention was very generally and very earnestly directed to the condition of the poor, and to the operation of the laws providing for their relief. In 1832 commissioners were appointed to inquire into these subjects in England, and the reader is referred to the 2nd volume of the ' *History of the English Poor Laws*' for information as to their Report on the occasion, and also for an account of the important measure which was founded thereon.

On the 25th September 1833, commissioners were appointed " to inquire into the condition of the poorer classes in Ireland, and into the various institutions at present established by law for their relief; and also whether any and what further remedial measures appear to be requisite to ameliorate the condition of the Irish poor or any portion of them." [f] An extensive field of inquiry was thus laid open to the commissioners, who forthwith entered upon the duties confided to them; and it must be admitted that there could hardly have been any more important, or more highly responsible.

1833.
Commission to inquire into the condition of the poorer classes in Ireland.

In July 1835 the commissioners made their first Report—" *as to the modes in which the destitute classes in Ireland are supported, to the extent and efficiency of those modes, and their effects upon those who give, and upon those who receive relief.*" A large body of evidence is appended to the Report, which evidence the commissioners say is now complete, containing parochial examinations made in one parish in each of seventeen counties, relative to the present modes of relieving—

1835.
The commissioners' first report.

---

[f] The commissioners were, the Archbishop of Dublin, Dr. Murray (the Roman catholic Archbishop), Rev. Charles Vignoles, Richard More O'Farrall Esq., Rev. James Carlisle, Fenton Hort Esq., John Corrie Esq., James Naper Esq. and William Battie Wrightson Esq. The Right Hon. A. R. Blake was subsequently added to the commission.

" Deserted and orphan children.

" Illegitimate children and their mothers.

" Widows having families of young children.

" The impotent through age or other permanent infirmity.

" The sick poor, who in health are capable of earning their subsistence.

" The able-bodied out of work.

" Vagrancy as a mode of relief."

An examination of every dispensary in nine counties is also given, and of every infirmary, and some dispensaries and hospitals in eleven counties. Likewise the examinations concerning institutions not medical, for the relief of different classes of the poor, which are said to be " principally mendicity institutions, houses of industry, almshouses, and societies for visiting the destitute and distributing food, money, or clothes," in all the large towns.

After thus enumerating the several heads or divisions under which their investigations were conducted, the commissioners proceed to state—

1st.—The difficulties they had to encounter from the extensive and complicated nature of the subject, and the peculiar social condition of the Irish people.

2ndly.—The course they pursued in collecting information, " showing how far it is full and impartial, and therefore how far worthy of confidence." And

3rdly.—The reasons why they are not yet able to report—" Whether any and what further remedial measures appear to be requisite to ameliorate the condition of the Irish poor, or any of them."

These points are all largely dwelt upon, especially the first. On every side, the commissioners say, they were assailed by the theories of persons who might be

supposed to possess means of forming a sound judgment
—" one party attributed all the poverty and wretchedness of the country to an asserted extreme use of ardent
spirits, and proposed a system for repressing illicit dis-
tillation, for preventing smuggling, and for substituting beer and coffee. Another party found the cause
in the combination among workmen, and proposed
rigorous laws against trades unions. Others again were
equally confident, that the reclamation of the bogs and
waste lands was the only practicable remedy. A fourth
party declared the nature of the existing connexion
between landlord and tenant to be the root of all the
evil. Pawnbroking, redundant population, absence of
capital, peculiar religious tenets and religious differences, political excitement, want of education, the mal-
administration of justice, the state of prison discipline,
want of manufactures and of inland navigation, with a
variety of other circumstances, were each supported by
their various advocates with earnestness and ability, as
being either alone, or jointly with some other, the
primary cause of all the evils of society ; and loan
funds, emigration, the repression of political excitement,
the introduction of manufactures, and the extension of
inland navigation, were accordingly proposed each as
the principal means by which the improvement of
Ireland could be promoted." The commissioners abstain
from expressing their opinion upon any of these propositions, but they determine " that the inquiry should
embrace every subject to which importance seemed to
be attached by any large number of persons."

Under the second division of their Report, the commissioners advert in considerable detail to the obvious
impossibility of collecting the necessary information
themselves, and the difficulty of finding Irishmen at
once competent and impartial to undertake the duty ;
and they determine as the only mode of combining
local knowledge with impartiality, to unite in the in-

quiry " a native of Great Britain with a resident native of Ireland." And in order that the evidence might be full and impartial, and be collected and registered in a satisfactory manner, the assistant-commissioners who had been appointed were desired to adopt in their investigations the following course of procedure :—

First—" To request the attendance of persons of each grade in society, of each of the various religious persuasions, and of each party in politics; to give to the testimony of each class an equal degree of attention, and to make the examinations in presence of all. Not to allow any person to join in conducting the examination, and to state at the opening of the proceedings, that any statement made by an individual, and not impugned by any person present, would be considered to be acknowledged as at least probable by all."

Second—" To note down at the time of examination, the replies given, or the remarks which occurred to him ; to register, as nearly as might be possible in the words of each witness, the statements which might be made ; to register the names of all the persons who attended the examination; and before proceeding to examine another district, to send the minutes of the previous examination to the office in Dublin, signed by both the assistant-commissioners."

With regard to the third head, that is the reasons for not yet being able to report " whether any and what further remedial measures appear to be requisite to ameliorate the condition of the Irish poor, or any portion of them"—The commissioners observe that the reasons are sufficiently apparent in the fact that they have not yet completed their inquiry into the causes of destitution. They would, they say, be little worthy of the high trust reposed in them, were they content with deciding upon the extent and nature of distress, or upon the means of only present alleviation. " We consider it our duty (they remark) to endeavour if possible, to investigate the causes of the destitution which we discover, and to ascertain why classes of his Majesty's subjects are from time to time falling into a state of wretchedness; why the labouring population do not provide against those events which seem inevitable; why the able-bodied labourer does not provide against the sickness of himself, or that of the various members of his family; against the temporary absence of employment; against the certain infirmity of age; against the destitution of his widow and his children in the contingent event of his own premature decease; whether these omissions arise from any peculiar improvidence in his habits, or from the insufficiency of employment, or from the low rate of his wages." It would not even be sufficient to answer that the limited amount of employment and the rate of his wages will not permit him. " It is our duty (they say) to carry the investigation further, and at least to endeavour to trace whether there be any circumstances which restrict the amount of employment, or the rate of wages; or in any other way offer impediments to the improvement of the people, which are such as can be remedied by legislation."

The commissioners accordingly in the first place directed their attention to agriculture, that being, they observe, the principal occupation of the Irish people. There was said to be much unreclaimed land which might be brought into cultivation, and throughout Ireland the land already in cultivation might be better worked, and thus the demand for labour be increased. The commissioners wish to ascertain the

extent to which such statements are well founded, and
whether the evil is attributable to want of capital or to
want of skill; and " whether there are any circumstances which have deterred British capitalists from
coming to Ireland, or have prevented the investment
in agriculture of capital existing in Ireland, and to
what extent those circumstances have proved injurious;
and in case the evil arises from a deficiency of skill in
the tenantry, to ascertain whether there are any means
by which a superior knowledge of agriculture can be
diffused." By endeavouring to prevent the occurrence
of destitution, they consider that they will more effectually fulfil their mission, than if they merely devised the
means for its alleviation after it had arisen. They
shall, they say, " feel deep pain should they be compelled to leave to any portion of the peasantry of
Ireland, a continuation of distress on the one hand, or
a mere offer of charity on the other—far more grateful
(it is added) would be the office of recommending measures by which the industrious labourer might have the
prospect of a constant field for his exertions, with a
remuneration sufficient for his present demands, and
admitting of a provision against those contingencies
which attach to himself and to his family." They declare
it to be their anxious wish to do more than diminish
the wretchedness of portions of the working classes, and
that they are most solicitous to place the whole of those
classes in the greatest state of comfort consistently with
the good of the rest of society.

In answer to certain complaints which appear to
have been made " within and out of parliament" of the
time and money consumed in the present inquiry, the
commissioners explain at some length the impossibility
of proceeding more rapidly. They however admit that
the time will exceed that occupied by several other inquiries, and particularly by that on the English Poor-

law, to which they specially refer—" because the highest estimate has been formed of the manner in which it was conducted, both as regards diligence and accuracy, and because they feel that in measuring their labours, and the time they are likely to occupy by such a standard, they shall have taken the surest mode of showing that they have used the utmost diligence."

The foregoing summary exhibits the general purport of the commissioners' first Report, which it will be observed aims rather at explaining what ought to be and what is further intended to be done, than pointing out remedies or deducing practical conclusions from the " large body of evidence " which had been taken. It is impossible not to concur in the views and reasonings expressed by the commissioners with regard to the spirit in which the inquiry should be conducted, and also as to the objects sought to be attained : but nothing definite is proposed, nor any practical suggestion offered ; and as the commissioners admit that they had been occupied a year and ten months in the inquiry, we can hardly wonder that some impatience should be manifested " both in and out of parliament" on the occasion. The evidence presented with the Report was no doubt important, and calculated to afford much valuable information on the several points to which it specifically referred ;[g] but the mere collecting and grouping of such evidence, unaccompanied by any condensed summary of its import, or practical deduction from its details, could not be expected to be very satisfactory or very useful, either to the legislature or to the public generally.

In the early part of the following year the commissioners made a second Report " on that part of the inquiry which respects the various institutions at present established by law for the relief

1836.
The com-
missioners'
second
report.

---

[g] See the seven heads of inquiry set out, ante page 119.

of the poor." These are said to be—medical institutions, lunatic asylums, houses of industry, and foundling hospitals; and although much of the information given respecting them has been anticipated by the Report of the select committee of 1830,[h] it will be convenient to insert in this place a short abstract of the Report on these institutions, the most numerous of which are the medical charities.

To establish an infirmary, 500*l.* must be first raised by voluntary contributions, to which a grant not exceeding 1,500*l.* may be made by government, provided the distance be not less than ten miles from any existing infirmary. The funds for its support are provided by grand-jury presentments not exceeding 600*l.* in any one year, and a grant of 100*l.* by government towards the salary of the surgeon. The number of county infirmaries is stated to be 31, in addition to which there are 5 city and town infirmaries. Each is governed by a corporation, consisting of certain official persons, together with the donors of twenty guineas and upwards, and annual subscribers of three guineas. The corporation of governors appoint the medical officers, regulate the admission of patients, enact by-laws, and have the entire control of the institution. *Infirmaries.*

Dispensaries were established for affording medical relief to those poor persons who are too distant to receive aid from an infirmary. They are governed by the same corporation, with the addition of subscribers of not less than one guinea annually, and are supported by such subscriptions, together with grand-jury presentments not exceeding a like amount. The number of separate dispensaries is 452, and there are 42 more united with fever hospitals. *Dispensaries.*

The great prevalence of fever in Ireland rendered

---

[h] Ante, pp. 95 to 108.

hospitals for the special treatment of fever cases, ab-
Fever
hospitals. solutely essential to the general security; and
for providing such hospitals, of which there
are 28, grand juries may present sums equal to double
the amount of voluntary subscriptions, and government
may also make advances for the purpose, to be subsequently repaid by instalments. By the 58*th* *Geo. 3rd,*
cap. 47,[i] provision is made for the appointment of a
board of health, with extensive powers, whenever fever
occurs in a town or district; but it appears that this
provision has been rarely acted upon.

The total expense of supporting these infirmaries,
dispensaries and fever hospitals, in the year 1833 as
stated in tables appended to the Report, was 109,054*l.*—
of which amount grand-jury presentments furnished
55,065*l.*—subscriptions 37,562*l.*—parliamentary grants
6,661*l.*, and petty-sessions fees and miscellaneous
funds 9,766*l.* The entire number of cases relieved
in the same year, was 30,634 intern, and 1,243,314
extern.

The lord-lieutenant is empowered to direct as many
Lunatic
asylums. lunatic asylums to be provided as he may think
fit, and the grand juries are required to pre-
sent such sums as may be necessary for defraying the
expense of erecting and supporting them. Eleven
were completed, or in progress towards completion;
and the total amount of expenditure on them in 1833
was 26,247*l.*

With regard to these institutions the commissioners
remark — " The medical relief at present afforded
throughout Ireland is very unequally distributed. In
the county of Dublin, containing exclusive of the city
about 176,000 inhabitants, and about 375 square miles,
there are 24 dispensaries, or one to every 7,333 inhabitants. In the county of Meath, containing about

---

[i] Ante, p. 77.

176,800 inhabitants, and about 886 square miles, there are 19 dispensaries, or one for every 9,306 inhabitants. In the county of Mayo, containing 366,328 inhabitants, and about 2,100 square miles, there is only one dispensary supported at the public expense." Such inequalities, it is observed, are the necessary consequence of a law which renders the establishment of a dispensary contingent upon voluntary contributions. In districts abounding in rich resident proprietors, a medical charity is least wanted, but subscriptions are there most easily obtained; whilst in districts where there are few or possibly no resident proprietors, the aid is most wanted, but there are no subscribers, and consequently there is no medical charity.

Houses of industry (or workhouses) are established and regulated under the provisions of the 11*th* and 12*th* Geo. 3*rd*, cap. 30,[k] the 46*th* Geo. 3*rd*, cap. 95,[k] and the 58*th* Geo. 3*rd*, cap. 47.[k] There are nine of these institutions in Ireland, and of some of them a brief account is given; but it is said to be difficult to judge of the economy with which they are conducted. The total income of the houses of industry in the year 1833 derived from grand-jury presentments, subscriptions, and miscellaneous sources, and including a parliamentary grant of 20,000*l*. to the Dublin institution, was 32,967*l*., and the number of inmates on the books was 2,732.

There were two large foundling hospitals, one in Dublin, the other in Cork, and a small one in Galway. With the exception of one child under peculiar circumstances, there have been no admissions for some time into the Dublin house, and the establishment is only used for the occasional accommodation of such children as are still on the books; and as these are disposed of, will cease altogether. The Cork hospital is

Houses of industry.

Foundling hospitals.

---

[k] Ante, pp. 51, 74, and 77.

supported principally by a tax on coals : it is still open, and has 1,329 on the books. At Galway the number of children is only eight. These institutions, the commissioners remark, are now acknowledged to be in their nature utterly indefensible. The expense of the Cork and Galway establishments in 1833, derived from miscellaneous sources, was 6,628*l.* The parliamentary grant to the Dublin foundling hospital in 1828 was 34,000*l.* Supposing it to have been 30,000*l.* in 1833, it would make the entire charge of these institutions, in the latter year, amount to 36,628*l.*

The total charge of the foregoing institutions as stated in the tables appended to the Report, is as follows :—

Infirmaries	
Dispensaries	£109,054
Fever hospitals	
Lunatic asylums	26,247
Houses of industry	32,967
Foundling hospitals	36,628
	£204,896

Of this sum upwards of 50,000*l.* appears to have been furnished by parliamentary grants, the remainder being derived from grand-jury presentments, voluntary contributions, and other local sources.

The commissioners think that some provision ought to be made for poor persons discharged from hospitals in a state of convalescence, and also for persons suffering from chronic and incurable disease, neither being proper objects of ordinary hospital treatment. They are likewise of opinion that a public provision should be made for the deaf dumb and blind poor, such persons being, they consider, peculiarly deserving of assistance.

The impatience of the public was not likely to be satisfied by the appearance of this second Report, which contained no recommendations, and added nothing to

what was previously known of the condition of the
Irish poor. For a series of years inquiry after inquiry
had been instituted by commissions and committees
into that condition, with a view to devise means for its
amelioration; but without leading to any satisfactory
result. And now, after two years and a half had been
spent in prosecuting like inquiries, and this moreover
by men specially selected for the task, and standing
deservedly high in public estimation for talent and
acquirements, people began to fear that the result
would be again the same, and that time labour and
money would have been expended in vain. It was
known, or at least generally surmised, that differences
of opinion existed among the commissioners, as to the
nature of the recommendations which should be made
by them conjointly; some being in favour of the imposition of a general rate for the relief of the poor, and
others advocating a system of voluntary contributions
for that purpose. The latter pointed to Scotland as an
example to be followed, and the former to England.
Under these circumstances it is not surprising that the
question should occupy a good deal of public attention,
and that those who possessed, or were supposed to
possess information on the subject, should be induced
or invited to express their opinions with regard to it.
Pamphlets were written, and speeches made, contrasting the advantages and disadvantages inherent in the
compulsory and the voluntary systems of relief, as well
generally, as with reference to the case of Ireland; and
the entire subject became a matter of very general discussion, of which the proceedings under the amended
Poor Law in England naturally formed a part, and thus
gave additional interest to the question.

The author being at that time a member of the
English Poor Law Commission, the subject was
necessarily much pressed upon his notice; and
having reason to believe that a statement of

'Sugges-
tions' by
the author,
January 21,
1836.

his views in reference to it would be acceptable, he prepared for the consideration of government, a series of
suggestions founded upon a general view of social requirements, and upon his experience of the working of
the English Poor Law. He did not pretend to any personal knowledge of the state of Ireland, but considered
that the information furnished by the evidence appended
to the commissioners' first Report, showed that destitution and wretchedness prevailed to such an extent among
the poorer classes in that country, that legislative interference could no longer be delayed without compro-
mising the general security; and contrasting the state
of the English poor with what existed in Ireland,
he attempted to point out a remedy, or at least a
palliative for the evils which prevailed there. This
he was induced to do without waiting for the final
report of the inquiry commissioners, as the mode of
comparison pursued by him was different from the
course which they would adopt, and likewise because
the commissioners indicated their intention of taking
the general circumstances of the country into consideration, whilst he proposed to limit his suggestions to one
object, with a view to a single and specific remedy.

These 'Suggestions' were framed in considerable
detail, and recommended the application of the amended
system of English Poor Law to Ireland, with certain
modifications, calculated to guard against the evils which
had. sprung from the old law in England, and at the
same time be sufficient for the relief of a large portion
of the destitute classes who stood most in need of it.
The 'Suggestions' were presented to Lord John Russell
in January, about the same time as the commissioners'
second Report; and on perusing them now, after so
long an interval, and with all the experience since acquired, the author finds little to alter in what he then
ventured to suggest.

The long-expected final Report was at length re-

ceived, embodying all the recommendations for ameliorating the condition of the Irish poor, which
after nearly three years of inquiry and deliberation, the commissioners felt themselves warranted in˙submitting to government. It commenced
by stating, that the evidence annexed to the former
Reports proves the existence of deep distress in all parts
of Ireland. There is not, it is said, the division of
labour which exists in Great Britain. The labouring
class look to agriculture alone for support, whence the
supply of agricultural labour greatly exceeds the demand
for it; and small earnings, and widespread misery, are
the consequence. Tables are given of the population
of Great Britain and Ireland respectively, of the classes
and occupations in each, the quantity of cultivated and
uncultivated land, the proportions of agricultural produce, and the wages of agricultural labourers—from
which, the commissioners say it appears—" that in
Great Britain the agricultural families constitute little
more than a fourth, while in Ireland they constitute
about two-thirds of the whole population; that there
were in Great Britain in 1831,—1,055,982 agricultural
labourers, in Ireland 1,131,715,—although the cultivated land of Great Britain amounts to about 34,250,000
acres, and that of Ireland only to about 14,600,000."
So that there are in Ireland about five agricultural
labourers for every two that there are for the same
quantity of land in Great Britain. It further appears
that the agricultural produce of Great Britain is more
than four times that of Ireland; that agricultural wages
vary from 6d. to 1s. a day; that the average of the
country is about 8½d.; and that the earnings of the
labourers come on an average of the whole class, to from
2s. to 2s. 6d. a week, or thereabouts, for the year round.

Thus circumstanced, the commissioners observe, " it
is impossible for the able-bodied, in general, to provide
against sickness or the temporary absence of employ-

ment, or against old age, or the destitution of their widows and children in the contingent event of their own premature decease." A great portion of them are, it is said, insufficiently provided with the commonest necessaries of life. " Their habitations are wretched hovels, several of a family sleep together upon straw, or upon the bare ground, sometimes with a blanket, sometimes even without so much to cover them; their food commonly consists of dry potatoes, and with these they are at times so scantily supplied, as to be obliged to stint themselves to one spare meal in the day. There are even instances of persons being driven by hunger to seek sustenance in wild herbs. They sometimes get a herring or a little milk, but they never get meat except at Christmas, Easter, and Shrovetide.[m] Some go in search of employment to Great Britain during the harvest, others wander through Ireland with the same view. The wives and children of many are occasionally obliged to beg, but they do so reluctantly and with shame, and in general go to a distance from home that they may not be known. Mendicity too is the sole resource of the aged and impotent of the poorer classes in general, when children or relatives are unable to support them. To it therefore crowds are driven for the means of existence, and the knowledge that such is the fact leads to an indiscriminate giving of alms, which encourages idleness, imposture and general crime."

Such is described as being the condition of the great body of the labouring classes in Ireland, and " with these facts before us (the commissioners say) we cannot hesitate to state, that we consider remedial measures requisite to ameliorate the condition of the Irish poor— What those measures should be is a question compli-

---

[m] To partake of meat at these seasons is enjoined upon all the members of the Roman catholic church.

cated, and involving considerations of the deepest importance to the whole body of the people, both in Ireland and Great Britain. Society is so constructed, its various parts are so connected, the interests of all who compose it are so interwoven, the rich are so dependent on the labour of the poor, and the poor upon the wealth of the rich, that any attempt to legislate partially, or with a view to the good of a portion only, without a due regard to the whole of the community, must prove in the end fallacious, fatal to its object, and injurious in general to a ruinous degree."

None will deny the truth of these propositions, which doubtless ought to be kept in view in legislating for the relief of the poor, or for any other matter of general interest or importance. Their enunciation does not however materially assist in discovering a remedy for the fearful amount of destitution and suffering shown to prevail in Ireland, the descriptions of which as given in the Report, are here brought together in one point of view, in order that the reader may have the extent of the evil laid open before him.

It has, the commissioners say, " been suggested to us to recommend a Poor Law for Ireland similar to that of England, but we are of opinion that the provision to be made for the poor in Ireland must vary essentially from that made in England." The English law, it is said, requires that work and support should be found for all able-bodied persons who may be out of employment, and such work and support will now be provided for them only in a workhouse; so that if workhouses were to be established in Ireland as a means of relief, they must be sufficiently capacious for setting vast numbers of unemployed persons to work within them. The commissioners state that they " cannot estimate the number of persons in Ireland out of work and in distress during thirty weeks of the year, at less than 585,000, nor the number of persons dependent upon them at less than 1,800,000, making in the whole 2,385,000—This therefore (it is added) is about the number for which it would be necessary to provide accommodation in workhouses, if all who require relief were there to be relieved;" and they consider it impossible to provide for such a multitude, or even to attempt it with safety. The expense of erecting and fitting up the necessary buildings would, they say, "come to about 4,000,000*l.*, and allowing for the maintenance of each person 2½*d.* only a day (that being the expense at the mendicity establishment of Dublin) the cost of supporting the whole 2,385,000 for thirty weeks would be something more than 5,000,000*l.* a year; whereas the gross rental of Ireland (exclusive of towns) is estimated at less than 10,000,000*l.* a year, the net income of the landlords at less than 6,000,000*l.*, and the public revenue is only about 4,000,000*l.*"

The commissioners do not however think that such an expense would actually be incurred. On the contrary they are convinced that the able-bodied and their families would endure any misery rather than make a workhouse their domicile; and they add—" now if we thought that employment could be had provided due efforts were made to procure it, the general repugnance to a workhouse would be a reason for recommending that mode of relief, for assistance could be afforded through it to the few that might from time to time fall into distress, and yet no temptation be afforded to idleness and improvidence; but we see that the labouring class are eager for work, that work there is not for them, and that they are therefore, and not from any fault of their own, in permanent want." This, it is said, is just the state to which, on the authority of a passage quoted from the English Poor Law Commissioners,[n]

---

[n] The entire of the paragraph quoted would not bear out the interpretation here put upon it.

the workhouse system is held not to be applicable;
and if it were established in Ireland, would, the commissioners are persuaded, " be regarded by the bulk of
the population as a stratagem for debarring them of
that right to employment and support with which the
law professed to invest them." It is unnecessary, the
commissioners add, to point out the feelings which must
thus be created, or the consequences to which they
might lead; and they conclude this section of their
Report by saying—" We cannot therefore recommend
the present workhouse system of England as at all
suited to Ireland."

Having thus rejected the workhouse, the commissioners next consider how far the objections applicable
to a provision for enforcing in-door work, would be
applicable to one for enforcing out-door employment;
and they come to the conclusion, that having regard to
the number of persons for whom work must be found,
and the experience of the consequences to which out-
door compulsory employment led in England, any
attempt to introduce it into Ireland would be attended
with most pernicious results. " If (it is said) the
farmers were compelled to take more men than they
chose or thought they wanted, they would of course
reduce the wages of all to a minimum. If, on the other
hand, magistrates or other local authorities were empowered to frame a scale of wages or allowances, so as
to secure to each labourer a certain sum by the week,
we do not think they could, with safety to their persons
and property, fix a less sum than would be equal to the
highest rate of wages pre-existing in the district for
which they were required to act; nor would anything
less enable the labourer to support himself and his
family upon such food, with such clothing, and in such
a dwelling, as any person undertaking to provide permanently for human beings in a civilized country could
say they ought to be satisfied with. It would therefore

(the commissioners think) be necessary to fix different
scales of wages or allowances, which would average
for the whole of Ireland about 4s. 6d. a week. This
would be to double the present earnings of the body
of labourers, and these appear to amount to about
6,800,000l. a year. The additional charge would therefore come to about that sum."

The tenantry, the commissioners say, cannot be expected to bear this burden. They have not capital for
it, and the charge must therefore fall upon the landlords.
Rents would diminish, commerce would decay, and the
demand for agricultural produce and all commodities
save potatoes and coarse clothing would contract, while
the number of persons out of employment and in need
of support would increase, and general ruin ensue. The
well-known case of " Cholesbury" is then cited, and
held up as an example of what would follow in Ireland, " at the end of a year from the commencement
of any system for charging the land indefinitely with
the support of the whole labouring part of the community."

" With such feelings," the commissioners observe,
" and considering the redundancy of labour which now
exists in Ireland, how earnings are kept down by it,
what misery is thus produced, and what insecurity of
liberty property and life ensues, we are satisfied that
enactments calculated to promote the improvement of
the country, and so to extend the demand for free and
profitable labour, should make essential parts of any
law for ameliorating the condition of the poor. And
for the same reasons, while we feel that relief should be
provided for the impotent, we consider it due to the
whole community, and to the labouring class in particular, that such of the able-bodied as may still be unable
to find free and profitable employment in Ireland,
should be secured support only through emigration, or
as preliminary to it—those who desire to emigrate

should be furnished with the means of doing so in safety, and with intermediate support when they stand in need of it at emigrant depôts. It is thus, and thus only, that the market of labour in Ireland can be relieved from the weight that is now upon it, or the labourer be raised from his present prostrate state." Long quotations are then given from the several Reports of the assistant-commissioners, showing that, " the feelings of the suffering labourers in Ireland are also decidedly in favour of emigration." They do not desire workhouses, it is said, but they do desire a free passage to a colony where they may have the means of living by their own industry.

The commissioners conclude this section of their Report by saying, that they do not look to emigration as an object to be permanently pursued upon an extensive scale, nor as the chief means of relief for the evils of Ireland, but " as an auxiliary essential to a commencing course of amelioration." They then " proceed to submit a series of provisions for the improvement of Ireland, and the relief of the poor therein, including in the latter means of emigration."

The recommendations extend from section 5 to 15 inclusive, and are all more or less connected with agriculture, which is said to be the only pursuit for which the body of the people of Ireland are qualified by habit, and that it is chiefly through it that any general improvement in their condition can be effected. It is recommended—

1st. That a board constituted on the principle of the Bedford Level Corporation should be established, for carrying into effect a system of national improvement in Ireland, having a president and vice-president with suitable salaries, and who together with two of the judges to be appointed for the purpose, are to form a court of review and record, with power to hear and determine all matters connected with such improvements.

2nd. The "Board of Improvement" is to be authorized to appoint commissioners, who are to be armed with the usual powers given to commissioners under Enclosure Acts, and are from time to time to make surveys and valuations, and partitions of waste lands, the Board of Works making such main drains and roads as may be required, and taking, in consideration thereof, an allotment of a certain part of each waste in trust for the public, in proportion to the expense incurred in making the survey, partition, drainage, and roads.

3rd. With regard to land under cultivation, it is recommended that both draining and fencing should be enforced by law, and that the " Board of Improvement" should be empowered to appoint local commissioners for the purpose, for any district they may think proper. If the outlay to be incurred should exceed what the landlords or occupiers may be able to pay, 5 per cent. on the amount may be annually assessed and made payable to the Board of Works, which in consideration thereof is to advance the requisite sum—the funds placed at its disposal being proportionally increased.

4th. The " Board of Improvement " to be enabled to cause cabins which may be nuisances to be taken down, and to require the landlords to contribute towards the expense of removing the occupants and providing for them.

5th. The " Board of Improvement" to establish an agricultural model school, with four or five acres of land attached, in so many parishes or districts as may be thought necessary, the master to undergo due examination, and to give instruction in letters and in agriculture.

6th. Tenants for life, with the approval of the

" Board of Improvement," to be empowered to grant leases for thirty-one years, and to charge the property with the amount expended in effecting permanent improvements.

7th. A fiscal board to be established in every county, with the powers to make presentments for public works now vested in grand juries, and to be required to present such sums as may be appointed by the Improvement Board.

8th. The Board of Works to be authorized to undertake any public works " such as roads, bridges, deepening rivers, or removing obstructions in them, and so forth," that within certain limitations may be approved by the " Board of Improvement."

A dissertation is then introduced on the effect of Irish immigrants on the labour-market of England, and ending with this quotation from Burke—" England and Ireland may flourish together. The world is large enough for us both. Let it be our care not to make ourselves too little for it." The commissioners say it was their intention " to inquire relative to trade and manufactures, to the fisheries, and to mining ; but that it has been found impossible to go into those matters through want of time."

The foregoing summary of the commissioners' recommendations can hardly be said to come within the province of poor-law legislation, but it has been thought right to insert them here, in order that the reader may see what were the commissioners' views with regard to the state of Ireland, and especially with regard to its wants, which apparently consist in a want of capital, and a want of skill. The first is proposed to be furnished by government through the Board of Works, the last it is proposed to supply by constituting a " Board of Improvement."

The 16th section of the Report commences with the

declaration " *We now come to measures of direct relief for the poor.*" After adverting to the Poor Laws of England and Scotland, the one carried into universal effect by local assessments, and the other "in general supported by voluntary contributions administered by officers known to the law and responsible to it "—the commissioners say "they have shown by their second Report that the institutions existing in Ireland for the relief of the poor are houses of industry, infirmaries, fever hospitals, lunatic asylums, and dispensaries ; that the establishment of these, except as to lunatic asylums, is not compulsory, but dependent upon private subscriptions, or the will of grand juries; that there are but nine houses of industry in the whole country ; that while the provision made for the sick poor in some places is extensive, it is in other places utterly inadequate ; and that there is no general provision made for the aged, the impotent, or the destitute." Much, it is added, is certainly given in Ireland in private charity, " but it is not given upon any organised system of relief, and the abundant alms which are bestowed, in particular by the poorer classes, unfortunately tend to encourage mendicancy with its attendant evils."

The commissioners then declare that upon the best consideration they have been able to give to the whole subject, they think that a legal provision should be made, and rates levied, " for the relief and support of incurable as well as curable lunatics, of idiots, epileptic persons, cripples, deaf and dumb and blind poor, and all who labour under permanent bodily infirmities—such relief and support to be afforded within the walls of public institutions; also for the relief of the sick poor in hospitals, infirmaries, and convalescent establishments, or by extern attendance and a supply of food as well as medicine where the persons to be relieved are not in a state to be removed from home ; also for the purpose of emigration, for the support of penitentiaries to which vagrants may be sent, and for the maintenance of deserted children ; also towards the relief of aged and infirm persons, of orphans, of helpless widows with young children, of the families of sick persons, and of casual destitution."

For effecting these several purposes, it is recommended that powers should be vested in Poor Law Commissioners as in England, " for carrying into execution all such provisions as shall be made by law for the relief of the poor in Ireland, and that they shall be authorized to appoint assistant-commissioners to act under their directions." It is proposed that the commissioners should divide the country into relief districts, and cause the lands of each to be surveyed and valued, with the names of all proprietors of houses or lands and of all lessees and occupiers thereof, and the annual value of such houses and lands respectively, the same to be lodged at such place within the district as the commissioners shall appoint, and public notice thereof to be given.

It is also recommended that a board of guardians should be elected for each district by the ratepayers, consisting of proprietors, lessees, and occupiers, a certain number of the board to go out each year and others to be elected in their stead. The board of guardians to have the direction of all the institutions for the relief of the poor within the district which are supported by local rates, and to cause them to be duly upheld and maintained. If any district refuse or neglect to appoint guardians, or when appointed if the guardians refuse or neglect to act, the Poor Law Commissioners to be empowered to appoint assistant-commissioners for such district with suitable salaries, who are to exercise all the powers of the board of guardians. The salaries to be paid by a rate on the district.

It is likewise proposed that there should be so many asylums in Ireland for the relief and support of lunatics

and idiots, and for the support and instruction of the
deaf and dumb and blind poor, so many depôts for
receiving persons willing to emigrate, and so many
penitentiaries for vagrants, as the Poor Law Commissioners shall appoint—that these several establishments
should be national, and that for maintaining them &c.
the commissioners should be empowered to rate the
whole of Ireland, and to require the boards of guardians
to raise a proportional share thereof in each district,
according to the annual value of its property. It is
moreover recommended that there should be in each
district an institution for the support and relief of
cripples, and persons afflicted with epilepsy or other
permanent disease; also an infirmary, hospital and convalescent establishment, and such number of dispensaries as may be necessary, the whole to be provided
for by local assessment. A loan fund administered
according to regulations approved by the commissioners, is likewise recommended to be established in
every district.

With regard to emigration, as the whole United
Kingdom will, it is said, " be benefited in a very great
degree, and particularly in point of revenue, by the
improvement which extensive emigration coming in aid
of a general course of amelioration cannot fail to produce in Ireland, one-half of the expense should, the
commissioners submit, be borne by the general funds
of the empire." And considering the particular benefit
which Ireland will derive from it, and especially those
landlords whose estates may thus be relieved from a
starving population, it is proposed that in rural districts
the other half should be defrayed partly by the national
rate, and partly by the owners of the lands from which
the emigrants remove, or from which they may have
been ejected within the preceding twelve months. It
is further proposed that all the necessary arrangements
for carrying on emigration, should be made between the

Poor Law Commissioners and the Colonial Office; " and that all poor persons whose circumstances require it, shall be furnished with a free passage and with the means of settling themselves in an approved British colony ;" and likewise—" that the means of emigration shall be provided for the destitute of every class and description who are fit subjects for emigration ; that depôts shall be established, where all who desire to emigrate may be received; that those who are fit for emigration be there selected for the purpose, and that those who are not shall be provided for under the directions of the Poor Law Commissioners ;" who will moreover be authorized to borrow moneys from the Exchequer Bill Loan Commissioners for the purposes of emigration, or for defraying the cost of any buildings they may think necessary, and also " to secure the repayment thereof by a charge upon the national rate."

The commissioners likewise propose that the laws with respect to vagrancy should be altered. " At present," they say, " persons convicted of vagrancy may be transported for seven years—our recommendation is that penitentiaries shall be established to which vagrants when taken up shall be sent; that they be charged with the vagrancy before the next quarter sessions, and if convicted shall be removed as free labourers to such colony, not penal, as shall be appointed for them by the Colonial Department." But the wages earned in the colony are to be attached until the expense of their passage be defrayed ; and it is added by way of summary, that by such provisions as are now suggested, " all poor persons who cannot find means of support at home, and who are willing to live by their labour abroad, will be furnished with the means of doing so, and with intermediate support, if fit to emigrate ; and if not, will be otherwise provided for, while the idle who would rather beg than

labour, will be taken up, and the evil of vagrancy suppressed."

The 58*th* *George* 3*rd*, *cap.* 47, and an Act of the following year (*cap.* 41)° amending the same, are then
referred to, and the commissioners recommend that the
powers given by these Acts to vestries should be transferred to the boards of guardians of each district, and
that officers of health should be elected by them for
every parish within their jurisdiction—such officers of
health to grant tickets of admission to the next emigration depôt to any poor inhabitants of their parish who
may, on behalf of themselves or their families, demand
the same; and also, where necessary, to procure means
for passing such persons to the depôt. The officers of
health are moreover to pass all persons taken up under
the provisions of the above Acts to a penitentiary, and
also to cause all foundlings to be sent to nurse, "and
when of a suitable age to cause them to be removed
to an emigration depôt, from whence they may be
sent to an institution in some British colony, which
shall be appointed for receiving such children, and
training and apprenticing them to useful trades or
occupations." The officers of health are also to provide
in like manner for all orphan children,ᵖ and the funds
for the several purposes are to be raised by local assessment in the district. Provision is likewise to be made
at each depôt for receiving the persons sent thither
by the officers of health, such persons to be there supported and set to work until the period for emigration
arrives; and any persons who after entering an emigration depôt shall leave it, "without discharging such
expenses as may have been incurred with respect to
them, or who shall refuse to emigrate, shall be sub-

° Ante, pp. 77 and 78.

ᵖ The duties here proposed to be performed by the officers of health, are
similar to what are required from the relieving officer under the amended Poor
Law in England.

jected to the provisions recommended with respect to vagrants."

With respect to the relief of the aged and infirm, of orphans, helpless widows with young children, and destitute persons in general, it is stated that there is a difference of opinion—some of the commissioners " think the necessary funds should be provided in part by the public through a national rate, and in part by private associations, which, aided by the public, should be authorized to establish mendicity-houses and almshouses, and to administer relief to the indigent at their own dwellings, subject however to the superintendence and control of the Poor Law Commissioners ; while others think the whole of the funds should be provided by the public, one portion by a national rate and another by a local rate, and should be administered as in England by the board of guardians of each district." The majority are however of opinion, " that the plan of voluntary associations, aided by the public, should be tried in the first instance." Recommendations are then made as to the mode of raising and apportioning the rate. The commissioners have, they say, " anxiously considered the practicability of making the rate payable out of property of every description ; but the difficulty of reaching personal property in general by direct taxation, except through very inquisitorial proceedings, has obliged them to determine on recommending that the land should be the fund charged in the first instance with it."

There being, the commissioners say, reason to believe that the landed property of Ireland is so deeply encumbered, that a rate might absorb the whole income of some of the nominal proprietors, the Masters of the Court of Chancery were consulted on the subject, and from the facts they stated, " it appears that the average rent of land is under 1l. 12s. 6d. the Irish acre, equal to about 14s. 2d. the English ; that the gross landed rental of Ireland amounts to less than 10,000,000*l.*; that the expenses and losses cannot be taken at less than ten per cent., nor the annuities and the interest of charges payable out of the land at less than 3,000,000*l.* a year; so that the total net income is less than 6,000,000*l.*" The commissioners think therefore, that the encumbrancers should bear a share of the burden, and recommend " That persons paying any annual charge in respect of any beneficial interest in land, shall be authorised to deduct the same sum in the pound thereout, that he pays to the poor-rate." They also recommend " that the original rate shall never be raised by more than one-fifth, unless for the purpose of emigration."

As regards voluntary associations, it is proposed that the Poor Law Commissioners shall frame rules for their government, and that each association shall transmit to the commissioners an estimate of its probable expenditure and its funds for the year ensuing, and that they shall award such grant to it as they think proper. The commissioners to be also authorised " to advance to any voluntary association, out of the national rate, the whole sum which may be necessary for the building and outfit of a mendicity or alms house for any parish;" and if such mendicity or alms house be not afterwards duly maintained, the sum so advanced is to be repaid by the parish to the credit of the national rate.

Certain recommendations are then made with the view of promoting sobriety, and lessening " the inordinate use of ardent spirits"—also with reference to the Board of Charitable Bequests, whose functions may, it is suggested, be advantageously transferred to the Poor Law Commissioners—likewise the details of a plan for purchasing the tithe composition, and vesting it in the Poor Law Commissioners as a fund for the relief of the poor, by doing which, it is said, " there would be a surplus of 313,000*l.* a year applicable to the purposes of the national rate." In conclusion, the commissioners express their belief, that upon the whole there is a rising spirit of improvement in Ireland, which however requires to be stimulated by sound legislation, " or it cannot speedily relieve the country from the lingering effects of the evil system of former times." At present, it is observed, with a population nearly equal to half that of Great Britain, Ireland yields only about a twelfth of the revenue to the state that Great Britain does, nor can it yield more until it has more to yield. Increased means must precede increased contribution, and to supply Ireland with these is, the commissioners say, the great object of their recommendations.

Such was the commissioners' final Report on the condition of the Irish poor and the means for its amelioration, the substance and general import of which I have endeavoured to give with the fulness and completeness the importance of the subject demanded. The Report was not however signed by all the commissioners. Three of their body withheld their signature, and recorded their " reasons for dissenting from the principle of raising funds for the relief of the poor by the voluntary system, as recommended in the Report." [q] The ' Reasons ' are set forth in thirteen propositions, the most material of which are the following.

" Because—in the lamentably distressed state of the Irish poor, any system of relief to be effectual must be comprehensive, uniform, and prompt; whilst the very constitution of voluntary associations proclaims that their operations must be tardy; and circumstanced as Ireland is in the distribution of her population, must be partial and precarious.

" Because—it is notorious that many contributions, in name voluntary, are frequently obligations of the severest character. The pressure of such a tax must be unequal. The class least removed from want, would furnish as it now does, the largest number of contributors, and to the greatest amount; whilst

---

[q] These were Dr. Vignoles, J. W. S. Naper Esq., and Lord Killeen.

the wealthier classes, resident as well as absentee, would in a great measure be exempted from the liability of contributing in proportion to their wealth, or even from contributing at all.

" Because—viewing the peculiar state of society in Ireland, the extent to which religious zeal prevails, as well as the influence it must exercise, we consider the difficulties attendant on the raising of a voluntary fund in the first instance, and of an impartial distribution of relief in the next, all but insurmountable.

" Because—the mendicity institutions of Dublin, Limerick, Newry, Birr, Sligo, Waterford and Londonderry, as well as the voluntary poor's fund established in some of the rural districts, afford strong proofs of the inefficiency of the support afforded to these institutions; for although they have not totally failed, yet their subscriptions are falling off, and they are by no means adequate to the relief of the objects they contemplate.

" Because—although we admit that there are districts in Ireland in which voluntary societies might be established, and which would afford means of constructing a local administration for the management of the poor's fund—still we feel satisfied that in the present state of society, and under the existing distribution of the population, such a system cannot be either comprehensive or uniform. We are therefore of opinion that the fund should be obtained by an assessment, wholly and not partially compulsory; and that it will be most efficiently managed by elective boards of guardians as in England, directed by responsible public officers whose proceedings shall be subjected to the strictest public scrutiny."

These are no doubt weighty reasons in favour of certain means being provided to meet a certainly recurring contingency. But reasons were also adduced on the opposite side of the question, the other eight commissioners having in a series of sixteen propositions likewise recorded their " reasons for recommending voluntary associations for the relief of the poor;"[r] of which ' Reasons' the following are the chief :—

---

[r] The commissioners who signed this schedule of reasons are, the Archbishop of Dublin, Dr. Murray the Roman catholic archbishop, Rev. Mr. Carlisle, Mr. F. Hort, Mr. John Corrie, Mr. W. B. Wrightson, the Right Hon. A. R. Blake, and Mr. J. J. Bicheno. The two latter had been subsequently added to the original commission.

" Because—there are and must necessarily be continually arising, many cases of real destitution which cannot be relieved by a compulsory assessment, without bringing claims upon it to an unlimited extent. The attempt was made in England to meet all cases of distress by a compulsory rate, and the consequence was, that in one year the rate amounted to the enormous sum of more than 7,800,000*l.* sterling ; and besides the oppressive amount of the assessments, it did much evil in pauperising a large portion of the labouring population.

" Because—although such cases of distress might, and probably would be, relieved by spontaneous charity, yet the leaving of such cases of distress to be relieved by the operation of undirected benevolence, inevitably leads to an extensive vagrancy. This is now the state of Ireland. On the most moderate computation the amount of spontaneous alms given, chiefly by the smaller farmers and cottars, is from one to two millions sterling annually ; but being given without system or without inquiry to the good and to the bad, the really destitute and the pretenders to destitution receive alike their maintenance out of the earnings of the industrious, to their great impoverishment, and to the great injury of the morals and good order of the kingdom.

" Because—the most direct and effectual, if not the only means of avoiding these two great evils, namely, an extensive and ruinous pauperism created by an attempt to make compulsory provision for all cases of destitution, and an extensive and equally ruinous vagrancy created by the want of public provision, is to endeavour to bring voluntary almsgiving under regulations and system, so as to direct it to the relief of real distress exclusively.

" Because—the best means of systematising and regulating voluntary almsgiving, is to hold out the offer of a measure of public aid for all voluntary associations, based on certain principles, and governed by fixed regulations approved by a central board.

" Because—while a fund thus founded upon voluntary contributions would provide effectual relief for those who are really destitute, the very nature of it would debar the poor from establishing legal claims upon it ; since the contribution to a voluntary fund being wholly spontaneous, the contributors could at any time withhold them, if an attempt were made to compel an appropriation of the joint fund contrary to their instructions.

" Because—the example of an organised system of relief for the poor by voluntary contribution is afforded in Scotland, where it has been eminently successful.

" Because—although the system of providing for the poor by means of voluntary associations, aided by the public purse, and constructed upon well-digested principles, may not succeed at once in every part of the country—yet that, so far as it does succeed, it will tend to bring the population into a sound state with respect to the poor, and will we trust gradually work its way over the face of the island, and probably supersede in many places, as the Scottish system does so extensively, the necessity of a compulsory rate. Whereas we are convinced, that although a compulsory rate might be rendered general more rapidly, and be administered by artificial means, it would every day become more difficult to manage, and tend to bring the country into a worse state than our inquiry has found it."

The arguments for and against establishing a system of relief in Ireland founded upon voluntary contributions, are here deliberately stated by the advocates of such a procedure on one side, and by its opponents on the other. The question is vitally important with regard to the relief of the Irish poor, and deserves the most careful consideration. If the voluntary system be susceptible of the organisation and the certainty its advocates assume, it might doubtless be made to a considerable extent available, although still open to the objection that it would operate unequally upon the absentee and the resident proprietor, upon the liberal man and the niggard. The majority of the commissioners, we see, attach much weight to the example of Scotland, where they believe the voluntary system to have " been eminently successful." How little ground there was for such belief, is shown in the recent working of that system ;[a] and as regards the combining public aid with voluntary contributions which is recommended, it may be

---

[a] See ' History of the Scotch Poor Law.' The number of parishes assessed to the relief of the poor in Scotland in 1855, was 700, and the number unassessed, in which the relief is raised by voluntary contributions, was 183. The latter are continually diminishing, and will probably ere long cease altogether.

remarked, that such a combination has always led to the whole charge being eventually borne by the public.

In addition to the two schedules of 'Reasons' already noticed, another document was appended to the Report, entitled 'Remarks on the Evidence &c., by one of the Commissioners.' This was prepared by Mr. Bicheno, as an exposition of his own peculiar views, and fills upwards of forty closely printed folio pages. It contains a good deal of information upon the state of the country, and the condition and habits of the people, selected from the evidence furnished by the assistant-commissioners ; but is too long for insertion. The concluding paragraph however indicates the spirit in which the 'Remarks' were written, and may therefore have a place ; it is as follows—" After all the assistance that can be extended to Ireland by good laws, and every encouragement afforded to the poor by temporary employment of a public nature, and every assistance that emigration and other modes of relief can yield, her *real* improvement must spring from herself, her own inhabitants, and her own indigenous institutions, irrespective of legislation, and English interference. It must be of a moral nature ; the improvement of the high and the low, the rich and the poor. Without this, her tenantry will be still wretched, and her landlords will command no respect ; with it, a new face will be given to the whole people."

Mr. Bicheno's remarks on the evidence.

Another paper, entitled 'Remarks on the Third Report of the Irish Poor Inquiry Commissioners,' was submitted to government shortly after the delivery of that Report. It was dated in July 1836, and was drawn up by George Cornewall Lewis Esq.,[t] who had been one of the assistant-commissioners for prosecuting the inquiry in Ireland. The objections to the system, or rather the several systems of relief

Mr. G. C. Lewis' remarks on the third report.

---

[t] Now Sir George Cornewall Lewis Bart., and Chancellor of the Exchequer.

recommended by the commissioners, are stated by Mr. Lewis with great force and clearness, and he comes to conclusions on the whole question very similar to those contained in the 'Suggestions' which had been submitted by the author in the month of January preceding.[u] He proposes to apply the principle of the amended English Poor Law to Ireland, including the workhouse, with regard to the rejection of which by the commissioners, he remarks—" as the danger of introducing a poor-law into Ireland is confessedly great, I can conceive no reason for not taking every possible security against its abuse. Now if anything has been proved more decisively than another by the operation of the Poor Law Amendment Act in England, it is that the workhouse is an all-sufficient test of *destitution*, and that it is the only test; that it succeeds as a mode of relief, and that all other modes fail. Why therefore, this tried guarantee against poor-law abuses is not to be employed, when abuses are, under the best system, almost inevitable, it seems difficult to understand. If such a safeguard were to be dispensed with anywhere, it would be far less dangerous to dispense with it in England than in Ireland."

An account of the further steps taken with reference to the commissioners' Report, and as regards the whole of the very important question to which it applies, will be given in the next chapter.

---

[u] Ante p. 129.

CHAPTER III.

Recommendation in the king's speech — Motions and other proceedings in the House of Commons — Lord John Russell's instructions to the author — The author's first Report — Lord John Russell's speech on introducing a bill founded on its recommendations — Progress of the bill interrupted by the death of the king — Author's second Report — Bill reintroduced and passed the Commons — Author's third Report — Bill passes the Lords, and becomes law.

THE impatience generally felt for the Report of the Irish Poor Inquiry Commissioners, was not a little increased by the uncertainty as to what would be its nature. It was known that there were great differences of opinion among the commissioners with regard to the remedy, although they were all agreed as to the existence of the evil, and the necessity for something being done towards its mitigation ; but what that something should be, was a question on which it was understood they by no means coincided. It was feared therefore, that the present inquiry would end, as others had ended, without any practical result. An impression had long prevailed, and was daily becoming stronger, of the necessity for making some provision for the relief of the destitute poor in Ireland. The perpetually-increasing intercourse between the two countries, brought under English notice the wretched state of a large proportion of the people in the sister island ; and the vast numbers of them who crossed the Channel in search of the means of living, and became more or less domiciled in the large towns and throughout the western districts of England, made it a matter of policy, as it assuredly was of humanity, to endeavour to improve their condition ; and nothing seemed so equitable or so readily effective for the purpose, as making property liable for the relief of destitution in Ireland, as was the case in England—in other words, establishing some description of poor-law.

On the assembling of parliament, the subject was
The king's speech on opening parliament, February 4, 1836.
thus referred to in the Royal speech—" a further Report of the Commission of Inquiry
into the condition of the poorer classes in Ireland will speedily be laid before you. You
will approach this subject with the caution due to its
importance and difficulty; and the experience of the
salutary effect produced by the Act for the amendment
of the laws relating to the poor in England and Wales,
may in many respects assist your deliberations." A
few days after (February 9th) Sir Richard Musgrave
moved for leave to bring in a bill for the relief of the
poor of Ireland in certain cases—" He himself," he said,
" lived in an atmosphere of misery, and being compelled
to witness it daily, he was determined to pursue the
subject, to see whether any and what relief could be
procured from parliament." On the 15th of February
another motion was made by the member for Stroud for
leave to introduce a bill for the ' Relief and Employment
of the Poor of Ireland ;' and on the 3rd of March following, a bill was submitted by Mr. Smith O'Brien,
framed upon the principle that in a system of poor-laws
for Ireland, there ought to be local administration, combined with central control—" local administration by
bodies elected by, and representing the contributors to
the poor-fund, and general central supervision and control on the part of a body named by the government,
and responsible to parliament."

These bills were all introduced, it will be observed,
Lord John Russell's observations on the commissioners' Report, April 18, 1836.
irrespective of the final Report of the Commis-
sioners of Inquiry, which indeed had not yet
been presented. But on the 18th of April, in
answer to a question respecting it, Lord John
Russell, then Secretary of State for the Home
Department, said " that the Report had been under
the consideration of government, and they certainly
had found in it a great variety of important matters;

at the same time he must add, that the suggestions in it were not of that simple and single nature as to allow them to be adopted without the caution which was recommended by the commissioners themselves." He could not, he said, conclude without adding, "that the Report was not only of extreme importance, but that the subject of it was of a nature to render it absolutely necessary that some measure should be brought forward and adopted. It would be anxiously considered by the government with a view to such measures, and there were none as affecting Ireland, either at present or perhaps within the next hundred years, which could possibly be of greater magnitude." On the 4th of May Mr. Poulett Scrope moved a series of resolutions expressive of the necessity for some provision for the relief of the Irish poor—in commenting on which, Lord Morpeth[a] admitted "that the hideous nature of the evils which prevailed amongst the poorer classes in Ireland, called earnestly for redress, and he thought no duty more urgent on the government and on parliament than to devise a remedy for them." Government were now he said engaged in determining on the steps proper to be taken, and at the first moment they were in a condition to propose such a general measure as they could recommend for adoption on their own responsibility, they would do so. On the 9th of June following, on the motion for postponing the consideration of Sir Richard Musgrave's bill, Lord Morpeth again assured the house "that the subject was under the immediate consideration of government; and that he was not without hope of their being enabled to introduce some preparatory measure in the present session; but at all events they would take the first opportunity

Lord Morpeth's observations in reference to the Poor-Law question.

---

[a] The present Earl of Carlisle, then Secretary for Ireland, and now Lord Lieutenant.

in the next session, of introducing what he hoped would be a complete and satisfactory measure ;" and here the matter rested for the present.

Parliament was prorogued on the 20th of August, without anything having been done, either with the bills introduced by individual members, or in regard to the Report of the commissioners of inquiry. The recommendations of the commissioners seem indeed to have increased rather than lessened the difficulties attending any measure for the relief of the Irish poor, owing probably to the recommendations " not being of that simple and single nature" to which the home secretary adverted in his address to the house on the 18th of April. Public attention nevertheless continued to be directed to the subject with undiminished earnestness, and government felt the necessity of coming to some early and definite conclusion as to the steps to be taken in regard to it.

Parliament prorogued August 20, 1836.

We have now reached a portion of our narrative when the author will be compelled to speak of himself, and the part taken by him, first in devising a poor-law for Ireland, and next in superintending its introduction into that country; and he is very anxious to bespeak an indulgent consideration for the difficulty in which he is placed, by having been thus personally engaged in the transactions which he will have to describe. The great social importance of the Irish Poor Law, imposes upon him the duty of giving a full and complete account of all that took place with regard to it; and he feels that this duty cannot be rendered less imperative, by the fact of his official connexion with the measure. He will therefore proceed to detail the circumstances as they severally occurred; and it will be more simple, and may save circumlocution for him to speak in the first person, on the occasions in which he was himself immediately concerned.

The author's connexion with the subject.

On the 22nd of August I received directions to proceed to Ireland, taking with me the Reports of the
commissioners of inquiry, and there to examine
how far it might be judicious or practicable to
offer relief to whole classes of the poor, whether of the sick, the infirm, or orphan children—whether such relief might not have the effect of promoting
imposture, without destroying mendicity—whether the
condition of the great bulk of the poorer classes would be
improved by such a measure—whether a rate limited in
its amount rather than its application, might be usefully
directed to the erection and maintenance of workhouses
for all those who sought relief as paupers—whether
any kind of workhouse can be established which should
not give its inmates a superior degree of comfort to
the common lot of the independent labourer—whether
the restraint of a workhouse would be an effectual
check to applicants for admission; and whether, if the
system were once established, the inmates would not
resist, by force, the restraints which would be necessary.
Supposing the workhouse system not to be advisable, I
was directed to consider in what other mode a national
or local rate might be beneficially applied; and to
examine the policy of establishing depôts where candi-
dates for emigration might resort. My attention was
also specially directed to the machinery by which rates
for the relief of the poor might be raised and expended;
and to the formation and constitution of a central
board, of local boards, of district unions, and of parochial vestries. I was also directed to inquire whether
the capital applied to the improvement of land, and the
reclaiming of bogs and wastes was perceptibly or notoriously increasing or diminishing, and to remark generally upon any plans which might lead to an increased
demand for labour; and lastly, to " carefully read the
bills which had been brought into the house of commons on this subject during that year, and the draft

[margin note:] Lord John Russell's letter of instructions, August 22, 1836.

of a bill prepared by one of the commissioners of inquiry in conformity with their Report."

It will thus be seen that the proposed inquiry was sufficiently extensive; and I hardly need say that I entered upon the duty assigned me with a deep sense of the responsibility it involved. The working of the English Poor Law, afforded means for obtaining some insight into the character and habits of such of the Irish as had become resident in the metropolis and the larger towns of England, and I immediately instituted inquiries on the subject among the workhouse masters and other officers of several of the London parishes where the Irish labourers principally resided. They all assured me as the result of their experience, that the discipline of a workhouse operated with the Irish precisely as it did with the English poor. There was in fact no difference in this respect, nor any greater difficulty with regard to the one, than there was in the management of the other. This was so far satisfactory; but further examination and inquiry were necessary for giving entire confidence on this point, and these could best be pursued in Ireland whither I accordingly proceeded early in September.

The evidence collected by the late commissioners of inquiry and appended to their Report, established so conclusively the existence of a state of poverty throughout Ireland, amounting in numerous cases to actual destitution,[b] that I felt it to be unnecessary to adduce any aditional proofs on the subject. To this extent moreover, the evidence was fully borne out by previous investigations of committees and commissions on the state of Ireland. The fact of wide-spread destitution

---

[b] Whether the number of persons in distress and requiring relief during thirty weeks in every year, amounted to 2,385,000, as estimated by the commissioners, may admit of question; but there can be no doubt that much distress prevailed, and that occasionally it was exceedingly severe.

was therefore notorious, and its existence was universally admitted; so that in reporting to government at
the end of my mission, I considered it enough to state as
the result of my own inquiries, " that the misery now
prevalent among the labouring classes in Ireland,
appears to be of a nature and intensity calculated to
produce great demoralization and danger;" and such
being the case, it was doubtless the duty of government and the legislature to endeavour to devise a
remedy for the one, and thus at the same time to guard
against the other.

My first Report was delivered on the 15th of November. It stated that after examining the
several institutions in Dublin, I had visited the
west of Ireland from Cork to Limerick Westport and Sligo, and back by Armagh—" everywhere
examining and inquiring as to the condition and habits
of the people, their character and wants; and endeavouring to ascertain whether, and how far, the system of
relief established in England, was applicable to the present state of Ireland." The above route was deemed the
most eligible, because the inhabitants of the manufac-
turing and commercial districts of the north and east,
more nearly resembled the English than those of the
southern and western parts of Ireland; and if the English system should be found applicable to them, there
could be no doubt of its applicability to the others.

The Report is divided into three parts or principal
divisions—

The first, gives the general result of inquiries into
the condition habits and feelings of the people, especially with regard to the introduction of a law for the
relief of the poor.

In the second part, the question whether the workhouse
system can with safety and advantage be established in
Ireland is considered, and also whether the means for
creating an efficient union machinery exists there.

The author's first report, Nov. 15, 1836.

Assuming these questions to be answered affirmatively, the chief points requiring attention in framing a poor-law for Ireland, are in the last part considered. It is now proposed to insert, under the above divisions, so much of the Report as will be sufficient for showing its general import, and the nature of its recommendations; but omitting such portions as are not necessary for this purpose—

First Report.—Nov. 15, 1836.

PART THE FIRST.—" The investigations and inquiries in which I have been engaged, have led to a conviction that Ireland has, on the whole, during the last thirty or forty years, been progressively improving. It is impossible to pass through the country without being struck with the evidence of increasing wealth almost everywhere apparent, although it is of course more visible in towns than in the open country. Great as the improvement in England has been within the same period, that in Ireland, I believe, has been equal. There are towns and districts there, as there are towns and districts in England, in which little improvement is seen, or which may even have retrograded; but the general advance is certain, and the improvement in the condition and increase in the capital of the country, are still, I think, steadily progressive. If it be asked how this accords with the misery and destitution apparent among a large portion of the people, the answer is obvious—The capital of the country has increased, but the increase of the population has been still greater; and it therefore does not follow that there is an increase of capital or comfort in the possession of each individual, or even of the majority. The reverse is unhappily the fact—Towns, exhibiting every sign of increased wealth, are encircled by suburbs composed of miserable hovels, sheltering a wretched population of mendicants. In the country, evidence of the extreme subdivision of land everywhere appears, and as a consequence, the soil, fertile as it naturally is, becomes exhausted by continual cropping; for the cottier tenant, too often reduced to a level little above that of the mendicant, is unable to provide manure for his land, and has no other mode of restoring its vigour but by subjecting it to a long and profitless fallow. Farmers of three hundred acres, or even of two or one hundred, except in the grazing districts, have become almost extinct in Ireland. A variety of circumstances seem to have contributed to bring about this change. In some instances the proprietor has himself subdivided his land into small holdings of five, ten, or fifteen acres, with a view of increasing his rent-roll, or adding to his political influence. In other cases the land has been let on lease to a single tenant on lives, or for a term of years, or both conjointly; and he has sublet to others, who have again gone on dividing and subletting, until the original proprietor is almost lost sight of, and the original holding is parcelled out among a host of small occupiers.

" The occupation of a plot of land has now gotten to be considered, by a great portion of the Irish people, as conferring an almost interminable right of possession. This seems to have arisen in great measure out of the circumstances in which they have been placed; for there being no legal provision for the destitute, and the subdivision of the land into small holdings having destroyed the regular demand for labour, the only protection against actual want, the only means by which a man could procure food for his family, was by getting and retaining possession of a portion of land; for this he has struggled—for this the peasantry have combined and burst through the restraints of law and humanity. So long as this portion of land was kept together, it was possibly sufficient to supply his family with a tolerable degree of comfort; but after a time he would have sons to provide for, and daughters to portion off, and this must all be effected out of the land—until the holding of ten or fifteen acres became divided into holdings of two, three, or five acres. After a time, too, the same process of subdivision is again resorted to, until the minimum of subsistence is reached; and this is now the condition of a large portion of the Irish peasantry. Land is to them the great necessary of life. There is no hiring of servants. A man cannot obtain his living as a day-labourer. He must get possession of a plot of land to raise potatoes, or starve. It need scarcely be said that a man will not starve, so long as the means of sustaining life can be obtained by force or fraud; and hence the scenes of violence and murder which have so frequently occurred in Ireland.

" One of the circumstances that first arrests attention on visiting Ireland, is the prevalence of mendicancy. It is not perhaps the actual amount of misery existing amongst the mendicant class, great as that may be, which is most to be deprecated; but the falsehood and fraud which form a part of their profession, and spread by their example. Mendicancy appeals to our sympathies on behalf of vice, as well as want; and encouragement is often afforded to the one, by the relief intended for the other. To assume the semblance of misery is the business of the mendicant, and his success depends upon the skill with which he exercises deception. A mass of filth, nakedness, and squalor, is thus kept moving about the country, entering every house, addressing itself to every eye, and soliciting from every hand; and much of the filth and indolence observable in the cabins, clothing, and general conduct of the peasantry, may I think be traced to this source, and I doubt even if those above the class of labourers altogether escape the taint. Mendicancy and filth have become too common to be disgraceful.

" The Irish peasantry have generally an appearance of apathy and depression. This is seen in their mode of living, in their habitations, in their dress, in the dress of their children, and in their general economy and conduct. They seem to have no pride, no emulation; to be heedless of the present, and careless of the future. They do not strive to improve their appearance, or add to their comforts. Their cabins are slovenly, smoky, dirty, almost without furniture, or any article of convenience or common decency. On entering a cottage, the woman and children are seen seated on the floor surrounded by pigs and poultry, the man is lounging at the door, which can only be approached through mud and filth. Yet he is too indolent to make a dry approach to his dwelling, although there are materials close at hand, and his wife is too slatternly to cleanse the place in which they live, or sweep the dirt and offal from the floor. If you point out these defects, and endeavour to show how easily they might improve their condition and increase their comforts, you are invariably met by excuses as to their poverty. Are a woman, and her children, and her cabin filthy, whilst a stream of water runs past the door—the answer invariably is, ' Sure, how can we help it? we are so poor!' With the man it is the same; you find him idly basking in the sun, or seated by the fire, whilst his cabin is scarcely approachable through the accumulation of mud—and he too will exclaim, ' Sure, how can we help it? we are so poor!' whilst at the very time he is smoking tobacco, and has probably not denied himself the enjoyment of whisky. Now poverty is *not* the cause, or at least not the sole cause, of this condition of the Irish peasantry. If they desired to live better, or to appear better, they might do so; but they seem to have no such ambition, and hence the depressed tone of which I have spoken. This may be partly owing to the remains of old habits; for bad as the circumstances of the peasantry now are, they were yet, I am persuaded, worse fifty or thirty years ago. A part also may be attributed to the want of education, and of a feeling of self-respect ; and a part likewise to their poverty—to which last cause alone, everything that is wrong in Ireland is invariably attributed.

" The desultory habits of the peasantry are likewise remarkable. However urgent the demands for exertion—if, as in the present season, their crops are rotting in the fields from excessive wet, and every moment of sunshine should be taken advantage of—still, if there be a market to attend, a fair, or a funeral, a horse-race, a fight, or a wedding, all else is neglected or forgotten ; they hurry off in search of the excitements which abound on such occasions, and with a recklessness hardly to be credited, at the moment that they are complaining of poverty, they take the most certain steps to increase it. Their fondness for ardent spirits is probably one cause of this, and another will be found in their position as occupiers of land. The work required upon their small holdings is easily performed, and may, as they say, ' be done any day.' Working for wages is rare and uncertain ; and hence arises a disregard of the value of time, a desultory sauntering habit, without industry or steadiness of application. Such is too generally the character, and such the habits, of the Irish peasantry ; and it may not be uninstructive to mark the resemblance which these bear to the character and habits of the English peasantry in the pauperised districts, under the abuses of the old Poor Law. Mendicancy and indiscriminate almsgiving have produced in Ireland, results similar to what indiscriminate relief produced in England—the like reckless disregard of the future, the like idle and disorderly conduct, and the same proneness to outrage having then characterised the English pauper labourer, which are now too generally the characteristics of the Irish peasant. An abuse of a good law caused the evil in the one case, and a removal of that abuse is now rapidly effecting a remedy. In the other case, the evil appears to have arisen rather from the want, than the abuse of a law ; but the corrective for both will, I believe, be found to be essentially the same.

" The objections usually urged against the introduction of Poor Laws into Ireland, are founded on an anticipated demoralization of the peasantry—and on the probable amount of the charge. The first objection derives its force from the example of England under the old Poor Law ; but the weight of this objection is destroyed by the improved administration under the new law, which is rapidly eradicating the effects of previous abuse ; and will, there is good reason to believe, effectually prevent their recurrence. This belief is founded

on the experience of the effects of the system in every instance in which it has been brought into operation, and particularly in two important parishes in Nottinghamshire, where
the workhouse principle was first established in its simplicity
and efficiency fifteen or sixteen years ago, and where it has
continued to be equally effective up to the present time.
Similar results have invariably attended its application in the
unions formed under the new law, which are conducted essentially upon the same principle, but with a superior combination of machinery, and administrative arrangement.

" With respect to the second objection, founded on the probable
amount of expenditure, it may be remarked that the Irish
population, like every other, must be supported in some way
out of the resources of the country ; and it does not follow
that the establishment of such a system of relief will greatly
increase the charge, if it increase it at all.   During the progress of my inquiries, I was often told that the recognition of
any legal claim for relief would lead to universal pauperism,
and would amount to a total confiscation of property.   Many
Irish landowners appeared to participate in this apprehension
—under the influence of which it seems to have been overlooked, that the only legal claim for relief in England is
founded on the actual destitution of the claimant, and that as
the existence of destitution is the ground of the claim, so is
its removal the measure of relief to be afforded.   This, if the
destitution be rightly tested, will be a sufficient protection to
property.   At present there is no test of destitution in Ireland.   The mendicant, whether his distress be real or fictitious,
claims and receives his share of the produce of the soil in the
shape of charity, before the landlord can receive his portion
in the shape of rent, and before the tenant has ascertained
whether he is a gainer or a loser by his labours and his risks.
The mendicant's claim has now precedence over every other.
If the whole property of Ireland was rated to the relief of the
poor, it would be no more ; but in such case the charge would
be equally borne, whereas at present it is unequal, and tends
to evil in its application.

" The voluntary contributions of Scotland have been recommended
as an example to be followed, rather than the compulsory
assessments of England ; and the Dublin Mendicity Association has been referred to, and its working described as at
once effective for the suppression of mendicancy, and for the
relief of the indigent within the sphere of its operations, without injury to the sensibilities of individual benevolence.   But
the feelings of charity and gratitude, which it is delightful to
contemplate as the motive and the fruit of benevolent actions,

can only exist between individuals. It matters not whether the fund to be distributed has been raised by voluntary contribution, or by legal assessment, or whether it has been devised for purposes of general charity. The application of the fund becomes, in each case, *a trust;* it is distributed as a trust, and it is received as a right, not as a gift. It may moreover be remarked, that the Dublin Mendicity Association has with difficulty been kept in existence by great exertions on the part of the committee, and by threats of parading the mendicants through the streets. If difficulty is thus found in supporting such an institution in Dublin, how impracticable must it be to provide permanent support for similar institutions in other parts of the country. Some persons contend that relief for the indigent classes in Ireland should be provided in ' houses of industry,' similar to those now existing in Dublin and a few other places. These institutions are in general not badly managed, and some classification is enforced in them, and the sexes are invariably separated. But they are certainly not entitled to the designation of ' houses of industry.' They are in fact places for the maintenance of a number of poor persons, mostly aged or infirm, and idiots, and lunatics; but as a general means of supplying necessary relief, and of testing the necessity, they are totally inefficient.

" Notwithstanding these objections, I found everywhere, after quitting Dublin, a strong feeling in favour of property being assessed for the relief of the indigent. At present, the burthen falls almost exclusively upon the lower classes, whilst the higher classes generally escape. A system of poor-laws, similar in principle to the English system, would go far to remedy this inequality—the people are aware of this—and, as the general result of my inquiries, I have been led to the conclusion, that poor-laws may be now established in Ireland, guarded by the correctives derived from experience in England, with safety and success. I think also, that such a measure would serve to connect the interest of landlords and tenants, and so become a means of benefiting both, and promoting the general peace and prosperity of the country. The desire now so generally expressed for a full participation in English laws and English institutions, will dispose the Irish people to receive with alacrity any measure tending to put them on the same footing as their fellow-subjects of England —a circumstance particularly favourable to the establishment of a poor-law at this moment. At another season, or under other circumstances, it might be difficult to surround a legal provision for the relief of the Irish poor, with sufficient guards against abuse; but at present, I think the legislature may venture to entertain the subject, having the experience of England before them, with a reasonable confidence of being able to bring the measure to a successful issue; and if the landed proprietors and gentry of Ireland will there perform the same part, which the proprietors and gentry of England are now performing in the administration of the new Poor Law, the result will be neither distant nor doubtful.

" If a poor-law were established in Ireland, it must not however be expected to work miracles. It would not give employment or capital, but it would, I think, help the country through what may be called its transition period; and in time, and with the aid of other circumstances, would effect a material improvement in the condition of the people. The English Poor Laws, in their earlier operation, contributed to the accomplishment of this object in England; and there seems nothing to prevent a similar result in Ireland. Facilities now exist in Ireland for helping forward the transition, and for shortening its duration as well as securing its benefits, which England did not possess in the time of Elizabeth, or for a century and a half afterwards. By 'transition period,' I mean that season of change from the system of small holdings, con-acre, and the subdivisions of land, which now prevails in Ireland, to the better practice of day-labour for wages, and to that dependence on daily labour for support, which is the present condition of the English peasantry. This transition is, I believe, generally beset with difficulty and suffering. It was so in England; it is, and for a time will probably continue to be so in Ireland; and every aid should be afforded to shorten its duration, and lessen its pressure. It has been considered that the existence of the con-acre system is favourable to such a transition. I am disposed to concur in this view, and think that the annual hiring of the con-acre, may help to wean the Irish peasantry from their present desire of occupying land, and lead them to become labourers for wages. The eager clinging to land, and its subdivision into small holdings, is at once a cause and a consequence of the rapid increase of the people, and of the extreme poverty and want which prevail among them. It is not because the potato constitutes their food, that a kind of famine occurs annually in Ireland between the going out of the old, and the in-coming of the new crop; but it is because the peasantry are the sole providers for their own necessities, each out of his own small holding; and being all alike hard pressed, and apt to under-calculate the extent of their wants, they thus often find themselves without food before the new crop is ripe. In this emergency there is no store provided to which they can have recourse, and misery and disease ensue. A poor-law would lighten the pressure under such a visitation, and the poor-law machinery might be useful in cases of extreme need, as well as for preventing a recurrence of the calamity.

" It is impossible to mix with the Irish people without noticing the great influence of the clergy, and it seemed important therefore to ascertain their views in regard to a poor-law. I discussed the subject with many of them, as well Roman catholic as protestant, in all parts of the country ; and I found them, with few exceptions, decidedly favourably to such a law. In the cases where they were not so, it appeared to be owing to an apprehension that their influence might be lessened, by taking from them the distribution of the alms which now pass through their hands ; but this feeling was of rare occurrence, and I am warranted in saying, that the clergy of every denomination are almost unanimously favourable to a system of Poor Laws for Ireland. This was perhaps to be expected, the duties of the clergy leading them to mix more with the people, and to see more of their actual wants, than any other class of persons. The shopkeepers too, and manufacturers and dealers generally, I found favourable to a poor-law. They declared that they should be gainers at the end of the year, whatever might be the amount legally assessed upon them ; for that they could neither close their doors, nor turn their backs upon the wretched objects who were constantly applying to them ; whilst the gentry, if resident, were in a great measure protected from such applications, and if non-resident, escaped them altogether.

" A legal provision for the destitute, is moreover an indispensable preliminary to the suppression of mendicancy. If the state offers an alternative, it may prohibit begging—it would be in vain to do so otherwise, for the law would be opposed to our natural sympathies, and would remain inoperative. This was the course adopted in England, where it was long endeavoured to repress vagrancy by severe enactments, but apparently with little advantage. At last the offer of relief was coupled with the prohibition of mendicancy, and until our Poor Law administration became corrupt, with perfect success. To establish a poor-law, then, is I believe a necessary preliminary to the suppression of mendicancy. That it will be, on the whole, economical to do this in Ireland, it is I think scarcely possible to doubt ; but whether it be so or not, the advantage both morally and socially of removing such an evil, is beyond question important.

" It may be regarded as a circumstance favourable to the introduction of a poor-law, that so much land is lying waste and
uncultivated in Ireland. Much of this land is susceptible of
cultivation, and the order and security which a poor-law
would tend to establish, will encourage the application of
capital to such objects. If capital were to be so applied, considerable tracts would be brought under culture, and thus
afford occupation to the now unemployed labourers. Most of
the reclaimed bog which I saw in the western counties, was
effected by the small occupiers, who partially drained and
enclosed an acre or two at a time ; but such operations were
without system or combination, and for the most part indifferently performed. In this way, however, the reclamation
of these wastes will of necessity proceed—constantly adding
to the number of small cottier tenants, and swelling the
amount of poverty and wretchedness in the country—unless
proprietors and capitalists shall be induced to take the matter
in hand, and by enclosing and effectually draining whole
tracts, secure the means of applying economical management
on a large scale. The enclosing and draining, and the whole
process of reclamation, would afford employment to labourers
who are now, for a great portion of the year, idling about
without occupation ; and when the land so reclaimed becomes
subjected to a regular process of cultivation, it will continue
to afford them regular employment at daily wages, instead of
the often miserably insufficient produce of their own small
holdings, to which they now are compelled to cling as their
sole means of support.

" It appears then, I think, that a poor-law is necessary for relieving the destitution to which a large portion of the population in Ireland is now exposed. It appears too, that
circumstances are at present favourable for the introduction
of such a measure. A poor-law seems also to be necessary,
as a first step towards bringing about improvement in the
habits and social condition of the people. Without such improvement, peace, good order, and security cannot exist in
Ireland ; and without these, it is in vain to look for that
accumulation of wealth, and influx of capital, which are
necessary for developing its resources, agricultural and commercial, and for providing profitable employment for the
population. Ireland is now suffering under a circle of evils,
producing and reproducing one another. Want of capital
produces want of employment—want of employment, turbulence and misery—turbulence and misery, insecurity—insecurity prevents the introduction or accumulation of capital—and
so on. Until this circle is broken, the evils must continue,

and probably increase. The first thing to be done is to give security—that will produce or invite capital—and capital will give employment. But security of person and property cannot co-exist with extensive destitution. So that, in truth, the reclamation of bogs and wastes—the establishment of fisheries and manufactures—improvements in agriculture, and in the general condition of the country—and lastly, the elevation of the great mass of the Irish people in the social scale, appear to be *all* more or less contingent upon establishing a law providing for the relief of the destitute.—How such a law may be best formed, so as to secure the largest amount of good, with the least risk of evil, it is proposed next to consider.

Part the Second.—" There are two points for consideration under this division of the subject which are of primary import, the question of a Poor Law for Ireland mainly depending upon them. First—Whether the workhouse system can be safely and effectively established in Ireland ; and secondly— Whether a machinery can be there established for their government, such as exists in the English unions.

" In my inquiries with regard to these points, I endeavoured to exercise a care and vigilance proportioned to their importance. The inquiry was entered upon under an apprehension that the workhouse would be less efficient in Ireland, than experience had shown it to be in England ; and that it would probably be applicable to the able-bodied in a limited degree only, if applicable to them at all. I was doubtful also, whether it would be practicable to control any considerable number of the able-bodied in a workhouse—whether the proneness of the Irish peasantry to outrage and insubordination would not, as had often been represented, lead them to break through all restraint, and perhaps demolish the building, and commit other acts of violence. The probability of such outrage is strongly insisted upon by the Commissioners of Inquiry, and the same argument was urged upon me by some persons with whom I communicated in Dublin. In the progress of my inquiries however, I soon found reason for concluding that there was no ground for apprehension, either as to the applicability of the workhouse for the purposes of relief, or as to any danger of resistance to such a system of classification and discipline within it, as would make it a test of destitution. In the several ' houses of industry ' established in Ireland, a strict separation of the sexes is enforced, and a discipline more or less approximating to our workhouse discipline is established. No spirits are admitted, and on the

whole, there is enough in these institutions to render them
distasteful as places of partial restraint. Yet from no governor
of a house of industry could I learn that resistance had ever
been made to their regulations, and surprise was even expressed at my thinking it necessary to make the inquiry. I
received the same opinion from the governors of gaols. In
short, every man whom I conversed with, who had any experience of the habits of the people, declared that the peasantry
are perfectly tractable, and never think of opposing authority,
unless stimulated by drink, or urged on by that species of
combination for securing the occupancy of land, which has
become so common in certain districts. Neither of these
influences will interfere with the establishment of a workhouse, or the regulation of its inmates, all of whom will have
sought refuge in it voluntarily, and may quit it at any moment. As regards the security of the workhouse, therefore,
and the establishment of a system of discipline as strict as
that maintained in the English workhouses, I believe that
there will be neither danger nor difficulty.

" How far the workhouse, if established, may be relied upon as a
test of destitution and a measure of the relief to be afforded ;
how far it will be effectual for the prevention of pauperism,
and for stimulating the people to exertion for their own support ;—how far, in short, the workhouse system, which has
been safely and effectually applied to dispauperise England,
may be applied with safety and efficiency to prevent pauperism in Ireland, now remains for inquiry. The governing
principle of the workhouse system is this :—that the support
which is afforded at the public charge in the workhouse, shall
on the whole be less desirable than the support obtained by
independent exertion. To carry out this principle, it might
seem to be necessary that the inmates of a workhouse should
be in all respects worse situated—worse clothed, worse lodged,
and worse fed, than the independent labourers of the district.
In fact, however, the inmates of our English workhouses are
as well clothed, and generally better lodged and better fed
than the agricultural labourer and his family : yet the irk-
someness of the discipline and confinement, and the privation
of certain enjoyments, produce such disinclination to enter the
workhouse, that experience warrants the fullest assurance that
nothing short of destitution, and that necessity which the law
contemplates as the ground for affording relief, will induce
the able-bodied labourer to seek refuge therein ; and that if
driven thither by necessity, he will quit it again as speedily
as possible, and strive (generally with increased energy and
consequent success) to obtain subsistence by his own efforts.

" It would perhaps be in vain, even if it were desirable, to seek to make the lodging, the clothing, and the diet, of the inmates of an Irish workhouse, inferior to those of the Irish peasantry. The standard of their mode of living is so low, that the establishment of one still lower is difficult, and would under any circumstances be inexpedient. In Ireland therefore, there would not perhaps be found the same security in this respect for the efficiency of the workhouse test, which may in some degree be operative in England. There are countervailing circumstances in Ireland however, which more than balance this drawback, even if it were greater than it really is. The Irish are naturally, or by habit, a migratory people, fond of change, hopeful, sanguine, eager for experiment. They have never been practically limited to one spot by a law of settlement, as has been the case with the English peasantry. They have never been enervated by a misapplied system of parish relief. Rather than bear the restrictions of a workhouse, the Irishman, if in possession of health and strength, would wander the world over to obtain a living. All the opinions I have collected from persons most conversant with the Irish character, agree in this. Confinement of any kind is even more irksome to an Irishman than to an Englishman. Hence, although he might be lodged, fed, and clothed, in a workhouse, better than he could lodge, feed, and clothe himself— he will yet, like the Englishman, never enter the workhouse, unless driven thither by actual necessity; and he will not then remain there longer than that necessity exists. The test of the workhouse is then, I think, likely to be as efficient in Ireland, as it is proved to be in England ; and if relief be there restricted to the workhouse, it will be at once a test of destitution, and a measure of relief, and will serve to protect the administration of a legal provision for the destitute poor, from those evils and abuses which followed the establishment, and led to the perversion, of the old Poor Laws in England. I speak of the workhouse as a test of destitution generally, without limiting its operation to age, infirmity, or other circumstances ; for independent of the difficulty of discriminating between those who may fairly be considered as aged and infirm, and those who are not—as well as certain other difficulties, practical and theoretical, in the way of making any such distinction—I have found in the state of Ireland, no sufficient reason for departing from the principle of the English Poor Law which recognises *destitution alone* as the ground of relief, nor for establishing a distinction in the one country, which does not exist in the other.

" The expense of providing workhouses, will not, I apprehend, be so considerable as has by some been anticipated. If the surface of Ireland be divided into squares of twenty miles each, so that a workhouse placed in the centre would be distant about ten miles from the extremities in all directions, this would give about eighty workhouses for the whole of Ireland. A diameter of twenty miles was the limit prescribed for the size of unions by Gilbert's Act, but it was often exceeded in practice—it may however, be assumed as a convenient size on the present occasion. In some cases, owing to the position of towns, or other local causes, the unions will probably be smaller; in others, especially in the thinly-peopled districts of the west, they may be larger : but still, there is, I think, every probability that the number of workhouses required will not greatly exceed eighty. In aid of this number, the houses of industry, and mendicity and other establishments, which will be unnecessary as soon as a legal provision is made for the relief of the destitute, will become available at probably a small expense. In some instances, moreover, barracks, factories, or other buildings suitable for conversion into workhouses, may perhaps be obtained on easy terms :—but excluding all such considerations, and assuming that instead of eighty workhouses, a hundred will be required, and that the cost of erecting each will be about the same as for the largest class of English workhouses, namely, about 7,000*l.*— this would give a gross outlay of 700,000*l.* for the whole of Ireland—a sum not disproportionally large, when the nature of the object is taken into account. If government were to advance the sum necessary for providing the workhouses by way of loan, as has been done to the unions in England, requiring an instalment of five per cent. of the principal to be paid off annually out of the rates, it would make the whole charge so easy, that it would scarcely be felt. The payment of 35,000*l.* per annum for twenty years, with the interest on the constantly-decreasing principal, could not be considered a hardship on Ireland ; and this is in fact the whole of the new or additional outlay proposed: for as regards the relief of the destitute, that would not be a new charge, the destitute classes being now supported, although in a manner calculated to injure and depress the general character of the people.

" As respects the means for local management in Ireland, if it were attempted to establish a parochial machinery similar to that which exists in England, I believe the attempt would fail. The description of persons requisite for constituting such a machinery, will not be found in the majority of Irish parishes. In some parts however, and especially in the north and the east, competent individuals would be found in many,

if not in most of the parishes. If an Irish Poor Law were
established, the uniting of parishes for the purpose of securing
the benefits of combined management, is therefore more
necessary even than it was in England; and by making the
unions sufficiently large, there can be no doubt that in almost
every instance, such a board of elected guardians may be
obtained as would secure the orderly working of the union,
under a due system of supervision and control.

" In the first instance, and until a rate for the relief of the destitute is established, the contributors to the county-cess might
be empowered to elect the guardians. But in some cases an
efficient board may not be obtainable by election, and this is
most likely to occur at the commencement, when individuals
will be ill instructed as to their duties, and when the public
will perhaps have formed erroneous notions of what is intended
to be done. To meet such a contingency, it seems essential
that large general powers should be vested in some central
authority, to control and direct the proceedings of the boards
of guardians, and even to supersede their functions altogether,
whenever such supersession shall be necessary. Power should
also be given to declare unions, and to appoint paid officers
to conduct the business, under the direction of the central
authority, without the intervention of a board of guardians ;
and in order to guard against mistakes to be expected on the
first introduction of an entirely new order of things, and to
prevent the mischief that might ensue from failure or miscon-
duct at the outset, the central authority should also, I think,
be empowered to dispense with the election of the first board
of guardians, and to appoint such persons as may appear
most fit and competent to act as guardians of the union, until
the Lady-day next ensuing, or the Lady-day twelvemonths.
The number and selection of such specially-appointed
guardians to be at the discretion of the central authority.
These powers are greater than were given to the English
commissioners by the Poor Law Amendment Act : but they
are, in my opinion, necessary in the present state of Ireland.
With such powers confided to the central authority, no difficulty can arise for which it will not be prepared ; and it will,
I think, be enabled to establish the unions, and to constitute
an adequate machinery for their government throughout the
whole of Ireland, with certainty and efficiency.

" In England, the county magistrates residing and acting within
a union, are *ex-officio* members of the board of guardians.
The number and position of the magistracy in Ireland seem
to require some modification in this respect. The principle

of administration established in England by the Poor Law Amendment Act, is based essentially upon popular representation. The guardians are elected by the occupiers and owners of the property rated, and in the hands of the guardians the administrative power is vested. The county magistrates, it is true, in virtue of their office, sit and act as members of the board; but this does not destroy its elective character, as the number of elected so far exceeds that of the ex-officio guardians, that the popular character of the board is maintained; whilst the presence of the magistrates, who in virtue of their office are permanent members, and therefore connecting links between the successive boards of elected guardians, secures a stability and continuity of action, which, if based entirely upon election, the board might not possess. This is the constitution of the boards of guardians in England, and nothing can work better: but in Ireland, the number of magistrates who would be entitled under a similar provision to act as ex-officio guardians, would in general greatly exceed the number so qualified in England, and in some cases might outnumber the elected guardians. If this should occur, the elective character of the board would of course be destroyed; but even if this should not be the case, yet any undue preponderance of the permanent ex-officio guardians would detract from the popular character of the governing body, and lower it in the confidence of the people. With a view therefore of keeping as nearly as possible to the practical constitution of the English boards of guardians, I propose in the Irish unions,—1st. That the number of ex-officio guardians shall never exceed one-third the number of elected guardians: 2dly. That immediately on the declaration of a union, the county magistrates residing and acting within its limits, shall nominate from among themselves a number nearest to, but not exceeding, one-third of the elected guardians,—which magistrates so nominated by their compeers, shall be entitled to act as ex-officio guardians of the union, until the Michaelmas twelvemonth after such nomination: and 3dly. That at each succeeding Michaelmas, the magistrates entitled as aforesaid, shall proceed to a new election. These regulations will, I think, not only preserve a due proportion in the constitution of the boards of guardians, but also ensure the co-operation of the most efficient portion of the magistracy in the government of the unions; as the magistrates will doubtless nominate those members of their body who are most active and able.

" A different practice from that established in England, seems also to be necessary with respect to the Clergy. Under the

provisions of the Poor Law Amendment Act, ministers of
religion of every denomination are eligible for the office of
guardian, elected or *ex-officio*. In the present condition of
Ireland, I fear this would be attended with inconvenience,
and might destroy the efficiency of the boards of guardians.
I therefore propose that no clergyman, or minister of any
religious denomination, shall be eligible to act either as elected
or *ex-officio* guardian. This exclusion is not proposed from
any notion of the general unfitness of the clergy to fill the
office of guardian ; but with reference solely to the present
state of religious opinion in Ireland, and to the importance
of keeping the functions of the boards of guardians free from
the suspicion of sectarian bias. If the ministers of one persuasion were to be admitted, the ministers of every persuasion
must be so ; and then the deliberations would too probably
be disturbed by religious differences. On no point have I
taken more pains to arrive at a sound conclusion than on this,
being fully sensible of the objections, on principle, to the
exclusion of any class of men from office : but the great
majority of the clergy themselves with whom I have conversed,
Roman catholic and protestant, have agreed in thinking that
it will be, on the whole, inexpedient to admit any of the
ministers of religion to act as guardians ; and after the fullest
consideration and inquiry, I therefore recommend that they
should all be declared ineligible.

" In England, under the provisions of the Poor Law Amendment
Act, every parish or township rated for the maintenance of
its poor, and included in a union, is entitled to return a
guardian. In Ireland it will, I think, be essential that the
central authority should be empowered to fix the limits of a
union, without being restricted to parish boundaries. It
should be enabled to divide parishes, either for the purpose
of electing guardians, or for joining a portion of a parish to
one union, and another portion to another union. It should
also be empowered to consolidate parishes for the purpose of
electing one or more guardians, and likewise to form election
districts for this purpose, without reference to parochial
boundaries. And lastly, the central authority should be empowered to add to, take from, and remodel unions, whenever
such change might be found necessary. These powers would
have enabled the English Poor Law Commissioners to make
their unions more compact and convenient than they at present are, local prejudices and local interests having frequently
compelled them to abandon the arrangement which would
have been best for the general interest. In Ireland, full
powers in these respects are, I think, indispensable for en-

abling the central authority to deal with the various circumstances under which the unions will there have to be formed. But with adequate powers, and with such modifications as are before described, the principle of union which has been established in England by the Poor Law Amendment Act, may I think be advantageously extended to Ireland; and as it has been shówn that no insurmountable difficulty exists to prevent the introduction of the workhouse as a test of destitution—so neither will there be any insurmountable difficulty in establishing an adequate machinery for the government of the unions when formed.

PART THE THIRD.—" Assuming that a system of Poor Laws ought to be established in Ireland; that the workhouse system may there be relied upon, as a test of destitution; and that the means of forming and governing unions exist there, as well as in England—It now remains to describe the several points which require attention in framing a measure comprising these objects; and also to offer such further observations, as did not seem to come within the scope of the preceding divisions.

" The governing principle to be observed in dealing with this portion of the subject is, that the Poor Law of Ireland should assimilate in all respects as nearly as possible to that established in England,—varying only in those instances, in which the different circumstances of the two countries require it. In conformity with this principle, the first point for consideration would naturally be the constitution of the central or chief authority, and the powers to be confided to it; but I postpone this part of the subject—assuming only that a central authority is to be established, with powers similar in kind to those conferred upon the English Poor Law Commissioners. The other points for consideration are the following—

1st. *Of Relief.*—" The only legal claim for relief in England, is founded upon the destitution of the party claiming it. I propose to extend the same principle to Ireland; and as a test of the actual existence of such destitution, and to guard against the evils which have invariably attended the distribution of out-door relief, (that is, of relief administered either in money or in kind to parties out of the workhouse) I further propose that, in Ireland, no relief should be given except in the workhouse. I do not propose to impart a *right* to relief, even to the destitute poor. The claim to relief in England, is founded on prescription, rather than enactment; for although the 43rd *of Elizabeth* provides for the levying a rate for the purpose of relieving the destitute poor, it invests them with no right to claim relief, the administration of which is left to the local authorities, who are of course responsible for its due exercise. The promulgation of rules for the administration of relief will therefore rest with the central authority, limited by the proviso that relief is only to be administered in the workhouse. The central authority will declare when the workhouse shall be so applied in each union, and will also take care that no time be lost in providing suitable workhouse accommodation, as well as to establish such regulations as may be necessary for the guidance of the local authorities in the interim; but it will be most safe to prohibit all relief whatever, until the test of the workhouse can be applied.

" The strict limitation of relief to the workhouse may possibly be objected to, on the ground that extreme want is found occasionally to assail large portions of the population, who ought then to be relieved at the public charge, without being subjected to the restraint of the workhouse. But this is an exceptional case, and it would not, I think, be wise to adapt the regulations of poor-law administration in Ireland to the possible occurrence of such a contingency. In a period of famine, the whole population may be said to become destitute; but it surely would not be expedient to hold out an expectation, that if this should unhappily occur, support for *all* would be unconditionally provided at the public charge? —During such a visitation, the workhouse might not be sufficient for the numbers who were anxious to crowd into it; but to the extent of its means of accommodation it would help to relieve the general distress, and the union machinery would probably be found useful in other respects. The occurrence of a famine, however, if general, seems to be a contingency beyond the powers of a poor-law to provide for. There is then an actual deficiency of supply; and as there is less to consume, less must be consumed. It is however, I think impossible to contemplate the continuance of such a state of things in Ireland, as that in which any considerable portion of its population would be subjected to the occurrence of famine. As the habits and intelligence of the people improve, these visitations will be guarded against or averted; and I do not propose to make any exception permissive of out-door relief in such cases, but recommend that relief should be limited strictly to the workhouse. It is moreover necessary that no individual of a family should be admitted, unless all its members enter the house. Relief to the father or husband is equivalent to relief to the child or the wife, and *vice versâ;* and, while they continue one family, a part cannot be considered as destitute, and the rest not so ; a family must be taken as a whole, and so admitted or excluded. The provisions of *the* 43*rd of Elizabeth*, requiring parents to support children, and children to support parents, should also be extended to Ireland ; and I think relief by way of loan, as provided for by the 58*th section* of the Poor Law Amendment Act, might in certain cases be useful, and if exercised with discretion, can scarcely be productive of mischief.

2*ndly. Of the Local Machinery.*—" I propose that the local machinery for the administration of relief to the destitute in Ireland, under the direction of a central authority, should be the same as is provided in England by the Poor Law Amendment Act; namely, the union of a district for common management, under a board of guardians elected by the ratepayers, with paid officers appointed or approved by the central authority.

" In forming the unions, it will be necessary to observe the civil, rather than the ecclesiastical boundaries of parishes ; but cases will arise, in which it may be requisite to disregard all such boundaries—it being obviously more important that the district to be united should be compact, convenient, and accessible, and be naturally connected with its centre, than that the old and often inconvenient boundaries should be observed. This applies no less to county or baronial boundaries than to those of parishes or other divisions. The principle which has governed the formation of the English unions, whenever the commissioners have not been driven from it by local circumstances, has been to fix upon some market-town conveniently situated as a centre, and to attach to it the whole surrounding district, of which it may be considered the capital, and in which the general business of the district, both public and private, for the most part centres. The roads of a district always converge upon the market-town. The communications with it are constant, and the people settled within the range of its influence constitute almost a distinct community. To form such a district into a union, seems an obvious course, and I recommend its being adopted in Ireland. There may be parts of the country in which such a convenient centre does not exist, but this will be of rare occurrence, and the general powers of the central authority will be competent to deal with it.

" Much of what appeared to be necessary with reference to the members of the boards of guardians, both elected and *ex-officio*, is given in the second part of this Report : but the important question—in whose hands the right of appointing guardians shall be confided, and in what way that right shall be exercised, still remains to be considered. In this, as in other cases, the principle established in England, should, I think, be applied to Ireland, and the election of guardians be vested in the ratepayers and owners of property within the union ; but the circumstances of Ireland require some modification of the English practice, in this respect. The owners of property in England, are entitled to vote according to the scale which was established by the Select Vestry Act, and which ascends by gradations of 25*l*. each, from a rated value of 50*l*. per annum up to 150*l*. per annum, giving one vote for the former, and six votes for the latter. This scale seems open to some objection, on the grounds of complexity and over-minuteness. It moreover differs from the scale of voting fixed for the ratepayers by the Poor Law Amendment Act, which provides that ratepayers, if rated under 200*l*. shall have one vote ; if rated at 200*l*. and under 400*l*., two votes ; and if at 400*l*. and upwards, three votes. Such a scale seems on the whole well adapted to the condition of ratepayers in England, but the amounts specified are too high for Ireland ; and the scale is not sufficiently minute in its graduation, for the subdivision of property which prevails there. Instead of adopting these English scales, therefore, I propose to establish one scale in Ireland, by which simplicity of detail, and a right result will I think be more effectually secured ; and I recommend the following for regulating the votes of owners of property, as well as occupiers,

above 5*l*. and under 50*l*.	..	one vote.
50*l*. and under 100*l*.	..	two votes.
100*l*. „ 150*l*.	..	three votes.
150*l*. „ 200*l*.	..	four votes.
200*l*. and upwards	..	five votes.

3rdly. Of Rating.—" The power to assess the property and levy a rate within a union for the purpose of relieving the destitute, must, I think, be confided to the board of guardians, by whom such relief is to be administered. The mode of assessing and collecting the rate, as well as its application, will be prescribed by the central authority. The Parochial Assessments Act passed last session, establishes the principle that the rates are to be paid upon the net annual value of property. This was always the law, although it had not always been acted upon. As regards the principle by which the assessment of property should be regulated, it will therefore be only necessary to extend the provisions of that Act to Ireland, substituting the union for the parish authorities. The valuation of property for rating need not, I apprehend, be made in every instance by surveyors or professional valu-ators. The fairly-estimated value of the property is all that is necessary. In many instances a valuation has already been made for the purpose of tithe commutation, and wherever that, or any other fair valuation has been made, it will be available for rating to the relief of the poor. Hitherto there has been no such rate in Ireland. The destitute classes have gone on increasing in numbers, but still there has been no recognised or legal provision for their relief. Property has been acquired, capital invested, and contracts made, under this state of things, and it will be impossible now to impose a rate upon property, without affecting existing arrangements: but I believe the effect will be slight, and that in a few years it will cease altogether. If it were far greater than I anticipate however, all objections to the imposition of a rate on this ground must be overborne by considerations of the public welfare.

" The question as to who shall pay the rate, and in what propor-tions, is next to be considered. The parties immediately interested are the owner or person possessing the beneficial interest of the property assessed, and the tenant or occupier. Between these therefore, it seems both equitable and expe-dient to apportion the rate. Where the two are combined, the same person would be answerable for the entire rate. The Irish Poor Inquiry Commissioners appeared to be of opinion that the owner should pay two-thirds of the rate, and the occupier one-third; and it seemed to me, at first, that this would be a suitable division: but after further con-sideration and inquiry, I thought that each should be called upon to pay half the rate.[c] I was mainly influenced to adopt this view, by the consideration that at present nearly the whole support of the destitute falls upon the tenantry. It is to the occupiers that the mendicant resorts, and from them he receives his daily rations. There is thus in reality, a rate now levied, although not sanctioned by legal enactment; and no occupier, however limited may be his means, turns away the mendicant empty-handed from his door. The pressure of these continual calls upon the occupiers, help to bear them down, and keep them at their present low level; but if the destitute classes were relieved by means of a general rate upon property, of which the occupiers were called upon to pay half, they would be relieved from nearly one-half their pre-sent burthen. A poor-law, if rightly administered, although it ensures relief for the destitute, will not increase their number, or eventually swell the fund appropriated to their

---

[c] In Scotland the rate is divided equally between the landlord and tenant.

support. On the contrary, I believe it will help to lessen both. But admitting that the number and the amount remain the same, still the occupiers will then have to pay only one-half, the landlord the other; whereas now the occupier contributes nearly the whole.

4*thly. Of Settlement.*—" Parochial settlement, as established in England, is almost universally admitted to have been productive of great mischief. It has led to much litigation and expense; and by fixing the peasantry to the narrow limits of their parish, beyond which the world was to them almost a blank, it has done more to injure their character, to destroy its elasticity, and to banish self-reliance and resource, than any other portion of the old Poor Law system. It will not, therefore, I presume, be considered right to establish parochial settlement in Ireland. The habits of the Irish are migratory, their movements depending upon their own volition. To establish a law of settlement, would be to fix them to one locality. No such law has yet been established there; and it is therefore open to the legislature to prescribe the limits, if a settlement shall be deemed advisable; or else to dispense with settlement altogether.

" Without a law of settlement, it is true, vagrants from other districts may congregate in particular unions, and may claim relief, or be sent to the workhouse; but if the workhouses are all regulated upon the same scale of diet and discipline, there would be no inducement for the vagrant classes to prefer one union to another, and they would probably remain scattered throughout the country, in much the same proportion as at present. If such a preference was in any instance shown by them, it might be taken as a proof of inefficient management or lax discipline on the part of the favoured union, and would be a signal for the central authority to interfere. Thus, if there should be no law of settlement, the number of inmates in the several workhouses would serve as a kind of index to the management of each; and the local authorities would be compelled in self-defence to keep their unions in good order, to prevent their being overrun with paupers. Such a competition, if well regulated, might go far to ensure the general efficiency of the unions.

5*thly. On Mendicancy*—" Whenever relief is provided for the destitute, mendicancy may be suppressed. A law which says, ' You shall not beg or steal, but you shall starve,' would be contrary to natural justice, and would be disobeyed; but if the law first makes provision for the destitute, and then says, ' You shall not beg, but you shall be relieved at the public charge,' the alternative thus offered will entitle the community to suppress a practice which is held to be injurious. On these grounds, I think the law which establishes a system of public relief for destitution, should at the same time prohibit mendicancy. The present state of Ireland however, and the habits and feelings of the Irish people, throw considerable difficulty in the way of an immediate suppression of mendicancy. The number of mendicants is very great, and they are therefore of some importance as a class, and support and keep each other in countenance whilst following, what they consider, no disreputable vocation. They enter the cottages of the peasantry as supplicants, it is true, but still with a certain sense of right; and the cottager would be held to be a bold, if not a bad man, who resisted their appeal. In fact, the appeal never is resisted,—if there is only a handful of potatoes, they are divided with the beggar; and there is thus perhaps levied from the produce of the soil in Ireland for the support of mendicancy, as large a contribution as it is now proposed to raise by an assessment of property for the relief of destitution. The ' sturdy beggars,' noticed in the 14*th of Elizabeth*, must have been very similar to those now common in Ireland. Indeed the state of society at the ·two periods seems to have been nearly the same in both countries, the prevalence of begging in each being accompanied by the same general disposition to give, and this disposition of course increasing the number of beggars.

" The evils of mendicancy in Ireland are certainly very great, and its suppression should be provided for at the earliest practicable period. The best mode of effecting this would probably be, to enact a general prohibition, and to cast upon the central authority the responsibility of bringing it into operation in the several unions, as the workhouses became fitted for the reception of inmates. The central authority might, I think, so regulate their proceedings, as that the now itinerant mendicants who may be really unable to provide for themselves, should be placed in the several workhouses with the least degree of coercion and inconvenience; and that the ablebodied vagrants and disorderly persons should be compelled to provide for their own subsistence, by the application of strict workhouse discipline. Time and forbearance will doubtless be necessary in carrying such a measure into operation in Ireland, and these the powers of the central authority will enable it to afford. The present generation will probably pass away before the disposition to encourage begging by indiscriminate almsgiving, which now prevails so generally among all classes in Ireland, will be corrected by the adoption of a more enlightened benevolence. It will then we may hope be seen, that the real friends of the people are those who lead them to independent exertion, to a reliance upon themselves and their own efforts for support—not those who, by the constant doling of miscalled charity, entice the people into a state of dependence. It may minister to human pride, to be surrounded by a crowd of such dependents ; but it surely is inconsistent with genuine benevolence to encourage, or even to permit this, if it can possibly be prevented.

6thly. *Of Bastardy.*—" As far as I had opportunity of observing and inquiring, the Irish females are generally correct in their conduct. I am aware that opinions somewhat different have been expressed ; but my own impression of the moral conduct of the Irish females is highly favourable. Their duties appear to be more laborious than those of the same class in England. Their dress, too, is inferior, and so likewise seems their social position ; yet they universally appear modest, industrious, and sober—I state this as the result of my own observation ; and if the Irish females have preserved their moral character untainted hitherto, as I believe in the main to be the case, it affords an argument for ' letting well alone.' If it had been otherwise however, and if the extent of bastardy, and its demoralising influence on public manners had been greater, I should still have recommended that the Irish females should be left, as now, the guardians of their own honour, and responsible in their own persons for all deviations from virtue. The abuses under the old English bastardy law, and our brief experience of the improved practice established by the Amendment Act, warrant the recommendation that no such law should be applied to Ireland ; but that bastards, and the mothers of bastards, in all matters connected with relief, should be dealt with in the same manner as other destitute persons solely on the ground of their destitution.

7thly. *Of Apprenticeship.* — " The experience which England affords with regard to apprenticeship, is of a somewhat conflicting character, although the preponderance of testimony is opposed to it. It is open to much abuse, and has operated mischievously in several parts of the country, by increasing that dependence upon the parish which under the old Poor Law had become so characteristic of the English peasantry. It must however I think be admitted, that the apprenticing of orphan and destitute children, as provided for by *the 43rd of Elizabeth,* has in many cases been productive of good ; and if judiciously limited, so as not to be regarded as the ordinary mode of providing for the children of the labouring classes, but merely as a resource for the destitute and the orphan, it might still I think be continued with advantage. I am aware that this opinion differs somewhat from that of the members of the late English Poor Law Inquiry Commission ; but the evidence of abuse submitted to the commissioners was taken in the time of the old Poor Law, which converted everything it touched into an abuse ; and it does not follow, because apprenticeship added to the accumulation of evils under such circumstances, that it is incapable of producing good under others. It is on the different application of apprenticeship, and on the different circumstances in which it would be applied, that I now rely. None of the abuses exist in Ireland which prevailed under the old parochial management in England ; and by the aid of the union machinery apprenticeship may, I think, be safely applied to the placing out of destitute and orphan children, the number of whom in Ireland is very considerable. The Poor Law Amendment Act empowers the commissioners to frame regulations for apprenticing the children of poor persons ; and I propose to extend this provision to Ireland, by which it may be hoped that all the beneficial effects of the law may be secured, whilst the evils which certainly have resulted from it in England will in great measure be avoided.

8thly. Of Pauper Idiots and Lunatics.—" For individuals of this description, if not dangerous, the union workhouses will be available. Dangerous lunatics, and insane persons, must of course be sent to asylums, as at present ; and it is important, I think, that these institutions should be kept distinct from poor-law administration. The deprivation of reason is a misfortune so extreme, that special efforts are called for on behalf of individuals subjected to such a visitation. The careful supervision of such unhappy persons is necessary for the protection of the community. But with respect to pauper idiots and lunatics not dangerous, these might, I think, be advantageously provided for in the several workhouses, where a lunatic ward should be prepared for such of them as might be unfitted to mingle with the other paupers. Idiots, labouring under a deficiency, rather than a deprivation of reason, appear in general to feel contentment in proportion as they are employed on something of a nature suitable for them. In a workhouse, such employment might always be found, and they would probably there partake as largely of comfort as their unhappy state is susceptible of. I propose, therefore, that the provision of the Poor Law Amendment Act, permissive of the retention in a workhouse of idiot and lunatic paupers, not dangerous, be extended to Ireland, and that their mode of treatment and employment be in all cases subject to the direction of the central authority.

9thly. Of Emigration.—" A country may be so circumstanced, as to require that a portion of its population should migrate from one part of it to another, either permanently or occasionally ; and may still, on the whole, have no actual excess of population. A country may also, with reference to its means of employment, labour under an excess of population ; or both these circumstances may exist at the same time, which appears, in fact, to be the state of Ireland at present. The Irish population is excessive, compared with the means of employment ; and the effect of this excess would be more felt, were it not for the opening which England presents for migration. Where the population is in excess, it must be exceedingly difficult to effect any material improvement in the condition of a people ; for as long as the labourers exceed the number required, so long will their competition for employment serve to depress their condition, and counteract whatever efforts may be made to improve it. The only alternative in such case is, either to increase the amount of employment, or to decrease the number of labourers depending upon it. To bring about by direct interposition any material increase of permanent employment, is in every view difficult, and under common circumstances, perhaps impossible ; but something may be done indirectly in this respect, by the removal of impediments and the establishing of increased facilities for the application of capital, and something also perhaps by the intervention of government : but all such aids must of necessity be limited in their application, as well as remote in their effects—it is from spontaneous or natural employment alone, that the labouring classes can look for permanent occupation, and the means of support.

" To aim directly at effecting an increase of employment in Ireland, is beyond the powers if it be not foreign to the province of a poor-law, the immediate object of which is to provide for the relief of the destitute. Now destitution may be caused by an excess of labourers, or by a deficiency of employment, which are in truth convertible terms. If an able-bodied labourer becomes destitute through want of employment, he must be relieved at the common charge, like any individual reduced to a state of destitution by age or infirmity. If the want of employment and destitution be owing to an excess of population, to relieve that excess by emigration must be a good. Yet it may be doubted whether the parent stock is not enfeebled by the remedy, for in general the most active and enterprising emigrate, leaving the more feeble and less robust at home ; and thus a continual drain of its best elements will lower the tone and reduce the general vigour of a people, at the same time that it imparts an additional stimulus to their increase.

" Emigration however, not only may, but I believe must be had recourse to as a present means of relief, whenever the population becomes excessive. The excess will be indicated by the pressure of able-bodied labourers on the workhouse. If any considerable number of these enter the workhouse, and remain there subject to its discipline, it may be taken as a proof of their inability to provide for themselves, and of the consequent excess of labourers beyond the means of employment. Under such circumstances, emigration must be looked to as the only present remedy ; and provision should be made for defraying the expense which this would occasion, as well as for the regulations under which it should be carried into effect. With regard to the expense, I propose that the charge should in every case be equally borne by the government, and the union from which the emigrants proceed. This division of the charge appears equitable, for although the union only is immediately benefited, yet eventually the whole empire is relieved, excess in one portion of it tending to occasion an excess in the whole. But the emigration should, I think, be limited to a British colony, and should be conducted under the control of the central authority, and be subjected to such regulations as the government may deem it right to establish.

10*thly. Of Houses of Industry, and Charitable Institutions.*— " There is now a kind of poor-law established in Ireland, under which the 'houses of industry' are managed, but it is partial and ineffective ; and the several statutes providing for these houses of industry, and the other institutions intended for the relief of the poor, should be repealed, and the management of such establishments placed under the central authority. Institutions strictly charitable, and supported by voluntary contribution or otherwise, would of course remain as at present ; but it would, I think, be extremely desirable to invest the central authority with such a power of revising their rules and superintending their practice, as would ensure their acting in unison with, or at least prevent their acting in contravention of, the principles which the Act establishes for poor-law administration in Ireland. The 'houses of industry' would generally become available as union workhouses, for which they are for the most part well adapted ; and the other establishments, where they are public property, or supported by government, or by local grants from the county-rates, may be appropriated in like manner, under direction of the central authority.

" The foregoing appear to be the only points requiring especial attention, in framing a poor-law for Ireland, although there are several other matters of minor interest not to be overlooked. The 'Poor Law Amendment Act' should, I think, be taken as a guide in framing the measure, and the language, order, and general provisions of that Act should be adhered to, except where the contrary is herein indicated, or where a variation is obviously necessary. There will be much practical convenience in thus assimilating the two statutes, which provide for poor-law administration in the two countries. A measure framed on the principles developed in this Report, is I think necessary for Ireland. Unless the people are protected from the effects of destitution, no great or lasting improvement in their social condition can be expected. The establishment of a poor-law is, I conceive, the first step necessary to this end; and followed as it will be by other ameliorations, to the introduction of which it is a necessary preliminary, we may hope that it will ultimately prove the means of securing for Ireland the full amount of those benefits which ought to arise from her various local advantages, and the natural fertility of her soil.

" The proposed measure may, I believe, be carried into effect, either by means of a separate commission in Ireland, or by the existing English Poor Law Commission. One of these modes, I presume, must be adopted; and before deciding which, it will be necessary to consider the advantages and disadvantages of each. In doing this, it is important to bear in mind, that it is the English Poor Law system which is now proposed to be established; and that the knowledge and experience acquired in working that system, can be best made available for Ireland, by employing individuals conversant with the English practice. If there should be a separate commission for Ireland, it would be necessary that the commissioners should be acquainted with the English Poor Law, as now administered; and this, I apprehend, would exclude most of those Irishmen who might otherwise be deemed qualified for the office. Such exclusion, however necessary, would have an ungracious appearance, and might excite angry comment. But independent of this consideration, if there were a separate commission, the law would be similar in both countries, but the practice might become widely different, as was the case in different parts of England under the old Poor Law administration. With two commissions, there might possibly be no unity of principle,—there would certainly be no unity of action,—and probably no identity of result. Unless the existing English Poor Law Commission should be unequal to the additional duty of introducing the proposed law into Ireland, or unless it should appear that the commissioners ought not to be intrusted with the performance of this duty, the above reasons would seem to be conclusive against a separate commission.

" It must be admitted that the official duties of the English Poor Law Commissioners have been, and in fact still are, very heavy. As a member of the commission, and one too not unaccustomed to work, I may be permitted to say, that the labour has been throughout unceasing and excessive, to an extent that nothing but the hope of accomplishing a great public good would have rendered bearable. The success of the measure, however, in lessening the pressure on the rate-payers, and in improving the condition of the labouring classes, coupled with the support which has been afforded by government, and by nearly all the intelligent portions of the community, have given the commissioners encouragement and confidence ; and when the process of forming unions shall be completed, their labours will become lighter. Under these circumstances, there would seem to be no insuperable difficulty in the way of the present Poor Law Commissioners being made the instruments of establishing the new law in Ireland ; and whatever may be the difficulty at first, it will lessen as the amount of English business decreases, and the organisation of the Irish machinery is perfected. If, then, no other grounds of objection exist, and if it shall be deemed desirable, I see no reason to doubt that the English Poor Law Commissioners are competent to the additional duty of introducing the proposed measure into Ireland."

Such was the substance of my first Report, which it has been here endeavoured to condense as far as was consistent with a full exposition of its import ; and this it is necessary to give, in order to prepare the reader for correctly appreciating the important measure which was founded upon it. After undergoing much consideration, the Report was finally adopted by government on the 13th of December 1836, and on the following day I was directed to have a bill prepared embodying all its recommendations. This was accordingly done, and after being scrutinised clause by clause in a committee of the Cabinet specially appointed for the purpose, and receiving various emendations, the bill was introduced on the 13th February 1837.[d] The public and parliament had been prepared for the measure by the Royal speech at the commencement of the session, in which his Majesty recommended for early consideration "the difficult and pressing question of establishing some legal provision for the poor in Ireland, guarded by prudent regulations, and by such precautions against abuse as their experience and knowledge of the subject enable them to suggest."

Lord John Russell[e] introduced the bill in a comprehensive and very able speech—It appears, he said, from the testimony both of theory and experience, that when a country is overrun by marauders and mendicants having no proper means of subsistence, but preying on the industry and relying on the charity of others, the introduction of a poor-law serves several very important objects. In the first place it acts as a measure of peace, enabling the country to prohibit vagrancy which is so often connected with outrage, by offering a substitute to those who rely on vagrancy and outrage as a means of subsistence. When an individual or a family are unable to obtain subsistence, and are without the means of living from day to day, it would be unjust to say they shall not go about and endeavour to obtain from the charity of the affluent, that which circumstances have denied to themselves. But when you can say to such persons—here are the means of subsistence offered to you—when you can say this on the one hand, you may on the other hand say, "you are not entitled to beg, you shall no longer infest the country in a manner injurious to its peace, and liable to imposition and outrage." Another way, he observed,

Lord John Russell's speech, February 13, 1837.

---

[d] The author's Report was presented to the house at the same time.

[e] Then secretary of state for the home department, and leader in the house of commons.

in which a poor-law is beneficial is, that it is a great promoter of social concord, by showing a disposition in the state and in the community to attend to the welfare of all classes. It is of use also by interesting the landowners and persons of property in the welfare of their tenants and neighbours. A landowner who looks only to receiving the rents of his estate, may be regardless of the numbers in his neighbourhood who are in a state of destitution, or who follow mendicancy and are ready to commit crime ; but if he is compelled to furnish means for the subsistence of persons so destitute, it then becomes his interest to see that those around him have the means of living, and are not in actual want. He considered that these objects, and several others collateral to them, were obtained in England by the Act of Elizabeth. Almost the greatest benefit that could be conferred on a country was, he observed, a high standard of subsistence for the labouring classes, and such a benefit was secured for England chiefly by the great Act of Elizabeth. His lordship then alluded to the abuses which subsequently arose, and to the correction of those abuses then in progress under the provisions of the Poor Law Amendment Act; and said that " we ought to endeavour to obtain for Ireland all the good effects of the English system, and to guard against the evils which had arisen under it."

The Report of the Poor Inquiry Commissioners for Ireland was next adverted to. They had, he said, recommended many measures of improvement for Ireland, and suggested certain measures with regard to the indigent. It was to the latter he wished to call the attention of the house, as being the principal object of the present bill. The other suggestions for the general improvement of Ireland he proposed to leave for future consideration. With regard to the question of immediate relief for the destitute, the commissioners, he said, propose in the first place, that a large class of persons

should be provided for at the public expense by means
of a national and local rate. They advise also that there
should be money afforded for emigration, and that depôts
should be provided for persons preparing to emigrate.
In considering that Report, great doubts occurred to his
Majesty's ministers whether it was a good principle to
provide only for certain classes, and whether those
depôts for emigration could be safely and advantageously
adopted. It appears, he observed, from every reflection
on the subject, that the real principle is to afford relief
to the destitute, and to the destitute only ; and it would
be quite as wrong to refuse relief to the able-bodied
person in that situation, as to afford relief to the cripple,
the widow, or a deaf and dumb person who had other
means of support. It is not then the peculiar circumstances which excite public or individual compassion that
we are to regard ; but if we have a poor-law at all, it
ought to be grounded on destitution, as affording a plain
guide to relief. Then with regard to the emigration
depôts, that part of the commissioners' recommendations
could not be adopted without a great deal more of consideration than the plan proposed by them appears to
have received. And, he added, " deeply impressed as
we have been with the responsibility that attaches to a
government which proposes a law upon this subject, it
occurred to us that the best method was to see whether
the law which, as amended, has been applied to England,
could be introduced with advantage in Ireland." For
this purpose Mr. Nicholls, one of the Poor Law Commissioners, was requested to go to Ireland, and ascertain
on the spot whether anything resembling the machinery
of the English Poor Law could be there applied ; and
the result of Mr. Nicholls's inquiry is, that supposing it
to be expedient to extend a poor-law to Ireland, there
was no insurmountable obstacle or objection to the establishment of a law in many respects resembling the
amended Poor Law in England. The reasons for that

opinion are stated in the Report which has been laid on the table, and on which the bill is founded. His lordship then adverted to the chief portions of the Report, and stated generally his own views on the subject.

There is no doubt, he said, that there have occurred in Ireland many outrages consequent upon vagrancy and destitution, and the people's being left without remedy or relief; and also that a large portion of the people, especially those not having land, do practise mendicancy for a great portion of the year. He had made some inquiry with respect to the amount of the relief thus afforded to mendicants, and the result is that in most cases a shilling an acre is paid in course of the year by farmers for the support of mendicants. In some cases it has been 6d. an acre, in others 9d., and in others 1s.; but in one case it amounted to 2s. an acre. This is a heavy tax, which cannot upon the whole amount to less than between 700,000l. and 800,000l., perhaps a million a year. But this practice of mendicancy, which raises so vast a sum, is not like a well-constituted poor-law, which affords relief to the really indigent—that which seems to afford relief to the distressed, also promotes and keeps up imposture, and in Ireland where mendicancy is so general, and relief so freely given, the number of impostors must be enormous.

His lordship then proceeded to consider whether the workhouse system was applicable to Ireland; and after noticing the objection made by the commissioners of inquiry, and urged by others, that the workhouse would not be safe—that there would be too much violence—that there would be such a dislike of restraint that it could not be enforced—he came to the conclusion " that there was no reason to apprehend anything of the sort." In some of the houses of industry, he remarked, they have carried the system of restraint further than in the old English workhouses, and have established the separation of sexes such as exists in the new English work-

houses; and no regulation was proposed which did not
now exist, so " there need be no fear that violence would
be used, or that we could not protect the workhouses in
Ireland, as well and as securely as the workhouses in
England."

It had been much urged, he said, as a means of preventing undue pressure on the workhouse, that a residence in the district of three years or some other definite
period should be a condition to any person's being relieved therein; but he declared that he was opposed to
establishing a law of settlement in Ireland, being quite
convinced that it is one of the greatest evils of the poor-
laws in England. It circumscribes the market for industry. It has led to immense litigation, and any person,
he observed, "who has attended the quarter sessions,
and there witnessed the disputes that arise between
parishes as to whether a person had been hired for a
year and a day, whether he had been ordered to go
home on the day before the expiration of the term so as
to destroy the settlement, or whether he had served a
full year and a day, and various other similar questions
—any person who has attended to this litigation and
those disputes, will not have any wish that I should
introduce the question of settlement into this bill."

When the whole of the workhouses are in operation,
and we are enabled to relieve all that are entitled to it,
we may then, he observed, prohibit vagrancy; but until
we can do the one, it will not be just altogether to prohibit the other. It is not therefore proposed to prevent
persons asking alms, if they can show they have applied
for and failed in obtaining relief. This is a necessary
step in the transition from one state to another. If
it succeeds, we shall hereafter be able to prohibit
vagrancy.

His lordship then went over the ground more fully
discussed in the Report, with regard to the local machinery, the question of rating, the extent of the unions,

cost of the workhouses, emigration, and some other minor points; and then stated that the safest way of introducing such a law as had been described, would be to use the simple machinery which had been found so advantageous in England. It was therefore proposed, instead of forming a separate commission for Ireland, that the Poor Law Commissioners for England should have the power of intrusting to one or two of their body, the power of acting in Ireland for carrying the law into operation. This would he thought be better than establishing a separate commission. A lengthened discussion then took place in reference to the proposed measure, in which Mr. Shaw, Mr. O'Connell, Lord Howick, Sir Robert Peel, Lord Stanley, and other members took part. Doubts were of course expressed, and objections stated; but on the whole the measure was not received unfavourably, and the bill was ordered to be read a first time.

The bill read a first time.

On the 25th of April Lord John Russell moved the second reading of the bill, and the debate thereon was continued by adjournment to the 1st of May, when the second reading was carried without a division, although not without long and somewhat hostile discussion. On the 9th of May the house went into committee on the bill, and the first fourteen clauses were passed with only a few verbal alterations. On the 11th the committee got to the end of the 20th clause, after two unimportant divisions. It had been announced that on the 12th of May the question of settlement should be considered. Many members were still of opinion that a settlement law was necessary; but after a long and temperate discussion of the subject in all its bearings, the committee decided against the introduction of settlement by 120 to 68. On the 26th of May the bill was again in committee, when the clauses up to the 35th were agreed to. On the 2nd, 5th, 6th and 7th of June, the committee proceeded in

The bill read a second time and committed.

considering the clauses of the bill up to the 60th, but the vagrancy clauses (53 to 58 inclusive) Vagrancy clauses were postponed. These clauses provided for the postponed. repression of mendicancy in the unions, as the work-houses were successively completed and in operation; but there appeared to be a strong feeling in the house that nothing should be done to prevent begging, until the poor-law was everywhere fully established. The clauses were therefore postponed for further consideration.

At this time the king's illness had so much increased that his recovery became highly improbable, Death of and the business of parliament was conse- William IV. June 20, quently suspended. William the Fourth died on 1837. the 20th of June, and was succeeded by his niece the Princess Victoria, our present gracious sovereign. On the 17th of July parliament was prorogued by the youthful queen, in a speech from the throne, which the manner of its delivery and the occasion combined to render more than ordinarily interesting. The Irish Poor Relief bill, and the other measures then in progress, were therefore put an end to, and would have to be commenced anew on the re-assembling of parliament.

The interval thus interposed, afforded opportunity for further consideration and inquiry, and it was determined that this should be taken advantage of, and that the author should again proceed to Ireland for the purpose of visiting " those districts which a want of time prevented his inspecting last year." I was also directed to bear in mind the discussions which had taken place during the progress of the bill in the late session, and generally to report whether the circumstances of the districts about to be visited, or any new matter that I might discover, " shall have caused me in any way to alter or modify the recommendations set forth in my last Report."

Accordingly at the end of August I proceeded to Ireland, and continued in the active prosecution of my inquiries until early in October. I moreover took advantage of the opportunity afforded me in going and returning, to inquire very carefully at Bristol, Liverpool, Manchester, and Birmingham, into the habits of the large number of Irish congregated in each of these towns, and into the mode of dealing with such of them as become destitute, or stand in need of relief, on which points I obtained much valuable information, for the most part confirmatory of my previous views. On the 3rd of November I reported the result of my further inquiries;[f] and I will now, as was done in the case of the ' First Report,' give an abstract of this ' Second Report,' although much less fully, it not being now necessary to go so much at length into what may be considered matters of detail, as was requisite in the first instance—

Second Report.—Nov. 3, 1837.

" The investigations which I have just concluded, have not afforded ground for any material change of opinion. I may perhaps estimate the difficulty of establishing a poor-law in Ireland somewhat higher than I did before, but of the necessity for such a measure, I am if possible more fully convinced ; and now, after a more extended inquiry, both in England and in Ireland, I am enabled substantially to confirm the statements in my Report of last year, to which I can add but little in the way of recommendation, although it may be necessary to notice certain objections which have been made to portions of the Report, and to some of the provisions of the bill of last session. No material change in the bill however appears to be called for, and I presume government will again proceed with it as then proposed. The measure is essentially based upon the English workhouse system ; and as, notwithstanding the facts and reasonings which were adduced in proof of its applicability to Ireland, doubts were still expressed both in and out of parliament upon this vital point, it seemed important to ascertain whether any grounds for such doubts really existed.

---

[f] The Report was accompanied by appendices containing important evidence on several of the points to which it referred; and in particular a communication from Mr. Stanley, on the extent of destitution among the poorer classes in Ireland, in which he shows that the estimate of the inquiry commissioners was founded on erroneous data.

" With this view I visited Bristol, Liverpool, Manchester, and
Birmingham, through which places nearly the whole of the
Irish migrants pass and repass, and in all of which there is a
large resident Irish population, and where therefore their
habits are well known. All the persons whom I consulted in
these places, were unanimous in declaring their belief, that
nothing but absolute inability to provide for himself would
induce an Irishman to enter the workhouse. But it may
be objected, that although disinclination to the workhouse is
characteristic of the Irish when in England, such would not
be the case if the system were established in Ireland. This
objection does not admit of an answer founded on direct
experience; but judging from analogy, and making due
allowance for the circumstances of the two countries, there
seems no reason to doubt that the result would be the same
in one as in the other. The Irishman is by habit and tem-
perament more roving and migratory than the Englishman;
but this is surely not calculated to reconcile him sooner
to the restraints of a workhouse. I made it my business to
inquire, and obtain information from all classes of persons,
and was everywhere assured that the Irish would not go into
the workhouse, if they could in any way obtain support out
of it. The result of my investigations in the several houses
of industry and mendicity establishments has been to the
same purport, all tending to show that if the workhouse
is properly regulated, it will be resorted to only by the actually destitute. It is not less important to state however, that
I found the same persons decidedly opposed to anything in
the shape of out-door relief. I have not met with an individual conversant with the subject, either in England or in
Ireland, who did not declare against out door relief. 'Confine relief to the workhouse,' was the general reply, 'and you
will be safe ; but if you once grant out-door relief, your
control is gone, and the whole Irish population will become a
mass of paupers.'

" It has been argued that the workhouses will eventually fail in
Ireland, as they have failed in France, at Munich, and at
Hamburgh ; but there is no analogy between the two cases.
The workhouse principle was never recognised in these establishments, which were all either poorhouses for the maintenance of the aged and infirm, or manufactories for setting to
work vagrants, mendicants, and other idle persons. All these
institutions were established under the notion that profitable
labour could be always found, and that pauper labour could
be made profitable to the community, and their management
had reference to these objects. There were certain variations in practice to suit local circumstances, but this was the

view under which the institutions were founded, by Count Rumford, at Munich, by the imperial government in France, and by Baron de Voght, at Hamburgh. I need scarcely say that this view is essentially different from the workhouse system established in England, and as it is proposed to establish it in Ireland. Experience has proved that pauper labour can never be profitable. The workhouse is here used merely as a medium of *relief*; and in order that the destitute only may partake of it, the relief is administered in such a way, and on such conditions, that none but the destitute will accept it. This is the workhouse principle, as first established in the two parishes of Bingham and Southwell eighteen or twenty years ago, and as it has recently been established in the unions formed under the Poor Law Amendment Act ; and we have the experience of these parishes, and the more varied, though less prolonged experience of the English unions, in proof of the efficiency of the system, which has worked hitherto without a single instance of failure. It is not therefore upon mere hypothesis, that it is proposed to proceed with regard to the Irish Poor Law, but upon the surer ground of experience.

" It has been further argued, that there is always a tendency to deterioration in such institutions, and that after a time they fall away from the principle on which they were originally established—to which it may be answered, that no such deterioration occurred in the two parishes above named —on the contrary, the workhouse principle continued to operate in these parishes in all its simplicity and efficiency, up to the day when they were each constituted the centre of a union. May it not therefore be inferred, that if established as a test of destitution, the workhouse will continue to be effective, and the principle free from deterioration, as in the two cases named above? But the proposed measure does not depend on this inference alone—a safeguard is provided by the Poor Law Amendment Act in the appointment of commissioners, who under the control of the executive, and the supervision of parliament, are to superintend the working of the measure, and to apply from time to time such correctives, whether local or general, as may be necessary for securing its efficiency. Whatever doubts may have arisen on either side of the Channel, as to the sufficiency of the workhouse for relieving the destitute, as well as for protecting the ratepayers, I therefore feel warranted in expressing my conviction, not only that the workhouse system is applicable to Ireland, but that it is the only mode in which relief can be safely administered to the destitute classes in that country.

" The question of the workhouse being thus disposed of, I shall now proceed to notice such objections as have been made to the bill generally, or to any of its provisions; and in doing this, I will endeavour to introduce such illustrations as seem to be called for, and such further information as I have been able to collect during my recent visitation, which extended from Waterford to Belfast and Londonderry, and the counties of Donegal, Fermanagh, Cavan, and Meath.

" The chief objections which have been made to the measure, as it was introduced in the last session, are comprised under the heads hereafter specified, to each of which a full explanation is appended ·in the Report. From these several explanations, so much is here given, as will, it is hoped, serve to lessen, if not altogether to remove, the weight of the objections which were raised during the discussion on the bill, or which may have appeared in pamphlets or in any other shape.

The measure is said not to be applicable to the North of Ireland.— " It has frequently been asserted, both in and out of parliament, that the condition of the people in the north of Ireland differs so essentially from those in the south, that a poor-law which might be applicable in one case, would be inapplicable in the other; and it was urged as a ground of objection to the measure of last session, that it had been framed exclusively with reference to the southern and western districts. This objection seems to have been made mainly on the ground, that no specific information had been obtained as to the north of Ireland; whereas, in fact, a large mass of information had been collected by the commissioners of Irish Poor Inquiry, with respect to the north, as well as the other parts of the country; and this information, coupled with what I had obtained from other sources, and supported by my own observation in those of the northern counties which I had visited, appeared to be sufficient, without further examination of the northern districts. An opportunity for such examination having however been afforded by the postponement of the bill, I have now visited most of the northern counties, and carefully examined the condition and habits of the people, with special reference to the contemplated measure; and I can with entire confidence state, in my opinion, it is as well adapted to the circumstances existing in the north, as to those which prevail in the south. The habits of the people are there in some degree fitted for its reception. The necessity of relieving the destitute is there admitted, and in most of the northern towns of any note, there is now a kind of voluntary poor-law established. In Monaghan, in Armagh, at Newry, Belfast, Coleraine, Londonderry, I found provision made for relieving destitution, and the principle virtually recognised, that it is the duty of a civilised community to protect its members from perishing by want. Indeed, if any doubt existed as to establishing a poor-law in Ireland, an inspection of the northern counties would, I think, remove the doubt, and show the expediency of such a measure. The extent of poverty is there less than in the south and west ; but the amount of destitution is probably as great. There is this important difference however—in the *south* and *west* the destitute depend for support upon the class immediately above them, the small cottiers and cultivators ; but in the *north*, the sympathy existing between the different ranks of society—between the opulent and the needy—has led to the making of some provision for the relief of the latter class. If the charge of this provision was fairly spread over the whole community— if the relief afforded was sufficient, and permanent, and equally distributed, it would be equivalent to a poor-law ; but the charge is unequal, the provision uncertain, and the relief partial and inefficient. To apply the proposed measure to the north of Ireland, will therefore be little more than carrying out, in an equal and effective manner, that which has been long but unequally and ineffectually attempted by the communities themselves.

" In speaking of the north of Ireland, I ought to except the county of *Donegal*, the inhabitants of which differ materially from those of the other northern counties, and approximate to those of the west and south. Small holdings, and minute subdivisions of land, prevail in Donegal to a greater extent than I have found in any other part of Ireland ; and the consequent growth of population there presses so hard upon the productive powers of the soil, as to depress the condition of the people to nearly the lowest point in the social scale—exposing them, under the not unfrequent occurrence of an unfavourable season, or a failure of the potato-crop, to the greatest privations. This has unhappily been the case during the last four years, in each of which, and especially in the last, there has been a failure of the crops in Donegal. In May, June, and July last, nearly the whole of the population along the northern and western coasts of the county, were reduced to a state bordering on starvation ; and had not government sent a supply of meal and medical aid, numbers of the people would have fallen victims to famine and disease. The surface of Donegal is generally covered with bog, susceptible of profitable cultivation wherever lime or sea-sand or sea-weed is obtainable, and the people have in consequence congregated wherever these elements of fertility abound—along the coasts, and on the shores of the numerous bays and inlets opening upon the Atlantic, along the banks of the rivers, and up the narrow valleys and ravines with which the country is intersected—everywhere, in short, where the soil is most easily reclaimed by individual exertion. But wherever combined effort, or an outlay of capital is necessary for draining, fencing, and reclaiming—there nothing has been done, and the surface is permitted to lie waste and unproductive. The process of reclamation in such circumstances is above the limited means of the people; each one of whom just manages to cultivate land enough to raise potatoes for his family—a patch of oats to supply them, mostly I fear, with whisky—and then, as to rent (for they all pay rent), they rely for raising that upon a few cattle or sheep running wild upon the mountains.

" Nothing can exceed the miserable appearance of the cottages in *Donegal*, or the desolate aspect of a cluster of these hovels, always teeming with a crowded population. Yet if you enter their cabins, and converse with them frankly and kindly, you will find the people intelligent and communicative, quick to comprehend, and ready to impart what they know. They admitted that they were too numerous, ' too thick upon the land,' and that, as one of them declared, ' they were eating each other's heads off,'—but what could they do? There was no employment for the young, nor relief for the aged, nor means nor opportunity for removing their surplus numbers to some more eligible spot. They could only therefore live on, ' hoping,' as they said, ' that times might mend, and that their landlords would sooner or later do something for them.' To improve the condition of such a people would increase the productive powers of the country, a point well deserving the attention of the great landowners, with whom it mainly rests. But no material or lasting improvement can be effected, so long as the present subdivision of land continues. This practice, wherever it prevails, forces the population down to the lowest level of subsistence—to that point where subdivision is arrested by the dread, or by the actual occurrence of want ; and it is alike the duty and the interest of the landowner, so to exercise the right of property as to guard his tenantry from such depression. In the case of Donegal, a two-fold remedy seems to be necessary, that is, emigration, and an extension of cultivation. There is abundant room for the latter, and if undertaken with spirit and intelligence, it will not only ensure an ample return on the capital expended, but also afford employment, and provide suitable locations for a part of the surplus population. If a portion of this surplus were removed by emigration, and another portion placed on new grounds, effectually reclaimed, a consolidation of the present small holdings might be effected. This would be a great point gained, where the average rental of such holdings does not exceed 2*l.*, and numbers are under 1*l.* per annum. A poor-law would facilitate this change, so necessary for the landowners, as well as for the great mass of the people of Donegal. The principle of a poor-law is to make the property of a district answerable for the relief of destitution within it; and the application of this principle would serve to connect the several orders of society, and teach them to act together—it would show them that they have reciprocal interests, reciprocal duties—that each is necessary to the other—and that the cordial co-operation of *all* is necessary to the well-being of the whole. I therefore augur much good from the establishment of a poor-law, under circumstances similar to those now existing in Donegal; and believe that such a law, whilst it provides for the relief of the destitute, will be a safeguard to property, and facilitate the introduction of other ameliorations.

There ought to be a law of Settlement.—" There is no part of the subject to which I have given more attention than to the question of settlement. Of the evils arising from settlement in England, there can be no doubt, and the grounds on which it was proposed to establish a poor-law in Ireland without settlement, are explained in my former Report. But it appears that many persons still consider some law of settlement necessary for securing local co-operation based upon local interests, for the protection of particular unions from undue pressure, and for guarding the towns on the eastern coast from being burdened with the destitute who may flock thither, or be sent thither from England or Scotland, or with the families of the large body of migrants who proceed to Great Britain in the harvest season and return at its conclusion. If there were danger from all or any of these sources, it might be right to make provision against it in the bill; but I am satisfied that, in carrying out the measure as now proposed, none of these inconveniences would arise, beyond what the commissioners could meet by special regulations, without recurring to a settlement law. There is this primary objection to settlement, that it impedes the free distribution of labour, and interferes with the fair and open competition which is alike necessary for protecting the employer and the employed, and by which an equalisation of supply and demand in the labour-market can alone be maintained. Its direct tendency is to depress the social condition and character of the people; for by narrowing the field of labour, and binding individuals to a particular locality, not perhaps favourable to the development or most profitable employment of their faculties, improvement is checked, independence is destroyed, and the working classes, without resource or elasticity of spirit, are led to depend upon their place of settlement in every contingency, instead of upon themselves. If therefore the bill as at present proposed, by requiring the rate to be levied upon the union for relief of the actually destitute within it is sufficient, as I believe it to be, for securing attention to the business of the union, there can be no necessity to establish a law of settlement for such purpose; and nothing short of absolute necessity in that or some other respect, could justify the introduction of a law, the direct tendency of which would be in other respects so injurious.

Out-door Relief should have been provided for.—" Much has been said as to the necessity of providing out-door relief in Ireland; but most of the arguments in favour of an extension of relief beyond the workhouse appear to be founded, either upon a misapprehension of the objects of a poor-law, or upon an exaggerated estimate of the number of destitute persons for whom relief would be required. The object of a poor-law is to relieve the destitute—that is, to relieve those individuals who from sickness, accident, mental or bodily infirmity, failure of employment, or other cause, may be unable to obtain the necessaries of life by their own exertions. Under such circumstances, the destitute individual, if not relieved, might be driven to beg or to steal; and a poor-law, by providing for the relief of destitution, prevents the necessity or the excuse for resorting to either. This is the legitimate object of a poor-law, and to this its operations are limited in the bill of last session. But if, disregarding this limitation, it be attempted to provide relief for all who are needy, but not destitute—for all who are poor, and whose means of living are inferior to what it may be desirable that they should possess—if property is to be taxed, not for the relief of the destitute only, but for ensuring to every one such a portion of the comforts and conveniences of life as are assumed to be necessary—the consequence of any such attempt must be in Ireland, as it notoriously was in England, not only to diminish the value of property, but also to emasculate and demoralise the whole labouring population.

" The evidence collected by the Commissioners of Poor Law Inquiry in England, establishes the conclusion that out-door relief is inevitably open to abuse, and that its administration entails consequences prejudicial to the labouring classes, and to the whole community—in short, that there is no security for the prevention of abuse, nor any mode of ensuring a right administration of relief, but by restricting it to the workhouse. The facts and reasonings contained in the Reports on this subject, have been confirmed by the experience of the present Poor Law Commission ; and although out-door relief has not yet been totally prohibited in any of the English unions, there can be no doubt that the intention of the Poor Law Amendment Act points eventually to the workhouse as the sole medium of relief, and requires that it should be so restricted as early as circumstances permitted. To establish out-door relief in Ireland, would therefore be in direct con-tradiction to English experience, and to the spirit of the English law. It would introduce a practice in the one country, under the prejudicial effects of which the other has long been suffering, and from which it has not yet entirely recovered. Some persons have recommended that out-door relief in Ire-land, should be restricted to the aged, sick, and infirm ; but even with this limitation, how is abuse to be prevented, and how is the precise limit to be defined of the age, sickness, or infirmity, entitling an individual to be relieved out of the workhouse ?—I believe it to be impossible so to define the conditions as to prevent the occurrence of gross abuses, which would not only be a source of demoralisation, but would also serve to engender strifes jealousies and ill feeling in every locality. After the best consideration which I have been able to give the subject, in all its bearings, I still re-tain the opinion that in Ireland relief should be restricted to the workhouse, or in other words, that out-door relief in any shape should be prohibited.

The mode of Rating is objected to.—" The question of rating is obviously open to much contrariety of opinion. The mode of valuation, of assessment, of collection, and the proportions in which the rate shall be paid, are all questions on which dif-ferent opinions might possibly be formed by different persons ; and accordingly the views expressed upon these points have been various and conflicting. Some have contended that the whole of the rate should be charged upon the owner, on the ground that the tenant derives little profit, often no profit what-ever from the occupation, and ought not therefore to be called on to pay any part of the rate. Those taking this view, appear to overlook the fact that the destitute classes in Ire-land are now supported almost entirely by the occupiers, who will be relieved from this charge when the proposed measure shall have come into operation. To require the occupiers to pay half the rate, is not therefore to impose on them a new charge, but a portion only of an old charge, to which they had long been accustomed. Moreover the occupiers have an interest in the property rated—not permanent indeed like the owners, but more immediate ; and on this ground also they are fairly chargeable with a portion of the rate. If the owners paid the whole, the occupiers would of course not be entitled to take part in the distribution of the funds, nor in the management of the business of the union—they would have no interest in common with their landlords, and would to a certain extent be arrayed against them ; for their interest and their sympathies would probably lead them to increase the amount of the burthen, rather than lessen it. Even if there were a sufficient number of resident owners, it would be inexpedient to place the whole control of the unions in their hands, thus constituting them a separate class, and at the same time lowering the position of the occupiers ; but in the present state of Ireland, such a proposition seems especially open to objection. The exemption in favour of occupiers of 5l. value and under, and the charging the owners of such property with the entire rate, forms an exception to the above reasoning, and will probably be disapproved by those whose interests may appear to be affected by it. But every such charge is eventually borne by the property, and in the long run it is perhaps not very material whether the rate is paid by the owner or by the tenant, it being in fact a portion of the rent. This arrangement is proposed, partly as a matter of convenience, on account of the difficulty and expense of collecting a rate from the vast number of small holdings of 5l. value and under which exist in Ireland, and partly also with the view of relieving this description of occupiers, who are for the most part in a state of poverty bordering on destitution, from a portion of the burthen ; and it is gratifying to find that this proposition has on the whole been favourably received.

The Unions as proposed are too large.—" In almost every discussion during the progress of the bill last session, the proposed number and size of the unions were objected to. Yet the discretion of the commissioners is unfettered in these respects. They are left at liberty to form the unions, as may appear best adapted to the circumstances in each case. The same discretion was confided to the commissioners in England, and it must be equally necessary that they should possess it in Ireland. The objections to the intended size of the unions, do not therefore apply to the bill, but to my first Report, in which it is stated that, ' If the surface of Ireland be divided into squares of twenty miles each, so that a workhouse placed in the centre would be about ten miles from the extremities in all directions, this would give about eighty workhouses for the whole of Ireland.' Instead of eighty workhouses however, I assumed that a hundred might be required, and calculated the probable expense accordingly. But this was mere assumption, for it is obviously impossible to state what will be the precise number of unions, until some progress has been made in the work of formation. The commissioners are bound to form the unions in the best manner, according to the best of their judgment. Their credit as public functionaries would be compromised by any failure in this respect; and it may be fairly presumed that they will use due vigilance and impartiality, and avail themselves of all the experience which England affords in this matter.

The suppression of Mendicancy objected to.—" Objections have been made to the vagrancy clauses, and it has been contended that if such provisions were necessary, they should be established by a separate Act. Whether the suppression of mendicancy be provided for in the Poor Law Bill, or by a separate bill, does not seem very material; but it is important that the provision should be made concurrently with the Poor Law measure. To establish a poor-law, without at the same time suppressing mendicancy, would be imperfect legislation, especially with reference to the present condition of the Irish people. It is true there are now vagrancy laws in Ireland, which enact whipping, imprisonment, and transportation as the punishments of mendicancy; but these laws are inoperative, partly from their severity, and partly from other causes. Ireland wants a vagrancy law that shall operate in unison with the Poor Law, for without such concurrent action, both laws would be in a great measure ineffective. The suppression of mendicancy is necessary for the protection of the peasantry themselves. No Irish cottier, however poor, closes his door whilst partaking of his humble meal. The mendicant has free access, and is never refused a share. There is a superstitious dread of bringing down the beggar's curse, and thus mendicancy is sustained in the midst of poverty, perpetuating itself amongst its victims. Much of the feeling out of which this state of things has arisen may, I think, be traced to the absence of any provision for relieving the destitute. A mendicant solicits charity on the plea of destitution. His plea must be admitted, for it cannot be disproved; and to refuse relief, may occasion the death of a fellow-creature, which would be a crime of great magnitude. Hence the admission of the mendicant's claim, which is regarded in the light of an obligation by the Irish peasantry. To make provision for relieving mendicants at the public charge, without at the same time preventing the practice of begging, would leave the peasant exposed to much of the pressure which he now sustains from this source ; for the mendicant class would generally prefer the vagrant life to which they are accustomed, to the order and restraint of a workhouse. To suppress mendicancy, is therefore necessary both as an adjunct of the proposed Poor Law, and for the protection of the labouring classes throughout Ireland.

Objections to cumulative voting, &c.—" It might perhaps be sufficient to say, in answer to the objections which were made to cumulative voting, voting by proxy, and constituting magistrates *ex-officio* guardians, that the Irish bill follows in these cases the example of the English Poor Law Amendment Act. There are, however, weighty reasons in favour of each of these provisions, some of which it may be useful to notice.

" With respect to cumulative votes, it may be observed, that the raising and disbursing of a poor-rate involves nothing political, but is to be regarded rather in the light of a mutual assurance, in which the community joins for the purpose of being protected against the effects of pauperism, each member contributing in proportion to his means, and each having an interest according to the amount of his contributions. If therefore the amount contributed be the measure of each ratepayer's interest, it ought in justice also, within certain convenient limitations, to be the measure of his influence ; and these limitations the bill provides, by fixing a scale according to which every ratepayer is entitled to vote. As regards the voting by proxy, such a power is necessary for enabling the owner to protect his property, his interest in which is permanent, although he may not always be present to represent it by his personal vote ; and the bill therefore provides for his doing so by proxy. The occupier is always present, and may vote in person ; not so the owner, whose interest would be unprotected without this power of voting by proxy. That the owner's interest ought to be represented will not be denied. The rate is levied upon property, and thus in fact becomes a portion of the rent, which would be increased by the amount of the rate, if this were not levied for Poor Law purposes ; so that in reality it is the landlord, the permanent owner of the property, who finally bears the burthen of the rate, and not the tenant or temporary occupier. It seems consonant with justice therefore, that every facility should be afforded to the owner for protecting his interest by his vote.

" There are many reasons why magistrates should form a portion of every board of guardians. The elected guardians will for the most part consist of occupiers, or renters, not the owners of property ; and their interest will be temporary, whilst the interest of the owner is permanent. Some union of these two interests seems necessary towards the complete organization of a board of guardians ; and as the magistrates collectively may be regarded as the chief landed proprietors of the country, the bill proposes to effect this union by creating them *ex-officio* members of the board. The elected guardians are moreover subject to be changed every year, and their proceedings might be changeable, and perhaps contradictory, and confusion might arise through the opposite views of successive boards. The *ex-officio* guardians will serve as a corrective in this respect. Their position as magistrates, their information and general character, and their large stake as owners of property, will necessarily give them much weight ; whilst the proposed limitation of their number to one-third of the elected guardians, will prevent their having an undue preponderance. The elected and the *ex officio* members may be expected each to improve the other, and important social benefits may arise from their frequent mingling, and from the necessity for mutual concession and forbearance which such mingling cannot fail to teach. Each individual member will feel that his influence depends upon the opinion which his colleagues entertain of him, or upon the respect or regard which they feel towards him ; and hence will arise an interchange of good offices, and a cultivation of mutual goodwill, beginning with the board of guardians, and extending throughout the union, and eventually it may be hoped throughout the country ; and thus the union system may become the means of healing dissensions, and reconciling jarring interests in Ireland. On these grounds, I consider that the establishment of *ex-officio* guardians, voting by proxy, and cumulative voting, as provided in the bill, should be adhered to.

" Many measures, local as well as general, have been suggested, either for removing restrictions to the application of capital, or for giving direct encouragement to its application in Ireland ; and some of these measures, I understand government intend taking into early consideration. In the survey which I have been able to take of the state of Ireland, and of the condition of the Irish people, it has appeared to me that quiet, and the absence of excitement, is the object chiefly to be desired. With repose would come security, and the investment of capital, and thence would arise employment, and the development of the productive powers of the country. The proposed Poor Law will not of itself accomplish these objects, but it will be found a valuable accessory ; and with the progress of education, and that orderly submission to lawful authority which is at once the cause and the consequence of peace and prosperity, all those other objects will, we may hope, be eventually secured for Ireland."[g]

My Report was considered by the Cabinet,[h] and the whole subject was again very fully discussed, and several minor alterations in the bill were decided upon. It was also determined to bring it forward as the first measure of the session. The subject continued to occupy

---

[g] The following estimate was prepared during the progress of the bill, and was printed by order of the house of lords.

Assuming that there will be a hundred unions, each having a workhouse capable of accommodating 800 persons, the paid officers, with their respective salaries in each union, may be stated as follows :—

Clerk of the union	from £60 to	80
Master and mistress of the workhouse ..	60 ,,	80
Chaplains	50 ,,	80
Medical officers and medicines	100 ,,	150
Auditor	20 ,,	30
Returning officer	10 ,,	20
Collector	50 ,,	70
Schoolmaster and schoolmistress	50 ,,	80
Porter and assistant-porter	20 ,,	30
Other assistants in the workhouse and union, say	30	30
	£450 to	650

For the hundred unions, this would give a total expenditure in salaries of from 45,000l. to 65,000l. per annum ; or say 55,000l. on an average.

In addition to the above, it may be further assumed, that on an average throughout the year the workhouses will be three parts full, and that the total cost of maintenance clothing bedding wear and tear &c., will amount to 1s. 6d. per head per week, which is equal to 3l. 18s., or say 4l. per head per annum ; this will give an expenditure of 240,000l. per annum for maintenance &c., in the hundred unions : which added to the 55,000l. for salaries, will make a total charge of 295,000l. annually for the relief of the destitute, under the provisions of the bill.

The money for building the workhouses is to be advanced by government, free of interest for ten years ; and is to be repaid by annual instalments of five per cent. The cost of the workhouses has been stated at 700,000l., but assuming it to amount to 1,000,000l., this would impose an additional charge of 50,000l. annually for the first twenty years (exclusive of the interest after the first ten years on the then residue of the principal), which, added to the above, makes an aggregate charge of 345,000l. per annum.—G. N.

[h] It was laid on the table of both houses on the assembling of parliament.

a good deal of public attention, as well in England as in Ireland. It was discussed in the papers, and pamphlets were written upon it. In this instance however, as in most others, the opponents were the most active, and much ingenuity was displayed in animadverting on the asserted incongruities of the proposed Irish Poor Law. The inquiry commissioners also had their advocates, and in Ireland especially their recommendations were, as might be expected, more popular than the government bill. However, on the whole, the measure may be said to have held its ground, and to be regarded as a matter of first-rate importance.

Parliament assembled on the 10th of November, and on the 1st of December Lord John Russell reintroduced the bill, in an argumentative speech of considerable length. After going through and commenting on the several recommendations of the inquiry commissioners,[i] and noticing the objections to which they were all more or less open, he explained by way of contrast the principle on which the present bill was founded, much in the same manner that he had done on the first introduction of the measure. The statement was generally well received, although there were some marked exceptions in this respect, and the bill was read a first time without a division. It was in like manner read a second time on the 5th of February 1838. But on the motion for going into committee on the 9th, Mr. O'Connell strongly opposed the bill, and moved that it be committed that day six months. The amendment was however negatived by 277 to 25, a majority which made the passing of the measure in some form pretty certain. On the 23rd of February the question of settlement was again very fully discussed, and its introduction decided against by 103 to 31, the latter number comprising all who could be

The bill reintroduced, December 1, 1837.

---

[i] Ante, pp. 137 to 146.

brought to vote for a settlement law of any kind. The vagrancy clauses were now also withdrawn from the bill, on the understanding that there would hereafter be a separate measure for the suppression of medicancy. The bill continued to be considered in successive committees until the 23rd of March, when all the clauses having been gone through and settled, it was ordered to be reported, which was done on the 9th of April. On the 30th of April the bill was read a third time and passed by the commons, and on the day following was introduced and read a first time in the lords. *The bill passed the commons and read a first time in the lords.*

It had been thought desirable that during the Easter vacation I should visit Holland and Belgium, with the view of ascertaining whether there was anything in the institutions of those countries, or in the management of their poor, that could be made available in the present measure of Irish Poor Law ; and it was arranged that Dr. Kay, one of our assistant-commissioners should accompany me. The time at our disposal was short, and our investigations were necessarily hurried ; but the letters with which we were furnished procured for us ready access everywhere, and enabled us to obtain information which would not otherwise have been accessible. On our return, I reported to government the result of our inquiries.[k] The first portion of the Report was chiefly furnished by my companion, and had reference to the subject of education, in which Dr. Kay[m] felt a deep interest, and in the promotion of which he afterwards took a distinguished part. The latter portions of the Report applied more immediately to our present subject, and from these portions I will now abstract so much as seemed calculated to be useful with regard to the question of Irish Poor Law, or to bear in any way upon the state of Ireland—

---

[k] The Report was printed, and laid before parliament.
[m] Now Sir James Kay Shuttleworth, Bart.

Third Report.—May 5, 1838.

" The institutions for the relief of indigence are numerous in Holland, and consist of hospices for the aged and infirm, orphanhouses, workhouses of towns, depôts de mendicité, or district workhouses, the poor colonies, and private charitable institutions. The funds for the support of these establishments are to a great extent derived from endowments and voluntary contributions, the direct tax not being more than about 1,800,000 guilders, or 150,000*l.* per annum. Among the classes having ability to labour, a state of even temporary dependence is considered disgraceful, and great exertions are made by the labouring population to avoid it. But no sense of degradation attaches to the orphan establishments, which are calculated to invite rather than to discourage dependence. The depôts de mendicité, or provincial workhouses bear so close a resemblance to the old English workhouses and those established under Gilbert's and the various local Acts, as to warrant a belief that the English workhouses must have been formed upon a Dutch model; but however this may be, the result has certainly been the same in both countries, the evil of pauperism having been increased rather than diminished by these institutions, in which the profitable application of pauper labour has been sought for, rather than the repression of pauperism.

" The workhouse of *Amsterdam* is a vast building, capable of containing upwards of 1,500 inmates. The imposing character of its exterior, the elegance of its entrance-hall, and the decorations of the rooms appropriated to public business, were in marked contrast with the aspect of the several wards. The inmates chiefly consisted of the lowest and least moral part of the population of the great cities, who had sought refuge in the workhouse because they had forfeited their claim to regular employment, and the vigilance of the police did not permit them to subsist by mendicancy. The sexes were strictly separated at all times, but the children were in the same apartment with the adults of each sex. The males and females each occupied separate day-rooms, in which the dirt and disorder were very offensive. In these rooms the inmates ate their meals, without any attention to regularity or propriety. Here also they worked in the looms, or at other occupations. The first group of men to whom we advanced, were seated at a table playing at cards; we found another party playing at draughts, and a third at hazard. Others were idly sauntering up and down the room. The women's day-room presented a scene of similar disorder. Both men and boys were clothed in a coarse kind of sacking. The chief article of their diet is rye-bread, almost black, and not over-abundant, with an indefinite quantity of boiled butter-milk ; but they are permitted to work at certain rates of wages, and to spend a portion of their earnings at a canteen in the house, where coffee tobacco gin &c. may be obtained. On application for admission, the paupers undergo a strict examination as to their ability to maintain themselves ; and while inmates they are not permitted to go abroad, ' unless they give positive hopes that on re-entering society, they will render themselves worthy of their liberty, by diligently endeavouring to gain their own livelihood by honest means.'

" The establishment at La Cambré, near *Brussels*, was superior in its internal arrangements to the workhouse at Amsterdam, particularly in the separate classification of the aged, the children, and the adults, and also in the good arrangement and cleanliness of the sleeping-rooms. The sexes are strictly separated, as is invariably the case in all the other Dutch and Belgian institutions. By the penal code, a mendicant once condemned to a depôt de mendicité for begging, may be kept there during the remainder of his life ; but in practice, he is allowed to leave the establishment whenever the commission of superintendence are satisfied that he is disposed to labour for his subsistence, without resorting to mendicancy.

" There are three great workhouses for the whole of *Holland*, which are situated, one at Amsterdam, another at Middle-burgh, and a third in the commonalty Nieuve Pekel A, in the province of Groningen. *Belgium* has five great work-houses, situated respectively at La Cambré, near Brussels, for the province of Brabant ; at Bruges, for the two Flanders ; at Hoogstraeten, for the province of Antwerp ; at Mons, for Hainault, Namur, and Luxembourg ; and at Reickheim, for Liege and Limburgh. Under their present regulations, these provincial workhouses, or depôts de mendicité, both in Holland and Belgium, are I think, judging from what we could learn and what we saw, very defective institutions ; and hence seems to have arisen the necessity for resorting to some stricter measures, which ended in the establishment of the poor colonies. In England, the defects of the old work-houses were remedied by the introduction of regulations calculated to render them efficient tests, by the aid of which we ' have succeeded in establishing the distinction between poverty and destitution : for the latter we have provided relief, but we have left the former to its own natural resources. In Holland and Belgium no such distinction has been made, or test established. Their workhouses remain as they were originally formed—nurseries for indolence, and stimulants to pauperism. But in order to correct this evil, the Dutch have had recourse to the establishment of penal colonies, to which all persons found begging (or committing vagabondage as it is termed) are sent, if able to work, and compelled to labour for their subsistence, under strict discipline and low diet. Had the workhouses been made efficient, there would have been no occasion for these establishments; but the workhouses not being efficient, recourse has been had to the penal colonies, where the test of strict discipline, hard labour, and scanty diet, is so applied as to be held in the greatest dread by the vagrant classes. All beggars are apprehended by the police; if able to work, they are sent to the penal colonies; if aged or infirm, or unable to perform out-door work, they are sent to the workhouses; and although the discipline of the workhouses is defective, and the management in many respects faulty, yet with the aid of the penal colonies they secure the repression of mendicancy.

" In the workhouses of the penal colonies to which the able-bodied mendicants are sent, one ward is used in common as a dormitory, refectory, and workshop. The inmates sleep in hammocks, and are very coarsely clad. They labour in the fields, or in making bricks, or at manufactures in the house, under the superintendence of an inspector. Each colonist is furnished with a book, in which is entered the work executed daily, the amount of food and clothes furnished, his share of the general expenses of the establishment, and whatever he has received in the paper-money of the colony. Guards on horseback to patrol the boundary of the colony, rewards given for bringing back any colonist who has attempted to escape, and an uniform dress, are the means adopted to prevent desertion from the colony. Mendicants when arrested, may choose whether they will be brought before the tribunals as vagabonds, or be sent to the coercive colony, where they must remain at least one year. These rigorous measures for the suppression of mendicancy, have been adopted in the absence of any acknowledgment of a right to relief, and notwithstanding that a large portion of the relief actually administered arises from endowments and voluntary contributions. This forms an important feature in the Dutch and Belgian system; and if, as I believe, the rigour of this part of their institutions has been caused by the imperfect organization of the others, the true remedy would have been, not in the establishment of penal colonies, but in such an improvement of those other institutions as would have rendered them efficient for the repression of mendicancy, as well as for the administration of relief. On comparing the modes of relief existing in Holland and Belgium, with the system of relief it is proposed to establish in Ireland, the latter will I think be found to be much more simple and complete, and consequently to promise greater efficiency. No right to relief exists in Holland or Belgium, yet mendicancy is suppressed in both those countries. It is proposed not to give a right to relief in Ireland, and it is intended to suppress mendicancy,—in this respect therefore the circumstances are similar. But in Ireland, it is proposed to divide the whole country into districts of convenient extent, with a workhouse to each, so that every destitute and infirm person will be within easy reach of adequate relief; and this arrangement is obviously preferable to the various, and in some respects conflicting modes of relief which exist in Holland and Belgium, and will be more effective in its operation. The example of Holland and Belgium may therefore be cited, in addition to that of England, in support of the proposed Irish Poor Law.

" Another matter of much interest, is the different condition of the smaller class of cultivators in the two countries. Small farms of from five to ten acres abound in many parts of Belgium, closely resembling the small holdings in Ireland ; but the Irish cultivator is without the comforts and conveniences of civilised life, whilst the Belgian peasant-farmer enjoys a large portion of both. The houses of the small cultivators in Belgium are generally substantial, with a sleeping-room in the attic, and closets for beds connected with the lower apartment, a dairy, a store for the grain, an oven, a cattle-stall, piggery, and poultry-loft. There is generally decent furniture and sufficient bedding, and although the scrupulous cleanliness of the Dutch may not be everywhere observable, an air of comfort and propriety pervades the whole establishment. In the cowhouse the dung and urine are preserved in the tank ; the ditches are scoured, the dry leaves potato-tops and offal of every kind are collected for manure, and heaps of compost are in course of preparation. The premises are kept in compact order, and a careful attention to economy is everywhere apparent. The family are decently clad, none are ragged or slovenly, although their dress may be of the coarsest material. The men universally wear the bleuse, and wooden shoes are in common use by both sexes. Their diet consists chiefly of rye-bread milk and potatoes. The contrast of what is here described, with the state of the same class of persons in Ireland, is very marked. Yet the productive powers of the soil in Belgium are certainly inferior to the general soil of Ireland, and the climate does not appear to be superior. To the soil and the climate therefore, the Belgian does not owe his superiority in comfort and position over the Irish cultivator.

The difference is rather owing to the greater industry economy and forethought of the people.

" A small occupier, whose farm we examined near Ghent, paid 225 francs per annum for about two bonniers, or six acres of land, with a comfortable house, stabling, and other offices attached, all very good of their kind; this makes the rent (reckoning the franc at 10*d*.) equal to 9*l*. 7*s*. 6*d*. sterling per annum; and, if we allow 3*l*. 7*s*. 6*d*. for the rent of the house, stabling, and other offices, there will be 6*l*., or 1*l*. per acre for the land, which accords with the information we obtained at other places. This farmer had a wife and five children, and appeared to live in much comfort. He owed little or nothing, he said, but he had no capital beyond that employed on his farm. We questioned him respecting his resources in case of sickness. He replied that if he were ill, and his illness was severe and of long duration, it would press heavily upon him, because it would interrupt the whole farm-work; and in order to provide for his family and pay the doctor he feared he should be obliged to sell part of his stock. If his wife and family were long ill, and he retained his strength, the doctor would give him credit, and he should be able to pay him by degrees in a year or two. We suggested that the Bureau de Bienfaisance, or charitable individuals, might afford him aid in such a difficulty, but he replied cheerfully that he must take care of himself. If a sick club, or benefit society, were established among these people, to enable them by mutual assurance to provide for the casualty of sickness, the chief source of suffering to their families would be obviated, and there would be little left to wish for or amend in their social condition. The Belgian peasant farmer here described, is not very different from the small Irish occupier as respects his position in society, but how much better is his condition as regards the comforts and conveniences of life. The cause of this difference I believe to be, the more skilful system of culture pursued by the six-acre farmers of Belgium, the rigid economy which characterises them as a class, and the persevering industry and forethought with which they adjust their limited resources to their wants; and one of the first steps to the improvement of this important class in Ireland should be, to endeavour to assimilate their farming operations and domestic management, to that of the same class in Belgium.

" It is not necessary to discuss the comparative advantages of small and large farms, it being notorious that the former abound in all parts of Ireland, in some districts almost to the exclusion of the other; and that any attempt at a rapid consolidation of these small holdings would occasion great misery and suffering. Changes of this nature cannot be successful, without special regard to local circumstances; and the obstructions which arise from fixed habits and old social arrangements, generally render any great organic change impracticable, excepting in the lapse of years. An improved management of the small farms in Ireland, would however afford the means of increasing the comfort, and ameliorating the condition of the cottier tenantry, and at the same time facilitate the progress of other changes conducive to their general well-being. It would, in fact, be beginning at the lowest point of the scale—improved management would bring increase of capital and improved habits, and thence would arise an enlargement of occupancies, which the vast extent of now waste but reclaimable land in Ireland would greatly facilitate. The establishment of a poor-law, by removing the burthen of supporting mendicancy which now presses almost exclusively on the class of small cultivators, will afford them relief and encouragement, and facilitate the improvement of their condition : but the Poor Law alone will not effect the necessary ameliorations, which can only be accomplished by a combination of efforts, of which the establishment of a poor-law is one, possibly it is the chief; for a poor-law will unite the interests of the other classes with the well-being of the poorest, and thus secure for the least intelligent, and therefore the most dependent portion of the community, the sympathies and the assistance of the most competent and intelligent of the middle and higher classes. The Poor Law will in this way, I believe, become the means of combining the now discordant elements of society in Ireland, for the promotion of the common interest; but the first impulse in the career of amelioration must be given by the landed proprietors, who should unite in promoting improvements among their tenantry, as well as in carrying out the provisions of the law."

The feeling in the house of lords with regard to the bill, was decidedly more adverse than had been the case in the house of commons. Many of the Irish peers whose properties were deeply en- Bill read a first time in cumbered, were alarmed at the threatened im- the lords, May 1, 1838. position of a poor-rate, which they feared would swallow up a large portion of their incomes. These fears were appealed to, and the danger declaimed against and magnified, both by the economical opponents of any poor-law whatever, and by the opponents of the present measure. It was evident therefore from the first that the bill would encounter a strenuous opposition in the lords, and that its passing was far from certain. On the 21st of May the bill was read a second time, after a long and stormy debate, which lasted nine hours. Lord Melbourne moved the second reading in a judicious and temperate speech, touching skilfully on most of the leading points, and deprecating the intervention of party feeling. The bill was, he said, founded on the amended system of the English Poor Law. It was in fact an adaptation of the Act of 1834 to the circumstances of Ireland, with such alterations as were required by the peculiar condition of that country, and as the experience of its working suggested. He thought the establishment of the measure would be the beginning of a system of order, and that it would introduce order in a beneficial form. It would among other things form the foundation of a measure for the suppression of mendicancy; and one great advantage to which he looked as arising from it was, that the struggle for land, and the violent means the people took of enforcing what they conceived to be their right with regard to it, would be much lessened, if not extinguished. The writings of eminent political economists had, he said, led him at one time to doubt whether the evil effects attending a system of poor-laws, did not more than counterbalance any advantage to be derived from them; but a full and careful consideration of the subject had convinced him, that it was most beneficial for the landlords to be made to take an interest in the condition of the people on the land. The principle on which a poor-law should be established, was that of the general benefit of the country— we should relieve the destitute, but not do so in a way to paralyze the feeling of energy and enterprise which ought to be paramount in every man's bosom; and for this purpose he thought the workhouse system was the

(marginal note) Bill read a second time in the lords.

one best adapted for testing the necessity and means of the applicant.

The Marquis of Londonderry spoke strongly against the bill, and moved that it be read that day six months. Many other peers joined in denouncing the measure, but none more violently than Lord Lyndhurst, who declared that it would lead to a dissolution of the Union. The Duke of Wellington supported the second reading, with a view to amending the bill in committee, and rendering it better fitted for its objects. The distress existing in Ireland was he said undoubted. There had been inquiry after inquiry on the subject, and on the outrages of every description to which it led. He expected from this bill that it would improve the social relations of the people of Ireland, and prevent the distress which now so often prevailed there. Another result he anticipated from the measure was, that it would induce the gentry of Ireland, whether resident or not, to look after their properties, and pay some attention to the state of the population on their estates. This, the duke observed, would improve the social relations between landlord and tenant—between the occupier and the labourer of the soil. If the Poor Laws had not been amended in England, he should have hesitated before consenting to the introduction of a poor-law into Ireland; but seeing the results the measure of 1834 had produced in this country—seeing the great advantage which had occurred from the working of that system—and seeing how it has improved the relations of landlord and tenant, he could not help desiring some such measure for Ireland, in order, if possible, to remedy in like manner the evils of that country. With regard to settlement, he was firmly convinced that its establishment in connexion with the bill, would be productive of unbounded litigation and expense, and lead to disputes of which no one could foresee the end. At the same time, he thought care should be taken that all parishes should

be required to pay the expenses connected with the
relief of their paupers, "that being one of the principles of the Poor Law in this country; and such an
amendment should be introduced into the present bill."
The measure being thus supported by the duke, the
second reading was carried by a majority of 149 to 20.

It was proposed that the bill should be committed on
The bill in   the 28th of May, but the debate was exceed-
committee.   ingly violent and was continued by adjournment to the 31st. It is difficult to describe the scene
which took place, on the motion for going into committee on the bill. The confusion then, and indeed
during the whole night, surpassed anything one could
have expected in such a deliberative assembly. The
alarms of the Irish peers as to the effects of the measure
exceeded all bounds, and they were joined by several
English peers who are supporters of the English Poor
Law. On the resumption of the debate on the 31st
however, and after a further discussion for eight hours,
the house resolved by 107 to 41 to support the principle
of the bill, as embodied in the 41*st clause*. This clause
provided that relief to the destitute might be administered in the workhouses, at the discretion of the boards
of guardians, subject to the condition—in the first place
of a preference being given to the aged and infirm
poor, and to destitute children; and in the second place
to persons residing in the union before those not so
resident, when there is not sufficient accommodation for
all the destitute.

These latter provisions were introduced at the instance
of the Duke of Wellington, in order to meet the objections and mitigate the hostility of the opponents of
the bill, as was also the provision in the 44*th clause*
charging the cost of relief to the several electoral divisions, instead of to the unions at large, as it before stood.
These changes were arranged between the duke and
myself, with the approval of government, previous to

the second reading. The bill was considered in committee on the 7th, 21st, 22nd, and 26th of June, and was read a third time on the 6th of July. On the 11th I find it recorded in my journal— *The bill read a third time.* " The bill is now clear of the lords, altered and in some respects improved, although the localisation of the charge upon the electoral divisions approximates too nearly to settlement to be quite satisfactory. I wish this had been left as it at first stood; but so long as no right to relief, and no power of removal are given, we shall I trust be able to avoid the infliction of actual settlement."[n]

Although so far " clear of the lords," there nevertheless remained much to be done in reconciling differences between the two houses with regard to some of the amendments, and in particular with regard to the schedule of rating, which it was desired to make available for the purposes of the municipal franchise. Several conferences were held, and " reasons" *pro* and *con* were delivered in, and it was not until the 27th of July that the bill was ready for the royal assent—This was given on the 31st, and thus a law was at length established, making provision for the systematic and efficient relief of destitution in Ireland.

---

[n] This quotation is from a journal which I had kept of the proceedings with regard to the Irish Poor Law, from the commencement of my connexion with the question in August 1836, and which has been very useful in framing the present narrative. In this journal is recorded from day to day, the progress of my inquiries in Ireland and elsewhere, the deliberations and consultations with government on the subject, the discussions with different public men in reference to it, and also the various interviews with the Duke of Wellington after the bill had passed the commons, in which it was my good fortune to be the medium of communication for settling the points at issue between his grace and the government. I say " my good fortune," for without the duke's assistance the bill would not have passed the house of lords, and without the part taken by myself in negotiating and bringing about a right understanding on the subject, I doubt if that assistance would have been accorded. If therefore the enactment of the Irish Poor Law was, as I believe, a measure of great social importance, and as subsequent events have moreover I think shown it to be, it cannot but be regarded as a great privilege to have been permitted to assist in any way towards the accomplishment of such an object. With this privilege I was so fortunate as to be invested, and I feel happy in the consciousness of having spared no pains to fulfil the obligations it involved.

CHAPTER IV.

Summary of the ' Act for the more effectual Relief of the Poor in Ireland,' and of the ' Amendment Act '— Arrangements for bringing the Act into operation — First and second Reports of proceedings — Dublin and Cork unions — Distress in the western districts — Third, fourth, fifth, and sixth Reports — Summary of the Act for the further amendment of the Law — Seventh Report — Cost of relief, and numbers relieved — Issue of amended orders.

HAVING in the last chapter described the progress of the bill from the commencement till it became law, I now propose, as in the case of the English and Scottish Acts,[a] to give a summary of the Irish statute sufficiently in detail for enabling the reader, with the aid of the Reports on which the measure was founded, to understand clearly both the import and the object of the several provisions—

Summary of the 1st and 2nd Victoria, cap. 56,

Entitled ' An Act for the more effectual Relief of the Poor in Ireland'—31st July 1838.

Sections 1, 2, 3.—Empower the Poor Law Commissioners for the time being to carry the Act into execution, and to issue such orders for the government of workhouses, the appointment and removal of officers, the guidance and control of guardians, and for keeping and auditing of accounts, as they shall think proper.

Sections 4, 5, 6, 7, 8.—General rules issued by the commissioners are to be submitted to the secretary of state, and not to take effect until the expiration of forty days, and are to be laid before parliament at the commencement of every session. The rules are to be made public, and to be open to the inspection of the ratepayers ; and whenever disallowed, the disallowance is also in like manner to be made public.

---

[a] See the author's Histories of the English and Scotch Poor Laws.

Sections 9, 10, 11.—The assistant-commissioners, secretary, and other officers appointed by the commissioners, are to be officers under the present Act. The commissioners may with the approbation of the secretary of state, delegate their powers (except the power to make general rules) to one of the commissioners, or to one or more of the assistant-commissioners acting in Ireland, subject to such regulations as the commissioners may direct.

Sections 12, 13, 14.—The assistant-commissioners are empowered to summon and examine witnesses on oath, and persons refusing to attend, or giving false evidence, or altering or concealing documents required for the purposes of the Act, are to be deemed guilty of a misdemeanor. The commissioners may order reasonable expenses of witnesses to be defrayed.

Sections 15, 16.—The commissioners may by order under their seal, unite so many townlands as they think fit to be a union for the relief of the destitute poor ; and may add to, take from, or dissolve the same, and may determine the proportionate amount chargeable in any such case, as shall appear to them to be just. But no such dissolution or alteration of a union is to take place without the consent of a majority of the guardians, and a copy of every order for the same is forthwith to be transmitted to the secretary of state.

Sections 17, 18, 19.—Whenever a union is declared, a board of guardians is to be elected, for which purpose the commissioners may divide the union into electoral divisions, and from time to time alter the same ; but in making or altering such electoral divisions, no townland is to be divided. The commissioners are to determine the number of guardians, having regard to the circumstances of each electoral division ; and also the qualification, which in no case is to exceed a rating of 30*l*. net annual value—" provided always that no person being in holy orders, or being a regular minister of any religious denomination, shall be eligible as a guardian."

Sections 20, 21, 22.—The first election of guardians is to take place at the time fixed by the commissioners, and afterwards on the 25th of March in each year. Outgoing guardians may be re-elected, and in case of vacancy occurring through death removal or resignation, the remaining guardians are to act.

Sections 23, 24.—Every justice of peace not being a stipendiary magistrate or assistant-barrister or minister of any religious denomination, is an ex-officio guardian of the poor of the union in which he resides, and after the board of guardians is duly constituted may act as a member of the board, in like manner as an elected guardian. But when the justices duly qualified and residing in the union exceed one-third the number of elected guardians, they are at a meeting specially assembled for the purpose, to appoint from among themselves a number nearest to but not exceeding one-third of the elected guardians, to act as ex-officio guardians from the time of such apppointment, until the 29th of September following, and so annually on each succeeding 29th of September—the number of ex-officio guardians being in no case permitted to exceed one-third the number of the guardians elected by the ratepayers.

Sections 25, 26.—If an election of guardians does not take place, or if any of those elected shall neglect or refuse to act, the commissioners may order a fresh election, and on failure thereof may appoint another to fill the place of any guardian so failing, until an election of guardians takes place under the provisions of the Act. And if regular meetings of the guardians be not held, or if their duties be not effectually discharged according to the intentions of this Act, the commissioners may dissolve such board, and order a fresh election; and if the guardians then elected likewise fail, the commissioners may appoint paid officers to carry out the provisions of the Act, and define their duties, and regulate their salaries, which are to be paid out of the poor-rates of the union.

Sections 27, 28, 29, 30.—The board of guardians is declared a body politic and corporate for all the purposes of the Act. The commissioners and assistant-commissioners may attend the meetings, and take part in the discussions of the boards of guardians, but are not entitled to vote. The guardians are to assemble at such times as the commissioners direct, and no guardian, whether ex-officio or elected, has power to act, except as a member, and at a meeting of the board, for constituting which the presence of three members is necessary. No defect in the election or qualification of a guardian, is to make void the proceedings of any board in which he may have taken a part.

Sections 31, 32, 33.—The commissioners may direct the appointment of such paid officers, with such qualifications, as they think necessary in every union, and may define their duties and determine their continuance in office or dismissal, and regulate their salaries. The commissioners are further empowered, with or without the concurrence of the guardians, to remove any paid officer whom they deem unfit or incompetent, and to require the appointment of a fit and competent person in his room, failing in which the commissioners may themselves make the appointment.

Sections 34, 35, 36.—When a union is declared, every house of industry, workhouse, and foundling hospital within its limits, and supported wholly or in part by parliamentary grant &c., with all things thereto belonging, is to become vested in the Poor Law commissioners, subject to the debts and encumbrances thereof—in trust for, and subject to, the powers and provisions of this Act. The commissioners may from time to time as they see fit, build or cause to be built a workhouse or workhouses for any union, or may hire any building or buildings to be used as a workhouse, and may enlarge and alter the same, in such manner as they deem most proper for carrying the provisions of the Act into execution, and may purchase or hire any land not exceeding twelve acres to be occupied with such workhouse, and may order the guardians to uphold and maintain, and to furnish and fit up the same, and provide means for setting the poor to work therein—for all which purposes the guardians are required to raise and levy the necessary sums as a poor-rate, or to borrow the money and charge the same on the future poor-rate, as the commissioners shall direct. But after the workhouse has been declared fit for the reception of the destitute poor, the commissioners are restricted from ordering the expenditure of more than 400*l*. without the consent of the guardians.

Sections 37, 38, 39, 40.—Incapacitated persons empowered to convey land &c.—the powers of 7*th George* 4*th, cap.* 74, regarding the purchase and valuation of sites extended to this Act—Where the purchase-money is paid into the bank of Ireland, the commissioners exonerated from liability as to its application—The commissioners may sell lands &c., and apply the proceeds in purchase of other lands &c.; but are restricted from selling the workhouse of a union without the consent of the guardians.

Section 41.—When a workhouse has been declared fit for the reception of destitute poor, and not before, the guardians, subject to the orders of the commissioners, are to take order for relieving and setting to work therein, in the first place, such destitute poor persons as by reason of old age infirmity or defect, may be unable to support themselves, and destitute children; and in the next place, such other persons as the guardians deem to be destitute poor, and unable to support themselves by their own industry or other lawful means— provided that in any case where there may not be sufficient accommodation for all the destitute persons who apply, the guardians shall relieve such as reside in the union, in preference to those who do not.

Sections 42, 43, 44.—A register-book in a prescribed form, is to be kept by the master of every workhouse of the persons relieved therein, and such register is to be examined, corrected and signed by the chairman at every meeting of the guardians, and countersigned by the clerk—Accounts of the expenditure are to be kept and made up every six months, charging to every electoral division the proportion incurred in respect of persons relieved who are stated in the registry to have been resident in such electoral division; the expenses incurred in respect of all others are to be charged against the whole union. At the end of three years, any two or more electoral divisions may, with the commissioners' concurrence, agree to bear the expense of the relief chargeable to each in common, a copy of every such agreement to be deposited with the commissioners, and another copy with the clerk of the peace.

Sections 45, 46, 47.—On the declaration of a workhouse in any union, all local Acts relating in any way to the relief of the poor therein, are to cease and determine. The commissioners are to inquire into the state of fever hospitals and dispensaries, and report thereon to the secretary of state, stating the number of such institutions which in their opinion ought to be provided. They are also to examine into the administration of hospitals and infirmaries, and give directions for the more effective management thereof.

Sections 48, 49.—The commissioners are to take order for the due performance of religious service in the workhouse, and are to appoint fit persons to be chaplains for that purpose, one being of the established church, another a protestant dissenter, and another of the Roman catholic church, and they are to fix the salaries of such chaplains. But no inmate of a workhouse is to be compelled to attend any religious service contrary to the religious principles of such inmate, or to which his or her parents or guardians object.

Section 50.—The board of guardians are to appoint a fit person in each parish or townland within the union to be the warden thereof, who is to provide for the conveyance to the workhouse of such destitute poor persons as the guardians shall direct, and perform such other duties as the orders of the commissioners shall prescribe.

Section 51.—If a meeting of the ratepayers of any electoral division agree to the raising of a rate to assist emigration, the commissioners may direct the guardians to raise such sums (not exceeding 1s. in the pound in any one year) as they think requisite for the purpose, either by a rate under this Act, or by a charge on the future rates; and the money so raised is, under the direction of the commissioners, to be applied by the guardians of the union in assisting the emigration to British colonies of poor persons residing in such electoral division.

Section 52.—The money raised under authority of the Act, is only to be applied as is expressly provided for in the Act.

Sections 53, 54, 55, 56.—Every husband is made liable for the maintenance of his wife, and every child under the age of 15, whether legitimate or illegitimate, which she may have ; and every father is liable to maintain his child, and every widow to maintain her child, and the mother to maintain her bastard child, until such children respectively attain the age of fifteen. Relief given to a wife or child, is to be considered as given to the person liable to maintain such wife or child. Relief may be declared to be a loan, and be recoverable accordingly, and when given to a person entitled to any pension or other allowance, the guardians may require the next payment thereof to be made to them for indemnity of the union, and are then to repay the surplus to the person entitled thereto.

Section 57.—Every child of a poor person who may be unable to support himself, shall be liable according to his ability to support his parents, and if any relief under this Act be afforded to such parents, it may by order of two justices be recovered by the guardians from such child, together with such other relief as shall subsequently be given.

Sections 58, 59, 60.—Every person absconding from a workhouse and leaving his wife or child to be relieved therein, or who refuses to work, or is guilty of drunkenness or disobedience to the rules prescribed for the government of the workhouse, or who shall introduce spirituous or fermented liquors into any workhouse, is on conviction to be subjected to imprisonment with hard labour for not exceeding one month. Any person who deserts and leaves his wife or child so that they become chargeable, is on conviction to be subjected to hard labour in the house of correction for not exceeding three months ; and every justice of peace may issue his warrant for apprehension of the offenders.

Sections 61, 62, 63.—For defraying the expenses incurred under this Act, the guardians are empowered to make and levy such rates as may be necessary on every occupier of rateable hereditaments within the union, regard being had to the proportion previously charged upon any electoral division.   The

rateable hereditaments are then enumerated. But it is provided that no church chapel or other building exclusively
dedicated to religious worship, or used for education of the
poor, nor any burial-ground or cemetery, nor any building
used for charitable or public purposes shall be rateable,
except where any private profit or use is derived therefrom,
in which case, the person deriving such profit or use, is to
be rated as an occupier according to the annual value of the
same.

Sections 64, 65.—Every rate is to be a poundage rate, made upon
an estimate of the net annual value of the several hereditaments—" that is to say, of the rent at which, one year with
another, the same might in their actual state be reasonably expected to let from year to year, the probable annual
average cost of repairs insurance and other expenses, if any,
necessary to maintain the hereditaments in their actual state,
and all rates taxes and public charges, if any, except tithes,
being paid by the tenant." The particulars of every rate are
to be entered in a book (the form of which is given in a
schedule annexed) and the guardians and other officers whose
duty it may be to make the rate, are to sign the declaration
at the end of the same, after which it is to be evidence of the
truth of the particulars contained therein.

Sections 66, 67, 68, 69, 70.—Existing surveys and valuations may
be used, but if these are not deemed sufficient, the guardians
may cause new ones to be made. All proprietors of tolls and
profits liable to be rated are to keep accounts thereof, which
the guardians are to have liberty to inspect. The commissioners may direct the cost of any survey and valuation to be
defrayed by a separate rate, or by a charge upon the poor-
rate, as they see fit. Twenty-one days' notice to the ratepayers for inspecting the valuation is to be given before
making a rate, copies of which may be taken at all reasonable
times.

Sections 71, 72, 73.—The poor-rate is to be paid by the occupiers,
but in cases where the property is rated at less than 5*l.* and
where the parties have agreed thereto, the lessor may be
rated instead. County-cess collectors may be appointed to
collect the poor-rate on giving security and being approved
by the commissioners—failing in which the rate may be collected by any other officer appointed for the purpose with like
approval.

Sections 74, 75, 76, 77.—Every occupier may deduct half the
poundage rate paid by him, from the rent payable to the
owner ; and where any person so receiving rent, shall also

pay a rent in respect of the same property, he will be entitled to deduct from such rent a sum proportionate to what was deducted from the rent he received. The entire rate is to be deducted from tithe ; and all agreements to forego the deduction of rate are declared void.

Sections 78, 79.—If a rate is not paid within two months after it has been made, the guardians may levy the same by distress, or sue for such rate by civil bill. The receipt for poor-rate is in all cases to be accepted by persons entitled to receive rent or tithe, in lieu of such sum as the person tendering the receipt is entitled to deduct from such rent or tithe. But no deduction is to be made from any rent-charge or terminable annuity.

Sections 80, 81.—Every occupier paying rate, and every receiver of rent from which a deduction has been made on account of rate, and every owner of tithe, is to be deemed a ratepayer ; and at the election of guardians in any union, every ratepayer is entitled to vote[b] according to the following scale—

Where the annual value of the property rated shall not
amount to 20*l*.	One vote.
Where it amounts to 20*l*. and not to 50*l*.	Two votes.
„ to 50*l*. and not to 100*l*.	Three votes.
„ to 100*l*. and not to 150*l*...	Four votes.
„ to 150*l*. and not to 200*l*...	Five votes.
„ to 200*l*. and upwards	Six votes.

Where the occupier is also the owner, he will be entitled to double the above number of votes ; and where the net annual value of the property rated exceeds the rent paid by the occupier, he is in addition to his votes as occupier, to be entitled to vote for such excess as if it were rent received by him.

Sections 82, 83, 84, 85.—Where two or more ratepayers are jointly liable, each is to be entitled to vote according to the proportion borne by him, but one may claim to vote for the whole. The votes are to be given in writing in such manner as the commissioners may direct, and the majority returned in each electoral division is to be binding on such division.

---

b In altering the bill to localise the charge upon the electoral divisions respectively (see ante, p. 220) it was omitted to substitute the term Electoral Division for that of Union in the 81st sect. ; so that a person who might pay a rate in every electoral division of the union, could only as the clause stood vote in one, although each electoral division was separately chargeable. This would be contrary to what was intended by the Duke of Wellington's amendment, and the error was remedied as soon as discovered by the 2nd *Vict. cap.* 1, *sec.* 5. See post, p. 233.

Votes may be given by proxy, but no occupier can vote unless all rates assessed upon him of six months' standing be first paid.

Sections 86, 87, 88.—The members of a corporation or joint-stock company are not entitled to vote, but their officers may do so if duly authorised by the governing body. Where a rate has not been made, the cess-payers are to form a constituency for electing guardians, with the same proportion of votes as is prescribed for ratepayers, each shilling of county cess to be reckoned as one pound of annual value. The commissioners are to appoint a returning officer, and prescribe the duties to be performed by him in the election of guardians.

Sections 89, 90, 91.—The guardians may with consent of the commissioners borrow money for purchasing and providing a workhouse, either from the Exchequer Bill Loan Commissioners, or any persons willing to advance the same on security of the rates. The money so borrowed is to be repaid in twenty years by annual instalments, together with the interest accruing thereon. The securities for money so advanced to a union may be transferred or assigned on notice thereof being given to the guardians.

Sections 92, 93.—Contracts made by the guardians are not valid, unless conformable to the rules of the commissioners ; and no guardian, paid officer, warden or other person engaged in collecting the rates, or in the management of the union, is either directly or indirectly to furnish supplies of any kind for the use of the union, under penalty of 100*l.* with full costs of suit to any person who shall sue for the same.

Sections 94, 95, 96, 97.—Guardians treasurers and other officers are to render a true account of receipts and payments &c., at such times and in such a form as the commissioners shall direct. Auditors are to be appointed to examine such accounts, and are to disallow all payments made contrary to the Act, or at variance with the orders of the commissioners. Bonds contracts advertisements &c. for carrying the Act into effect are exempted from stamp-duty, and letters relating exclusively to the execution of the Act, sent by or addressed to the commissioners, are exempted from postage.

Sections 98, 99, 100, 101, 102.—Justices may proceed by summons for recovery of penalties— penalty on officers disobeying guardians—penalty on officers and others purloining goods &c. belonging to any union—penalty on persons wilfully disobeying the orders of the commissioners or assistant-commissioners.

Sections 103, 104, 105.—Forfeitures costs and charges may be levied by distress under warrant of two justices, and are to be applied to the use of the union—ratepayers are competent witnesses—distress not to be deemed unlawful for want of form in the proceedings—plaintiff not to recover for wrongful proceeding, if tender of amends be made.

Sections 106, 107, 108, 109.—Persons aggrieved may within four months after the cause of complaint, appeal against the poor-rate, or against a conviction where the penalty exceeds 5*l.*, and the justices and assistant-barrister before whom the appeal is brought, are empowered finally to determine the same ; but fourteen days' notice of the appeal is to be given.

Sections 110, 111, 112.—Notwithstanding any appeal or notice thereof, the rate is to be paid, unless and until it be actually quashed or amended.   Persons appealing are to enter into recognisance to prosecute the same at the next sessions, and to abide the order and pay such costs as the justices and assistant-barrister shall award.

Section 113.—No action to be commenced against any person for anything done under authority of the Act, until after twenty-one days' notice thereof, nor after sufficient satisfaction has been tendered to the party aggrieved, nor after three months from the time the action complained of was committed; and the defendant may plead the general issue.

Sections 114, 115, 116, 117.—No order of the commissioners, assistant-commissioners, or guardians, is removable by writ of certiorari except into the Court of Queen's Bench in Dublin, and every order or rate[c] so removed is to continue in force until declared to be illegal.   No application for writ of cer-tiorari to be made, unless ten days' notice of the particulars thereof shall have been delivered in writing to the commis-sioners, who may thereupon show cause against such applica-tion, and the court may if it think fit, proceed at once to hear and determine the case.   Recognisances must be entered into previous to application for a writ of certiorari, and if the order be quashed, notice thereof is to be given to the unions to which it was directed ; but the judgment is in no case to annul existing contracts.

Sections 118, 119, 120, 121.—The Poor Law Commissioners for England and Wales are declared to be " The Poor Law Com-

---

[c] A rate was excepted from such removal by the Amendment Act passed shortly afterwards, 2*nd Vict. cap.* 1.   See post, p. 233.

missioners" under the provisions of this Act, and are
empowered to carry the same into effect. A fourth commissioner may be appointed, and any two or more of the
commissioners may sit as a board in England and Wales, or
in Ireland, as they shall deem expedient. They are to have
a common seal, and all orders or copies thereof purporting to
be sealed therewith, are to be received as evidence that the
same have been duly made.

Sections 122, 123.—When required by the secretary of state, or
when the board shall think fit, one of the commissioners may
act in Ireland, and have all the powers given to the board of
commissioners, except the power of making general rules;
but the whole of the commissioners are to assemble in London
once at least in every year, for the purpose of submitting a
report of their proceedings, which report is to be made on or
before the 1st of May, and is to be annually laid before parliament, "together with an account of the expenditure upon
the relief of the poor in each union, and of the total number
relieved in each union during the year ended the 1st of
January preceding."

Section 124.—Interpretation clause.

Notwithstanding all the care that had been taken
in framing this Act, it was found on proceeding to
carry it into operation that there were several defects, partly owing to a want of information with regard to certain peculiarities existing in Ireland, but
principally arising out of the changes made in the passage of the bill through parliament. Thus, on the
assumption that the division into townlands was universal, an alteration was made in the Lords constituting
a townland the unit in the formation of unions; but in
some places it was found that no townland existed, and
in very many cases the extent of the townland was not
known. There was uncertainty also with regard to
parishes, their limits being in many instances unde-
fined. It became necessary therefore with as little
delay as possible to take steps for remedying these
defects, and to pass a short Act amending the former,
which was accordingly done; and as this last was

essential to the one which preceded it, so that the two Acts may be said to form one statute, it will be convenient to insert a summary of it here in continuation of the above—

Summary of the 2nd Victoria, cap. 1, *to amend the 1st and 2nd Victoria, cap.* 56.—15*th March,* 1839.

Section 1.—The boundaries of many townlands not being accurately known, and there being places which are not known as townlands—it is enacted that the provisions in the preceding Act relating to townlands, shall " apply to every place in Ireland whether known as a townland or not."

Section 2.—Where the population of any city borough or town exceeds ten thousand, or where the population of any other place within an area of three miles exceeds ten thousand, the commissioners may constitute such city borough town or other place, or any part or parts thereof respectively, an electoral division ; and may divide such electoral division into wards for the purpose of conducting the election of guardians.

Sections 3, 4.—The commissioners may by order under seal declare any place not known as a townland, to be a townland ; and where the boundaries of a townland are not known, may declare and determine the boundaries thereof.

Sections 5, 6.—In the election of guardians, every ratepayer who under the last rate made shall have paid or be liable to pay rate in respect of property in any electoral division, " shall have a vote or votes in the election of guardians in such electoral division, according to the scale of votes prescribed." And where needful expenses are incurred before any rate can be levied for defraying the same, a sum not exceeding 200*l.* may be borrowed and charged upon the first rate made.

Sections 7, 8. — Conveyances of land &c. to the Poor Law commissioners are to be made according to the form set forth in the schedule annexed to the Act, or as near thereto as circumstances admit. The purchase-money is to be paid into the Bank of Ireland to account of the accountant-general of the Court of Chancery, " ex parte the Poor Law commissioners."

Sections 9, 10.—Appeals may be made heard and determined at general or quarter sessions of the peace, although an assistant-barrister be not present. So much as relates to the removal by writ of certiorari of any rate made under the previous Act, is by the present Act repealed.

We will now resume our narrative, in the order of date. It has been stated that the Irish Poor Relief Act was passed on the last day of July. A fortnight afterwards it was arranged that I should proceed to Ireland for the purpose of carrying the new law into operation. I had an interview with Lord John Russell on the occasion, and urged the necessity of proceeding vigorously and without delay in the introduction of the measure, and expressed my conviction that our so doing was essential to success. His lordship assured me that government approved of our at once going forward with the formation of unions and providing workhouses, and were prepared to afford every assistance that we might require. It was settled that I should go to Ireland at the end of the month, taking with me four of our assistant-commissioners, whose experience in the administration of the English Poor Law would, it was thought, be found highly useful in Ireland.[d] I quitted London on the 1st of September, and as soon as the assistant-commissioners had assembled in Dublin, one of them was sent to Belfast, another to Limerick, a third to Cork, and one was retained in Dublin. They were furnished with instructions in which the objects to which their attention should be chiefly directed were pointed out. The mode of commencing operations was one of the first things which had to be considered. Would it be better to commence by forming unions of the chief towns, and then work back from them to the interior of the country ; or else to begin in the interior, and work up to the great towns ?—This, the assistant-commissioners were told, was an important question, requiring to be decided as quickly as possible ; and in order to obtain the requisite data for so deciding, it was necessary that

1838.

Proceeds to Ireland to bring the Act into operation.

---

[d] The gentlemen selected for this purpose, were Mr. Gulson, Mr. Earle, Mr. Hawley, and Mr. Voules.

some of the chief towns should be first examined, in doing which, they were desired at the same time to endeavour to obtain such a knowledge of other parts of the country, as would assist them in forming a judgment upon the question.

The investigations in which the assistant-commissioners would thus be engaged, would it was considered, serve to bring them acquainted with the condition and habits of the people, and prepare them for entering upon the formation of unions as soon as arrangements for the purpose were sufficiently advanced. The position size and character of the towns, the existence of barracks or other buildings readily convertible into workhouses, the disposition of the inhabitants with respect to the new law, whether favourable or otherwise, were all to be noted, as constituting materials for judging of when and where the unions should be formed; it being important to begin, where the least difficulty or opposition would have to be encountered.

The principle adopted in the formation of unions in England was considered applicable to Ireland, namely, that the union should consist of a market town as a centre, and the district surrounding and communicating with it. The unions so formed would, it was supposed, be pretty equally distributed throughout the country, and be of a size not materially differing from what had been stated in the Reports to be the most eligible, that is embracing a radius of about ten miles. Some persons had contended for smaller unions, but the smaller the union, the larger in proportion would be the establishment charges; and as the provisions introduced in the house of lords for localizing the rate upon each electoral division, had removed one of the objections to large unions chiefly insisted upon, it would now probably be considered, that in taking the market town as a guide, the commissioners could not be far wrong, since the people who frequent the market would find no difficulty in attending at the union workhouse, whether as guardians or applicants for relief. At the same time however, local interests were not to be disregarded in the arrangement of unions and electoral divisions; but the boundaries of private property, and of counties and baronies were to be observed, as far as might be consistent with the general interest and convenience.

The assistant-commissioners were likewise cautioned as to the sensitiveness of the Irish people, and the importance of conciliating their feelings and gaining their confidence, which would be best accomplished by observing a simple straightforward line of conduct towards them, a scrupulous fulfilment of promises, and not raising or encouraging expectations unless they were pretty certain of being fulfilled. " We know," it was added, " that the object of the law we are called upon to administer is kind and beneficent, and calculated to better the condition and improve the social habits of the people ; and knowing this, we cannot feel otherwise than confident in its application, and earnestly zealous in working out the results contemplated by the legislature in its enactment."

The assistant-commissioners re-assembled in Dublin on the 9th October, and reported the result of their investigations; and being joined by four others who had been appointed in the interim,[e] the whole question as to the mode of bringing the law into operation was very fully discussed and considered. The assistant-commissioners shortly afterwards proceeded to Cork, Limerick, Londonderry, and Belfast, furnished with full instructions for their guidance in the formation of unions in and around those places, it being considered that clusters of unions so formed would be better protected

---

[e] These were Mr. Clements, Mr. Hancock, Mr. O'Donoghue, and Mr. Phelan, the latter with an especial view to the medical charities. Mr. Stanley had been appointed secretary to the board in Dublin.

from undue pressure at the outset, than if they stood singly and isolated.   Mr. Earle remained in Dublin for a like purpose.   With regard to the formation of unions, the instructions previously given were confirmed, but careful consideration, they were told, would be required in arranging the electoral divisions, as well as in determining the number; for although the commissioners were empowered "to alter the electoral divisions from time to time as they may see fit," it was important that the divisions should be so formed at the outset as to render subsequent alteration unnecessary.   As a general rule the board considered that there should be as many electoral divisions as there were elected guardians, and that the divisions should be all nearly of the same size. There might however be cases, owing to the extent of individual properties or other cause in which this rule could not be observed, and in such cases, the larger divisions might properly have more than one guardian, as in the larger English parishes : but it would be well to deal with such cases as exceptions, and as far as practicable to form the several electoral divisions of the same size, and each to return one guardian.

The townland being the unit, and some townlands being heavily charged with pauperism, while others were comparatively free, it was thought that difficulties might sometimes arise in determining upon the townlands of which an electoral division should consist.   Landed proprietors might be naturally desirous of having all their land in one division, unmixed with the land of others, especially where they have taken pains, or incurred expense to improve their properties.   The board deemed it impossible to lay down any unvarying rule that would be applicable to all such cases, but considered that the wishes of the proprietor, where the lands are contiguous, should be attended to whenever it could be done without injury or inconvenience to others; and in grouping pauperised and unpauperised townlands together, it should be endeavoured so to arrange the district, as to make the junction as little oppressive as possible to the latter. In Dublin, Limerick, and a few of the older towns, it was thought likely that the electoral divisions could not be so formed as to maintain an equality of pressure, owing to some parishes being exclusively inhabited by the poor and mendicant classes, whilst others were entirely free from them. The board declared that it was " very sensible of the magnitude of this difficulty, which will receive its best attention with the view of endeavouring to devise a palliative, if not a remedy ; and it is much to be desired that the efforts of the assistant-commissioners should be directed to the same end."

As respects the number of elected guardians to be Number and assigned to a union, it was on the whole consi-qualification of guardians. dered, having regard to the satisfactory despatch of business as well as the importance of there being an executive so extended as to command the confidence of the ratepayers, that a number varying according to circumstances from 16 to 24, would be best calculated for carrying into effect the provisions of the Act. These numbers, with the proportion of one-third ex-officio guardians, would give to each union a board of from 21 to 32 members, which would be sufficient for the purpose of deliberation, and yet not so numerous as to impede efficient action. The qualification of guardians must of course depend very much upon the circumstances of the district. " In some parts of Ireland a 5l. qualification would not be too low, whilst in others the maximum of 30l. would not be much if at all too high ;" and the assistant-commissioners were told to use their discretion between these extremes in the recommendations they might make. The board however considered that it would be advantageous to assume 10l. as a preferable medium to be observed, except in cases where a greater or a smaller amount of qualification appeared to be required. Recommendations were then made as to the selection and duties of returning-officers, the nomination of parish wardens, and the appointment of clerks to the boards of guardians, and also as to the necessity for observing strict economy in all the arrangements connected with the formation and working of the unions. The board likewise, under the heavy responsibility devolved upon it, considered it to be a duty " to point out to the assistant-commissioners the vast importance of their avoiding even the semblance of party bias, either in politics or religion."

The commissioners being by the 35th *section* of the Act made responsible for providing the workhouses, very particular instructions were given to the assistant-commissioners on the subject, which constituted in fact the foundation of the whole measure. They were directed " at the formation of every union to make a careful survey, not only of the present state of destitution and mendicancy within it, and of what will be the extent of workhouse accommodation required immediately, or in the first two or three years, but also what was likely to be necessary afterwards; so as to frame such plans and adopt such arrangements in the construction of the buildings, as should afford the earliest present accommodation, and at the same time afford facilities for enlargement whenever it should become necessary." In cases where barracks or other buildings should be taken for workhouse purposes, care ought likewise to be taken that the necessary alterations and additions were so framed that a portion only need be constructed in the first instance, and that the whole of the plan as designed might be completed whenever it should afterwards be found necessary, without materially interfering with the parts already in use. The quantity of land to be occupied with the workhouse is by the Act restricted to twelve acres, and the assistant-commissioners were recommended to endeavour to convince the guardians of the inexpediency of occupying more land than was sufficient for the purposes of a garden, or than could be conveniently managed by the boys and aged and infirm men.

Next in importance to the workhouse, was the establishing an assessment founded upon the actual value of all the rateable property within the union, in conformity with the 54*th* *section* of the Act. The assistant-commissioners were directed to call the attention of the boards of guardians at their first and second meetings to this important duty, for the performance of which they were responsible. Suggestions were then offered with regard to the government valuation, and that made under the Tithe Composition Act, and also to the probable necessity in some cases of procuring a new valuation; although in general it was considered that it would be found practicable at the outset to establish a fair and equitable assessment for the poor-rate, without resorting to the expensive process of a valuation by professional men.

The board next determined upon the kind of returns, statistical and otherwise, to be required from the assistant-commissioners, and the extent of information in all cases to be obtained before any unions should be declared; and a circular containing full directions on every point, together with a form for tabulating the several heads of information, was addressed to the assistant-commissioners for their guidance in this highly important part of their duty.

Whilst the assistant-commissioners were pursuing their inquiries and collecting information preparatory to forming unions, the commissioner acting as a board in Dublin was occupied in preparing the several forms and orders for declaring unions, governing elections, and regulating the proceedings of boards of guardians. These were all framed, as nearly as circumstances admitted, on the model of those issued in England, and were transmitted to the board in London for revision and approval. And here it may be well to state, that although under the 122*nd section,* I was when acting singly in Ireland invested with all the powers of a board, and might make and issue all orders and regulations with the exception of " general rules," yet I never directly exercised this power, but forwarded every such instrument to be approved and sealed by the board in London. This course was adopted in consideration that it afforded greater certainty of keeping up a unity of action, and a more complete interchange of information between the two boards, than would be likely to exist if the commissioner acting in Ireland were to frame and issue orders without the participation of his colleagues acting in England.

At the commencement of their proceedings, the assistant-commissioners found that vague and often very exaggerated notions prevailed with regard to the new law, and their approach was at first everywhere viewed with more or less of suspicion and alarm. By great patience and perseverance however in explaining the objects and intentions of the Act, and by the examples they were enabled to cite of the working of the amended law in England, they generally succeeded in removing these impressions, and in obtaining a willing co-operation; so that ere long, the requirements of the law, if not universally popular, were at least very generally acquiesced in. Perhaps this change may also have been in some degree owing to the magistrates and the clergy of each denomination having been furnished with copies of the Act, elucidated by copious explanatory notes, and likewise with copies of the Reports on which the Act was founded. The extensive correspondence which was continually going forward, and the frequent personal communications with the board in Dublin, contributed moreover to diffuse information as to the nature objects and working of the law, and not only helped to prepare the way for its introduction, but proved likewise the means of raising up zealous administrators for carrying it into execution.

Having thus generally stated the nature of the preliminary arrangements for bringing the law into operation, it is now proposed, as in the author's ' History of the English Poor Law,' and as is also done in his ' History of the Poor Law of Scotland,' to take the Commissioners' annual Reports as the groundwork of the narrative. Their first Report of proceedings in Ireland is dated 1st May 1839.[f] It comprises only a short period, and will not require a lengthened notice ; but it is of considerable interest, as showing the steps earliest taken in the introduction of the measure.

1839.
First report
of proceed-
ings in
Ireland.

As the time approached for declaring Unions, and for constituting boards of guardians, it was necessary to be prepared for conducting the elections. Arrangements were accordingly made, with the sanction of the Irish government, for the distribution and collection of the voting-papers by the constabulary ; and as the commissioners were immediately responsible for the appointment of returning officers to conduct the elections, the assistant-commissioners were directed to seek for and recommend competent individuals for the purpose, that is, some one in each district about to be united who was well known, and possessed the confidence of the ratepayers ; and the Report states that there is every reason to be satisfied with the manner in which the selections have been made.

Election
proceedings.

To aid the returning officers in the performance of their novel duties, they were furnished with ample instructions on every point not provided for in the

---

[f] This is included in the fifth annual Report of the Poor-Law Commissioners, but I shall continue to number the Reports of proceedings in Ireland separately, without regard to the number of the commissioners' general Reports.

election order; and the assistant-commissioners were required to attend at all the early stages of the proceedings in every union, to afford such further assistance and counsel as might be necessary. Some few irregularities occurred, but not more than was to be expected under the circumstances. There were likewise a few instances of party or sectarian feeling, but in no case were improper individuals returned as guardians; and allowance being made for the want of previous training, the Irish boards will, it is said, " fairly bear a comparison with the boards in England," and a hope is confidently expressed that the measure will not fail through the want of an efficient executive.

Relief in the workhouse being the only mode of relief sanctioned by the Act, it was evident that until a workhouse is provided the law must be practically inoperative. Attention was therefore early directed to this object, for the due execution of which the commissioners were alone responsible ; and much pains were taken to ascertain the kind of buildings that would be most suitable, having regard to the circumstances of the country and the habits of the people. After extensive inquiry, as well in England as in Ireland, and a careful consideration of the whole subject, it was determined to engage an architect experienced in the construction of English workhouses, and to employ him in conjunction with the assistant-commissioners, and with the aid of the best local information that could be obtained, in devising a series of plans for the Irish workhouses, of different sizes, together with descriptive specifications and estimates for each.[g] This was accordingly done, and the proceeding was fully justified by the result. The style of building adopted for

The work-houses.

---

[g] The architect engaged for this service was Mr. Wilkinson, who had erected several of the English workhouses, and who continued to superintend the building operations in Ireland until all the workhouses were completed, and for some years subsequently.

the workhouses, was of the cheapest description compatible with durability; and effect was sought to be obtained through harmony of proportion and simplicity of arrangement, all mere decoration being studiously excluded. The unoccupied barracks were originally proposed to be converted into workhouses, and at first a few of the unions were arranged with a view to this object. But after repeated discussions with the Ordnance authorities, it became evident that very few if any of these buildings could be obtained, the whole appearing to be considered necessary for military purposes.[h]

Valuations and rating. One of the first duties to which a board of guardians is required to attend, was the valuation of the property within the union for the purpose of its being rated to the relief of the poor. This under any circumstances is a matter of some difficulty, but in Ireland the difficulty was increased by the condition of the country, and the absence in many parts of any reliable data for framing such a valuation. To assist the guardians in the performance of their duties in this respect, they were furnished with very full instructions, pointing out in detail the principle on which the valuation and the rating were to be conducted, and all that was necessary to be attended to, in order to fulfil what the law required.

Shortly after the commencement of operations in Ireland, it was discovered, as has been before stated, that there were certain defects in the Act, which it was necessary forthwith to remedy; and this it has been shown was accordingly done by the passing of the 2nd Vict., cap. 1,[i] until after which no union could be

---

[h] A portion only of one barrack was ultimately taken, that of Fermoy; and it turned out to be neither satisfactory nor economical. At the end of a few years it was restored to its original use, and a new and more convenient workhouse was provided for the union.

[i] Ante, p. 233.

formed in Dublin and some of the other chief towns, owing to the townland division not being there known.

On the 25th of March, the end of the usual parochial year, the Report states that—" the number of unions declared was 22, and that in 18 of these boards of guardians had been elected. The requisite statistical details were also completed for nine other unions, which would shortly be declared, and considerable progress had likewise been made in arranging nine more." Such were the results of somewhat less than six months' operations in the introduction of the Irish Poor Law, and they were generally regarded as satisfactory, and as warranting an expectation of the successful introduction of the measure.

Unions declared.

The Report of the second year's proceeding is dated 30th April 1840, and is considerably longer than the preceding Report. It was moreover accompanied by an Appendix containing copies of Orders and Reports, in fact a copy of each class of important documents issued or received by the Dublin board, thus showing not only everything that was done for bringing the law into operation, but also the mode of doing it, and whatever took place in connexion with it.

1840. Second report of proceedings in Ireland.

The first Report brings the proceedings down to the 25th of March 1839. The second Report brings them down to the same date in 1840, at which time the number of unions declared was 104, and it was thought that 30 more would probably complete the number into which it might be desirable that the country should be arranged. This would be a greater number than was at first contemplated, but a strong desire for small unions was found to be very general; and this desire, added to the want of convenient centres, and other local circumstances, led to an increase of the number beyond the original

Unions declared, and workhouses in progress.

estimate. Sixty workhouses had been contracted for, and were in progress of building, and arrangements for ten others were considerably advanced.

It soon appeared to be on many accounts exceedingly desirable, not only that the formation of the unions, but also that the necessary arrangements for administering relief, should be urged forward as rapidly as possible. The government concurred in this view, and Three additional assistant-commissioners. sanctioned the appointment of two additional assistant-commissioners,[k] who after a short training in England, were assigned to their respective duties in Ireland, whither also another of the English assistant-commissioners was transferred.[k] The valuable services of Mr. Earle were in the present year withdrawn from the commission, and he was succeeded in the charge of the Dublin district by Mr. Hall, who had previously been acting in England.

Formation of unions. Great pains were taken in forming the unions, and for the most part the arrangements made were satisfactory to the parties interested, but not always so to the extent desired; for it was not always found possible " to adapt the limits of the union to the limits of individual properties, and at the same time adhere to other local boundaries and pay a due regard to general convenience." Difficulties likewise arose in determining the portion of rural district to be included in the same electoral division with towns, or with other places where the destitute and mendicant classes were numerous. Such places were regarded as likely to bring a burden upon whatever else they might be combined with. It does not follow however because mendicancy prevails in a town, that the poor-rates will be heavier there than in the neighbouring country districts. The reverse will often be the case, the larger amount of

---

[k] These were Mr. Burke and Mr. Otway ; and Mr. Muggeridge was transferred from England.

property rateable in a town, being more than equivalent to its comparatively greater charge of pauperism.
The practice generally adopted on such occasions, was
to attach to a town as much of the adjoining district as
seemed naturally to belong to it, and over which the
town mendicants habitually levied contributions. No
part of an electoral division so formed would be subjected to any new burden. It had supported the mendicant classes heretofore—it would have to pay rates
for supporting the destitute thereafter; and of the two,
the latter would probably be found the lighter.

Before submitting a proposal for establishing a union,
the assistant-commissioners in every instance called
a meeting of the inhabitants of the district, and explained the nature and intent of the law, together with
the proposed arrangements for carrying it into effect,
and also took into consideration whatever objections or
suggestions there might have been made on the occasion ; and it was not until after this public exposition
of the course proposed to be pursued, and a careful
sifting of testimony for and against it, that the arrangements for the several unions were proposed to, and
received the sanction of the board in Dublin. The
Reports of the assistant-commissioners on these occasions were sometimes long and minute, entering into
a detail of the circumstances of the district, and thus
forming " a valuable body of information general and
statistical, which may hereafter serve to test the working of the measure, and its effects upon the population."
A copy of one of these Reports furnished by each of
the assistant-commissioners, was inserted by way of
example in the Appendix to the annual Report.

The Board's attention was early directed to the state
of the charitable institutions in Dublin, and The Dublin
house of
especially to the house of industry and the industry.
foundling hospital, both of which became vested in the
commissioners under the 34*th section* of the Poor Re-

lief Act. The house of industry consisted of an asylum
for aged and infirm poor and incurable lunatics, together
with the Hardwick, the Whitworth, and the Richmond
Hospitals, and the Talbot Dispensary. It was constituted
under the Irish Act of 11*th and* 12*th Geo.* 3*rd, cap.* 11,[m]
and was expected to be supported by voluntary contributions, but these soon failed, and in 1777 it received
a grant of 4,000*l.* from parliament, and had continued
ever since to be supported in like manner. In 1816
it was determined to appropriate the house of industry
to the reception of the aged and infirm and the sick
poor, orphan children, and lunatics and idiots. This
led to the introduction of a large number of persons
requiring medical treatment, and made it necessary to
provide hospitals for the purpose. The expense of the
entire establishment was defrayed by parliament, and
the grant for each of the preceding five years had been
20,000*l.* The estimate for 1839 was 21,136*l.* The
number of inmates was as follows—

Aged and infirm poor	888
Incurable lunatics and epileptics	474
	1,362
Sick in the hospitals	303
Total	1,665

The foundling hospital was established in 1704 by
the 2*nd Anne, cap.* 19, and was re-constituted
in 1772 by the 11*th and* 12*th Geo.* 3, *cap.* 11.[n]
With the exception of a small rent from property devised to it, the institution had been supported by parliamentary grants, which during the last five years had
averaged 14,765*l.* The estimate for the current year
was 11,255*l.* Infants were at first, and for many years
subsequently, received into the hospital without payment or inquiry, the annual number varying from 1,500
to 2,000. In 1822 a deposit of 5*l.* was required with

The Dublin foundling hospital.

---

[m] Ante, p. 45.   [n] Ante, pp. 35 and 45.

each child, which soon had the effect of reducing the admissions to below 500; and in 1829 a committee of the house of commons recommended that admissions should cease altogether, which they accordingly did in the following year. The previous admissions however had been so numerous, that on the 25th of March 1839 the dependents on the institution still amounted to 4,258, viz.—

Children at nurse in the country, of whom 446 are under
    ten years of age 1,484
Apprentices 2,528
In course of being apprenticed, or under medical treat-
    ment in the house 40
Adults on the invalid list 206

                             4,258

The invalid class consisted of 150 females and 56 males, and had accumulated principally since 1797, only 13 having been admitted previous to that year. " Many were blind, some crippled, others were severe cases of scrofula, and a few were deaf and dumb. They were quartered in the country, and were annually visited by the inspectors."

The capacity of the house of industry and foundling hospital for being converted to workhouses, Arrangements with regard to the house of industry and foundling hospital. and the great prevalence of mendicancy in Dublin, made it expedient to introduce the new law with as little delay as possible; and steps were taken for this purpose, as soon as the passing of the Amendment Act[o] enabled the board to unite districts not being townlands. Arrangements were, with the approbation of government, made for the lunatic inmates of the house of industry, amounting with their attendants to 523, by preparing certain old barracks at Island Bridge for their reception; and as the hospitals and the dispensary, when detached from the house of industry, would stand in need of kitchen and other office accommodation, these essentials

o Ante, p. 233.

were accordingly provided, and the appointments in connexion with them were consigned to the Irish government. With regard to the foundling hospital, a suitable residence was provided for the officers, and for such of the children as it might be occasionally necessary to bring to Dublin. The expense attendant upon making these various changes was very considerable, but the whole was accomplished " without calling for any advance beyond the money already voted by parliament for the house of industry and foundling hospital, the balance remaining from the vote of the year preceding, and the saving of expenditure by enforcing a rigid economy during the past year, having afforded sufficient funds to effect all that was necessary." This result is declared to have been chiefly owing to the confidence which government placed in the commissioners with regard to a matter of much intricacy, and which did not perhaps strictly come within the line of their duty. It was also in no slight degree owing to the prompt support afforded by his excellency the lord lieutenant, whose cordial co-operation and assistance on all occasions is gratefully noticed in the Report.[p]

A full account of the measures adopted with regard

The two Dublin unions.   to the Dublin foundling hospital and house of industry, is given in the assistant-commissioners' Report[q] on these institutions, and also of what was required to be done preparatory to their being used as the workhouses of the two Dublin unions, for which they were well suited both as to size and situation. One of the unions comprised the district on the south side of the Liffey, with a population of 182,767; and the other comprised the district on the north side,

---

[p] Lord Ebrington (now Earl Fortescue) was lord lieutenant at this time, and I feel it a duty to state that much of our success in the early part of our proceedings, was owing to the aid and countenance he was ever ready to afford us. He knew the difficulties with which the commission had to contend, and never withheld assistance when it was needed.

[q] This is inserted in the Appendix to the Annual Report.

having a population of 125,245. The workhouses would each be made capable of accommodating 2,000 inmates, and were very conveniently placed, with a sufficiency of land attached to them. A belt of unions had been formed nearly encircling the city, so that the Dublin unions would be protected from undue pressure. The guardians exhibited a good spirit, and promised an active co-operation in carrying out the law. The unions were both declared on the 6th of June 1839; and the order declaring the workhouses fit for the reception of paupers was issued on the 25th of March 1840, the interval being occupied in making the necessary preparations. Dublin workhouses declared, March 25, 1840.

Cork possessed a foundling hospital and a house of industry as well as Dublin; but both were much smaller than the metropolitan ones, and the house of industry alone was susceptible of being used as a workhouse, and that only temporarily until an adequate building could be provided for the purpose. With respect to the foundling hospital, steps were taken as in the case of that of Dublin, to bring it to a close at the earliest period compatible with the wellbeing of the children maintained in it. The Cork guardians entered with alacrity on the discharge of their new duties, and took immediate steps for obtaining a valuation, and levying a rate. It was therefore determined in compliance with the desire strongly expressed by them, and by the inhabitants generally, to bring the law into full operation in the Cork union with the least possible delay, although it was not unlikely that some inconvenience might arise from relief being administered there so much sooner than it would be practicable to provide for its administration in the neighbouring districts. The union was declared on the 3rd of April 1839; and on the 15th of February 1840 an order was issued declaring the old house of industry to be the temporary workhouse of the The Cork union. Cork workhouse declared temporarily, February 15, 1840.

union for administering relief. Full instructions were furnished to the guardians on the occasion, and an intention was expressed of watching the progress of the Cork and the Dublin unions, with a view to the prompt exercise of the powers provided by the law for mitigating "whatever inconveniences might arise from thus early bringing the law into operation." The proceeding was one of great interest, and of great anxiety also to those on whom the responsibility rested, so much depending on the success of the first unions. The author has a vivid recollection of all that passed on the occasion, and of the deep thankfulness experienced on witnessing the efficient working of these unions, and this moreover under difficulties far greater than would be likely to arise when the course of procedure was more matured.

As the period approached for bringing the Cork and the Dublin workhouses into operation, it became necessary to prepare a code of workhouse regulations, and a system of union accounts. The latter, it was endeavoured to make as simple as possible, having regard to accuracy and to a proper discrimination of subjects; and the former it was determined to frame on the model of the English workhouse regulations, making such changes only as were necessary for adapting them to the circumstances existing in Ireland. The "order for regulating the workhouse, and for keeping and auditing accounts," [r] was accordingly prepared, and was issued successively as the unions became sufficiently advanced for its reception. With regard to the dietaries, an "order" for which it was also necessary to prepare, the Board instituted inquiries into the mode of living in different parts of Ireland, so as to be able to establish dietaries in the different unions that should accord with

Marginal notes: Workhouse regulations and order of accounts prepared.

The workhouse dietaries.

---

[r] A copy of the order is appended to the 2nd Annual Report.

the general habits of the people, and yet "not be in any case superior to the ordinary mode of subsistence of the labouring classes in the neighbourhood." On this principle the Board continued to frame the workhouse dietaries, as being essential adjuncts of workhouse management. But for the efficiency of the workhouse, reliance was chiefly placed on the enforcement of order, sobriety, cleanliness, daily occupation, the observance of decency and decorum, and the exclusion of all stimulants to excitement—these constitute the real strength of the workhouse as a test of destitution, and would be in a great degree effective, even if the diet, clothing, and other merely physical appliances were superior to what is seen in the neighbouring cottages; and these essentials the workhouse regulations are calculated to maintain.

Very exaggerated notions prevailed as to what would be the effect of the Poor Law, when brought into full operation. Some declared that all the charitable institutions would be immediately annihilated, as people would cease to subscribe as soon as they were called upon to pay a poor-rate, and compensation was claimed on behalf of certain functionaries, on the ground that they would be deprived of their means of living when the workhouses were opened. Numerous applications were made on the subject, and among others by the officers of the Dublin Mendicity Association who claimed to be compensated on this account. They were however told that the association might still be continued with advantage, as an independent auxiliary to the Poor Law; for that it was highly probable there would be a class of persons whose destitution would not be so urgent as to compel them to become inmates of the workhouses, and who yet would be proper objects of such charitable assistance as it came within the province of the mendicity institution to bestow.

Exaggerated expectations as to the effects of the Poor-law.

The measures connected with the erection of work-
Erection of workhouses. houses required much care and circumspection,
and a constant watchfulness of the prices of
labour and materials in the several districts. The
buildings were proceeded with in such a way as to
create the least disturbance in the labour-market, and
it was endeavoured to spread the operations as equally
as possible throughout the country. Notwithstanding
these precautions however, a tendency to advance in
prices was sometimes manifested; but on such occasions
the Board made it to be understood, that it was prepared to put out repeated advertisements, or to postpone
building altogether for a season, rather than submit to
terms above what it considered to be the fair market
price. On the other hand, the Board did not bind
itself to accept the lowest tender, and generally gave
a preference to builders resident in the district, when of
good character and possessing a sufficient command of
means. The extreme wetness of the previous season
was very unfavourable to building, and also delayed
the valuations, so that the completion and opening of
the workhouses was delayed longer than had been at
first contemplated; but an assurance was given, that no
effort would be spared to effect this object at the earliest
possible period.

Numerous representations were addressed to the
Repression of mendicancy. board on the subject of mendicancy, urging
that provision should be made for its being put
an end to simultaneously with the commencement of
relief under the Poor Law. The question was very
generally discussed by the boards of guardians, and
forty of them, for the most part unanimously, passed
resolutions in favour of a measure for the suppression
of mendicancy; but three of the boards took a different
view, and were adverse to such suppression. The correspondence which took place on these occasions appears
in the Annual Report, and also a minute which the

Dublin board addressed to the assistant-commissioners on the occasion. In this minute, after pointing out the necessity for repressing vagrancy and mendicancy as a measure of police, the repression is declared to be likewise necessary for ensuring the effective operation of the Poor Law; for so long as the vagrant classes were permitted to levy contributions on the plea of destitution, the ratepayers, although taxed for the relief of the destitute, would not be protected from the daily demands of the mendicant, nor be exonerated from those compulsory contributions which the mendicant so well knows how to exact. Unless mendicancy were repressed therefore, great injustice would be inflicted on the ratepayer, whose payment of the poor-rate entitles him to protection from such demands. The most expedient way of effecting this object, was considered to be by establishing a law founded on the English Vagrancy Act, with such modifications as might be necessary for adapting it to the state of Ireland.[s]

The subject of emigration was generally regarded with great interest in Ireland, and had latterly occupied more than usual attention, partly on Emigration. account of a persuasion that it would be necessary to have recourse to it as the corrective for a redundant population, and partly also in consequence of the efforts which were made by certain associations to promote it. In answer to the various representations on the subject, the Board did not offer any opinion as to whether an extensive and organized system of emigration were necessary or not, but considered that there might be localities over-densely peopled, to which it might be applied with advantage. When the unions were all in operation, and when the effects of the Poor Law had been fully developed, the Board would be prepared to

---

[s] Clauses to this effect had been inserted in the original bill, but were withdrawn, as has been before stated. Ante, p. 195.

state its views on the subject—"but pending the introduction of the Poor Law, one object of which was to establish an identity of interest between the owners and occupiers of property and the working classes, and to hold out to the former the strongest inducements to extend the field of employment at home"—pending the development of this great impulse upon the home energies of the country, it was considered that it would be premature to offer any opinion on the general question of emigration.

As the summer of 1839 advanced, severe distress began to prevail in several districts of the west of Ireland, and the government deputed Captain Chads of the Royal Navy to investigate its extent, and furnished him with means for affording such present relief as might be found imperatively necessary.[t] It was at first thought, that where poor-law unions had been formed, use might be made of the union machinery in dispensing the relief which government was prepared to furnish; but it soon appeared that this would be inexpedient if not impracticable, and that the administering of government aid must be kept totally distinct from the poor-law executive, except only as regarded information and advice and whatever other facilities the assistant-commissioners might be able to afford. The relief distributed by the agent of government on this occasion, was in every case made contingent upon an equal amount being raised by persons resident or having property in the district; and notwithstanding the danger from fraud and misrepresentation to which a person so deputed was obviously liable, and the still greater danger of creating an undue dependence upon government aid, there is reason to believe that a considerable amount of good was effected,

Marginal note: Distress in the western districts— relief afforded by government.

---

[t] The money expended on this occasion amounted to 5,441*l*. See 'The Irish Crisis,' by Sir Charles Trevelyan, p. 18.

and that little mischief was caused by what was done by the agent of government in this instance.

The extremely wet and ungenial summer and autumn of 1839, caused great apprehension throughout Ireland as to the effect upon the crops, and steps were taken to obtain correct information on the subject, particularly with regard to the potato crop, it being the one most universally important to the Irish people. The result of these inquiries through the assistant-commissioners and other sources, showed that there was much ground for alarm, " the crop appearing to be deficient in quantity in some districts, whilst owing to the almost incessant rains the quality would it was feared be found inferior in all, and probably so far inferior as not to admit of the potatoes being kept for the usual time." If such should turn out to be the case, distress wide spreading and severe would inevitably ensue, and the distress would moreover be aggravated by the want of fuel, the people having been prevented by the continual wet from gathering in their turf. *Unfavourable season.*

Many applications were addressed to the Poor Law board, and to the Irish government on this subject, several of them containing schemes and suggestions for rendering the Poor Law available, in case the danger apprehended should actually arise ; and it was therefore deemed advisable that the views of the Board in reference to this question should be made known. This was accordingly done by a minute, calling attention to the provisions by which relief was to be governed. *Suggestions for relieving the distress.*

The minute states, that the 3*rd section* of the Act directed that relief should be administered " ac- cording to such laws as shall be in force at the time being;" and that the 41*st section* provides— " That when the commissioners shall have declared the workhouse of any union to be fit for the reception of destitute poor, *and not before*, it shall be law- *Board's minute, Dec. 5th 1839.*

ful for the guardians to take order for relieving and
setting to work *therein* destitute poor persons &c."
Nowhere else is power given to the guardians to administer relief—their functions in this respect are limited
to receiving destitute persons into the workhouse, and
relieving and setting them to work "*therein.*" And by
the 5 2nd *section* it is further provided, " that it shall not
be lawful for the commissioners, or guardians, or other
persons acting in execution of this Act, to apply directly or indirectly any money raised under authority
of this Act, to the relief of destitute poor in any other
manner than is herein expressly mentioned, or to any
purpose not expressly provided for in this Act."
Whether the relief so provided for be or be not in the
opinion of the guardians -suitable or sufficient, the Act
under which they are constituted, and whence their
administrative functions are derived, is thus seen to be
precise and definite in its provisions; and they were
told that they could not legally deviate in the slightest
degree from the course it prescribes, neither did
there reside in the Poor Law Commissioners any power
or discretion to authorize any such deviation. Some
persons however suggested that the law should be
altered early in the next session, so as to allow of other
modes of relief as a temporary measure, to meet the
then apprehended exigency. But this, it was said, would
be re-opening a question upon which the deliberate
sense of the legislature had been recently recorded;
and parliament having deemed it right to prohibit all
relief except in the workhouse, the commissioners could
not encourage an application which had for its object
the reversal of that decision.

Such was the general purport of the minute, although
considerably more in detail, and embracing some minor
points not noticed above. It was circulated among the
boards of guardians, and was thought to have produced
a good effect by directing attention to the principle as
well as to the provisions of the Act. There was reason

to believe moreover, that the potato crop, although scanty in some districts, was on the whole not materially deficient in produce, and that although the quality was generally inferior, the potatoes would keep nearly as well as in ordinary seasons. There was likewise reason to believe that the dread of scarcity had influenced the people to be more careful and economical in the use of their stores than they probably otherwise might have been, and that they would thus by provident fore-thought avert the occurrence of any very serious amount of distress, notwithstanding that a general de-ficiency in the grain crops was superadded to the other evils arising out of the extreme wetness of the season.

The third Report of proceedings in Ireland is dated May 1st, and contains an account of all that was done during the previous parochial year, ending March 25th 1841. At the date of the second Report 104 unions had been declared. At the date of the third Report we find the number in-creased to 127, and it is stated that only 3 more will be required, and that these will be declared in the course of the present month, making the entire number of unions in Ireland amount to 130. At the date of the last Report 60 workhouses had been contracted for, and the buildings were in different stages of progress. The number of workhouses con-tracted for and built or in process of building up to the 25th of March 1841, was 115, of which a particular account is given in a Report by the architect inserted in the Appendix to the present Report.

1841. Third report of proceed-ings in Ireland.

Unions and workhouses.

The providing of the Irish workhouses was a large and difficult operation, involving a great variety of details, and requiring constant attention. The contracts were as stated in the last Report entered into so gradually, and the works were spread so equally throughout the country, that although the number ac-tually in progress at one time was greater than it might

Erection of the workhouses.

at first have been considered safe or expedient to undertake, it yet was not found that prices were materially
affected, or that any other material inconvenience had
arisen. One of the chief impediments was the delay
and difficulty encountered in obtaining sites for the
workhouses, owing to encumbrances and other circumstances connected with landed property in Ireland, and
to the Act's containing no special provision for the
purpose. At one time indeed it was thought that it
would have been necessary to apply to parliament on the
subject; but by determined perseverance sites were at
length everywhere obtained, and although not in every
case so good as might be wished, no union was left without one sufficient for its object. The winter of 1841
began early, and continued late, and was unusually
severe, which greatly retarded the progress of the
buildings; but the contractors were generally sensible
of the value of time, and whenever the weather permitted, exerted themselves to recover what was unavoidably lost through unfavourable seasons. It may perhaps not be deemed irrelevant to mention, that the
author being then the resident commissioner in Ireland,
he made a point of examining every workhouse site
purchased, or intended to be purchased, and also inspected once at least in every year each of the workhouses, whether built or in progress of building. These
inspections were no doubt a great addition to his other
labours, but they were very necessary for correcting the
defects and omissions which are sure to occur in carrying out so extensive an operation.

     Eleven workhouses were completed and opened for
the relief of the destitute poor during the year
1840-41 in addition to those of Dublin and
Cork opened in the preceding year, and making fourteen in all. Two of these belonged to the important
unions of Londonderry and Belfast. The Londonderry
house had been open throughout the winter, and con-

Fourteen workhouses in operation.

tinued to work in all respects satisfactorily. The others had been too recently declared to afford reliable indications as to their future working, but nothing had occurred to excite apprehension with respect to them.

The two Dublin workhouses had been opened upwards of twelve months, and the guardians The Dublin had attended to the administration of relief unions. and the union business generally, in a very exemplary manner. Before the houses were thoroughly completed and organized, the closing of the Dublin mendicity institution threw a sudden pressure upon these establishments, especially upon that of the South Dublin union, as many as 500 poor persons having been admitted there in one week, and 1,473 within the first month, a great majority of whom had been previously supported in the Dublin Mendicity. Such an influx could hardly fail of causing embarrassment and confusion, and it may be regarded as a proof of the efficiency of the workhouse system, that notwithstanding the want of preparation which necessarily prevailed, and the inexperience of the guardians and union officers, so large an admission was provided for, and order speedily established. Even after the first influx of mendicity paupers had ceased, there was great pressure for admission, on which account a cautionary letter was addressed to the guardians, recommending that from the numerous applicants they should at one time select such a moderate number only "as could be conveniently cleansed, classified, placed in their proper wards, and registered in course of that and the following day;" and likewise, that the visiting committee should report as to the condition of the inmates, and whether they had been disposed of in accordance with the regulations, previous to further admissions taking place on the days fixed for the purpose. In the absence of strict discipline, the workhouse will, they are told, become a place to which the idle would resort to the

exclusion of those who are real objects of charity; and
this was the more to be apprehended in the Dublin
unions, from the circumstance of their workhouses being
open while no relief was given in the neighbouring
unions, and were consequently attracting from the surrounding country those poor persons who needed or who
professed to need such relief. The number of inmates in
the South Dublin workhouse on the 25th of March was
2,080, and in the North Dublin the number was 1,837.

The case of Cork differed materially from the two

The Cork union. Dublin unions. These had each a capacious
workhouse in which classification could be established and order be enforced; but the Cork house was
small, ill-arranged, and altogether insufficient for these
purposes; and it was not without considerable mis-
giving, that in compliance with the wishes of the
guardians, it had been permitted to be used as the temporary workhouse of the union, until the new house
should be ready.[u] The inconvenience was certainly less
felt than might be expected, the guardians having
made the most of the old building, and established a
tolerable degree of order among the inmates under circumstances extremely unfavourable for the purpose.
The number of inmates on the 25th of March was
1,844, nearly the half of whom were former inmates of
the old house of industry. This number was much
beyond what could be properly accommodated, but
owing to the severity of the winter and the high price
of provisions there had been much distress among the
poor, and the pressure for admission had consequently
been very great. When relief shall be administered
in the neighbouring unions, the pressure upon Cork
may be expected to subside. The new house is calculated for 2,000 inmates, and will it is considered, when
completed, be sufficient to meet the wants of the union.

---

[u] Ante, p. 251.

The foregoing account of the proceedings in the Cork and Dublin unions, exhibits the actual working of the Poor Law in the only unions in which it had been in operation sufficiently long for showing any definite result. In each of these unions workhouse relief had been administered for upwards of a year, and the boards of guardians and other executives had mostly held office for double that period. The circumstances under which they had to act, were moreover peculiarly trying. These unions may therefore be regarded as average examples of the working of the law, and might be appealed to in proof of its sufficiency for the objects contemplated in its enactment. There was no doubt still in these three unions much to adjust and regulate, which it required time and watchfulness to effect. But the general establishment of the law throughout Ireland might now, it was considered, be looked forward to with confidence, nothing having hitherto occurred to raise a doubt as to its applicability; but on the contrary, all the proceedings had served to show that the system was suitable to the circumstances of the country, and adequate for the relief of the destitute poor.

By the 123rd section of the Relief Act it is directed, that an account of the expenditure upon the relief of the poor during the year, and the total number of persons relieved, in each union on the 1st of January, shall be annually laid before parliament, together with the commissioners' General Report. On the 1st of January 1841, the returns showed that the expense of relief in the previous year, and the numbers relieved in the four unions then in operation, were as follows—

		No. in the workhouse on the 1st Jan. 1841.
Cork	£12,453 8 0	1,549
North Dublin	10,407 12 7	1,601
South Dublin	12,732 3 8	1,987
Londonderry (two months)	1,464 4 5	331
	£37,057 8 8	Total 5,468

The education of the children maintained in the
Education and training of workhouse children. workhouse, was from the very outset felt to
be a matter of the utmost importance. In
the North Dublin workhouse there were 500
children under sixteen years of age, and in the South
Dublin workhouse there were 635. That these children
should be trained up in moral and religious habits, and be
fitted by education and by instruction in useful branches
of industry for earning their own living, all must admit
to be necessary; and for these purposes a protestant
and a Roman catholic chaplain, and a schoolmaster and
schoolmistress, were appointed to each workhouse. The
girls were taught sewing, and were employed in the
domestic work of the house, so as to fit them for service. The boys were taught tailoring, shoemaking,
carpentering, and some were set to work in the garden :
but the various employments to which boys reared in
the workhouse are likely in after life to betake themselves, hardly admit of their being specifically trained
for them, and little more can be done in the way of preparation than to send them forth imbued with habits
of industry, their frames strengthened and inured to
labour, their tempers and mental faculties duly cultivated, and above all with their minds duly impressed
with a sense of their moral and religious duties. When
thus prepared, they will be best fitted for entering upon
the duties incidental to their position, on the right performance of which their future condition in life must
depend. The earnest attention of the Dublin boards
was given to this subject, and arrangements were made
with the Commissioners of National Education for inspecting the workhouse schools, and for supplying them
with books and other requisites on the most favourable
terms. The Board likewise took advantage of every
opportunity for impressing upon the guardians and
union officers the great importance of attending to the
education and training of these children, and of getting

them out into service and other occupations as soon as they were fitted for it.

Shortly after the opening of the Dublin workhouses, a marked decrease was observed in the number of beggars, and persons before adverse to the Poor Law were then heard to speak in its favour. *Mendicancy.* Many of the beggars had in fact entered the workhouses, and thus the public were relieved from their solicitations ; but the relief was short-lived, for others soon flocked in from the neighbouring districts, and many who had entered the workhouses experimentally as it were, or through fear that their vocation might be suddenly put a stop to, again left them and resumed their former practice of begging ; and thus after a time, the streets and suburbs of Dublin were as full of beggars as before. This circumstance appears to have produced a very general conviction, not in Dublin only but throughout the country, of the necessity for suppressing mendicancy, and Lord Morpeth[x] introduced a bill for the purpose, which however was not proceeded with. The commissioners nevertheless again emphatically declared " that a law for the repression of mendicancy was essential to the well-working of the Poor Relief Act in Ireland."

Much attention was given to the valuations of the rateable property in the several unions, and such advice and assistance as appeared to be *The valuations.* necessary were afforded on the occasion. The valuations were said to be complete in fifty of the unions, and were in progress in most of the others; and notwithstanding that they were said to be too low, " there was on the whole reason to be satisfied with the manner in which this very important duty had been performed, although in so large an operation, entered upon under such a variety of circumstances, there must be variances

---

[x] Then secretary for Ireland.

and imperfections requiring time and experience to rectify." It was at this time proposed to found the parliamentary franchise upon the Poor Law valuations, and the author's opinion was asked as to their accuracy, and whether the commissioners possessed sufficient power for securing their correctness in future. A good deal of communication took place on the subject, and the author stated that he considered no further powers to be necessary—that strictly speaking the valuation was only applicable to one rate, and was constantly open to revision as the value of property changed, or as circumstances required it; so that supposing the valuations not to be accurate then, as provision was made for successive revisions, it could hardly be doubted that after a few rates had been levied, they would be made to approximate very closely to what was contemplated by the Act, and would also be kept in that state by the self-corrective principle with which they were imbued. With respect to any consequences likely to arise from basing the parliamentary or the municipal franchise upon the Poor Law valuations, if either should be determined on, he thought " that whatever influence such a connexion might have, must tend to raise the valuations; and as these were now confessedly too low, the effect would be so far beneficial."

Many irregularities had occurred in the election of guardians, and there had likewise been instances of improper interference with the distribution and collection of the voting papers. An inquiry was therefore instituted with a view to ascertain whether it might not be expedient to make some change in these respects. Under the Municipal Corporation Act, the suffrages are required to be given at polling-places appointed for the purpose, while by the Board's order for the election of guardians they are directed to be given by means of voting papers; and of the two modes, many persons thought the former best suited to the

Election of guardians.

state of Ireland. But although irregularities and improper influence had no doubt in some cases interfered with the distribution and collection of the voting papers, intimidation and undue influence of another kind might, it was thought, be as effectually practised, and in a more turbulent manner, when the electors proceed to polling-places to record their votes; and to make so important a change at the then early stage of the proceedings, unless it were absolutely necessary, would tend to weaken public confidence—on all which accounts, and after much consideration, it was determined to adhere to the mode of conducting the elections then established —endeavouring however at the same time to improve the details, and as far as possible to guard against irregularities and improper influences of every kind. Elections had taken place in 99 unions, and in 25 of these the guardians were returned without a contest. The other 74 unions comprised 1,234 electoral divisions, and ten divisions which were subdivided into 54 wards, making in all 1,288 election districts, in 254 of which contests took place, whilst in 1,034 the guardians were returned without a contest. These results seemed to augur well for the future elections under the existing order. A tabular statement showing the particulars of all these elections, with the names of the several returning officers, is given in the Appendix to the Annual Report.

A limited inquiry into the state of a few of the medical charities had been made in the previous year, but a more extended inquiry under the provisions of the Poor Relief Act appearing to be desired, and the time indicated by the 46th *section* for commencing such inquiry, namely " so soon as conveniently may be after the formation of the unions," having arrived, it was determined that the whole of the medical charities should forthwith be examined, and a series of instructions were accordingly prepared for the

The medical charities.

purpose.[y] At the date of the commissioners' third Annual Report the medical charities within 53 of the unions had been examined and reported upon, and as these were spread over every part of the country, and comprised every variety of circumstance usually connected with such institutions, they might be considered as presenting a fair sample of the wants, and of the actual state and condition of the whole. It was therefore thought that a sufficient amount of information had been obtained for reporting the same to government, and suggesting such corrective measures as appeared to be called for, although the inquiry had not been completed in all the unions; and this was soon afterwards accordingly done.

The 3rd and 4th Vict., cap. 29, ' to extend the practice Vaccination. of vaccination,' had been passed in the year preceding, and no time was lost in bringing the Act into operation in Ireland, so far as depended on the Poor Law executive. Letters were addressed to the unions, advising and instructing the guardians as to the steps to be taken by them on the occasion, and furnishing them with the necessary forms of contract &c. for carrying the law into effect. These were generally found sufficient for the purpose, and ninety of the unions had already contracted in the form and on the terms proposed; and the others would, it was expected, do the same, when their organization became sufficiently advanced. The rate of remuneration recommended for the medical practitioners, was a shilling for each case of successful vaccination treated during the year up to 200, and sixpence for each such case beyond that number; but the guardians were not restricted to these rates, if in any case they should appear to them to be unsuitable.

---

[y] The gentlemen to whom this very important duty was confided were Mr. Phelan who had been specially appointed with a view to this object, and Dr. Corr afterwards temporarily employed for the like purpose; and to them was joined the assistant-commissioner in charge of the district within which the particular inquiry took place.

It had always been considered that the union machinery would afford facilities for the introduc- Union
agricultural
tion of local improvements in Ireland. Hitherto societies.
there had been a want of means for carrying any such
object into effect. But the Union authorities now afforded
the means, and possessed sufficient local influence for
setting on foot and supporting whatever local measures
might be necessary for promoting the comfort and
well-being of the people. I had frequent communications on this interesting subject with persons residing
in different parts of the country, and I omitted no opportunity of adverting to the important considerations
which it involved. Agriculture is the chief staple of
Ireland, on which the welfare, and it may be said the
very existence of its inhabitants depended. Yet agriculture was, with few exceptions, confessedly in a very
backward state; and it appeared to me likely that this
backwardness might to some extent be remedied by the
establishment of union agricultural societies—that is,
associations for promoting improvements in agriculture
within the limits of the respective unions; but of course
to be in no way connected with the administration of
the Poor Law. Efforts were accordingly made for
accomplishing this object, and with considerable success,
several such associations having been formed at the date
of the third Report, the Ballinasloe union under its
chairman Lord Clancarty being the first, and others
likewise being in course of formation, with every prospect of beneficial results.

The prices of provisions were high during nearly
the whole of last year (1840), and there was Prevalence
of distress.
a good deal of distress in some districts. Applications for assistance were as usual made to government on the approach of summer in the present year,
and these being referred to the Dublin Board, were in
every instance fully inquired into. It was evident that
much pressure prevailed in some parts of the country,
owing to the exhaustion or short supply and conse-

quent dearness of the potato; but " it did not appear that the pressure was so great, or the distress in any district so urgent, as to call for extraordinary interference on the part of the government." The distress which usually took place in the western parts of Ireland between the months of June and September, from a failure of the old and pending the incoming of the new crop, will it may be feared continue more or less to prevail, so long as the potato continues to be the chief or nearly sole food of the population. The intensity of the distress is always in proportion to the length of the interval between the exhaustion of one crop and the maturity of the other; and this interval under ordinary circumstances can only be reduced by the exercise of forethought and prudential considerations by the people themselves. These qualities happily appear to be increasing and becoming more general, the pressure of the preceding year having been sustained, not only without the usual aid from government, but with less suffering and privation than had prevailed in former years, although the last year's crops were considerably under an average. The people therefore must have been more careful in husbanding their means, and were likewise, it may be presumed, better informed with regard to their social position, and the duties which it imposed upon them. Perhaps a portion of this improvement may be attributed to the frequent discussions with reference to the Poor Law question during the last five or six years, partly also to the organization of unions latterly in progress throughout the country, and partly likewise to the spread of temperance which had happily taken place of late.

The Report for 1842 brings the account of proceedings down to the 1st of May, instead of ending at the 25th of March, as in the case of the three preceding Reports. This was done in

1842.
Fourth
report of
proceedings
in Ireland.

order to assimilate the dates of the English and Irish
Reports, the statements of proceedings in each now ter-
minating at the same period.

At the date of the preceding Report, the unions had
all been declared excepting three, for the de- Unions
claring of which the preliminary arrangements declared.
had all been made, and these were declared shortly
afterwards.[z] The whole of Ireland must now therefore
be regarded as being divided into unions, with the extent
of each union defined, and its population and other circumstances ascertained and recorded. In each union
likewise, an administrative body had been formed on a
broad representative principle, and there could be no
doubt that the boards of guardians so elected would
possess the confidence of the people. A complete return of the 130 unions, with their area and population,
the number of electoral divisions, the number of
guardians elected and ex-officio, and the date of declaration of each union, is given in the Appendix to the
Report.

Next in order to the formation of the unions, and
it may be added next also in importance, The work-
is the erection of the workhouses; and to a de- houses.
scription of the steps taken in carrying forward this
extensive operation, several pages are devoted in the
fourth Report, at the date of which, all the workhouses
had been built, or were in progress of building, and 81
had been declared fit for the reception of destitute
poor. In all of these, excepting a few of the last
finished, relief was being then administered, and by the
end of the summer it was expected that at least 100 of
the workhouses would be completed and opened, and
the others far advanced towards completion. A hope
is also expressed that by the end of the following
spring, " or at latest by midsummer," the workhouses

---

[z] Ante, p. 259.

throughout Ireland would be all in operation. This it is observed was perhaps as much as could be expected under the most favourable circumstances; but the prevalence of wet weather during the last three years had greatly impeded the progress of the buildings, and much increased the labour and difficulty of superintendence. Even in favourable seasons, it would not be a light task to superintend and direct extensive buildings, proceeding simultaneously in every part of the country; but with such weather as had prevailed in the last three years, and with a hundred of these buildings in progress at one time, all requiring constant attention, the labour and the difficulty must obviously have been increased. The builders likewise were sufferers from the same cause, which made them lose much time, as well as incur much additional expense. Generally however the buildings were well finished, and the several contractors evinced, with few exceptions, an honest determination to fulfil their engagements, although this was in some instances done to their own loss.

The money required for providing the workhouses, Workhouse being under the provisions of the Relief Act, loans. and with consent of government, advanced by the exchequer-bill loan commissioners, arrangements had been made for its reception, safe custody, and correct appropriation, through the medium of the Bank of England and the Bank of Ireland. A separate loan was in the first instance granted to each union, and as the money was successively required to pay for land purchased, or to pay the stipulated instalments to the contractor, the amount was transmitted to the Bank of Ireland for the credit of the person to whom it was payable in Dublin; and thus these loans passed from her Majesty's exchequer into the hands of the parties severally entitled to receive them, without ever departing from the custody of one or other of the two great national banks, and consequently without risk, or the possibility of malversation. On the completion of the buildings, and after the accounts had been duly examined and certified, they were together with all the original documents laid before the boards of guardians, in order that every step which had been taken in the matter might be distinctly seen by them— the amount claimed, the amount deducted, and the quantity and price on which the deduction was founded or the claim allowed, all appeared on the face of the accounts; and a statement was at the same time delivered ·showing in detail the amount of the several receipts from the loan, and the expenditure on account of the union, and exhibiting the excess if there were a balance in hand, or the deficiency if there was not enough to cover the expenditure, in which case a further order to the guardians to raise or borrow the sum deficient was necessarily issued.

It was originally estimated that the cost of the workhouses would not exceed a million sterling, and Cost of the provision had been at the outset made to that workhouses. extent : but as the buildings advanced, it became evident that this amount would not be sufficient, and application was made for a further loan of 150,000*l.* One cause of the excess was, that it had not been originally proposed to finish and fit up the workhouses in so expensive a way as was afterwards found to be necessary. As the general condition of the people with respect to their habitations and mode of living, was inferior to that of the corresponding classes in England, it was thought that the workhouses might properly be of a somewhat less finished and costly character, and the arrangements for the buildings were framed in accordance with this view. Further experience however showed it to be necessary that the Irish workhouses should be made in all respects as complete as those in England. Indeed the guardians very generally wished that the finishing and fittings should be more costly and complete than was the case in the

English houses; and if the prevalent desire on this point had been complied with, the workhouses in Ireland would have been finished and fitted up after the model and with all the appliances of an hospital or infirmary. This will account for much of the excess beyond the original estimate in providing the Irish workhouses.

In connexion with the workhouses, the difficulty of always finding suitable employment for the inmates requires to be noticed. That pauper labour is unprofitable, was generally admitted; and if it were so in England where there is a constant demand for labour, it could not fail of being so in Ireland where the labour market was for the most part overcharged. All that had hitherto been done in this respect in the Irish workhouses, was to keep the inmates occupied as far as possible in employments of the commonest kind. The aged and infirm of both sexes who constituted a great majority of the inmates, were generally employed in oakum-picking, in the picking carding and spinning of wool, in knitting, and some few in making and mending the clothes belonging to the establishment. There were scarcely any able-bodied men in the workhouses, although there were many partially disabled, who were mostly occupied in the kitchen or doing the rougher work about the yards, and where this did not afford sufficient occupation they were employed in breaking stones. The able-bodied women were employed in household work, and there were not always a sufficient number of these to clean and keep the house in proper order; but where the number was greater than could be so employed, they were set to work with the needle, or in carding spinning or knitting. With regard to the children of both sexes, when not at school, they are employed in occupations suited to their age and strength —the girls under the matron in household work, or in working with their needle; the boys working in the

Workhouse employment.

yards, or in the garden, or at some trade in the house, thus accustoming their hands to labour, and fitting them for the everyday occupations of life. Much difficulty had always been found in getting young persons out into service or other occupation in Ireland. The better the workhouse children are trained and educated however, the better will be their chance in this respect. With the boys there will probably be less difficulty than the girls. Emigration would seem to be the suitable remedy for an excess of numbers in either case; but emigration, contrary to what was originally intended, was by the 51st *section* of the Relief Act made a charge upon the electoral division. The board of guardians collectively had no power to deal with it. And hence, although there were a number of friendless young persons, mostly females, the residuum of a former system, in the workhouses of the two Dublin unions, and at Cork, Waterford, Limerick, and Belfast, for whom no employment could be found, the money necessary for defraying the expense of their emigration could not be raised, and they continued a burden upon the unions instead of becoming useful as colonists.

The sanitary condition of the workhouses had generally been good, although they were in some instances much crowded during the winter. This was especially the case with the Dublin and Cork houses. Yet the inmates had on the whole been remarkably healthy, and fewer deaths occurred than might have been expected, looking at the advanced age and generally depressed physical condition of a large proportion of the individuals admitted. But the absence of all exciting influences, the regular hours, due supplies of food and clothing, and the warmth and ventilation which are found in a workhouse in a superior degree to what can be obtained by the same class out of it, no doubt conduce to the preservation of the health, and the extension of the life of its inmates. Such is not always

Sanitary state of the workhouses.

the case however with respect to children. In the Dublin workhouses, a large proportion of the infants were in a diseased or extremely emaciated state when admitted, and very many of them in their then condition could hardly be expected to live. The mortality which took place was accordingly so considerable as to lead to an inquiry being instituted, the result of which showed— " that although the mortality among the infants under two years of age in the workhouse was large, it yet had not exceeded, but rather fallen short of the average mortality among infants of the same age and class in foundling hospitals and other like institutions, or even at large under the care of their parents."

Audit of the accounts.

The accounts of the unions in which workhouses were in operation were severally audited by the assistant-commissioners, and duly reported upon. These reports showed the working of the system in all its details, pointing out and commenting upon the good and bad parts of the administration, and exhibiting and explaining the general results. The audit reports are in fact calculated to afford a complete view of the working of the Poor-law, wherever the administration of relief under its provisions had been brought into operation. Several of these were appended to the fourth annual Report.

Amount of expenditure and number relieved.

The expenditure on relief of the poor during the previous year, and the numbers relieved on the 1st of January, in the four unions then in operation, of which an account has been given,[a] was in the year ending January 1st 1842 as follows—

		Number in the house on the 1st January 1842.
Cork..	£11,775	1881
North Dublin	14,643	1940
South Dublin	15,613	2124
Londonderry	3,711	385
	£45,742	Total 6,330

[a] Ante, p. 263.

These unions may therefore be considered as being in orderly working, and equal to the duties imposed upon them by the Poor Relief Act. Thirty-three other unions in different parts of the country were likewise in operation during a portion of the year, longer or shorter according to the respective orders of declaration ; and the expenditure in these unions down to the same date as the above, had amounted to 64,535*l.*, the number of inmates in the several workhouses at that time being 8,916, of which number 1,310 were in the Limerick house. It thus appears that at the commencement of 1842, after somewhat more than two years' preparation, workhouse relief was administered in 37 unions, to 15,246 destitute persons, at an expense of 110,277*l.*—a result which, having regard to all circumstances, could hardly fail of being deemed satisfactory, and as holding out a promise of the early maturing of the other unions, all of which had been declared and were in progress of organization.

Apprehensions had been expressed, that in some parts of the country it would be difficult if not impos- Collection of sible to collect the poor-rates; but with very the rate. few exceptions no difficulty whatever occurred. There was nowhere any concerted resistance to the payment of the rate. " In a few instances, (it is observed) personal caprice or misapprehension of the law, has led individuals to refuse to pay the rate when it has been demanded ; but such refusals have not been persisted in, after the commencement of legal proceedings, or after due explanation has been given; and in no instance has any material difficulty arisen, where the magistrates have evinced a prompt and firm determination in carrying out the law." Whatever apprehensions may have been felt on this point, experience hitherto had therefore shown to be without foundation.

By the 53*rd and four following sections* of the Relief Act, the relatives of persons maintained in a workhouse are, when of sufficient ability, made liable for the cost of Liability of such maintenance ; and the boards of guardians relatives. were advised, whenever a case of this kind occurred, and the ability of the relatives was undoubted, to take the necessary steps for enforcing the law. That the guardians ought to do this can hardly admit of doubt, it being no less a legal than a social obligation. No fitting opportunity of pressing the fulfilment of this duty upon the guardians was therefore omitted, and an intention was expressed of continuing to do so—" in the conviction that the liabilities of natural relations, as established by the 53rd and following sections, were calculated to confer an important benefit upon the whole community."

The valuations of rateable property had now been The valua- completed in a hundred and ten of the unions, tions. and were in progress in all the others. Before the end of the present year they would it was expected be complete throughout Ireland, and confidence is expressed as to their general sufficiency, " without however venturing to assert that they are in every instance free from error." It was indeed said to be almost impossible that they should be so, the value of properties continually changing ; but they had attained a satisfactory state of average accuracy, and would, it was considered, become more and more correct through the successive revisions they will undergo previous to the imposition of every new rate. On the Municipal Corporations Act coming into operation in Dublin however, and when the poor-rate was taken as the basis of the municipal franchise, respecting the possession and exercise of which much excitement prevailed, the accuracy of the valuations was more closely scrutinised, and an inquiry with regard to the means for their revision was instituted. The result of the inquiry was, that although the valuations in their present state might be sufficient for poor-law purposes, yet with reference to the Municipal Act, it was desirable that a supervisor of the rates should be appointed in the unions comprising large towns. This was accordingly at once done in Dublin and Limerick, and was determined to be done in other places, as it should be found necessary. Instructions were at the same time prepared for the guidance of supervisors in the execution of this duty.

The Report on the medical charities in pursuance of the powers conferred by the 46*th and* 47*th sec-* tions *of the Poor Relief Act, was presented to* government shortly after the date of the last annual Report,[b] together with the evidence which had then been taken, and including " the heads of a proposed bill for the better regulation and support of the medical charities of Ireland." The remainder of the evidence was presented on the conclusion of the inquiry, and the whole was in due course laid before parliament. I was then the commissioner acting in Ireland, and being highly impressed with the importance of the numerous medical institutions, and with the necessity for their better support and regulation, I had bestowed much time and labour on the subject, and had earnestly endeavoured to devise the means of placing these valuable charities in a more secure condition with regard to their finances, and at the same time to improve the position of the medical practitioners by whose exertions they were in very many cases chiefly supported. All my efforts were directed to these ends, and to increasing the efficiency of the charities for the objects for which they were instituted. I was aware that there were difficulties to be overcome, arising from interested motives professional jealousies and misapprehensions; but there was no concealment, the course adopted was open, no pains were spared, able assistance had been obtained, and I was hopeful of success. The Report, with the heads of the proposed bill, was sent to every medical institution

Report on the medical charities.

---

b Ante, p. 268.

throughout Ireland, and had also been otherwise extensively circulated, without calling forth any expression of dissent, either from the medical profession or other parties; and with the sanction of government a bill was prepared in exact conformity with the headings set forth in the Report, and was about being introduced into parliament, when so violent an opposition was suddenly manifested by a great majority of the medical profession, that government deemed it inexpedient to proceed with the bill. The measure for "the better regulation and support of the medical charities in Ireland" was therefore suspended, but it was not abandoned; and the author had a few years afterwards the satisfaction of seeing a measure substantially the same as he had recommended, and founded on the inquiry which he had instituted, generally acquiesced in and become the law.[c]

Every attention was continued to be given for carrying Vaccination. into effect the provisions of the Vaccination Act, and no efforts were spared to realize the benevolent intentions of the legislature for extending the benefits of vaccination, and for preventing the occurrence and the spreading of smallpox. The Appendix to the Annual Report contains a return showing the numbers successfully vaccinated in each of 100 unions, the whole amounting to 104,713, a number fully equal to if not exceeding what could reasonably have been expected under the circumstances.

The prevalence of mendicancy continued to be felt as Mendicancy. a burden, and was very generally regarded as an evil which ought to be put an end to. It is true that the law did not confer an actual right to relief, and that the workhouses might possibly be sometimes inadequate for the reception of all who were in a state of destitution; but a rate was nevertheless made for the relief of the destitute, and the persons who were most helpless would be received into the workhouses. It was

---

[c] The 14th and 15th Vict. cap. 68. See post, p. 382.

therefore considered that means should be taken, if not
for putting an end to mendicancy altogether, at least for
its diminution in a ratio corresponding with the means
which had been provided for the relief of destitution.
Many of the boards of guardians had passed resolutions to this effect; and at a public meeting held in
Dublin for considering the subject, it was resolved to
apply to the Irish government, urging the necessity of
immediate steps being taken to put down the evil. The
prevalence of mendicancy was found to be a positive
obstacle to the working of the Poor Law. Thus in
some of the unions, after the stock of habitual mendicants had for the most part been taken into the workhouses, the ratepayers of particular electoral divisions
finding that the removal of what might be called their
own established poor did not protect them from mendicancy, but was followed by inroads of beggars from
other districts, deemed it better that their own poor
should be permitted to levy contributions from house to
house as theretofore, than that the ratepayers should
incur the charge of maintaining them in the workhouse,
and at the same time be called upon for contributions
to the mendicants by whom their doors were beset. If
the mendicancy clauses in the Poor Relief Bill as
originally framed had been retained, these evils would
have been prevented, and the repression of begging
would have kept pace with the administration of relief
under the Poor Law; but in the passage of the measure
through parliament, these clauses, as before stated, were
withdrawn, and no step had subsequently been taken for
their re-enactment in any shape, as was understood to
be intended at the time.[d]

During the greater portion of the last year, excessive
rains and a general prevalence of cold ungenial
weather affected both the grain and the potato
crops, which were in consequence neither so
early, so good, nor so abundant, as under more

Unfavour-
able weather,
backward
crops, and
consequent
distress.

---

[d] Ante, p. 211.

favourable circumstances they might have been. The same had been the case in the two or three previous years; and this succession of adverse seasons necessarily tended to increase the distress which usually more or less prevails in Ireland, especially in the western districts, during the months of June July and August. But notwithstanding the existence of much distress from these causes, it was in the present as in the preceding year met and overcome by the energies of the people themselves, without aid from government as on former like occasions; a circumstance which must be regarded as indicative of improved habits, and as warranting hopeful anticipations with regard to the future.

At the date of the last Report (May 1st 1842), the 1843. whole of Ireland had been formed into 130 unions, all the workhouses were either built or in progress of building, and 81 had been declared fit for the reception of destitute poor. It was then likewise expected that by midsummer of the following year all the workhouses throughout Ireland would be in operation.[e] This expectation however was not fulfilled, for at the date of the present Report (1st May 1843) no more than 110 of the workhouses had been declared, and in only 98 of these was relief administered. In the earlier proceedings, it had been the practice to declare and bring the workhouses into operation as quickly as possible, leaving certain minor matters to be more leisurely completed afterwards. This was done, often at some inconvenience, in order to give effect to the law at the earliest practicable period. But it was now deemed more expedient to have the workhouse and all the arrangements fully completed before bringing it into operation; and hence a period longer or shorter according to circumstances, would necessarily intervene between the declaration of the house and the

Margin note: 1843. Fifth report of proceedings in Ireland.

---

[e] Ante, p. 271.

actual admission of applicants by the guardians. This accounts for relief being administered in only 98 of the houses, although 110 had been declared. It may also account for the non-fulfilment of the expectation which had been expressed, as to the declaration of the whole of the workhouses.

In the 37 unions, the workhouses of which were in operation previous to the 1st of January 1842, the numbers then relieved and the amount of expenditure have already been stated.[f] On the 1st of January 1843 the numbers relieved in these unions amounted to 17,529, and the expenditure to 150,050*l*., thus showing an increase in the former of 2,283 persons, and in the latter of 39,773*l*. And in 55 other unions in which the workhouses had been brought into operation in course of the preceding year, the numbers relieved on the 1st of January 1843 amounted to 14,043, and the expenditure to 131,183*l*., making when added to the above—31,572[g] persons receiving relief in 92 workhouses, at a cost of 281,233*l*. The comparative amount of relief administered in the years 1840, 1841, and 1842 will thus stand as follows—

(marginal note: Cost of relief and numbers relieved.)

	No. of workhouses in operation.	No. of inmates.	Cost of relief in the previous year.
On the 1st of January 1841	4	5,468	£37,057
„ 1842	37	15,246	110,277
„ 1843	92	31,572	281,233

In connexion with this statement of the relief afforded during these three years, it should be borne in mind that the relief was administered in workhouses so re-gulated as not to deter the really destitute from availing themselves of the shelter afforded, whilst the discipline and regularity of the establishment made it an un-welcome residence for such of the able-bodied as had the means of supporting themselves by their own exertions.

---

[f] Ante, p. 277.

[g] Although this was the total number in the 92 workhouses on the 1st of January 1843, no less than 56,000 had been admitted and discharged, and consequently relieved for a longer or shorter period, during the previous year.

At the end of 1842, the author quitted Ireland. The
The author charge and direction of the proceedings in
quits Ireland. that country, had hitherto from the commencement been devolved upon him; and as these were so
far advanced as to leave no doubt with regard to their
completion, and as the commissioners were jointly responsible for carrying the law into effect, it was considered desirable that his colleagues should now take
their full share in the management of the Irish business.
It was intended that each of the commissioners should
reside for a time in Dublin, when and as it might be
found necessary, as had been recommended in the
author's first Report, and as is provided for by the 11*th*
section of the Act. This arrangement was accordingly
acted upon, but only for a short time, it not being
deemed satisfactory; and with the sanction of the Home
Office, it was determined to delegate to two of the
assistant-commissioners the powers necessary for conducting the Irish business,[h] this being considered, it is
said—" a course more consistent with the intention of
the legislature as expressed in the Irish Poor Relief
Act." The author will now therefore be relieved from
a difficulty he has hitherto experienced in regard to
the proceedings in Ireland. With these proceedings he
will no longer be individually connected, and may
advert to them with greater freedom, as being the acts
of the commission collectively.

Before leaving Ireland, I visited the several unions,
Inspection and inspected all the workhouses whether
of the work-
houses. completed or in course of erection, as I had
done in previous years, for the purpose of satisfying
myself with respect to the arrangements and management in the former case, and as to the condition
and progress of the works in the latter. The result
of this inspection was for the most part satisfactory.

---

[h] The gentlemen selected for this duty were Mr. Gulson and Mr. Power:
and the instrument of delegation is dated 20th April 1843.

There were exceptions, no doubt, and in two instances owing to the bankruptcy of the contractors, the houses had to be in great measure built, and entirely fitted up and completed by the Dublin Board. But on the whole, the contractors had fulfilled, and were fulfilling their engagements satisfactorily. The workhouses in operation were also managed in a creditable manner; and the guardians were generally attending to the business of their respective unions with regularity and efficiency. I quitted Ireland therefore without apprehending the occurrence of any material difficulty or delay, and looked forward with confidence to the early and universal establishment of the law, and with a deep sense of thankfulness for the prospect which was afforded of its successful operation.

In the early part of the summer of 1842, the weather having continued unfavourable, distress again Distress, and manifested itself especially in the western dis- government aid. tricts, as had been the case in the three preceding years; and it was considered necessary that some assistance should be afforded, and that the people should not be left entirely to their own resources, as on the two last occasions. Accordingly on the application of the Irish government, coupled with an intimation of its desire to extend its aid "in such a way as not to prejudice or embarrass the future proceedings of the commissioners," the assistant-commissioners in charge of the districts where the distress prevailed, were directed to give all the facilities in their power by making inquiries and furnishing information on the cases forwarded to them, preparatory to the distribution of such aid as the government might think fit to bestow.[i] But before the end of June the weather changed, and became so favourable as to promise abundant crops. The

---

[i] The amount distributed by government on this occasion, in aid of local subscriptions, was 3,448*l.* See 'The Irish Crisis' by Sir Charles Trevelyan, p. 19.

markets immediately fell, and the scarcity, which had arisen rather from the holding back of supply than from any general deficiency, no longer existed.

These facts appear to indicate, that a portion of the distress which periodically takes place in Ireland, may be referred to a cause, the operation of which is likely to be increased by grants of public money; for provisions are said to be sometimes accumulated in the stores of persons who will not bring them to market, under the expectation of being able to dispose of them at a famine price as soon as government shall be induced, on the plea of distress, to make an advance of public money for the purpose. Wherever the union workhouse was in operation, it proved of the greatest use throughout these periods of difficulty, from whatever cause arising. It not only afforded efficient relief in numerous cases where it was needed, but likewise effectually tested the representations of distress which were continually being made. The fluctuations in the numbers admitted and discharged, afforded moreover the means of forming from time to time a correct judgment on the condition of the poor in the surrounding district, and was thus an index of the intensity of the distress wherever it existed.

Applications had been frequently made both to the Pauper luna- Irish government, and to the Board in Dublin, tics. representing that if the idiotic and harmless lunatics then confined in the gaols or maintained in the lunatic asylums, were transferred to the workhouses of the unions to which they belonged, those institutions would be greatly relieved, more especially the asylums, which would then be enabled to receive more curable cases, and thus extend their usefulness. To such communications it had always been replied—" that the Irish Poor Relief Act made no provision for the support of insane and lunatic persons, specially as such; but that a destitute person, being insane or lunatic, might be admitted into the workhouse if the guardians so decided, in the same manner as any other destitute individual." To provide for cases of this description, idiot wards had been prepared in every workhouse, which were calculated to afford accommodation for about 2,400 of this class of paupers, whenever the guardians in the exercise of their discretion, should think fit to admit them. It had however been thought right to discourage any forced or immediate transfer of insane or idiotic persons or harmless lunatics from the asylums and gaols, but rather to wait for the gradual absorption by the workhouses of such of these unfortunates as could be properly relieved therein.

Fruitless efforts were made, particularly at Cork and Belfast, to raise the funds necessary for defraying the expense of emigration. In Cork, Emigration. Dublin, Waterford, Belfast, and certain other large towns, a considerable number of young persons chiefly females, and for the most part the remnants of a former system, had as has been before stated,[k] accumulated in the workhouses, for whom emigration would afford at once the most eligible, and it may almost be said the only outlet. Yet in the present state of the law, it was found nearly if not quite impossible to take advantage of it. The workhouses had not created the present burden, but they had gathered it into mass, and might be made useful auxiliaries to a well-directed plan of emigration. The commissioners declared that it would materially facilitate this object, if the boards of guardians were empowered to apply a portion of the rates for the emigration of such fit persons as had been resident sufficiently long in the workhouse for testing their actual helplessness and destitution. This would in fact be reverting to what was originally proposed, but which had been altered in the progress of the bill through the house of

---

[k] Ante, p. 275.

lords, by substituting divisional chargeability for that of the entire union—a change to which is mostly owing whatever difficulties have since occurred in the working of the measure.

The 18*th and* 44*th sections* of the Relief Act provide

Electoral divisions. for dividing the unions into electoral divisions, and for charging against each electoral division not only its proportion of the general expenses of the union, but also the expense incurred for the relief of persons stated in the registry to have been resident in such electoral division ; the relief of others not stated to have been so resident, being charged against the union at large. These provisions were inserted in the bill in the house of lords, on the motion of the duke of Wellington, with the professed view of assimilating the mechanism of the Irish unions to the unions in England ; but the circumstances in the two countries were widely different, and there would be little analogy between the long-established English parish, and the newly-created electoral divisions. This difference was however overlooked in the desire for assimilation, and the electoral division system was incorporated in the Act, together with a sort of quasi settlement as between the different divisions, approximating to settlement as between parishes in the English unions. Under these circumstances, it can hardly occasion surprise, that although arranged with the utmost care, and with every endeavour to give them a general harmony and coherence, the electoral divisions did not work smoothly. Their separate chargeability interfered with the efficient action of the unions for general purposes, as in the case of emigration, and led to struggles and contention in the boards of guardians as soon as the unions got fully into operation, each division endeavouring to relieve itself from the charge of a registered pauper, by fixing it upon some other, or by casting it upon the union at large ; and thus one of the evils of the English settlement-law was inflicted upon the Irish unions, contrary to the intentions of the original framers of the Act, and contrary likewise to what a more thorough knowledge of the condition of the two countries would it is believed have dictated.

There was moreover still considerable difficulty with respect to the valuations, and the difficulty was not a little increased by the complexity of the form in which the rate is directed to be made out. This form is expressly prescribed by the Amendment Act, and is rather calculated for the state of things in England, than for what exists in Ireland, although it is too minute and complex to admit of its working satisfactorily in either. The form was engrafted on the bill in the house of lords, with a view to other than poor-law purposes, and contrary to the author's earnest representations. As the number and the business of the unions increased, it was found nearly impossible to adhere to this form, owing to the extreme subdivision of property.[m] In all the 130 unions the number of persons rated whose valuations did not exceed 5*l.* was 630,272, whilst the number whose valuations were above that amount was 550,866, and those at 50*l.* and upwards 46,565 ; thus showing that a considerable majority of the ratepayers were valued at and under 5*l.*[n] Believing that such would turn out to be the case, the author had recom-

Valuation and rating.

---

[m] See the author's first Report on Irish Poor Laws, p. 160.

[n] These numbers were ascertained by returns which the author had obtained in 1842, and caused to be tabulated by desire of the Irish government, with a view to the parliamentary franchise. The same returns show that the net annual value of property assessed to the relief of the poor in Ireland, was 13,428,787*l.* ; but more exact returns subsequently obtained place the amount at 13,253,825*l.* The annual value of property assessed to the poor-rate in England and Wales at that time was 62,540,003*l.*—See return to an order of the house of commons dated 3rd May 1842. Both of these valuations are no doubt below the actual amount, probably by 20 or 25 per cent. ; but of the two, the Irish valuation is perhaps somewhat nearer the truth than the other.

mended that no occupier under 5*l.* should be called
upon to pay the poor-rate, but that the rate on all such
holdings should be paid by the landlord. It was however provided by the 72*nd section* of the Act, that
instead of the exemption of 5*l.* holdings, the landlord
might agree to pay the rate himself, and be allowed a
rebate of 10 per cent. for so doing : but this provision
has not been acted upon, and all the small tenements
are required to be rated in the complex form of the
2*nd schedule* of the Act, comprising no less than eighteen distinctive columns, under penalty of the rates
being deemed illegal. There can be no doubt that in
the abstract, as the commissioners observe, " all property should contribute to the rate, and the whole
population be interested in the prevention of pauperism,
and in the well-being of the class for whose immediate
benefit statutory provision has been made." But the
small ratepayers in Ireland are so numerous, and the
amounts to be severally collected from them are so
trifling, whilst the distinction between them and the
destitute is often so little perceptible, that Ireland seems
to constitute an exception to the general rule in this
respect ; and it would be a great convenience, and tend
to facilitate the working of the Poor Law, if as was
at first proposed, the burden of the rate on the smaller
holdings were to be thrown upon the owner or immediate lessor, rather than on the tenant himself.

The defects above noticed are explained and com-
mented upon at great length in the fifth Report. They
no doubt impede the orderly working of the law, and
add to the labours and embarrass the proceedings of
the entire executive ; but they do not affect the principle of the measure, nor very materially detract from
its usefulness. They are of a different origin from the
measure itself, having been grafted upon the bill in its
progress through parliament ; and they will no doubt
be removed, or so modified as to be less obstructive

than at present, to which end they were now brought prominently under notice.

The Report of 1844, like those preceding, is dated the 1st of May; and it will be convenient to commence the account of the year's proceedings with a summary of the Act for amending the law, which was passed on the 24th August 1843, and which what is said above will have prepared the reader to expect. 1844. Sixth report of proceedings in Ireland.

Summary of the 6th and 7th Vict. cap. 92.

For the further Amendment of the Law for the Relief of the Poor in Ireland.

Sections 1, 2.—That where the property rated is not of greater value than 4*l.*, or in certain boroughs named than 8*l.*, the rate on such property shall be made on the immediate lessor, and if his name be not known he may be rated as " the immediate lessor;" and the rate is to be recoverable together with costs, notwithstanding any defect or error in the name, by action, or by civil bill, or by complaint before a justice, but no action is to be brought without consent of the Poor Law Commissioners.

Sections 3, 4.—If a rate be not paid by the lessor in four months, it may be recovered from the occupier, who in such case may deduct the amount from the rent due to the lessor, or recover it from him. If a house be let in lodgings, the lessor is to be rated for the whole house, and if the rate be not paid within thirty-one days, it may be recovered from the occupiers, who will be entitled to deduct it from the rent due by them; but the Municipal Corporations Act is not to be affected by any of these provisions.

Sections 5, 6.—When the property rated is above 5*l.*, the lessors may in like manner be rated instead of the occupiers, if both enter into a written agreement for the purpose, and if the guardians consent thereto. All goods and chattels to whomsoever belonging, found on premises for which the occupier is liable to pay rate, may be distrained for the same.

Sections 7, 8.—To remove certain doubts with regard to valuators and valuations, the commissioners are empowered to appoint valuators, or they may direct the guardians to do so; and the person so in either case appointed, may enter premises for the purpose of making or revising any survey or valuation ; and rates are to be assessed on the valuations so made or revised, and sealed by the commissioners ; and are not to be altered unless appealed against, when on receiving a copy of the order of court amending such rate, the commissioners are to authorize its alteration in conformity therewith. The appeal in all cases is to be made to the sessions of the peace of the county, or county of a city or town within which the hereditaments are situate.

Sections 9, 10, 11.—Any person affected by a rate, may on all days except Sunday, between ten o'clock and four, inspect the valuation on which the rate is made, and take copies thereof. The form of rate prescribed by the Amendment Act is repealed, and the commissioners are empowered to prescribe the form in which the rates are to be made. The clerk to certify that the rate when made conforms to the valuation, and the chairman and two or more of the guardians present are to certify that they allow the same. In Dublin the poor-rate is to be collected in the same manner and with the like remedies as the grand jury cess.

Sections 12, 13.—The residence required in order that the expense of relief may be charged to an electoral division in any case, is the occupation of a tenement for eighteen months, or having usually slept within such division for twelve months before the person's admission to the workhouse. The expense of all others not having so occupied or slept, is to be charged against the whole union. If a person after quitting the workhouse be again admitted within six months, the expense of such person is to be charged as before. The charge of every child admitted, is to conform with that of the person liable for its maintenance. The guardian or any three or more ratepayers of an electoral division, may with consent of the commissioners appeal against its being separately charged in any case.

Sections 14, 15, 16.—The guardians, subject to the commissioners' approval, may send any poor deaf and dumb or blind child under the age of eighteen, to a deaf and dumb or blind institution, and defray the expense of its maintenance therein ; and may also defray the expense of conveying any poor person from the workhouse to a fever hospital or lunatic asylum and his maintenance therein. Persons affected with fever or other contagious disease, may be relieved in houses hired for the purpose under the commissioners' regulations, and the expense be charged upon the rates.

Section 17.—The guardians may charge the rates with any expense reasonably incurred, in apprehending or prosecuting offenders against the provisions of any of the Poor-law Acts.

Section 18.—Two-thirds of the guardians of any union, subject to the regulations of the commissioners, may assist any poor person who has been in the workhouse for three months, to emigrate to a British colony, and may charge the expense on the union, or on the electoral division to which such poor person has been chargeable ; but the entire amount of such expense is not in any one year to exceed sixpence in the pound on the net annual value of the rateable property of the union or the electoral division respectively.

Sections 19, 20, 21.—If the number of ex-officio guardians be reduced by death removal or disqualification, the commissioners may appoint a day for the election of another ex-officio guardian in the place of the one so removed. A person put in nomination for an elected guardian, may refuse by notice in writing to serve the office ; and in case of vacancy or refusal to act, the commissioners may order a fresh election if they think fit, but not otherwise.

Sections 22, 23.—A person convicted of felony fraud or perjury, or adjudged liable to forfeiture under the provisions of the Poor Law, is incapacitated for acting as a guardian. The commissioners empowered to inquire into and decide disputes in regard to the elections.

Sections 24, 25.—Notice of claims to vote by owners and proxies, extended from one week to one calendar month. Any person knowingly tendering a false claim to vote, or forging falsifying or altering any such claim, or altering carrying off destroying or defacing any voting-paper, subjected to a penalty of ten pounds.

Sections 26, 27.—In case of reasonable doubt in regard to any claim, the returning officer may refuse the vote until proof of its correctness be produced. Ratepayers, guardians, and union officers, not incapacitated for giving evidence.

Section 28.—This and the two previous Acts (1*st and* 2*nd, and* 2*nd Vict. cap.* 56 *and* 1) to be construed as one Act, except where otherwise provided.

The alterations made by the above Act relate exclusively to matters of detail. There is no change of principle in the measure. The electoral division system remains entire, except only as regards emigration, the expense of which the guardians have now the option of making either a union or a divisional charge. The definition of residence for establishing the chargeability of an electoral division, may be of some practical convenience, and would amount to a law of settlement if a power of removal were given; but as it is, it will merely in a slight degree facilitate the working of the divisional system. The abolition of the previous complicated form of rate is no doubt an advantage, as is also the power of rating the immediate lessors in certain cases, instead of leaving it optional with them to compound for the rates of their tenantry as before. The provisions in regard to fever cases will be of much use, especially as the measure proposed for regulating the medical charities was not carried into effect.° The additional powers given to the commissioners in election cases are likewise desirable; and it may indeed be said of the Act generally, that it is calculated to remedy certain minor defects and omissions, and to promote the more orderly working of the law.

We will now turn to the commissioners' Report of 1844, which commences by declaring that " The administration of relief of the poor in Ireland had been attended with some difficulties during the past year, arising in a great measure from the political influences which had agitated that country." The influences and agitations here alluded to, were connected with the great movement for a repeal of the Union, stirred up and organized by the late Mr. O'Connell, the consequences of which were in various ways exceedingly pernicious, diverting the people from their legitimate and necessary occupations, exciting jealousy and ill-feeling towards England, inculcating distrust of the government, weakening the authority of law, and inciting to a resistance of whatever was established, of course including the Poor Law. Some indications of this

---

° Ante, p. 280.

hostility appeared before the author quitted Ireland towards the end of 1842, but shortly afterwards it was openly manifested, and the Poor Law was declaimed against as being an intolerable burden inflicted and enforced by England and English officials, and that it ought consequently to be opposed by every true Irishman.

Under these circumstances, and in the then state of Ireland, it cannot excite surprise that there should be resistance to the law, and that efforts should be made to evade its provisions. As early as the end of 1842 there had been resistance to payment of the rates in some of the divisions of the Skibbereen and Waterford unions, which afterwards extended to Tipperary and several other unions in different parts of Ireland. At Skibbereen indeed a death had unhappily occurred, through the violent resistance made to the constabulary while assisting the collectors in levying the rates. In a return made to an order of the house of commons, 21 unions are named as having down to the 1st of January 1844, so far resisted the payment of the poor-rates as to require the intervention of the constabulary or the military to enforce the collection. In 11 of these unions, a military as well as constabulary force was deemed necessary. In the other 10, the constabulary alone were found sufficient to protect the collectors in the execution of their duty. But it was not alone resistance to the rates which obstructed the working of the law; in the Tuam union a rate was made in October 1842,[p] but no part of it had been collected on the 1st of January 1844. This was not owing to resistance on the part of the ratepayers, but to the unwillingness of the guardians to proceed in the administration of relief. The workhouse, capable

Resistance to the law.

---

[p] The rate amounted to 1,796*l*. The population of the union exceeded 70,000.

of accommodating 800 persons, had been declared fit for the reception of destitute poor in August 1842, a master matron medical officer and porter had been appointed, but such was the backwardness of the guardians in fulfilling the requirements of the law, that no case of destitution however urgent, was or could be relieved except by application to some neighbouring union.

Even after the workhouse had been opened, and relief therein administered, there were several instances of unwillingness on the part of the guardians to make rates of sufficient amount to meet the liabilities of the union, and at the same time to provide for the relief of the poor. Some of the boards moreover refused to borrow and charge the rates with the sums necessary to cover the expense of building the workhouses, on the alleged ground of dissatisfaction with the architect's certificates in favour of the contractors, or of the manner in which the work had been executed.[q] Legal proceedings against the guardians were in consequence taken on account of these refusals, and much expense was thus injudiciously incurred, whilst the poor were curtailed of their needful relief. The contracts entered into under such circumstances for supplying the workhouse, if they could be made at all, were necessarily made on extremely disadvantageous terms ; and thus the intentions of the legislature were frustrated, and disaffection towards the law was generated, by the very parties appointed to carry out the one, and guard against the occurrence of the other. Several unions are named in the Report, in which such was or had been the case, and in one (Carrick on Shannon) a poor

---

[q] The complaints of the architect's certificates were not confined to the guardians, for whilst these complained of his too liberal allowance of charges, the contractors complained that their charges were unduly cut down. Both complaints were however totally without foundation, and in fact one negatived the other.

man had died in consequence of being refused relief. Yet there can be no doubt that where the unions were properly in operation, a large amount of actual destitution and extreme suffering was effectually met by opportune relief afforded in the workhouses. In many cases however the poor people were so reduced as to be in an extremely debilitated state when admitted, and they often died shortly afterwards. In this worst extremity to which, in a physical sense, a human being can be exposed, an institution affording shelter, medical attendance, and the last consolations of religion, must surely be one of the most effective forms in which relief can be administered, more especially among a population such as exists in Ireland.

Much dissatisfaction continued to be expressed with regard to the apportioning the charge of relief upon the several electoral divisions. Those in which the rated property was large, and the number of poor inconsiderable, complained of the proportion they had to pay towards the common charges of the union, whilst the amount of relief required by them was so small. The divisions on the contrary in which the number of paupers was considerable, and the amount of relief bore a large proportion to their rated value, complained of the high rate of poundage to which they were subjected, in comparison with the other divisions. The change now made in the law may help gradually to reconcile although it does not remove these distinctions. As new admissions take place, the proportion charged upon the union at large would most likely increase, and there would thus be a closer approximation towards an equal rating of the whole union. But many boards of guardians expressed themselves as not satisfied with this gradual and partial change, and declared themselves favourable to a union rate, whereby all charges would be borne by an equal poundage-rate over the several electoral divisions. That these guar-

dians took a correct view of the question seems hardly
to admit of doubt. They had seen the evils of divisional chargeability, and wished to apply the obvious
remedy by bringing the law back to what was
originally proposed ; but the time for so doing had not
arrived, and the evils and inconveniences were still to
be continued, although perhaps in a somewhat mitigated form.

At the date of the present Report (1st May 1844)
Collection of resistance to the collection of the rates was in
the rates. great measure overcome, and the authority of
the law vindicated. The general results of the collection
are stated to have been as follows—In 98 of the unions,
in which the rates made previously to the 24th August
1843 amounted to 605,864*l.*, there remained uncollected
on the 1st January 1844 only 46,322*l.*, or something less
than 8 per cent. of the entire amount. But it must not
be supposed that even the whole of this arrear was col-
lectable. All tenements, whether occupied or not, are
usually included in the rate, the infinite number of
small tenements making it impossible to distinguish
with certainty what are unoccupied at the time the rate
is made ; and it is only the occupied tenements which
pay. Public property legally exempt is also often included in the rate, and the arrears in the South Dublin
union amounting to 4,479*l.*, are likely to include sums
of this nature. On the whole therefore, it appeared to
the commissioners, that " considering the great difficulty
of collecting the rates from the occupiers of very small
tenements, on which class a large portion of the entire
rate is laid, these results would not be regarded as un-
satisfactory."

In order to secure regularity and efficiency in the
Auditors ap- collections, and the proper keeping of the union
pointed. accounts, it was determined to appoint four
auditors, who would be employed exclusively in that
capacity ; and it is expected that they would be the

means of establishing a greater degree of uniformity as well as accuracy throughout all the unions in Ireland.

Fourteen workhouses had been brought into operation in course of the year 1843, the cost of relief administered in which amounted to 23,277*l*., Cost of relief, and numbers relieved. and the number of inmates to 1,529, on the 1st of January 1844—on which day the number of inmates in the 92 workhouses in operation prior to 1843 was 31,981, and the cost of relief 221,097*l*. So that the entire number of persons relieved on 1st January 1844 in 106 workhouses was 33,510, and the cost of relief during the year amounted to 244,374*l*. This appears less than in the preceding year, but the difference is probably owing to the much greater number of workhouses which were opened in 1843, and the extra expenditure always attendant upon first bringing the houses into operation. By a statistical table appended to the Report, the total number of inmates of all classes in the several workhouses on 31st January 1845, is shown to have been 43,293, of whom 9,231 were able-bodied (that is 2,809 males and 6,422 females) and 11,441 were disabled through sickness age or other infirmity. Another minutely framed table in the Appendix to the Report shows, that of 27,529 adults above the age of fifteen, and 22,585 children under that age, 5,942 of the former were widows, and 3,622 widowers; and that of the children 19,886 were legitimate (4,164 being orphans) and 2,639 were illegitimate.

The Report of 1st May 1845, commences by declaring that "the administration of the law in Ireland 1845. Seventh report of proceedings in Ireland.* had proceeded satisfactorily upon the whole since the date of the last Report." The instances of resistance to the collection of the rates, or in which violence had occurred, were comparatively few,

---

* This forms a part of the eleventh Report of the Poor Law Commissioners.

and the financial embarrassments which had operated prejudicially in several of the unions, had for the most part ceased. There were altogether 118 workhouses open for the purposes of relief. Of the 12 which remained, 3 were not yet declared fit for the reception of inmates, and in a few instances the guardians still neglected or refused to proceed in duly administering relief, although the workhouses had long since been declared. The most remarkable instance of this kind was in the Tuam union; but the commissioners had deemed it right to proceed against the Tuam guardians by mandamus, and their submission to the authority of the law was shortly expected. Meantime however they had, it is said, been sued for debts which they did not hesitate to incur, although they neglected to provide the means of payment.

Many of the unions had taken steps under the 15*th* Provision for *and* 16*th sections* of the late Amendment Act, fever cases. for providing for the relief of persons suffering from fever or other contagious complaints, either by building fever wards distinct from the workhouses, or hiring premises for the purpose, or by arranging for the reception of such cases into fever hospitals; and the result had in several instances been highly beneficial. " In Galway for example, during a severe epidemic, the guardians erected a temporary hospital near the workhouse, and received into it during a period of about six months 1,096 cases, of which 995 were discharged cured."

A statement is given in the Appendix to the Report, Vaccination. showing the progress made in bringing the Vaccination Act into operation in Ireland. By this statement it appears that, although not duly carried out in several of the unions, the measure had obtained a wide and beneficial operation, and was in course of gradual extension. The amount expended for vaccination in all the unions during the previous year, exceeded 4,000*l.*, the rate of payment being 1*s.* on each case successfully vaccinated for the first two hundred cases, and 6d. on each successful case afterwards. This is one of the charges for which the poor-rate is made liable, although not strictly appertaining to the relief of the poor; but it is no doubt calculated to prevent a far greater charge, by protecting the people against the smallpox, a fearful scourge which generally leaves disablement and destitution in its train.

In the 106 workhouses which had been opened prior to 1844, the number of inmates on the 1st of January 1845 was 37,701, and the expenditure on relief amounted to 251,467l.[s] In the 7 workhouses declared in course of that year, the number of inmates on January 1st 1845 was 1,474, and the expenditure 18,063l., making the total number of persons relieved on that day in 113 workhouses amount to 39,175, and the expenditure on relief during the year to 269,530l. The average weekly cost of the inmates of the workhouses was 1s. 5½d. per head for maintenance, and 2½d. for clothing, making together 1s. 8d. per head. The cost had at the outset been estimated at 1s. 6d. per head.[t] Rates were made in 126 of the unions, in all in fact excepting four[u] situate in the extreme west; but in 8 of the unions in which rates had been made, the workhouses were still not in operation. The commissioners trusted however, that they would " be enabled to report next year that the whole of the 130 workhouses in Ireland were open for the reception and relief of the destitute poor, in accordance with the intention of the legislature, and the provisions of the Irish Poor Relief Act."

On comparing the expenditure with the net annual value of property rateable in each union, it will be found that it does not on an average amount to sixpence

Cost of relief, and numbers relieved.

---

[s] No return could be obtained from the Athlone union, which is one of the 106, and its operations are therefore not included in these amounts.

[t] See author's memorandum at page 209 ante.

[u] These were Cahirciveen, Clifden, Glenties, and Milford.

in the pound. The expenditure moreover includes the instalments which had been repaid on account of the workhouse loans; but as there was a large arrear of these instalments then due, and few of the workhouses had their full complement of inmates, it was thought likely that the average might be higher by and bye, although not so much higher as to afford reasonable ground for dissatisfaction or alarm. The aggregate of the loans granted by government for building and fitting up the workhouses amounted to 1,140,350*l.*, or about 1*s.* 8*d.* in the pound, on the net annual value of rateable property in Ireland, that is a poundage of somewhat less than 1*d.* in the pound per annum for repayment of the money borrowed. The poundage varied considerably however in different unions, according to the proportion the cost of the workhouse bore to the value of the rateable property.

Advantage was at this time taken of the experience acquired during the five years that the law had been in operation, to revise the orders and regulations which were at first promulgated. And accordingly an amended order was issued for the election of guardians, together with a new circular of instructions to the clerks of unions with regard to the duties to be performed by them as returning officers. An amended general order was also issued regulating the proceedings of boards of guardians, and defining the duties of union officers; and likewise a general order containing amended regulations for the management of workhouses, together with a new form for the half-yearly abstract of accounts, with ample instructions thereon. In short, nothing in the way of regulation which came within the powers confided to the commissioners, was omitted or neglected; and all resistance to the payment of the poor-rates having ceased, it was hoped that henceforward the working of the law would everywhere proceed in an orderly and effective manner.

Issue of amended orders.

CHAPTER V.

Eighth Report of proceedings — Failure of the potato — A fourth commis-
sioner appointed — Ninth Report — Potato disease in 1846 — Public
Works Act — Distress in autumn 1846 — Labour-rate Act — Relief-works
— Temporary Relief Act — Pressure upon workhouses — Emigration —
Financial state of unions — First Annual Report of Poor-Law Commis-
sioners for Ireland — Extension Act — Act for Punishment of Vagrants —
Act to provide for execution of Poor Laws — General import of the new
Acts — Change of the commission — Dissolution of boards of guardians
— Report of Temporary Relief Act Commissioners — British Association
— Second Annual Report of Poor-Law Commissioners — Recurrence of
potato disease — Cholera — Rate-in-Aid Act — Further dissolution of
boards of guardians — Boundary commission — Select committee on Irish
Poor Laws — Expenditure, and numbers relieved.

THE Report for 1845-6, like those of preceding years, is dated on the 1st of May, and represents the progress of the law during the previous twelve months as being on the whole satisfactory. All the workhouses were open and the rates in course of collection, except in the two small unions of Clifden and Cahirciveen, in each of which however the guardians had taken steps for making a rate and opening the workhouse.

(marginal note) 1846. Eighth report of proceedings in Ireland.[a]

The number of persons relieved in the several workhouses continued to increase throughout the present year, the total number amounting to 114,205. In the week ending 27th December 1845 the number so relieved was 41,218, whilst in the week ending 28th March 1846 (the last for which the returns were complete) the number was 50,717, being an increase of 9,499 in three months, and indicating that the distress which had now become very general was beginning to press upon the workhouses. The number described as able-bodied was 8,246, that

(marginal note) Numbers relieved, and cost of relief.

---

[a] This eighth Report of proceedings in Ireland, is included in the twelfth Report of the Poor Law Commissioners; but as before stated it has been thought better to keep the Irish portion of the Reports distinct from the other, and to give them a separate number.

is 1,984 males and 6,262 females. The total expenditure on relief of the poor during the preceding year in the 113 unions of which the workhouses were opened prior to 1845, amounted on the 1st of January 1846 to 298,813*l.* The number of inmates at that date was 40,876. In the 10 other unions the workhouses of which were opened in the course of 1845, the expenditure on relief amounted to 17,213*l.*, and the number of inmates to 1,192,—so that on January 1st 1846 there were 42,068 poor persons relieved in 123 workhouses, and the entire cost of relief during the year amounted to 316,026*l.*

The financial state of the unions generally, appears to have been satisfactory. In the monthly returns for February 1846, comprising 128 unions, the rates collected during the month amounted to 41,871*l.*, leaving 206,664*l.* in course of collection. The aggregate of the balances against the guardians in 25 unions was 5,294*l.*, whilst in the remaining 103 unions, the whole of the balances were in favour of the guardians and amounted to 54,314*l.*, thus showing a net balance of 49,020*l.* in the hands of the treasurers. This sum added to what was in course of collection, making together 255,684*l.*, must be regarded as sufficient for covering an expenditure of say 320,000*l.* per annum, the rates in a great number of the unions being made half-yearly.

The number of electoral divisions amounted to 2,049, Electoral di- each on an average containing a population of visions.   about 4,000 persons. The dissatisfaction expressed in many instances with the divisional system, and with the inequalities of charge to which it gave rise, has already been noticed.[b] The 44*th section* of the Poor Relief Act seeks to provide a remedy for, or at least a mitigation of such inequalities, by enabling the guardians of the several divisions of a union to agree to a common rating : but it is evident that wherever the inequality

---

[b] Ante, p. 288.

of rating is greatest, there will be the greatest difficulty in effecting such an arrangement. In fact the only instance in which it has been effected is in the Dunmanway union, where the guardians of all the electoral divisions signed an agreement in the terms of the statute, that the charges should thenceforth be borne in common. In this union therefore one great source of contention will have been removed, although at a sacrifice in some degree of that local interest which attaches to guardians representing a district separately chargeable: but enough of such interest will remain in a common chargeability to secure attention to the general interests of the union, in which all that is exclusively local will become merged; and it may therefore be expected that the well-working of the Dunmanway board will not be impeded through a want of harmony among its members.

The Tuam guardians, against whom judgment had been pronounced under the proceedings by mandamus, as noticed in the last Report,[c] although professing compliance with the peremptory order issued by the court, were still backward in fulfilling the duties which the law imposed upon them, as were also the guardians of the Castlereagh union. The commissioners therefore deemed it right to dissolve both these boards, on whom it was evident that reliance could not be placed for an effective administration of the law, in the impending season of scarcity and distress through the failure of the potato crop; and it was at the same time intimated, that if the boards elected in lieu of those dissolved " failed to discharge effectually their duties as guardians of the poor," paid officers would be appointed under the 26*th section* of the Relief Act to carry its provisions into execution. " It is satisfactory (the commissioners observe), prepared as we are

The Tuam and Castlereagh boards dissolved.

---

[c] Ante, p. 300.

in case of necessity to resort to the exercise of those powers, that we have, in the first instance, always endeavoured to give effect to the views of the legislature, when resisted, by an appeal to judicial authority. We still trust that the decisions which the Court of Queen's Bench has pronounced in vindication of the law, and which have invariably been followed by submission elsewhere, will finally have their due effect in the Tuam and Castlereagh unions, and render unnecessary the appointment of paid officers to perform the functions of guardians in those unions."

Considerable progress had been made in providing for poor persons afflicted with fever. In 50 of the unions, fever wards in connexion with the workhouses were either built or in course of building, and in others houses had been hired for the purpose, or temporary provision was made until fever wards could be erected. Arrangements had likewise been made for sending fever patients from the workhouses to county fever hospitals, and no pains were spared in urging upon the guardians the necessity of their being prepared for the occurrence of fever, which experience had shown to be always prevalent in seasons of distress, from whatever cause arising.

Fever wards.

We are now arrived at the period of the potato failure, some account of which as affecting England and Scotland has been given in the respective histories.[d] " The potato disease," so called to distinguish it from the less general and entire failure of that root which has occasionally occurred, first appeared in America in 1844, but it did not show itself in Ireland until the autumn of 1845. The early crops generally escaped its ravages, but the late or main crop

Failure of the potato.

---

d See ' History of the Scotch Poor Law,' p. 199. See also ' History of the English Poor Law,' 2nd vol. pp. 391-393.

was found to be so far tainted with the disease, that although much of it was susceptible of being used at the time the potatoes were dug, they afterwards rotted in the pits, and became an offensive mass unfitted for the use of man or beast. This was especially the case in the western districts; and there as well as wherever the small cottier or the conacre systems prevailed, any failure in the potato crop, even although it were small and partial, would necessarily occasion much distress, the population being in such cases generally redundant, and subsisting nearly altogether on that root.

In the present instance there was not only a failure in the quantity raised, but the portion of the crop stored for future use was known to be in jeopardy, and the distress and alarm were proportionally increased. Both were in fact excessive, the one adding to the other, and causing the most serious apprehensions throughout the country. Government participated in these apprehensions, and took early steps for obtaining 100,000*l.* worth of Indian corn from America, in anticipation of the distress and difficulties sure to arise through the failure of the potato, and for which the country itself afforded no substitute.[e] This timely supply arrived in course of the spring of 1846, and in order to its distribution, depôts were established in various places along the coast under the direction of commissariat officers, with sub-depôts in charge of the constabulary and coast-guard.[f] Wherever the ordinary supplies of food were found to be deficient, Indian meal was sold from these depôts at a moderate price, to the relief

---

[e] In March 1846, on the introduction of the measure (*9th and* 10*th Vict. cap.* 2) for enabling the Treasury to make advances on security of grand jury presentments, Mr. O'Connell, whose knowledge of Ireland must be admitted, declared that government had acted wisely in causing a quantity of maize or Indian corn to be imported, to replace the damaged potatoes, as by so doing they had added to the quantity of food for the people.

[f] See 'The Irish Crisis,' by Sir Charles Trevelyan, reprinted in 1848 from the Edinburgh Review No. 175.

committees if any such had been formed, and likewise
to all who applied for it. The meal was not however
at first relished by the people, for although far more
nutritious than the potato, it was new, and they preferred that to which they had been accustomed. But
necessity is ever a successful controller of taste, and
Indian meal which was at first disliked, and about
which the most absurd stories were promulgated, became ere long, and after the mode of preparing it came
to be understood, a favourite description of food with
the Irish people.

Although the potato had thus failed, not only in
Ireland but in England and Scotland, and throughout
the greater portion of Europe, the grain crops were
generally abundant, and would in a great degree supply
the deficiency caused by such failure, except where the
potato constituted the chief or nearly sole article of
subsistence, as was the case in many parts of Ireland.
Here the void caused by the loss of the potato could
only be supplied by imports from abroad, and this circumstance was adduced by Sir Robert Peel in January
1846 as one of the reasons for a reduction of the corn-
duties, and led to Indian corn being admitted at a duty
of 1s. per quarter, instead of being charged the same
duty as barley, as it previously had been, and owing to
which charge probably, it was little used or known
either in England or Ireland.

In the autumn of 1845, as soon as the prevalence of
the " potato disease " had been ascertained, government
deputed three gentlemen of high scientific attainments[g]
to examine into its nature, and to suggest means for
checking its ravages. But the result showed that the
evil was beyond the reach of human skill, for notwithstanding the application of every remedy which science
could devise or experience dictate, the decay of the

---

[g] These were Professors Kane, Lindley, and Playfair.

root continued with undiminished rapidity. On the appearance of the disease, the Poor Law Commissioners entered into active communication with the several boards of guardians on the subject, and endeavoured to mitigate the consequences of the potato failure, by authorizing the use of other kinds of food in the union dietaries. These were for the most part modified accordingly, and bread, or stirabout prepared from Indian meal, was substituted for potatoes.

The circumstances of Ireland at this time, induced the government to exercise the power conferred by the 119*th section* of the Irish Poor Relief Act, and to appoint a fourth commissioner to act in that country. The gentleman selected was Mr. Twisleton, of whom mention has been made in connexion with the Scotch Poor Law;[h] and on his proceeding to Ireland, the powers previously delegated to the two assistant-commissioners[i] were revoked.

A fourth commissioner appointed.

The ninth Report (for 1846-7) is like the others dated on the 1st of May. It describes very fully the effects consequent on the potato disease of the previous autumn, so far as these effects bore upon the working of the Poor Law. The connexion between the two, although in one sense intimate, is in other respects limited; for where the land has ceased to be productive, the necessary means of relief cannot be obtained from it, and a poor-law will no longer be operative, or at least not operative to an extent adequate to meet such an emergency as then existed in Ireland. A poor-law, rightly devised and judiciously administered, will generally be found equal to the relief of destitution in the ordinary progress of events; but a state of famine, or a total failure of the

1847.
Ninth report of proceedings in Ireland.

---

[h] See ' History of the Scotch Poor Law,' pp. 130 and 165.
[i] Ante, p. 284.

means of subsistence is extraordinary, and the wide-spread destitution thence arising is beyond the powers of a poor-law effectually to relieve, although it may doubtless be applied to some extent in mitigation. Under the circumstances at that time unhappily exist-ing in Ireland, other aid was necessary beyond what could be derived from any modification of the Poor Law; and the nature of those circumstances, and the means pursued in dealing with them, will be explained in the following pages.

The potato disease made its appearance in 1846 much earlier than in the preceding year, and it was also much more general and destructive. Captain Mann in his narrative of events in the county of Clare at this period, says that the symptoms of the disease were first noticed in the latter part of July; but that the change which took place in one week in August was such as he shall never forget—" On the first occasion (he says) I had passed over thirty-two miles thickly studded with potato-fields in full bloom. The next time the face of the whole country was changed—the stalk remained a bright green, but the leaves were all scorched black. It was the work of a night. Distress and fear was pictured in every coun-tenance, and there was a general rush to dig and sell, or consume the crop by feeding pigs and cattle, fearing in a short time they would prove unfit for any use." And in a letter printed in the Parliamentary Papers, Father Mathew[k] states—" On the 27th of July I passed from Cork to Dublin, and this doomed plant bloomed in all the luxuriance of an abundant harvest. Returning on the 3rd of August, I beheld with sorrow one wide waste of putrifying vegetation. In many places the wretched people were seated on the fences of their

Margin note: The potato disease in 1846.

---

k Commonly known in Ireland as "the Apostle of Temperance," a worthy and benevolent man.

decaying gardens, wringing their hands and wailing bitterly the destruction that had left them foodless."

The disease made its first appearance in the form of little brown spots on the leaves of the plant. These continued to increase until the leaves became withered, leaving the stem bare, and so brittle that it snapped off on being handled. The whole was effected in less than a week, the fields appearing as if they were burnt, and the growth of the root entirely destroyed. No potatoes were pitted this year, and the wheat crop barely amounted to an average, whilst barley and oats were decidedly deficient. " On the continent the rye and potato crops again failed, and prices rose there early in the season above those ruling in England, which caused the shipments from the Black Sea, Turkey and Egypt to be sent to France, Italy and Belgium ; and it was not till late in the season that our prices rose to a point which turned the current of supplies towards England and Ireland. The Indian corn crop in the United States this year was however happily very abundant, and it became a resource of the utmost value to this country.[m]

In June 1846, *The 9th and 10th Vict. cap.* 22, was passed, providing for the gradual reduction of the import duty on corn, and fixing it at 1*s.* per quarter on every description imported after the 1st of February 1849. On the assembling of parliament in January 1847, two other Acts were passed[n] making further reductions in the duty on corn, and removing the restriction imposed by the Navigation Laws on the importation of corn in foreign vessels; and shortly afterwards the whole duty on rice and Indian corn and Indian meal was suspended.

In the early part of 1846, relief committees were

Reduction of duty on corn imported.

---

[m] See ' The Irish Crisis,' by Sir Charles Trevelyan, p. 41.
[n] The 10*th and* 11*th Vict. cap.* 1 and 2.

formed throughout Ireland, under the superintendence
Relief com- of a central commission established in Dublin,
mittees
formed. for the purpose of dispensing food, the requisite
funds being furnished by private subscriptions assisted
by donations from government. The months of June
and July was the period of heaviest pressure, during
which one of the central depôts established by government, issued in a single week no less than 233 tons of
meal to its various sub-depôts, and one of these latter
again retailed 20 tons to the public daily. If the people
had lived by wages like the labouring classes in England, the providing a cheap substitute for the potato
would have been sufficient for the present emergency.
But money-wages were comparatively little known in
Ireland, the people chiefly subsisting on produce raised
by themselves; and it was therefore necessary to adopt
some plan for enabling them to purchase the new
description of food which had been procured for them.

The plan adopted was by establishing public works,
as had been done on former somewhat like occa-
The Public sions; and an Act was accordingly passed
Works Act,
9th and 10th enabling the magistrates and principal cess-
Vict. c. 1. payers to obtain advances of public money for
this purpose, one-half as a free grant, the other half as
a loan to be repaid by the barony out of the grand-jury
cess. The greatest number of persons employed under
this system was 97,000. It was brought to a close in
the month of August, and may be said on the whole
to have answered its intended purpose, although not
without considerable drawbacks, partly through the misapplication of public money, and partly by increasing
the tendency which has always prevailed in Ireland to
rely upon government aid. The entire amount expended by the government down to the 15th of August
1846, in affording relief to the Irish people during this
season of distress was 733,372*l*., of which one-half was
a free grant, and the other half a loan. The sum raised

by voluntary subscription for like purposes was 98,000*l.*, making together 831,372*l.*, obtained from other than poor-law sources, and expended during this first season of severe pressure in relief of persons many of whom would else have perished through absolute want.

With the approach of autumn another period of distress commenced in Ireland, far heavier and more intense than the preceding, the potato crop having now almost universally and entirely failed. In the former season there were helps or palliatives, some districts having nearly escaped the disease and others being less generally affected by it; but in the present season there were no such exceptions, and neither help nor hope was to be found in the natural resources of the country. A new emergency may thus be said to have arisen, and the public works which had been put an end to in August were renewed in the following month, and the entire machinery of provision depôts and relief committees was reorganized on a more comprehensive scale than before. *The autumn of 1846. Severe distress.*

In order to check the exorbitant demands which had in many instances been made in the previous season, the whole expense of the public works was now under the new Labour-Rate Act made a local charge, to be defrayed by a rate levied and assessed in a manner similar to the poor-rate, which makes the landlord liable for the whole on tenements under 4*l.* yearly value, and for half the rate on tenements valued above that amount. It was also determined that as far as possible task-work should be adopted, and at a rate of payment below what was usual in the district. It was further determined in order to avoid embarrassing the operations of the private trader, that government should not order supplies from abroad, and that its interference should be confined to the western districts, in which no trade in corn for local consumption existed. Moreover, the government depôts were not to be opened *The Labour-rate Act, 9th and 10th Vict. c. 107.*

for the sale of food so long as it could be obtained from private dealers, and no purchases were to be made in the local market, where the appearance of government as a purchaser would be certain to raise prices.

Such generally was the plan proposed to be pursued under the pressure of famine, and the other distressing circumstances consequent on the failure of the potato crop at the end of 1846; and it was expected that the resident proprietors and ratepayers would perform their part, by ascertaining the extent of destitution in the several localities, and determining what was necessary to be done in the way of relief, and the best mode of doing it. This expectation however was not fulfilled, and in almost every instance these duties were left to be per- The board of formed by the board of works, which had thus to works. obtain the best information it could through hired agents, " to advance the necessary funds, to select the labourers, to superintend the works, to pay the people weekly, to enforce a proper performance of the labour, to ascertain the quantity of labour required for farm-works, to select and draft off proper persons to perform it, to settle the wages to be paid to them by the farmers and to see that they were paid, to furnish food not only for all the destitute out of doors, but in some measure for the paupers in the workhouses"—in short, " the board of works became the centre of a colossal organization, 5,000 separate works had to be reported upon, 12,000 subordinate officers had to be superintended, and their letters averaged upwards of 800 a day." °

The strain upon the executive through this system of The relief- centralization was excessive. Government had works. to bear the entire pressure of the masses on the sensitive points of wages and food. Task-work was

---

° See ' The Irish Crisis,' by Sir Charles Trevelyan, under whose able super-intendence the government aid was chiefly administered in Ireland, and on whose statements of what took place I have chiefly relied in this account of the dismal periods of 1846 and 1847.

generally objected to, and its enforcement gave rise to frequent struggles, in which the safety of the superintending officers was sometimes put in jeopardy. The number of persons employed on the works continued to increase—" Thousands upon thousands were pressed upon the officers of the board of works in every part of Ireland, and it was impossible for those officers to test the accuracy of the urgent representations which were made to them. The attraction of money wages regularly paid from the public purse, or ' The queen's pay,' as it was popularly called, led to a general abandonment of other descriptions of industry, in order to participate in the advantages of the relief-works. Landlords competed with each other in getting the names of their tenants placed on the lists; farmers dis- missed their labourers and sent them to the works; the clergy insisted on the claims of the members of their respective congregations; the fisheries were deserted; and it was often difficult even to get a coat patched or a pair of shoes mended, to such an extent had the population of the south and west of Ireland turned out upon the roads. The average number employed in October was 114,000, in November 285,000, in December 440,000, and in January 1847, 570,000." It was obviously impossible to exact from such a multitude the amount of labour that would operate as a test. Huddled together in masses they screened each other's idleness. It was thought that the enforcement of taskwork would stimulate their industry; but when after a hard struggle this point had been carried, an habitual collusion between the labourers and the overlookers appointed to measure their work revived the former abuse, and the labourers were as idle as ever.

Evils of the system.

The Labour-Rate Act (*9th and* 10*th Vict. cap.* 107) was founded on the assumption that the owners and occupiers of land would themselves make efforts commensurate with the magnitude of the crisis, and that only a manageable number of persons would have to be supported on the public works. But including the families of those so employed, more than 2,000,000 persons were maintained by the relief-works, and there were others behind including the most helpless, for whom no work could be found. The extent to which the rural population were thrown upon the relief-works, Failure of re-lief-works. threatened likewise to interrupt the ordinary tillage of the land, and thus to perpetuate a state of famine. In short, a change of system had become necessary, and at the end of January (1847) it was announced that government intended to put an end to the public works, and to substitute another mode of relief. The pressure nevertheless continued to increase. The 570,000 men employed daily in January, became 708,000 in February, and 734,000 in March, representing with their dependents upwards of 3,000,000 of persons. The expenses were in proportion, and exceeded a million sterling per month.[p] At the end of February however preparation was made for a change of system by passing the Temporary Relief Act (10*th* Vict. cap. 7). In March the numbers employed were reduced by 20 per cent., and successive reductions continued to be made as the change of system was brought into operation. In the first weeks of April, May and June respectively, the numbers employed were 525,000, 419,000, and 101,000; and in the week ending the 26th of June the number was reduced to 28,000. The necessary labour was thus returned to agriculture, and a foundation was laid for the ensuing abundant harvest. " The remaining expenditure was limited to a sum of 200,000*l*. for the month of May, and to 100,000*l*. a month for June, July, and the first 15 days of August, when the Act expired."

---

[p] In the month of March the expenditure upon relief-works including labour and plant, and the cost of the staff, amounted to 1,050,772*l*.

The system of affording relief through the agency of public works having broken down, while that of administering it in a direct form on the principle of the Poor Law had generally been found effective wherever it had been tried, it 26th Feb. 1847. Temporary Relief Act. 10th and 11th Vict. c. 7. was as above stated determined to give validity to this mode by passing the 10th and 11th Vict., cap. 7, which directs that a relief committee consisting of the magistrates, a clergyman of each persuasion, the poor-law guardian and the three highest ratepayers, shall be constituted in each electoral division, and that a finance committee of four gentlemen of character and knowledge of business should be formed to control the expenditure in each union. Inspecting officers are also to be appointed, and a central commission sitting in Dublin,[q] was to superintend and control the working of the whole system. The expense incurred was to be defrayed out of the poor-rates, and when these proved insufficient they might be reinforced by government loans, to be repaid by rates subsequently levied. But no loan is to be made, until the inspecting officer had certified that the guardians have passed a resolution for making the rate upon which the loan was to be secured. Such were the chief provisions of the Act, but free grants were also made in aid of the rates in the poorest unions, and when private subscriptions were raised the government made donations to an equal amount. The liability of the ratepayers would, it was considered, operate as a check to undue expenditure; and with regard to the recipients, the test applied consisted in requiring the personal attendance of all who needed relief, (excepting only the sick and impotent poor, and children under the age of nine) and that the

---

[q] Sir John Burgoyne was the chairman of this commission, and Mr. Twisleton the poor-law commissioner was a member. The other members were Mr. Redington the first under secretary, and Col. Jones and Col. M'Gregor the heads of the board of works and the constabulary.

relief should be given in cooked food,[r] in portions sufficient to maintain health and strength.

The cooked-food system of relief was found to a great degree efficacious in preventing abuse,

The cooked-food system of relief.

but it was objected to at first, and the enforcement of it was in some cases attended with difficulty. Undressed meal might be sold or exchanged for other articles. " Even the most destitute often disposed of it for tea tobacco or spirits," but stirabout soon becomes sour by keeping, and was not likely to be applied for except by persons who wanted it for their own immediate use. Depôts of corn and meal were formed—relief committees were established—mills and ovens were erected—huge boilers cast specially for the purpose were sent over from England for preparing the stirabout—and large supplies of clothing were collected. In July 1847 the system reached its highest point " 3,020,712 persons then received separate rations, of whom 2,265,534 were adults, and 755,178 were children." This vast multitude was however rapidly lessened at the approach of harvest,[s] which happily was not affected by the disease. Food became

Cessation of famine.

comparatively abundant, and labour in demand. By the middle of August relief was discontinued in nearly one-half the unions, and ceased altogether on the 12th September. It was limited by the Act to the 1st October.

This was the second year in which upwards of 3,000,000 of people had been fed " out of the hands of the magistrate " in Ireland, but it was now done more effectually than at first. The relief-works had been

---

[r] The best form in which cooked food could be given was " stirabout," made of Indian meal and rice steamed. It is sufficiently solid to be easily carried away by the recipients. The pound ration thus prepared swelled by the absorption of water to between 3 and 4 pounds.

[s] The price of Indian corn in the middle of February was 19*l.* per ton, at the end of March it was 13*l.*, and by the end of August it had fallen to 7*l.* 10*s.* per ton. The quantity of corn imported into Ireland in the first six months of 1847 was 2,849,508 tons.

crowded, often to the exclusion of numbers who were really destitute; but a ration of cooked food was less attractive than money wages had been, and it also proved a more effectual relief to the helpless poor. " The famine was stayed." Deaths from starvation no longer occurred. Cattle-stealing and other crimes connected with the want or insufficiency of food became less prevalent, and the system of relief which had been established is with allowable self-gratulation declared to be " the grandest attempt ever made to grapple with famine over a whole country." Organized armies, it is said, had been rationed before; " but neither ancient nor modern history can furnish a parallel to the fact that upwards of three millions of persons were fed every day in the neighbourhood of their own homes, by administrative arrangements emanating from and controlled by one central office." [t] The expense of this great undertaking amounted to 1,557,212*l*.,— a moderate sum in comparison with the extent of the service performed, and in which performance the machinery of the Poor Law unions was found to afford most important aid. Indeed without such aid, the service could hardly have been performed at all; and the anticipations of the advantage to be derived from the Poor Law organization in such emergencies,[u] were fully verified.

Fever as usual followed in the train of famine, and in order to check its ravages *the* 10*th and* 11*th* Fever. *Vict. cap.* 22 was passed, " making provision for the treatment of poor persons afflicted with fever," and enabling the relief committees to provide temporary hospitals, to ventilate and cleanse cabins, to remove nuisances, and to procure the proper burial of the dead, the funds necessary for these objects being

---

[t] See ' The Irish Crisis.' See also the Reports of the Irish relief commissioners, which give full information on this interesting but distressing subject.

[u] See the author's first Report, p. 167 ante.

advanced by the government in the same way as for furnishing food. Upwards of three hundred hospitals and dispensaries were provided under this Act, with accommodation for at least 23,000 patients, and the sanitary powers which it conferred were extensively acted upon. The expense incurred for these objects amounted to 119,055*l.*, " the whole of which was made a free gift to the unions in aid of the rates."

The amount expended under the Public Works Act Advances by government. (9*th and* 10*th Vict. cap.* 1) was 476,000*l.*, one-half being a grant, the other half to be repaid by twenty half-yearly instalments. The expenditure under the Labour-Rate Act (9*th and* 10*th Vict. cap.* 107) was 4,850,000*l.*, half of which was a grant and the other half to be repaid as before. The sum advanced under 9*th and* 10*th Vict. cap.* 2 for local purposes, was 130,000*l.*, to be repaid in various periods out of grand jury presentments. Lastly the sums expended under the Temporary Relief Act, 10*th Vict. cap.* 7, in the distribution of food, and under the 10*th Vict. cap.* 22 in medical and sanitary relief, amounted to 1,676,268*l.*, of which 961,739*l.* was to be repaid, and the remaining 714,529*l.* was a free grant. So that the entire amount advanced by government in 1846 and 1847 towards the relief of the Irish people under the fearful calamity to which they were exposed, was 7,132,268*l.*, of which 3,754,739*l.* was to be repaid within ten years, and the remaining 3,377,529*l.* was a free grant.[x]

But it was not the government alone that contri- Private subscriptions. buted to the relief of the Irish people in this trying emergency. Individual subscriptions were poured forth from all parts of the British empire. Associations were formed, local committees were appointed, all were active in sympathy and benevolent

---

[x] See 'The Irish Crisis,' p. 110.

efforts for the relief of Irish distress. The chief organ for receiving and dispensing these various contributions was " The British Association,"[z] which collected subscriptions to the amount of 269,302*l*., and to which was likewise committed the proceeds of two royal letters inviting contributions, amounting to 200,738*l*., making together no less than 470,041*l*., one-sixth of which was apportioned to Scotland,[a] and the remainder to Ireland.[b] Then there was the " Society of Friends" who collected 168,000*l*., which was distributed almost entirely in provisions, whilst a great number of persons in all parts of England acted independently of any association, but all directing their efforts to the same benevolent object.

In administering the funds placed at its disposal, the committee of the British Association acted concurrently with the government and the Poor-Law authorities, each of whom bore testimony to its great usefulness. It determined at the outset " That all grants should be in food, and not in money;" and " That no grant should be placed at the disposal of any individual for private distribution." The committee conclude their Report to the subscribers by declaring, that although evils of greater or less degree must attend every system of gratuitous relief, they are confident that any evils which may have accompanied the application of this fund, will have been far more than counterbalanced by the benefits which have been conferred upon their starving fellow-countrymen. " If ill desert has sometimes participated in this bounty, a vast amount of human misery and suffering has (it is said) been relieved."[c]

The British Association.

---

[z] The present Lord Overstone, then Mr. Jones Loyd, was chairman of the acting committee of the association, and Mr. Thomas Baring was the vice-chairman.

[a] See 'History of the Scotch Poor Law,' p. 202.

[b] In fact the amount applied to these objects by the association exceeded 500,000*l*., upwards of 130,000*l*. having been obtained by the sale of provisions and seed-corn in Ireland, and interest accruing on the money contributed.

[c] See Report of the British Association for the Relief of extreme Distress in Ireland and Scotland, 1st January 1849.

The foregoing account of proceedings by the government and by individuals for relieving the distress which prevailed in Ireland during the years 1846 and 1847, through the failure of the potato-crops, has been continued down beyond the date of the ninth Report in order to keep the subject together, and to obviate the necessity of again recurring to it. These proceedings form no part of the Poor Law administration, and are only so far connected with it as being directed to the relief of distress, and as having been latterly carried on very much in accordance with recognised Poor Law principles, and moreover to a considerable extent with the aid of the Poor Law machinery. We will now return to the detail of proceedings during the twelve months preceding the 1st of May 1847, as given in the commissioners' ninth Report.

All the workhouses had been opened for the relief of the poor, and every union had made a rate, so that the law might now be said to be in operation throughout Ireland. The amount of expenditure for the year ending 31st December 1846 was 435,001*l.*, and the number of persons then receiving relief in the several workhouses was 94,437, which exceeds by 52,369 the number in the preceding year, and the expenditure is greater by 118,975*l.* The entire number of persons relieved during the year was 243,933.

Amount of expenditure, and numbers relieved.

All the unions being now in operation, and their accounts being made up and audited half-yearly on the 25th March and 29th September, it is intended hereafter to substitute the latter dates for the return which has hitherto been made up on the 1st of January, at which time no perfectly authentic account of the expenditure could be obtained, owing to its not corresponding with either of the audit periods. This therefore is the last occasion on which that statement will be given; and it may here be convenient to exhibit in a tabular form its progress from the commencement, as shown in the several annual Reports—

The year ended December 31st.	Number of unions in operation.	Expenditure during the year.	Number in the workhouses on December 31st.	Total number of persons relieved during the year.
1840	4	£ 37,057	5,648	10,910
1841	37	110,278	15,246	31,108
1842	92	281,233	31,572	87,604
1843	106	244,374	35,515	87,898
1844	113	271,334	39,175	105,358
1845	123	316,026	42,068	114,205
1846	130	435,001	94,437	243,933

"The potato disease" having as before stated again appeared at the end of July (1846), letters were addressed to the boards of guardians requiring full information as to the state of the crop in the several electoral divisions. Early in September replies were received, which left no doubt as to the almost total destruction of the crop that had everywhere taken place, and the commissioners had anxiously to consider in what manner the poor-law could be made operative in mitigation of the distress which must inevitably ensue. Relief from the poor-rates being limited to accommodation in workhouses, it was manifest that such relief would be insufficient for meeting the present calamity, "and that the comprehensive remedial measures adopted by government in the establishment of a general system of public works, and the organization of relief committees, were to be looked to as the principal means." The commissioners nevertheless considered that it was imperatively necessary to use all the powers provided by the law on this occasion, and they addressed letters to the several boards of guardians, drawing their attention to the probability of a great increase of distress, and requesting them "to be prepared to make the utmost use of the means of relief which the law placed at their command." They were urged to look to the state of their contracts for provisions and other supplies, and to their stocks of bedding and clothing, and to base their financial and other estimates on the assumption that the whole accommodation in the workhouse would be required, probably for a considerable time. These recommendations were very generally acted upon. The total rates made in the months of September, October, November and December, amounted to 232,251*l.*, and much activity was manifested in the collection of the rates, as well as in providing the necessary supplies.

On the 29th August 1846, the returns for the week
Pressure upon the workhouses. showed that the inmates of the several workhouses amounted to 43,655, and the numbers continued to increase until on the 17th October, four of the workhouses were reported to be full,[d] and most of the others became so shortly after, although they fluctuated in this respect from time to time. The aggregate weekly returns however showed a continual increase down to the end of February 1847, when the inmates amounted to 116,321. From that time the number decreased, but the decrease was probably owing to the distressed circumstances in which the unions were themselves placed, rather than to any abatement of the general distress. There can, it is observed, be few situations more painful than that of a board of guardians in the present condition of Ireland, surrounded by an appalling extent of destitution, yet without the means of relieving the sufferers. " Possessed of a workhouse capable of holding a few hundred inmates, the guardians are looked to with hope by thousands of famishing persons, and are called on to exercise the mournful task of selection from the distressed objects who present themselves for admission as their last refuge from death." It was no longer a question whether the applicants were fit objects for relief, but which of them could be rejected and which admitted with the least risk of sacrificing life. Were persons in the last extremities of want to be denied admittance, or on the other hand were those already

---

[d] Those of Cork, Granard, Ballina, and Skibbereen.

admitted to be made the victims of over-crowding?—
The course which prudence dictated was the one most
opposed to human sympathies. Eyewitnesses of the
distress which was endured, the guardians could not
always resist the appeals made to them; and applicant
after applicant was admitted to the workhouse, long after
the sanitary limit had been passed.

It was the duty of the commissioners to resist all such
impulsive yieldings, and they failed not to urge
upon the guardians the necessity for such resistance on their part, without which the limited means
of relief at their disposal would be sacrificed. They
were told that effectual relief, even to the extent of the
existing accommodation could not be given, if contagious
disease took possession of the workhouse; and that in
attempting to go beyond due sanitary limits, the guardians would turn what was designed and adapted for
good purposes into an active evil, and deprive themselves of the power of using effectually those means of
relief which had been placed at their command. In
some instances orders under seal were issued, prohibiting
the guardians from admitting beyond a certain number.
The commissioners likewise " called into action the
proper functions of the medical officers of the workhouses, and placed upon them the direct responsibility
of advising and warning the guardians of those limits,
beyond which their admissions could not be extended
without danger." Notwithstanding these precautions
however, such was the fearful prevalence of distress,
especially in Connaught and the south of Ireland, that
all considerations of this nature were borne down, and
the workhouses became crowded to an extent far beyond
their proper capacity, the consequences of which were
in some cases very disastrous.

The workhouse hospitals were prepared for cases of
sickness occurring among inmates, presumed to be in an
average state of health, and they were generally found

(margin note: Overcrowd-ing of the workhouses.)

sufficient for the purpose. But now unhappily, almost every person admitted was a patient—was either suffering from dysentery or fever, or extreme exhaustion, or had the seeds of disease about him. Under such circumstances separation became impossible, diseases spread, and the whole workhouse was changed into one large hospital, without the appliances necessary for rendering it efficient as such. This state of things was not a little aggravated by the illness retirement or death of many of the principal officers. The usual difficulty of replacing a master or a matron, or medical officer when suddenly removed, was much increased by the dangerous nature of the service, there having been great mortality among these officers. During the first four months of the current year, at least a hundred and fifty were attacked with disease, of whom fifty-four had died, including seven clerks, nine masters, seven medical officers, and six chaplains—a number unusually large, and calculated no doubt to excite some indisposition to undertake such duties.

Mortality among the union officers.

The weekly mortality in the workhouses went on increasing from 4 in the 1,000 at the end of October 1846, to 13 in the 1,000 at the end of January 1847,—20 in the 1,000 at the end of February, and 25 in the 1,000 at the middle of April; the number of inmates at these periods respectively being 68,839—111,621—116,321—and 104,455. In the last week of February, when the number of inmates attained its maximum, the deaths amounted to 2,267; whilst on the 10th of April, when the inmates had been reduced to 104,455, the deaths of the preceding week were 2,613, thus showing an increase of mortality notwithstanding a reduction in the number of inmates. The people had in fact become so exhausted by the severity of the distress, that in many cases death occurred immediately after admission. This was the time when to escape famine and pestilence at home, the great rush of immigrants to Liverpool and the

Mortality in the workhouses.

western coasts of England and Scotland took place, and it is needless to say that the pressure must have been fearful to cause such an outpouring of the population.[e] We must not omit to state however, that at this time great exertions were being made in many, indeed it may be said in most of the unions to obtain increased accommodation for fever patients, by erecting or hiring buildings temporary or permanent according to the urgency and nature of the case; and also in like manner for increasing the means of workhouse accommodation, so as to bring it more nearly up to the wants of the period. The money expended upon these objects was in some instances obtained by way of loan, and in others was defrayed directly from the rates; but in all cases there was a considerable addition to the current expenditure by the provision thus made for affording additional relief.

Emigration was regarded by many persons as the most prompt and effective remedy, under the circumstances then existing in Ireland; and government was appealed to for assistance in promoting it, by defraying the expense of passage and outfit for the emigrants. But it was thought highly probable that the emigration which would take place independently of any such inducement, would be quite as large as the United States and Canada could with advantage receive; and the government therefore limited its interference to appointing additional agents to superintend the embarkation of the emigrants, and to increasing the fund applicable to the relief of the sick after their arrival in the colonies.[f] In 1846 the emigration from Great Britain amounted to 129,851. This was the largest ever then known; but in the first nine months of 1847 the

Emigration.

---

[e] See 'History of the English Poor Law,' vol. ii. p. 393, where however there is a misprint in the eighth line from the bottom, of 1846 for 1847, which the reader is requested to correct.

[f] Upwards of 100,000l. was expended in relieving the sick and destitute emigrants landed in Canada in 1847.

number of emigrants was 240,461, nearly the whole of them from Ireland, and proceeding to Canada and the United States, whence large remittances had been sent by former emigrants to enable their relations and friends in Ireland to follow them. Within the same period 278,000 immigrants reached Liverpool from Ireland, of whom only 123,000 sailed from thence to foreign parts; and the remainder must therefore have continued a burden on the inhabitants, or wandered about the country begging, or died of disease the seeds of which they had brought with them, and which proved fatal to a great number of other persons as well as to the immigrants themselves. It was the same everywhere.[g] In Mortality among the emigrants. the United States, in Canada and on the voyage out, the poor emigrants seeking to escape from famine at home, were assailed by disease whithersoever they turned, and very many of them sunk under its ravages. During this fearful crisis, the deaths on the voyage to Canada increased from 5 in the 1,000, to about 60; and so many more arrived sick, that the proportion of deaths in quarantine to the numbers embarked, increased from a little more than 1 to about 40 in the 1,000, besides still larger numbers who died at Quebec, Montreal, and elsewhere in the interior.[h]

Reference is made in the Report of 1846, to the Financial state of the unions. generally satisfactory state of the finances of the unions;[i] but such was no longer the case in 1847, the heavy pressure consequent on the potato failure having exhausted their resources, and in many cases caused the most serious embarrassment. The returns show, that instead of there being as before money in the hands of the treasurers to meet the current expenditure, there was now, taking in the whole of the unions, a considerable deficit. Even

---

[g] See 'History of the Scotch Poor Law,' p. 205. See also 'History of the English Poor Law,' vol. ii. p. 393.
[h] See 'The Irish Crisis,' p. 143.　　　Ante, p. 304.

those unions which were accustomed to maintain their
finances in a fair state of efficiency, had latterly failed
to obtain funds from the ratepayers proportioned to
their expenditure. In some instances, the commissioners say, they have been compelled by the extreme
urgency of the case, to supply the guardians with
bedding and clothing, and with the means of procuring
food to satisfy the immediate wants of the inmates,
" the means of doing so having been furnished by
government;" and they close their observations on
these financial difficulties by stating, " that while the
total expenses have been at the rate of at least 756,000*l.*
a year, the sums collected have not much exceeded the
rate of 609,056."

The effect upon prices caused by the failure of the
potato, may in some measure be judged of by the weekly
cost of maintenance in the workhouses, which instead
of being about 1*s.* 5*d.* per head as in former years,
averaged 1*s.* 8*d.* per head in March, and 1*s.* 9*d.* per
head in September 1846, after which it ex- Increase in
the cost of
ceeded 2*s.* per head. This increase of cost must relief.
have materially added to the difficulties of the unions,
not only by augmenting the pressure of the poor-rate,
but also by reducing the means of the ratepayers for
satisfying its demands. On every side there appeared
ground for alarm, and no one could venture to look
forward without feeling the most serious apprehensions. A third failure of the crops, should such unhappily occur, would be attended with consequences
the disastrous extent of which it must be alike impossible fully to estimate or guard against; and the period
was approaching when uncertainty on this vital point
would be removed—At the end of another three months
it would be seen whether want disease and misery were
again, but in a more aggravated form, to overspread the
land, or whether the earth would yield forth its increase
for the sustenance of man.

The Report for 1847-8 would, in the regular order,

1848.
First annual
Report of the
Poor-law
Commis-
sioners for
Ireland. have formed the tenth of the series. But it had now been deemed necessary to establish a separate commission for Ireland, entirely independent of the English commission, and the Report is consequently entitled the first of the new executive. This Report like the nine preceding, is dated on the 1st of May; and as three Acts making very important changes in the law for the relief of the Irish poor had been passed early in the period to which the Report applies, (namely on the 8th of June and the 22nd of July 1847), the insertion of the following summaries of these three Acts will be a fitting preliminary to our consideration of the Report itself.

The 10*th and* 11*th Vict., cap.* 31, is entitled ' An Act

The Exten-
sion Act, 10th
and 11thVict.
cap. 31. to make further Provision for the Relief of the Destitute Poor in Ireland '—8*th June* 1847.

Section 1.—Directs the guardians of the poor to make provision for the due relief of all destitute poor persons disabled by old age or infirmity; and of destitute poor persons disabled by sickness or serious accident, and thereby prevented from earning a subsistence for themselves and their families; and of destitute poor widows, having two or more legitimate children dependent upon them. Such poor persons, being destitute, are to be relieved either in the workhouse or out of the workhouse as the guardians may deem expedient; and the guardians are also to take order for relieving and setting to work in the workhouse when there shall be sufficient room for so doing, such other destitute poor persons as they shall deem to be unable to support themselves by their own industry.

Sections 2, 3.—Whenever relief cannot be afforded in the workhouse owing to want of room, or when by reason of fever or infectious disease the workhouse is unfit for the reception of poor persons, the Poor Law Commissioners may by order empower the guardians to administer relief out of the workhouse to such destitute poor persons, for any time not exceeding two months; and on the receipt of such order, the guardians are to make provision accordingly—Relief to able-bodied persons out of the workhouse, is however to be given in food only, and the commissioners may from time to time regulate its application.

Sections 4, 5, 6.—The commissioners may direct the guardians to appoint relieving officers to assist in the administration of relief; and also medical officers for affording medical relief out of the workhouse, whenever they shall deem such appointments to be necessary or expedient. The commissioners may likewise, on application of the board of guardians, wherever an electoral division is distant six miles from the place of meeting, form such division into a district, with a committee to receive applications, and to report thereon to the guardians.

Section 7.—Relieving officers are empowered to give provisional relief in cases of urgent necessity, by an order of admission to the workhouse or fever hospital of the union, or only affording such relief as may be necessary in food, lodging, medicine or medical attendance, until the next meeting of the board of guardians, to whom the case is then to be reported, and their directions taken thereon. The guardians are to furnish the relieving officers with the necessary funds for the above purposes, in such manner as the Poor Law Commissioners direct.

Sections 8, 9, 10.—Relief to a wife or child is to be considered as given to the husband or parent, as the case may be; and children are liable for the relief afforded to their parents. Relief at the cost of a union, is only to be given within the union. Occupiers of more than a quarter of an acre of land are not to be deemed destitute, nor to be relieved out of the poor-rates.

Sections 11, 12.—Regulate the mode of charging out-door relief; and provide that no person shall be deemed resident in an electoral division, unless three years before he applies for relief, he shall have occupied some tenement within it for three months, or usually slept within it for thirty months.

Sections 13, 14, 15.—Prescribe the conditions on which assistance may be given to emigration, and the proportion of the expense that may be defrayed out of the rates. The provisions of 6*th* and 7*th Vict. cap.* 92, *sec.* 18,[k] for the emigration of persons who have been three months in a workhouse, extended to poor persons not in a workhouse, or who have been there less than three months. The expense incurred in aid of emigration not to be deemed relief.

Section 16.—The limitation of ex-officio guardians to one-third the number of elected guardians is repealed; but it is at the same time provided that the ex-officios shall in no case exceed the number of the elected guardians.

---

[k] Ante, p. 293.

Sections 17, 18.—The commissioners empowered to dissolve or alter unions without consent of the guardians, and to form such other unions therefrom as they shall deem expedient, and to adjust the claims and liabilities consequent thereon. The commissioners also empowered to dissolve a board of guardians on their failing duly to discharge their prescribed duties, and to appoint paid officers to carry into execution the provisions of the law, without any intermediate election of guardians.

Section 19.—Enables the commissioners to provide a chapel, and to make such regulations as they deem expedient, for securing the religious worship of any denomination of Christians in the workhouses.

Sections 20, 21, 22, 23, 24.—Provide for the purchase of three additional acres of land to be used for a cemetery, or for the erection of fever wards. The commissioners are also empowered to hire or purchase, not exceeding 25 acres, for the purpose of erecting a school for the joint reception maintenance and education of the children of the North and South Dublin unions, the management of such school to be conducted by a board chosen from among the guardians of the two unions, in such manner as the commissioners shall by order direct. Other unions may also be formed into school districts in like manner, and for a like purpose.

Sections 25, 26.—The commissioners empowered to prescribe the qualifications and the duties of all officers, and to determine their continuance or removal, and to regulate their salaries, &c. The administration of relief is also subject to the commissioners' direction and control.

Sections 27, 28, 29.—Accounts are to be kept and audited as prescribed by the commissioners. Any payment disallowed by an auditor, is to be recovered from the party debited therewith. And on or before the 1st of May, in every year, an account is to be laid before parliament of the expenditure on relief of the poor, and of the total number relieved in each union, during the year ended on the 29th of September preceding.

The 10*th and* 11*th Vict. cap.* 84, is entitled ' An Act to make Provision for the Punishment of Vagrants, and Persons offending against the Laws in force for the Relief of the Destitute Poor in Ireland '—22*nd July* 1847.

The 10th and 11th Vict. cap. 84.

Sections 1, 2, 3.—After declaring it to be expedient to make further provision for the punishment of beggars and vagrants

&c., the 59*th section* of the Irish Poor Relief Act[m] is repealed, and it is enacted instead, that every person deserting or wilfully neglecting to maintain his wife or child, so that they become destitute and be relieved in or out of the workhouse of any union, shall on conviction be committed to hard labour for any time not exceeding three months. And persons wandering abroad begging or gathering alms, or procuring children to do so, and every person going from one union or electoral division to another for the purpose of obtaining relief, shall be liable on conviction to be committed to hard labour for any time not exceeding one month.

Sections 4, 5.—Offenders may be apprehended by any person whatsoever, and taken before a justice to be dealt with as is above provided. Or when apprehended, the offender may be delivered over to a constable or other peace officer, to be taken before a justice for like purpose. Justices may upon proof of offence, issue their warrant for the apprehension of any such offender, to be dealt with as the Act directs. Proceedings by or before any justice are not to be quashed for want of form, nor removable by writ of certiorari.

The 10*th and* 11*th Vict. cap.* 90, is entitled ' An Act to provide for the Execution of the Laws for Relief of the Poor in Ireland.' After reciting the several previous Acts under which the administration of relief to the poor in Ireland is subject to the direction and control of the Poor Law Commissioners, whose commission will shortly expire, it declares it to be " expedient that the control of the administration of the laws for the relief of the poor in Ireland should be wholly separated from the control of the administration of the laws for relief of the poor in England," and enacts that her Majesty may from time to time by warrant under the royal sign manual, appoint a fit person who, with the chief and under secretaries of the lord lieutenant shall have the control, and shall be styled " Commissioners for administering the Laws for Relief of the Poor in Ireland," and the person so appointed shall be styled the Chief Commissioner—

The 10th and 11th Vict. cap. 90, 22nd July 1847.

---

[m] Ante, p. 227.

Sections 2, 3, 4, 5.—The appointment of every chief commissioner is to be published in the 'Dublin Gazette.' The commissioners are to have a seal, which shall have the same force and effect as the seal of the Poor Law Commissioners; and they may appoint a secretary, inspectors, clerks &c., and may assign to the inspectors such duties, and delegate to them such powers as they may think necessary.

Sections 6, 7, 8.—One of the inspectors is to be appointed an assistant-commissioner, to assist in the business of the office in such manner as the commissioners direct; and to him may be delegated the powers and functions of the chief commissioner in the latter's absence. The inspectors are entitled to attend boards of guardians, and all meetings held for the relief of the poor, and may take part in the proceedings, but are not to vote. All salaries are to be determined by the Treasury.

Sections 9, 10.—The powers and duties of the Poor Law Commissioners are transferred to the new commissioners; and if any vacancy occur, the surviving or continuing commissioners or commissioner may continue to act. The commissioners are constituted a body corporate, and for all purposes connected with the administration of the laws for the relief of the poor throughout Ireland they are to be deemed successors of the Poor Law Commissioners, all property held by whom becomes vested in them accordingly.

Sections 11, 12, 13, 14, 15.—The commissioners are empowered to make rules orders and regulations, and to vary or rescind the same. Also to make general rules with the approbation of the lord lieutenant, who may at any time disallow the same or any part thereof, without prejudice however to things lawfully done under them before such disallowance. Every rule order or regulation directed to, or affecting more than one union, is to be deemed a general rule.

Sections 16, 17, 18.—The rules orders and regulations of the Poor Law Commissioners are to continue in force until varied or rescinded by the commissioners appointed under this Act, whose authority is in all cases to be substituted for the former, and is to have like force and effect in Ireland. Acts under seal not to be valid, unless signed by two of the commissioners, or by the chief commissioner, or in his absence by the assistant-commissioner.

Sections 19, 20.—The commissioners empowered to summon witnesses not exceeding twenty miles distant, and to make inquiries and call for returns, and examine on oath. Persons giving false evidence are subjected to the penalties of perjury;

and on refusing to give evidence, or neglecting to obey the commissioners' summons, or to produce books vouchers &c., are to be deemed guilty of a misdemeanour.

Sections 21, 22.—The commissioners are annually to report their proceedings to the lord lieutenant. The Report is to be laid before parliament, and is to contain a distinct statement of every order and direction issued in respect to out-door relief. All lawful proceedings of the Poor Law Commissioners, and all things done under previous Acts, and not varied or repealed by this Act, are declared valid.

Section 23.—The chief commissioner and other persons to be appointed and employed under this Act, are not to hold office or exercise any of the powers hereby given, "for a longer period than five years next after the day of the passing of this Act, and thenceforth until the end of the then next session of parliament," after which the power of appointing commissioners is to cease to operate or have effect.

These three Acts have, it will be seen, made very considerable changes in the law, and taken conjointly with the original Relief Act of 1838, and the Amendment Act of 1843,[n] may be considered as forming the entire code of Irish Poor Laws, and such moreover as they may be expected to continue, there being apparently no room for further alteration, or at least not to any material extent.

The sanction of out-door relief given by the first of the three Acts is a most important departure from the principle of the original statute, and was wrung from the legislature by the distressing circumstances in which the country was placed by the successive failures of the potato crop. With starvation raging almost universally around, it was felt that it would be impossible to maintain the restriction of relief to the limits of the workhouse. The concession made in the 1*st and* 2*nd sections* must however be regarded as exceptional, and as being intended to meet an exceptional case ; for the necessity of work-

General improport of the new Acts.

---

[n] That is *The* 1*st and* 2*nd Vict. cap.* 56, and *The* 6*th and* 7*th Vict. cap.* 92. Ante, pp. 222 *et seq.* and 291 *et seq.*

house relief being the established rule, never perhaps
commanded more general assent, than at the time when
a departure from it was thus sanctioned. The author
was examined before a committee of the house of lords
on this question, and he gave it as his deliberate
opinion that under the circumstances existing in Ireland
the concession was necessary, the preservation of life
being paramount to all other considerations; but at the
same time he considered, that the rule of in-door relief
should be departed from only so far, and in such a way,
as would secure its resumption with the least difficulty
and at the earliest possible period; and the two first
sections of the Act are not at variance with this view.[o]
In sanctioning out-door relief under the then emergency,
the legislature limited its application, imposing certain
conditions and restrictions, and at the same time in-
vesting the commissioners with large powers for checking abuse. Nay more, as if distrusting the discretion
of the commissioners themselves, *the 21st section of cap.*
90 provides that their Report, which is to be laid before
parliament, " shall contain a distinct statement of every
order and direction issued by them in respect to out-
door relief." The appointment of relieving and medical
officers and of district committees, was no doubt a considerable extension of the union machinery, but it was
necessary for giving effect to the law at the time, and
either or all might be discontinued when no longer

---

[o] The necessity for adhering to the principle of indoor relief was fully recognised by this committee, whose inquiries were for the most part limited to
that point, without going into the general question of the Poor Law. Any de-
tailed account of the committee's proceedings does not therefore appear to be
called for at this time, as no new light was thrown upon the subject by its
investigations. The same may be said of the commission for "inquiring into
the state of the law and practice in respect to the occupation of land in Ireland," (of which the Earl of Devon was chairman), and whose reports are exceedingly valuable; but they do not directly bear upon our subject, and have
therefore not been noticed. I have indeed endeavoured to confine attention to
the Poor-law itself, and to those matters immediately connected with it, and
calculated to elucidate its working, these collectively presenting a field sufficiently extensive.

required. The limitation of relief by the 9*th section*, and the extension of assistance for the purpose of emigration to persons not in a workhouse by the 14*th section*, are both likely to be of use, as may also be the provision in the 16*th section* with regard to ex-officio guardians. But the power given to the commissioners by the 17*th and* 18*th sections*, to alter unions, and to dissolve boards of guardians and appoint paid officers to carry the law into execution, is by far the most important of the provisions of this Act, with the exception of those sanctioning out-relief.

The second of the above Acts (*cap.* 84) is in fact a resumption of the vagrancy clauses which were intended to form part of the original Relief Act,[p] and which have now been rendered more necessary by the sanctioning of out-relief. The third of the above Acts (*cap.* 90) providing for the appointment of a separate commission for Ireland, may be regarded as a consequence of the unfortunate condition of that country, which was now said to require all the care and undivided attention of distinct functionaries. I have already stated that such was not my opinion, and after all that has passed I still am satisfied that the Poor Laws of England and Ireland might be administered under the superintendence of the same commission, as efficiently as under separate commissions; and that there would be a weight of authority influence and other advantages arising from the combination of the two, which would not be found in a separate commission. The example of Scotland was much relied upon as warranting the separation, but the cases are not similar, the Scottish Poor Law differing essentially from that of England, whereas the Irish law is directly founded upon it, and in its working must to a great degree be regulated by English ex-

---

[p] Ante, p. 211.

perience. But the separation having taken place, it
would be difficult to retrace the step, unless indeed
there should be, as has on high authority been proposed,
an entire amalgamation of the two governments by
abolishing the office of lord lieutenant, in which case
the Irish commission would naturally if not necessarily
become merged in the English. It is bootless however
to speculate upon these or other possible changes, and
we will therefore resume our task of tracing out the
progress of the law, and inquiring into the circumstances under which it has to be administered.

On the passing of the first of the above Acts (10*th*
and 11*th Vict. cap*. 31, commonly known as the Relief
Extension Act), copies of it were forwarded to all
the unions, and the attention of the several boards of
guardians was called to the necessity of making provision on a much larger scale than heretofore for the
relief of the poor, and pointing out the conditions on
which the relief was henceforward to be administered
to the classes of infirm and able-bodied. Five additional assistant-commissioners were also appointed [q] to
attend to the large increase of duties now devolved
upon the commission. On the 27th of August
the appointment of Mr. Twisleton as chief
commissioner, under the 10*th and* 11*th Vict.
cap*. 90, was notified in the Dublin Gazette, and on the
following day the administration of the law became
vested in the new commission established by that Act,
the ten gentlemen then acting as assistant-commissioners
were appointed inspectors, and Mr. Power was appointed
the assistant-commissioner.

Change of the
commission.
August 27,
1847.

The extent of sickness and mortality in the workhouses towards the middle of April, has already
been noticed.[r] The returns continued to show

Decrease of
sickness and
mortality.

[q] These were Mr. Crawford, Mr. Bourke, Mr. Stanley, and Mr. Barron.
Mr. Phelan had been appointed some months previously to superintend the
sanitary state of the workhouses. Mr. Stanley afterwards became secretary,
and was succeeded as inspector by Mr. Flanagan.
[r] Ante, p. 326.

a gradual decrease of deaths from that time, although there was no material decrease in the number of inmates or of fever patients until the month of July, when a decline rapidly took place in all three ; and in the last week of August the number of inmates was reduced to 76,319, of sick (including 5,782 fever patients) to 15,240, and of deaths to 646, or 8 in every 1,000 weekly. In the first week of October the inmates had again increased to 83,719, but the deaths were only 433, averaging 5 per 1,000 weekly. These numbers show the extent of the pressure on the workhouses in the earlier part of 1847. But the extent of assistance afforded under the Temporary Relief and the Fever Hospital Acts (10th and 11th Vict. caps. 7 and 22) must also be stated, in order to show the universality of the distress. Under the former Act, on the 8th of May rations were issued to 826,325 persons; on the Decrease of rations issued. 5th of June to 2,729,684; on the 3rd of July to 3,020,712; on the 1st of August to 2,520,376; on the 29th of August to 1,105,800 ; on the 12th of September to 505,984; and at the end of September the issues altogether ceased. Under the latter Act accommodation was provided for the treatment of 26,378 fever patients, and the average number in hospital was about 13,000. The proceedings under these Acts, when viewed in conjunction with those under the Poor Law, will sufficiently explain the magnitude of the crisis through which the country passed at this period, and the fearful suffering and privations to which the people were unhappily and it may be added unavoidably exposed.

The financial state of the unions became greatly depressed during this trying period. The fact of Financial state of the unions. the treasurers' balances having turned against the unions is noticed in the Report of the previous year,[s] and this continued down to the end of September, when owing to great exertions in the collection, the

---

* Ante, p. 328.

returns again showed a credit balance of upwards of 10,000*l.* in favour of the guardians. There was still however a large arrear remaining for collection, and this continued to be the case throughout the succeeding half-year, notwithstanding that the large sum of 961,354*l.* was collected and lodged with the treasurers, a proof that the guardians were not backward in making provision for carrying out the law, although the impoverished state of many of the unions rendered the collection difficult after the rates were made.

The harvest of 1847 proved to be a good one. Contrary to expectation the potato crop was free from disease, but the quantity grown was comparatively small, and the price continued so high that the peasantry were unable to purchase. The failure of the crop in the two previous years had discouraged them from planting, and they were consequently in great measure deprived of their usual means of living. The large importations of Indian meal had however so far reduced the price of that and other descriptions of food, that the general cost of subsistence was not much greater than in ordinary seasons, and in districts where the people found employment at moderate wages, they generally fared better than in former years. But in districts where there was no employment or money wages, and where the peasantry had been accustomed to subsist on potatoes raised by themselves, this resource being neglected, they would necessarily be in want of food, and would require assistance to preserve them from starvation. It was certain therefore, notwithstanding the non-appearance of the potato disease, that there would be much distress in many parts of the country long before the approach of harvest in the following year; and in order to be prepared for affording needful relief in such a contingency, without at the same time weakening the incentive to independent exertion in the labouring classes, it was necessary that a large increase of workhouse accommodation should be provided. This

A good harvest.

point the commissioners continued earnestly to press upon the attention of the several boards of guardians, and for the most part with success.

The extent and population of the Irish unions and the constitution of many of the boards of guardians, rendered it probable that the new and more laborious duties imposed upon them by the Extension Act (10*th and* 11*th Vict. cap.* 31) would not always be fulfilled, and that in some instances there might either be a failure of necessary relief, or a misapplication of the union funds. The power of dissolving a board of guardians, and at once appointing paid officers to discharge their duties, was given to the commissioners for the purpose of enabling them to deal with cases of this kind ; and being armed with such a power, they were responsible for its exercise whenever the occasion called for it— " Although reluctant in the highest degree, (they say) to interfere even temporarily with a system of self-government involving the great principle of popular representation in the raising and expenditure of a public fund, it appeared to them that in the immediate circumstances of the country, a more imperative object demanded for a time the sacrifice of those considerations, and that it was their paramount duty by every means which the legislature had placed at their disposal, to provide for the effectual relief of the destitute poor." Acting under these views, and on the occurrence of what they considered to be serious default on the part of the guardians, the commissioners dissolved thirty-two boards,[t] and appointed paid officers in their stead. The default in nearly every instance was either a failure to provide sufficient funds, or to apply them efficiently in relieving the destitute. Full

32 boards of guardians dissolved.

---

t These were—Athlone, Ballina, Ballinrobe, Bantry, Cahirciveen, Carrick-on-Shannon, Castlebar, Castlereagh, Cavan, Clifden, Cootehill, Enniskillen, Ennistymon, Galway, Gort, Granard, Kanturk, Kenmare, Kilkenny, Kilrush, Longford, Loughrea, Lowtherstown, Mohill, Newcastle, New Ross, Roscommon, Scariff, Trim, Tuam, Tullamore, Waterford, and Westport.

details of each case were laid before parliament, and the necessity of the proceeding was generally admitted, although it was no doubt much to be lamented that such a necessity should have arisen.

It is, however, satisfactory to find that in a great majority of the unions relief was provided and administered by the guardians in an orderly and efficient manner. There were some exceptions in addition to the above, it is true, and the commissioners had to exert all their influence and authority in procuring the appointment of relieving officers to receive and inquire into applications for relief, as provided by the Extension Act and directed by their own order. Another point on which the commissioners Out-door found much difficulty in winning the acquies-employment. cence of the guardians was with regard to the mode of employing poor persons, for whose relief out of the workhouse under the 2nd section of the Extension Act, a necessity had arisen in some unions. The guardians wished the employment to be of a productive or profitable nature, and that it should be applied mainly with that view. The commissioners were desirous that the employment should serve as a test of destitution, and recommended stone-breaking as open to least objection, the food to be given not as the price of labour but in relief of destitution, the labour being required simply as the condition of the relief; and in the unions where out-door relief in food was given to the able-bodied on this principle, the numbers are said to have been for the most part kept within moderate limits.

But although the labour-test might so far have suc-Increase of ceeded, the operation of the workhouse system workhouse accommoda- in the present difficult circumstances had been tion. found far less equivocal, and its efficiency was more universally acknowledged by those engaged in the administration of relief. A large extension of workhouse room, partly permanent partly temporary had been provided. The whole accommodation including additional

workhouses and fever hospitals connected with the workhouses would be sufficient for upwards of 150,000 persons, " being an addition of more than one-third to the
accommodation originally provided." In consequence
of this great increase of workhouse accommodation, it
appears that in 25 of the unions no relief was given out
of the workhouse, " except perhaps in the occasional
exercise of the provisional powers of the relieving
officers," and yet the workhouses of none of these unions
were said to be full. In 35 other unions, out-door relief
was afforded only under the 1st *section* of the Extension
Act, that is to the infirm, widows with two or more
children, and persons disabled by sickness or accident.
In the remaining 71 unions, orders had been issued
under the 2nd *section*, authorizing out-door relief in food;
but in only 23 of these was it authorized to be given
without distinction of class.

In proof of the efficiency of the workhouse in checking
applications for relief, when not caused by actual necessity, the example of Dublin may be cited. In the first
week of July, rations were gratuitously issued The Dublin
in the two Dublin unions to 57,509 persons, and unions.
the proportion of these classed as able-bodied amounted
with their families to 46,432. , In the South union the
number on the relief lists was greatly reduced before the
15th of August, the day on which the issues under the
Temporary Relief Act were ordered to cease; but in the
North union more than 20,000 persons continued to
receive rations, and the commissioners were entreated
to issue an order under the powers given to them by
the Extension Act sanctioning its further continuance,
the guardians being apprehensive that so large an
amount of relief could not with safety be suddenly discontinued. The commissioners deemed it to be their
duty to resist the appeal, and recommended the guardians
to convert a building then in their occupation and capable
of accommodating 400 persons, into a subsidiary work-

house. This was accordingly done, and admission was offered to such of the able-bodied and their families as applied for relief when the rations were discontinued; but the new subsidiary workhouse was not filled by those who accepted the offer, and all the others found the means of living by their own exertions. The class receiving out-door relief under the 1st section of the Act (i. e. the aged and infirm poor and widows with two or more children) were at the same time, with some assistance from the mendicity institution, reduced to about 4,000 persons; and no necessity afterwards arose for issuing an order under the 2nd section in either of the Dublin unions.

To this example of the efficiency of the workhouse in preventing undue applications for relief, may be added the testimony of the relief commissioners appointed under The 10th and 11th Vict. cap. 7,ᵘ as to' the extreme difficulty or rather impossibility in the state of Ireland at that time, of guarding against gross abuse in the administration of relief without the corrective of the workhouse test, even although in the shape of daily rations of cooked food. In their third Report dated 17th June 1847, the commissioners make the following remarkable statement — " In several instances the government inspecting officers found no difficulty in striking off hundreds of names that ought not to have been placed on the lists, including sometimes those of servants and men in the constant employ of persons of considerable station and property. These latter are frequently themselves members of the committees, and in some cases the very chairmen, being magistrates, have sanctioned the issue of rations to tenants of their own of considerable holdings, possessed of live stock, and who it was found had paid up their last half-year's rent." . . . " In

Report of commissioners appointed under the 10th and 11th Vict. cap. 7.

ᵘ Ante, p. 317.

other districts, the measure is subject to deception and
petty frauds practised by many of the order immediately above the class of actually destitute, and which
cannot be entirely checked by the best exertions of the
best committees.   Even in the districts where the
service is most correctly performed, the numbers on the
lists will no doubt exceed those of the really destitute."
It was perhaps to be expected under the circumstances
then existing in Ireland, that something like what is
here described might occur; but it could hardly have
been expected that it would have been to such an extent,
or that persons in the positions named would have
descended to practices at once so disgraceful and so un-
patriotic.   Against such frauds the workhouse seemed
to be the only safeguard.

The entire expenditure from the rates on relief of the
poor in the 130 unions during the twelve Expenditure
on relief
months ending 29th September 1847, was of the poor.
803,684*l*.   The number of inmates on that day was
86,376, and the total number relieved in the workhouses within the year was 417,139.   There was some
expenditure in a few of the unions shortly before the
29th September, although the issues under the Temporary Relief Act did not until then wholly cease.
The relief under the Extension Act (10*th and* 11*th
Vict., cap.* 31) which then commenced, continued to
increase as the distress arising from the exhaustion of
the small crops raised in many parts of the country
became more and more severe.   On the 12th Numbers in
the work-
February 1848 the number in the several work- houses.
houses amounted to 135,467, and the mortality reached
11 per 1,000.   This was perhaps to be expected from the
great pressure upon the workhouses, and the wretched
condition of very many of the poor persons at the time
they were admitted.   Contagious disease again prevailed, and the fatal effects again extended to the workhouse officers, ninety-four of whom died, chiefly of fever,

and also two of the Poor Law inspectors, and one vice-guardian in course of the year.

Although the numbers in the workhouses went on
Out-door relief. increasing in the latter months of 1847, it was not until February and March 1848 that the houses became filled, and that out-door relief was largely administered. In February the cost of out-relief in money and food amounted to 72,039*l.*, in March to 81,339*l.* The numbers and cost were then both at their maximum, and according to the best estimate which could be formed, the average daily number of out-door poor relieved was 703,762, and of in-door 140,536, making an aggregate of 844,298 persons. The description of food supplied to the poor in lieu of their habitual food the potato, consisted for the most part of a pound of Indian meal, that being the quantity of cereal food approved by the Central Board of Health in Ireland as necessary for the daily sustenance of an adult. The price of Indian meal was at that time about 1*d.* per lb., so that the cost of the food thus supplied probably did not exceed the cost of that to which the people had been accustomed. It appears therefore that in the early part of 1848 no less than 800,000 persons were relieved daily at the charge of the poor-rates, consisting chiefly of the most helpless part of the most indigent classes in Ireland; and the commissioners say they " cannot doubt that of this number a large proportion are by this means, and this means alone, daily preserved from death through want of food." The above 800,000 is irrespective of the children supplied with food and clothing by " The British Association," the number of whom in March 1848 amounted to upwards of 200,000.[x] So that the total number of persons then receiving eleemosynary support must have exceeded a million, or over one-eighth of the entire population.

---

[x] See Report of the association, p. 41.

The official returns of the collection and expenditure of the poor-rates are made up to the 31st March 1848, and comprise six months only of the parochial year which will end on the 29th September following. They show that in those six months 961,356*l.* had been collected, and 781,198*l.* expended, thus exhibiting an excess of collection over expenditure of 180,158*l.* The state of the balances appears therefore to have greatly improved,[y] and rates to the amount of 661,855*l.* still remained on the books for collection. " Up to this point therefore (the commissioners observe) the financial progress has been favourable "—But they add, " if we should have to sustain operations for five months longer, at the rate of expenditure exhibited for March, it is clear that great exertions have yet to be made in the collection of rates, in order to escape a large accumulation of debt at the close of the year." The above statements apply to the unions in the aggregate. There are however the commissioners say, certain unions which " cannot for some years be cleared from present debt under the most favourable circumstances, and in unions which on the whole are well provided with funds, many electoral divisions are in a state of almost hopeless bankruptcy."

Distress in certain unions.

The proceedings of the " British Relief Association " have already been noticed.[z] The committee of the association had still a considerable sum at their disposal in the latter end of 1847, and this it was determined to appropriate in aid of such of the distressed unions above adverted to as the Poor Law Commissioners should recommend for that purpose, and also in " affording food and clothing to children through the medium of schools." Accordingly grants to the amount of 143,519*l.* were successively made to

British Relief Association.

---

[y] Ante, p. 328.   [z] Ante, p. 321.

the distressed unions[a] in aid of their general expenditure ; and with regard to the school-children, it is said —" by the 1st of January 1848 the system was in full operation in thirteen of the more distressed unions, 58,000 children were on the relief-roll of the association, and this number gradually increased, until in the month of March upwards of 200,000 children, attending schools of all denominations in twenty-seven western unions, were participating in this relief. The total expenditure for feeding the children amounted to 80,885*l.*, in addition to which the sum of 12,083*l.* was spent in clothing, making a total expenditure during the second period of the relief operations of the association of 236,487*l.*"[b] Treasury grants to the extent of 114,968*l.* had also been made in aid of the distressed unions, during the present year.

It may not be irrelevant here to state, that the entire of the rates made in all the unions from the first introduction of the Poor Law down to the date of the present Report, have (exclusive of the last rate) amounted to 2,496,412*l.*, of which not more than 48,804*l.*, or 2 per cent., has been lost—143,046*l.*, or 6 per cent., of arrears having been carried into the rates last made. The last-made rates amounted to 1,462,878*l.*, which added to the above makes a total of 3,959,290*l.* assessed upon the property of Ireland for the relief of the poor, in course of the ten years since the introduction of the Poor Law, the last three being years of such intense distress as it was perhaps never before the lot of an entire people to be subjected to.

Total amount of rates raised.

---

[a] These were Ballina, Belmullet, Ballinrobe, Ballyshannon, Bantry, Boyle, Cahirciveen, Carrick-on-Shannon, Castlebar, Castlereagh, Clifden, Donegal, Galway, Glenties, Kenmare, Kilrush, Listowel, Manorhamilton, Milford, Mohill, Roscommon, Scariff, Skibbereen, Sligo, Swineford, Tralee, Dingle, Tuam, Westport, Athlone, Ennistymon, Gort, Nenagh, Loughrea and New Ross. This list somewhat differs from the one given in the commissioners' Report, but I quote from that furnished by the association, whose Report was made subsequently, being dated 1st January 1849.

[b] See Report of the British Relief Association, pp. 41 and 46.

The Report for 1848-9 is dated, not on the 1st May, as before, but on the 14th July. At the end of their last Report, the commissioners adverted to the great efforts which were made to restore the potato to its former position of the staple crop of Ireland, as being a circumstance at once hopeful and alarming. The policy of a people's relying for subsistence on a crop so uncertain in its produce, and which so soon decays, is no doubt a question of momentous importance. But this was lost sight of in the promise of an abundant harvest; and as the disease had done little mischief last year, it was hoped the country would be equally free from its ravages in the present. At the beginning of August however, the appearance of blight was reported from many parts of the country, and although not so general nor so destructive as in 1846, the disease proved much worse than in 1847, and there can be no doubt that a considerable proportion of the crop was destroyed by it. In October sound potatoes were sold at 8*d.* per stone, a price at which the ordinary rate of wages would not allow a labourer to purchase them for the support of his family. Another season of distress was therefore evidently impending. The out-relief lists had been reduced from 830,000 in July, to 200,000 on the 1st of October, when the numbers again began to increase, and on the last day of December they amounted to nearly 400,000. The numbers in the workhouses increased in the same period from 114,000 to 185,000, with a weekly rate of mortality of 6½ per 1,000. Statements of the numbers relieved, and the cost of the relief afforded, were periodically submitted to parliament throughout the whole of this trying period.

In the earlier months of 1849 there was greater privation and suffering among the population of the western and south-western districts, than at any time since the fatal season of 1846-7. " Ex-

Margin notes:

1849. Second annual report of Poor Law Commissioners for Ireland.

Recurrence of the potato disease.

Great distress and sickness.

haustion of resources by the long continuance of adverse circumstances, caused a large accession to the ranks of the destitute. Clothing had been worn out or parted with to provide food, or seed in seed-time; and the loss of cabins and small holdings of land, either by eviction or voluntary abandonment, rendered many thousands of families shelterless and destitute of fuel as well as food." The distress hence arising, aggravated by the inclement weather which then prevailed, was not we are told effectually met by the system of out-door relief. Where the workhouses were full, poor persons receiving out-relief were often compelled to part with a portion of their food to obtain a lodging. The cabins became crowded with ill-fed, ill-clothed, sickly people, and epidemic disease found victims prepared for its attacks. A great proportion of those who died in the work-houses at this period, had previously suffered from fever and dysentery, and entered the workhouse weakened by extreme privation, or in an advanced state of disease.

In the month of March a new enemy appeared, Cholera breaks out. cholera having broken out in the western and south-western unions, whence it afterwards extended to other parts of the country. The disease however assumed its most virulent form in the above unions, and proved extensively fatal to the inmates of the workhouses, as well as to the population generally. Great exertions were made to check its ravages; but the commissioners express their regret that a want of means had crippled their efforts, and in some urgent cases they had been obliged to apply for permission to appropriate a limited portion of the funds placed at their disposal by government, to provide the means of treatment for cholera patients, at a time when they were anxious to apply every sum remitted to them to the purchase of food for the in-door and out-door poor in the distressed unions. After a time the cholera disappeared from most of the unions in the west and south, but at the date of the Report it still prevailed with much virulence in other parts of Ireland.

The inmates of the several workhouses in the first week of March 1849 amounted to 196,523, and the weekly mortality to 9½ per 1,000. In the first week of May the number of inmates was 220,401, with a mortality of 12½ per 1,000. At the end of June the inmates were 214,867, and the mortality was reduced to 6¼ per 1,000. The numbers receiving out-relief at the three periods respectively were 592,705—646,964—and 768,902. These numbers show the extent of distress to which the people had been reduced by famine and disease in the last four disastrous years. This is also evidenced by the inquests held in cases of alleged death through actual want, the number of which in the first five months of 1849 amounted to 431. The suffering must necessarily indeed have been greater in each successive year than in the one preceding, since the general means were being continually reduced by the failure of the crops, the weakest and poorest of the people suffering first, then those a degree above them, and so on, until the comparatively well-to-do occupier of a few acres of land who had contributed to the relief of others, is himself dragged down to the condition of the lowest.

A conviction appears to have become very general, that the abuses and shortcomings incidental to out-door relief, especially when administered on a large scale, cannot be altogether prevented; and that in-door relief is preferable, not only under ordinary circumstances, but in seasons of severe distress like the present. Hence the guardians had hired building after building in aid of the workhouses at first provided; and the entire accommodation, which was originally calculated for 100,000 inmates, and which during the previous year had been increased to 150,000, had now been so far extended as to be equal to the accommodation

Extent of relief and mortality.

Extension of workhouse accommodation.

of 250,000. On this circumstance and the convictions out of which it arose, the commissioners chiefly founded their hope of securing an effective and economical administration of the law. It will be their duty, they say, to give a right direction to these views, by endeavouring to make the auxiliary establishments effective in point of classification and discipline, and to reduce where practicable the expenses of management; and if their efforts should be assisted by the gradual return of agricultural prosperity in the western and south-western parts of Ireland, they confidently expect at no very distant period to be enabled to withhold the exercise of the exceptional power confided to them in the *2nd section* of the Relief Extension Act,[c] or at least to confine its operation within very narrow limits.

The fact that in 25 of the unions no relief was given Restriction of except in the workhouse is mentioned in the relief to the workhouse. Report of the preceding year.[d] Several unions which then gave out-relief have since ceased to do so, and the number in which relief is restricted to the workhouse was now 35. In the great majority of these unions the result of such restrictions had been in all respects satisfactory. The applications of proper objects were not refused, and yet there had been sufficient means for relieving all the really destitute, whilst except in cases where epidemic disease had prevailed in the neighbourhood, and been thence imparted to the inmates, the workhouses of these unions had generally been healthy. In some instances however where the destitution was severe and wide-spreading, and where the auxiliary houses had been insufficient or defective, the adherence to in-door relief exclusively was less satisfactory. The insufficiency of workhouse accommodation led to overcrowding, and thence arose disease, fed and aggravated by the continual influx of destitute persons in a state of utter

---

[c] Ante, p. 330.   [d] Ante, p. 343.

exhaustion, or bearing about them the seeds of the prevalent malady. In all such cases, and they were not many, the guardians were urged to resort to those provisions of the Act which empower them to afford out-door relief, until they had provided the necessary accommodation for enabling them to restrict it to the workhouse without endangering life, or violating the principle of the Poor Law.

In connection with workhouse relief, the mortality which took place among the officers and other poor-law officials ought to be noticed, as illustrating the duties which the exigencies of the service required from them. The subject has already been adverted to as creating difficulty in obtaining suitable persons to fill these offices.[e] Although not so great in the present year as in 1846-7, the deaths of workhouse officers by fever or cholera amounted to no less than seventy, including nine chaplains and eight medical officers. Seven of the vice-guardians likewise fell victims to disease in the discharge of their arduous duties, as well as eight of the temporary inspectors, together with Mr. Hancock, who had acted under the commission from the commencement, first as assistant-commissioner and then as inspector.[f] *Mortality among the administrators of the law.*

An increased disposition had latterly been evinced by the boards of guardians for promoting emigration, under the provisions of the Extension Act.[g] The steady progress of the measure for sending orphan girls from the Irish workhouses out to the Australian colonies, the commissioners considered highly satisfactory. The number of these girls embarked for Adelaide and Sydney since the spring of 1848 was 2,219, at a cost to the unions of about 5l. each for outfit and *Emigration.*

---

[e] Ante, p. 326.
[f] The vacancy caused by the lamented death of Mr. Hancock, was filled by the appointment of Mr. Lynch, the temporary inspector of the Westport union.
[g] Ante, p. 331.

conveyance to Plymouth, the remainder of the charge being defrayed from the colonial funds. Many other unions were desirous that the orphan girls from their workhouses should participate in this arrangement, but the number at first was limited to 2,500. A hope is however expressed that means will be found for continuing to remove from this country a class of emigrants so eligible in every respect, and so much required in the colonies. The entire amount expended on emigration during the year ending on the 29th September 1848, was 2;776*l.*—a sum, it is observed, " less important in its direct effects, than as showing a growth of opinion in favour of this method of relief." Spontaneous emigration, chiefly to the United States, and irrespective of aid from the poor-rates, was exceedingly active from all parts of Ireland at this time, the natural love of country having been deadened by the pressure of want and disease.

In the session of 1848 two short Acts were passed which it is necessary to notice. The 11*th and* 12*th Victoria, cap.* 25, extends the powers for hiring or purchasing land for the use of workhouses to 25 acres, in addition to the 15 acres previously authorized. It likewise empowers the commissioners to combine unions for the maintenance and education of poor children, and also enables boards of guardians to provide for the burial of deceased poor persons. The 11*th and* 12*th Vict., cap.* 47, provides " for the protection and relief of the destitute poor evicted from their dwellings," and directs relieving-officers forthwith to take order for the relief of such persons, either in or out of the workhouse, and to report the circumstances to the guardians at their next meeting. The power of purchasing an additional 25 acres of land given by the first of these Acts, was chiefly with a view to the establishment of industrial schools, and was not intended to be used as a means of employing the workhouse inmates. Few things

The 11 and 12 Vict. caps. 25 and 47.

would be more objectionable on principle, or more conducive to lax management, than adding such a quantity
of land to a workhouse for the purpose of being cultivated by the inmates.

In the session of 1849 likewise two Acts were passed
requiring our attention. The first of these,— The 12 *and*
13 *Vict.*
The 12th and 13th Vict., cap. 4, relates to the   *cap.* 4.
appointment of vice-guardians. It provides that when a
board of guardians shall have been dissolved, and paid
officers appointed, before the 25th of March 1848, the
commissioners may direct the continuance of such paid
officers until the 1st of November 1849, and no election
of guardians is to take place in the interim. But it also
provides that the commissioners may if they think fit
discontinue the paid officers, and direct the election of a
board of guardians at any time. The second of these
Acts is known as ' The Rate-in-Aid Act,' and its provisions require to be more fully explained.

The ' Rate-in-Aid Act,' *12th and 13th Vict. cap.* 24,
makes provision for levying " a general rate in The Rate-in-
aid of certain unions and electoral divisions in Aid Act.
12 *and* 13
Ireland," and it enacts as follows :— *Vict. cap.* 24.

Section 1.—The Poor Law Commissioners, with the approval of
the lord lieutenant, may during each of the years ending
the 31st of December 1849 and 1850, from time to time
declare the amount they deem necessary for the above purposes, and may assess the same upon the several unions in
proportion to the annual value of the property in each rateable
to the relief of the poor ; but the sum levied in any union in
either of the two years is not to exceed 6*d.* in the pound on
such annual value. The commissioners are to transmit to the
guardians of each union an order under seal, stating the
amount so assessed, and the portion leviable in each electoral
division, according to the value of its rateable property.

Section 2.—In the rate next made on each electoral division, the
guardians are to provide for the sum so leviable ; and the
treasurer of the union, out of all lodgments made with him of
such rate, or any subsequent rate, on account of any division,
is to place one moiety thereof to the credit of such division in
an account to be entitled " The Union Rate-in-Aid Account,"

until the whole sum leviable on such division shall have been so placed. And the treasurer is to pay over all sums so from time to time received by him to a separate account at the bank of Ireland, entitled "The General Rate-in-Aid Account."

Sections 3, 4, 5.—The commissioners of the Treasury may order the whole or any part of the money standing in such separate accounts at the bank of Ireland, to be paid to such persons, at such times, and under such conditions as they may think fit, for affording relief to destitute poor persons in any union or electoral division, or for assisting emigration, or for repaying advances made for any of these purposes. And for the more speedy affording of such relief, the commissioners of the Treasury are empowered to advance out of the consolidated fund, any sums not in the whole exceeding 100,000*l.*, the same to be repayable out of any rates levied in pursuance of the Act. Accounts of all receipts and payments under the Act are to be made up to the 31st December, in the present and the following year respectively.

This Act was passed on the 24th May 1849, and its duration is limited to the 31st December 1850. It must therefore be regarded as a temporary measure directed to a temporary object, and it was accompanied by a vote authorizing an advance by the Treasury of 50,000*l.* for relief of the distressed unions in the west of Ireland. The calls which had been made upon England during the three preceding years, amounting altogether to probably little short of 10,000,000*l.* in the shape of loans advances or donations by the government, and contributions and subscriptions of one kind and another by individuals, for the relief of Irish distress, had evidently excited alarm, and appear to have given rise to a determination on the part of the legislature to revert to the precedent of the Elizabethan law, and to make the property of Ireland answerable for the relief of Irish poverty. This was certainly open to no objection in point of principle, although it may be questioned whether the most suitable time was selected for its application. We have seen the calamities to which Ireland had been exposed by the successive failure of the potato crop. Such failures were unprecedented and exceptional. The calamity had been emphatically designated as imperial; and if it were so, there would be no violation of principle, but rather the fulfilment of a duty, in one part of the empire coming to the assistance of the other. It was in fact a common cause, and was so regarded throughout England, until the repeated failures caused apprehensions as to the perpetuity of the burden, and seemed to point to the necessity of compelling the Irish people to abandon the treacherous potato, which it was thought they would hardly do, so long as they could turn to England for help whenever it failed them. The rate-in-aid was calculated to effect this object, by casting the consequences of the failure entirely upon Ireland itself, which in such case would be unable to persist in its reliance upon a crop so treacherous and uncertain as the potato.

Such it is believed were the impressions under which the Rate-in-Aid Act was passed. Its duration was limited to a little over a year and a half, and yet within that period, indeed within less than a month after it had passed, a subscription was set on foot by the government, each of its members subscribing 100*l.* and her Majesty 500*l.*, in the belief, it is declared, " that there are ways in which this money may be expended most usefully, without interfering with the relief administration through the Poor Law, such as the supply of clothing, which has now become a matter of paramount importance, especially to the children." The prospects of the next harvest were said to be favourable, but the promoters of the subscription declare " that the short intervening period must be one of such overwhelming misery, as to afford a strong claim for the exercise of private charity." [h] The distribution

A subscription promoted by government.

---

[h] This is quoted from the heading of the subscription list, as published in the ' Times ' of 16th June 1849. The money raised was confided for distribution in Ireland to Count Strzelecki.

of the money subscribed on this occasion, which did not quite amount to 10,000*l.*, was intrusted to the same benevolent gentleman who had superintended the application of the funds of the " British Relief Association," and who deservedly possessed the confidence of all parties, as well in Ireland as in England. That the urgency was great, as is above stated, there can be no doubt; and if it were susceptible of effectual relief by such means, it may be lamented that the remedy was not earlier resorted to, as it probably would have been but for the alarms which gave rise to the Rate-in-Aid Act, and prevented the intervention either of the government or individuals in furnishing eleemosynary aid.

It must not however be supposed that the whole of Ireland was in a state of "overwhelming misery." Distress more or less severe was doubtless very prevalent, and everywhere arising from the same cause; but distress so intense and overwhelming as to require immediate assistance from some extraneous source, only prevailed in certain of the western unions, where the people had depended entirely on the potato, and when that crop failed became poverty-stricken and helpless in the highest degree. The potato constituted the chief, or it may almost be said the only source of wealth in these unions, and its failure left them without other resource. Rates could not be levied, for the land yielded no available produce; and the population, accustomed to subsist in a semi-civilized state upon the potatoes raised by themselves, would nearly all have perished, as numbers of them did perish, but for the assistance which was afforded to them from England.

It was chiefly with reference to these western unions The western unions. that the Rate-in-Aid Act was passed. There were 22 of them,[i] comprising a population of

---

[i] These were Ballina, Ballinrobe, Bantry, Cahirciveen, Carrick-on-Shannon, Castlebar, Castlereagh, Clifden, Ennistymon, Galway, Glenties, Gort, Kenmare, Kilrush, Mohill, Roscommon, Scariff, Sligo, Swineford, Tuam, West-

1,468,248, thus giving an average of nearly 67,000 to each union ; and they stood in much the same relation to the other unions in Ireland, as a pauper stands in towards the independent labourer. The other unions were generally equal to the occasion, trying as the period undoubtedly was, and supported themselves through it, although not without undergoing severe privations. But these western unions were utterly destitute and without resource, and aid of some kind was necessary to prevent a fearful sacrifice of life. The aid had hitherto been furnished by England, and chiefly from the imperial treasury. The legislature now determined that it should be derived from Ireland itself, a determination that seems only open to objection, on the ground of the distress being so general and severe as to constitute an exceptional case, warranting a recurrence to extraneous sources.

The power which had been given of levying a rate in aid was forthwith acted upon, a general order being issued on the 13th of June, declaring the sum to be levied in each union and electoral division throughout Ireland, according to the value of the rateable property for the year 1849. The whole amount so assessed was 322,552*l.* 11*s.*, being at the rate of 6*d.* in the pound. The commissioners say that the resources thus placed at their disposal, and the advances by the Treasury on security of the rate in aid, " have been most seasonable, and have enabled the guardians of the unions assisted, to provide the necessaries of life during the last two months for a large mass of recipients of in-door and out-door relief, who must otherwise have been without food, the money and credit of the unions having been previously quite exhausted," and the continuance of such assistance until the period of harvest, is declared to be necessary for the relief of pressing destitution in these impoverished and overburdened districts.

A rate in aid of 6d. in the pound.

---

port, and Dingle. All the distressed unions had either paid guardians, or temporary inspectors, appointed by the commissioners.

In the year preceding 32 boards of guardians had been
Boards of
guardians
dissolved. dissolved, and paid officers appointed to execute
the law.[k]   It became necessary likewise to dis-
solve some others in the present year;[m] but two of the
preceding boards (Trim and Cavan) were revived under
the provisions of the original Relief Act, and another
(Mullingar) was revived under the 12*th and* 13*th Vict.*,
cap. 4.   By the operation of the latter Act, the boards of
guardians will, on the 1st November next, be reinstated
in all the unions now under the management of paid
officers, except the five last dissolved, which will continue
under paid officers until the 25th March 1850, unless
previously re-established by order of the commissioners.

The orders issued authorizing out-relief under the
Sanction of
out-relief. 2*nd section* of the Extension Act had, the commissioners say, been more numerous during the
present year than was intended at its commencement.
" But the rapid filling of the workhouses in certain
unions, and the pressure of the representations of distress, left them no alternative but to intrust once more
this extraordinary and exceptional power of affording relief to the able-bodied out of the workhouse, to
those charged with the administration of relief in the
western and south-western unions."   The financial state
Distressed
unions. of many of these unions was a source of continual anxiety.   In the last year 23 of them had
been furnished with assistance in aid of their rates, by
grants from government and from the funds of the
British Association, and they required like assistance in
the present.   The sums remitted for this purpose from
time to time by the Treasury, were guarded by the condition that they should not be used in payment of debts
already incurred, but be applied in purchasing the means
of preserving the lives of the people, when in danger of
perishing through want of the necessaries of life.   There

---

[k] Ante, p. 341.
[m] These were Mullingar, Boyle, Cashel, Thurles, Listowel, and Tipperary.

were other unions also whose finances were much embarrassed, although they had not yet received assistance; but all, whether assisted or not, are said to require perpetual watchfulness on the part of the commissioners and their inspectors.

The difficulties and distresses to which the country had latterly been exposed through the failure of the potato, together with the sanction given to out-door relief by the Extension Act,[n] had led many persons to consider that the unions and electoral divisions, as originally formed, were too large for the convenient and effectual administration of relief under existing circumstances. Representations to this effect were made to the government, and in March 1848 commissioners[o] were appointed for the purpose of inquiring and reporting—"whether the size and other geographical circumstances of the unions, are such as to prevent the guardians and relieving officers from attending the boards without serious interruption to their other duties" —"whether the same circumstances prevent the applicants for relief, who desire or who may be required to attend the board, from doing so without serious inconvenience"—"whether the amount of population and pauperism in each union is greater than would render it possible for the guardians in ordinary times to transact the business of the union conveniently in one day of the week"—and lastly, "what alterations it would be advisable to make in the boundaries of existing unions, and what new unions it would be desirable to form, in order to meet the wants of the country on the points adverted to, or any others which may present themselves in the course of the inquiry: due regard being had to the position of the existing workhouses, and the charge to be incurred in the erection of new workhouses."

The Boundary Commission.

---

[n] Ante, p. 330.
[o] The commissioners were Captains Larcom and Broughton of the engineers, and Mr. Crawford a poor-law inspector.

Similar inquiries were likewise to be made with respect
to the electoral divisions. Early in 1849 the commissioners reported the result of their inquiries, and recom-

Fifty new unions recommended. mended the formation of 50 new unions, the
details of which, together with maps explana-
tory of the system on which the recommendation was
made, were appended to the Report.

Early in the session of 1849, a select committee on

Select committee on the Irish Poor-laws. the Irish Poor Laws was appointed in the commons, and empowered " to report their opinion
and the minutes of evidence taken before them
from time to time, to the house." Many intelligent
witnesses were examined, and much information was
elicited with regard to the immediate object of the
inquiry, and as to its bearing upon the state of the
country generally. The recommendations of the boundary commissioners were also much canvassed, and there
appeared to be considerable diversity of opinion on the
subject, some preferring large areas both for unions and
electoral divisions, and others being favourable to small
ones. This is of course in some measure a question of
degree, and must likewise depend very much upon local

Size of the unions. circumstances. The size of a union or an electoral division might be perfectly suitable at one
time, or under one class of circumstances, and yet may
be unsuitable at another. When the unions were formed,
we were aware that some of them were too large, and
we reckoned upon these being afterwards divided, and
the district readjusted. For instance, in the case of
Ballina, the materials for constituting two efficient
boards of guardians could not be found, and so an extent
of territory sufficient for two unions, was formed into
one, until adequate executives could be found for two,
when a division might readily be effected. It was so
likewise in other cases, that of Dingle, now taken from
Tralee union and constituted a separate union, being
one ; and for my own part I always reckoned upon five

or six additional unions being created after the law had come into orderly working. I certainly never thought it likely that 50 new unions, or anything like that number, would be required; but neither did I foresee the fearful visitations to which Ireland has latterly been subjected, or the sanctioning of out-door relief under the Extension Act.

The expenditure from the rates on relief of the poor in the 131 unions, (Dingle being now added to the former number) during the twelve months ending 29th September 1848, was 1,835,634*l*. The number of inmates on that day was 124,003, and the total number relieved in the workhouses within the year was 610,463. The number receiving out-door relief on that day was 207,683, and the total number relieved out of the workhouse during the year was 1,433,042. There is here a large increase both of expenditure and numbers relieved, over the amounts in the preceding year; but the excess is perhaps in neither case greater than might be expected under the circumstances, the cause of the distress continuing, and its pressure consequently becoming year by year more severe. In proof of the great efforts which had been made to meet this distress, it is only necessary to state the amount of the poor-rates collected during the three last years, each ending on the 29th September, viz. :—

Amount of expenditure, and numbers relieved.

1846	..	..	..	..	..	£371,846
1847	..	..	..	..	..	638,403
1848	..	..	..	..	..	1,627,700

Mr. Twisleton who had ably discharged the duties of chief Poor Law Commissioner since the separate establishment of the Irish board, resigned office in the month of May in the present year, and was succeeded by Mr. Power, the assistant-commissioner, whose vacated office was filled by the appointment of Mr. Ball, one of the inspectors.

Change in the commission.

CHAPTER VI.

Third Annual Report of Poor-Law Commissioners — Further Amendment Act — Fourth Annual Report — New unions and electoral divisions — Consolidated Debts Act — Rates in aid — Fifth Annual Report — Annuities under Consolidated Debts Act — Treasury minute — Act to amend Acts relating to payment of advances — Medical charities — Medical Charities Act — First Report of Medical Charity Commissioners — Census of 1851 — Retrospection — Sixth Annual Report — Rate of wages — Expenditure, and numbers relieved — Changes in Poor-Law executive — New order of accounts — Author's letter to Lord John Russell, 1853 — Present state and future prospects of Ireland.

THE period comprised in the last chapter was one of great suffering and privation. Famine and pestilence prevailed throughout Ireland, to an extent only equalled by what is said to have occurred in some rare instances among eastern nations, if indeed it has ever been equalled in the world's history. It was altogether a fearful visitation. I have endeavoured to compress the chief incidents of the period, more especially those at all connected with the administration of the Poor Law, into one chapter, in order to place consecutively before the reader such a condensed account of the great calamity, as will prevent the necessity of again recurring to it. We will now turn to the brighter and more hopeful period which followed—when famine and disease having disappeared, the energies of the country revived, and all classes united in making strenuous efforts to remedy the evils which had taken place, and as far as possible to prevent their recurrence.

The third Annual Report of the commissioners is dated 25th May 1850, and continues the narrative of events and proceedings from the date of the preceding Report.

1850.
Third annual report of the Poor-law Commissioners for Ireland.

The maximum number in the workhouses during the year 1849–50, was 227,329 on the 16th June Decrease of relief. of the first-named year, and the maximum on the out-relief lists was 784,367 on the 7th July. From these dates the numbers went on rapidly decreasing throughout the succeeding months, until on the 6th October the inmates of the workhouses were reduced to the minimum of 104,266, and the number on the out-relief lists to 124,185, all orders for relief under the *2nd section* of the Extension Act being likewise then withdrawn. This sufficiently proves the change which took place shortly after the date of the last Report.

The crops in the autumn of 1849 turned out generally sound and abundant, and famine no longer cast The crops generally sound and abundant. its blight upon the land. Yet while all other parts of the country, including Mayo and Galway heretofore the most depressed and suffering, rejoiced in the favourable change, we are told that the unions in the county of Clare, especially those of Kilrush and Scariff, continued to exhibit a lamentable extent of destitution. There were still 30,000 persons on the out-relief lists in the Clare unions, nearly twice the number so relieved in the whole province of Connaught; "and the rate of mortality in the workhouses, and the number of inquests, although less than in former seasons, attest the indigent and suffering state of a great part of the population." A hope is nevertheless expressed " that the ground has been laid for a further very considerable reduction of expendi- Reduction of expenditure anticipated. ture after harvest, and that a material allevia- tion of the burden of poor-rates throughout Ireland, will be experienced during the year which will end on the 29th September 1851."

The large increase of workhouse accommodation which the last Report states to have been provided,[a] and the

---

[a] Ante, p. 351.

opinion which generally prevailed as to the importance

Increase of workhouse accommodation. of limiting relief as much as possible to the workhouse, appear to have realized the hope then expressed of successfully contending with the difficulties of the period. The large expenditure, amounting to 1,498,047*l*., connected with in-door relief in 1848-9, shows the determined character of the struggle, and although only partial success in establishing the system was obtained, events have shown the prudence of the course then pursued. When the boards of guardians which had been dissolved, resumed the charge of their unions in November, as provided by the 12*th and* 13*th Vict. cap.* 4,[b] they not only evinced a desire to limit relief to the workhouse, but were also with few exceptions prepared to make a further increase of their workhouse accommodation wherever it appeared to be necessary. So that ." the change from out-door relief to the safer system of relief in the workhouse, has (it is said) been found practicable throughout a large part of Ireland, not excepting some districts which suffered most severely during the famine." The conclusion of the harvest was as usual followed by an increase of applicants for relief, but the extent of workhouse accommodation being now greater by 70,000 than in the previous year, out-door relief instead of increasing *Decrease of out-door relief.* actually continued to decrease until the end of December, when the numbers so relieved amounted to 95,468, the number in the workhouses being then 194,547. At the end of March 1850, the number on the out-relief lists was 131,702, and in the workhouses 224,381, the sanitary state of the houses being at the same time satisfactory. No out-door relief whatever was then administered in 51 of the unions, and at the date of the Report the number of unions thus exempt was increased to 58.

---

[b] Ante, p. 355.

The recommendations of the Boundary Commissioners have been already noticed.[c] In carrying out these recommendations, the proposed arrangement of the electoral divisions . was generally adhered to ; but with regard to the new unions, it was not thought advisable to make the entire of the changes recommended. The commissioners have, they say, " refrained from forming such new unions in districts where it appeared that there was a preponderance of opinion against it, on the part of those who would be locally affected by the change, unless where the necessity for new union centres appeared, in a territorial point of view, to be placed beyond doubt." Orders were however issued for the formation of 24 new unions,[d] and forms of procedure were prepared for adjusting the liabilities of townlands in unions and electoral divisions of which the boundaries were altered, in accordance with the provisions of the 12th and 13th Vict. cap. 104. This Act now requires our attention, some of its provisions being of considerable importance.

The 12th and 13th Vict. cap. 104, was passed on the 1st August 1849, ' to further Amend the Acts for the Relief of the Destitute Poor in Ireland ;' and the following is a summary of its provisions :—

Section 1.—Provides that every person applying for relief, is to be deemed chargeable to the electoral division in which during the last three years he has been longest usually resident, whether by occupying a tenement or usually sleeping therein ;— provided that if he have not been so usually resident for at least one of the said three years, the expense of his relief is to be borne by the union at large.

Section 2.—Requires the Poor Law Commissioners in all cases where a change is made in the boundaries of any union or electoral division, to make such order under seal as appears

24 new unions formed.

The 12th and 13th Vict. cap. 104.

[c] Ante, p. 361.
[d] These were Belmullet, Killala, Dromore West, Newport, Oughterard, Skull, Castletown, Clonakilty, Tulla, Killadysert, Corrofin, Ballyvaghan, Portumna, Mount Bellew, Glennamaddy, Strokestown, Claremorris, Tobercurry, Glin, Croom, Millstreet, Mitchelstown, Bawnboy, and Ballymahon.

to them to be necessary for the adjustment of the liabilities existing at the time of such change, and the proportionate share thereof to be borne by any townland affected thereby, and likewise for indemnifying any union electoral division or townland for any loss on exchange of property occasioned by such alteration of boundaries.

Sections 3, 4, 5.—On the formation of new unions, the commissioners are empowered to prescribe the arrangements for the joint use of the existing workhouses, until the new unions are provided with workhouses of their own, and from time to time to alter or rescind the same, and to enforce payment of the expenses consequent thereon ; and for the purpose of providing workhouses, 'the Lands Clauses Consolidation Act' (*8th and 9th Vict. cap.* 18) is declared to be incorporated with the Poor Relief Acts.

Sections 6, 7, 8, 9.—In fixing the qualification of elected guardians, the commissioners are empowered to fix a different amount for different electoral divisions of the same union. The full number of ex-officio guardians may be made up from non-resident justices, if the number resident be not sufficient. Two or more electoral divisions may be combined for the purpose of electing a guardian ; and upon the request of a board of guardians the commissioners may appoint an assistant-guardian for such union, whom they are also empowered to remove or discontinue.

Sections 10, 11, 12.—Rents arising from exempted property, are to be rated to the extent of half the poundage. Occupiers are not to deduct from their rent more than one-half the amount of the rate paid by them ; and the provisions making void all agreements to forego deductions from rent are repealed.

Sections 13, 14.—The valuations are not required to be signed and sealed by the commissioners. " To encourage the employment of labour in improving the value of land," the valuation is not to be increased in consequence of improvements made under the Land Improvement Act, within seven years after such improvements.

Sections 15, 16, 17, 18, 19.—A short form of declaration is prescribed, and costs are limited in actions for recovery of rates. Judges may make rules and orders regulating proceedings in actions for poor-rates. Civil bill decrees for poor-rates may be filed, and have force as judgments of superior court. Judgments for poor-rates are to be registered, and take priority as charges on the land, with the exception of crown

the condition of Clare being at this time much worse than any other part of Ireland. The people had there suffered more, and the revival of the potato crop had brought them less relief. They exhibited in fact an ex- State of ception to the improvement elsewhere happily Clare. apparent, and nowhere more so than in Connaught, the unions in which province were among the most forward in recovering from the effects of the famine.

A portion of the fund raised by the rate-in-aid,[h] was applied to assist the emigration of poor persons from the workhouses of some of the overbur- Emigration. dened unions. But in order to prevent such assistance from operating injuriously, and serving as an induce-ment to persons to claim admission to the workhouse, the commissioners directed that it should be afforded only to those who had been inmates for one year at least. Certain of the unions were thus relieved from the charge of maintaining persons able to work, but unable to find employment; and by the removal of such persons additional workhouse room was obtained, without incurring the charge of providing additional buildings. The number thus assisted to emigrate during the present year, was 360 adult males, 844 females, and 517 children, at an expense of 21,075*l.*

Since the last Report eight more new unions[i] had been formed, which with the 24 formed last year, and New unions the 131 previously existing make 163 in all. and elec-toral divi-The old unions in which the boundaries either sions. of the Union or its electoral divisions had been altered, were 86; and the number of electoral divisions had been increased to 3,404, instead of 2,049 as originally constituted. Some of the recommendations contained in the boundary commissioners' Reports, were disap-

---

[h] Ante, p. 355.
[i] These were Borrisokane, Castlecomer, Donaghmore, Kilmacthomas, Tor-nastown, Urlingford, Youghal, and Castletowndelvin.

proved by the guardians of the unions to which they applied. This was particularly the case in the north of Ireland, and in several instances the Poor Law Commissioners deemed it expedient to yield to the objections which were made to any change; so that instead of 50 new unions as recommended in the boundary Reports, no more than 32 had been created; and to these, advances to the extent of 200,000*l.* were made by the exchequer loan board, for enabling them to provide the necessary workhouses.

It was likewise considered inexpedient to proceed further in making alterations in the unions or electoral divisions, " until the task of consolidating the debts due for workhouse loans, relief advances, labour-rate, and the advance of 300,000*l.* authorized by the 13*th and* 14*th Vict., cap.* 14, had been completed." The proceedings under this Act are said to be far advanced. They are of considerable importance, as is the Act itself, of which the following is an abstract—

The 13*th and* 14*th Vict., cap.* 14, was passed on the 17th May 1850, and after reciting the several Acts under which advances had been made, and declaring that considerable sums in respect of such advances remained unpaid, but that it was nevertheless expedient to authorize a further advance of public money to assist certain distressed unions and electoral divisions in Ireland &c., it empowers—

The 13 and 14 Vict. cap. 14.

Section 1.—The commissioners of the Treasury to make advances from time to time not exceeding in the whole 300,000*l.*, to such unions as they shall think fit, such advances to be paid to the Poor Law Commissioners, and by them applied towards the discharge of the debts or liabilities of the union or division &c., as the Treasury shall direct. All sums so advanced are to bear 3 per cent. interest, and be repaid out of the poor-rates at such times as the Treasury prescribe.

Sections 2, 3, 4.—The commissioners of the Treasury may cause the debts and liabilities of the several unions and electoral divisions &c. to be ascertained, and may cause the same to

be consolidated and proportionably charged upon such unions
or electoral divisions, and may charge such an annuity upon
the same as shall be equivalent to such proportionate amount.
A statement of the annuities so charged is to be transmitted
to the Poor Law Commissioners, who are to issue orders to
the guardians directing the punctual payment thereof.

Sections 5, 6.—If payment be not so punctually made, the treasurer
of the union is to reserve a third part of the moneys collected
and lodged with him on account of the electoral division, and
place the same to a separate account, to be entitled the
" Loans Repayment Account," until all arrears have thereby
been discharged. But the rate in aid under the 12*th and*
13*th Vict. cap.* 24, is to be paid, before the annuities charged
under this Act.

Sections 7, 8.—The Treasury are further empowered to make additions to the annuities chargeable under this Act, in respect of
loans for building or enlarging workhouses ; and may likewise
suspend the recovery of workhouse loans, and moneys directed
to be levied by grand-jury presentments.

The consolidation of the various claims upon the
unions and electoral divisions, and converting them
into annuities on terms which, whilst they secured the
government from loss, would make the repayment as
little burdensome as possible, must no doubt have been,
as was intended, an easement and an advantage to the
borrowers. The financial difficulties of many of the
western unions were however, it was apprehended, such
as would not only disable them from making any payment for some years, but such as would render further
aid necessary, in order to keep them in operation as
dispensors of relief to the destitute poor.

A statement is given in the appendix to the Report,
of the appropriation of the loan of 300,000*l.* advanced
under the above statute, which was, the commissioners
say, " a most seasonable relief to many unions and electoral divisions that were deeply embarrassed by debt in
the early part of 1850." But in addition to Second rate
this loan of 300,000*l.*, a second rate in aid of in aid of 2*d.*
in the pound.
2*d.* in the pound, amounting to 99,362*l.* 3*s.* 3*d.*, was

levied under an order issued on the 23rd December 1850, " for the further assistance of distressed unions and electoral divisions." The Rate-in-Aid Act would expire on the 31st of December, and it had been hoped that the raising a second rate under it might have been avoided. " But after the conclusion of the harvest of last year (the commissioners say) they perceived indications of the continuance of distress in so serious a degree in the counties of Clare and Kerry, that they could not, with the small balance at their disposal, feel justified in omitting to avail themselves of the power of declaring a further rate ;" and subsequent experience, they observe, confirmed the propriety of the step thus taken. The two rates in aid amounted together to 421,990l. The distribution of this large sum among the distressed unions was, under direction of the government, intrusted to the Poor Law Commissioners, by whom an account of its application was furnished in detail.

An expectation had been held out in the last Report of a very considerable reduction of expenditure taking place in the following year,[k] and this expectation was fulfilled. In the 163 unions the total expenditure from the rates for the relief of the poor during the year ending on the 29th September 1850, was 1,430,108l. The number of inmates on that day was 155,173, and the total number relieved in the workhouses during the year was 805,702. The number then receiving out-door relief was 2,938, and the number who received out-door relief during the year was 368,565.—It is seen therefore that, as was expected, a very considerable decrease had taken place ; but to show this clearer, I will recapitulate the several amounts for the three preceding years. In the year ending 29th September 1848, the total expenditure for relief of the poor was 1,835,634l.—in 1849 it was 2,177,651l.—and in

Amount of expenditure, and numbers relieved.

---

k Ante, p. 365.

1850 it was 1,430,108*l.* The total number relieved in
the workhouses in these years respectively, was 610,463
—932,284—and 805,702 ; and the total number who
so respectively received out-door relief, was 1,433,042—
1,210,482—and 368,565. The decrease in the numbers
who received in-door relief, may perhaps seem dispro-
portionately small ; but this is accounted for by the fact of
the workhouse being more extensively used for the purposes of relief, than had been the case in former years.

The generally improved circumstances of the country
must doubtless be regarded as the chief cause of the
present decrease of pauperism ; but the commissioners
consider that it is likewise in no small degree attributable
to the extension of workhouse accommodation. Extension of
This extension has, it is said, " enabled the workhouse accommoda-
administrators of relief throughout Ireland, with tion.
very few exceptions, to meet the actual destitution
existing, without having recourse to out-door relief."
The progress of the extension may thus be tabulated :—

Extent of Workhouse Accommodation.

Year.	On March 25.	On Sept. 29.
1847	114,129	114,865
1848	154,429	169,142
1849	228,458	244,942
1850	276,073	289,931
1851	308,885	—

And at the date of the Report (5th May 1851), the
aggregate of the workhouse accommodation available,
beyond the numbers then receiving in-door relief, was
60,491. Improvement in the sanitary state of the
workhouses, and of the labouring population generally,
is said always to follow the increase of workhouse
accommodation, and the substitution of in-door for
out-door relief; so that although a great reduction of
expenditure took place in the last year, a still further
reduction may be expected in the present.

The Report of the commissioners for 1851–52 is

1852.
Fifth annual
report of the
Poor Law
Commis-
sioners for
Ireland. dated on the 1st of May, as had been theretofore generally the practice, although this date
was not adhered to in the three preceding
Reports.

The transition from out-door to in-door relief was ,said
to be now complete throughout Ireland, accompanied
by a reduction in the number of applicants, as well as
a most satisfactory decrease in workhouse mortality.

Improved
circum-
stances of
the country. The crops generally had everywhere regained
their usual state of productiveness. Famine or
the fear of famine no longer prevailed, and its
effects were only perceptible in the decrease of the population, and the consequent increased demand for
labour. All in short was prosperous and promising
compared with the state of things five years ago.
There was however one exception, several of the western
unions being still much embarrassed in their finances,
and continuing to require assistance. This was especi-
The Munster
unions an
exception. ally the case in Munster; for the Connaught
unions had passed successfully through the
ordeal, and were comparatively prosperous. " Thus on
the 23rd February 1850, while the whole number receiving out-door relief in Ireland was 148,909, the
unions in the province of Munster contained 101,803 of
that number, and those in Connaught only 19,261 ;
and again, on the 26th April 1851, when the number
on out-relief was reduced to 10,935, the eight unions in
the county of Clare comprised 6,846, and the 29 unions
in the province of Connaught only 232."

During the progress of the important change which
Increase of
workhouse
relief. was now taking place in the circumstances of
the country, the number of persons relieved
in the workhouses had always considerably increased
in the spring and early part of the summer. These
persons were generally in a state of great exhaustion, and the aid and shelter they received enabled them

afterwards in most cases to leave the house with their health and strength restored. Some however remained, especially females and the children of both sexes, by whom it appears the workhouses continued to be unduly burdened. So long as there was an expectation of out-door relief being administered, a considerable amount of disease and mortality often prevailed, owing to the way in which persons really destitute persisted in hanging upon that expectation, instead of earlier seeking for admission to the workhouse; but when all hope for relief otherwise than in the workhouse was removed, " the sequel has invariably been a reduced number of applicants, a decreased rate of workhouse mortality, and an improved sanitary state of the population."

The increased extent of workhouse accommodation which has been noticed, had been obtained, either by means of permanent additions to the original workhouses, or by building new ones in the newly-formed unions, or by the erection of a cheap kind of temporary structure to meet the emergency; or else by hiring premises for the purpose. The latter of these expedients had been resorted to more extensively than was consistent either with economy or with efficient management, and most of these premises were now given up, or shortly would be so. Anxiety is expressed that the succeeding year should be commenced with the workhouse establishments concentrated as far as practicable in each union, " so as to avoid the disadvantage of using auxiliary buildings." Such a concentration was no doubt essential to efficient management, and it was only by such management, the commissioners observe, and by a further reduction of expenditure, " that some of the distressed unions in the west can be expected to become so far solvent as to support their own pauperism without further external aid."

It is certainly important on many accounts that there should be only one workhouse in a union, and that it should have been expressly constructed for the accommodation of the classes to be relieved therein, with all suitable means for their separation and employment. Without these essentials, a workhouse can hardly be effective either as a test of destitution or a medium of relief; and there is always danger of an inefficient workhouse becoming a stimulant, instead of being a check to pauperism.

Most of the unions made provision for the payment of the first annual instalment under the Consolidated Debts Act (13*th and* 14*th Vict. cap.* 14),[m] the arrangements under which, including the advance of 300,000*l.*,[n] appear to have been all completed by the end of September. But in the following month a Treasury minute was issued, delaring that although "my lords" are of opinion that the present state of the greater part of Ireland does not call for any relief from the operation of the Act, yet they cannot doubt that there are districts in which relief must be given—" in the case of those districts, for instance, where the local resources are insufficient to meet the ordinary expenditure for relief of the poor, and where it is necessary to have recourse to assistance from the relief-in-aid fund for this purpose, it cannot be expected that further sums for payment of the consolidated annuities can be raised." With regard to *postponement,* their lordships are of opinion that it would only tend to prolong a feeling of uncertainty as to future payments, whilst it is deemed of great importance to restore confidence in the owners and occupiers of land in the distressed districts, to which end the demands should be definite both in amount and in time. It is thought therefore that a remission of payment, either altogether or in part according to circumstances, is preferable to postponement, and

Annuities under the Consolidated Debts Act.

---

[m] Ante, p. 374.

[n] A statement of the appropriation of this loan is given in the Appendix to the commissioners' fourth Report.

an intimation is given of its being intended to apply to parliament with this view. Meantime however, the Poor Law Commissioners were authorized to direct the treasurers of the unions to retain the whole annuity payable by electoral divisions of which the expenditure in relief was ascertained to be 4s. in the pound, or more; and also to direct " so much only of the annuity to be paid in other divisions as might, together with the relief expenditure, amount to 4s. in the pound."

This was doubtless a considerate, but it was at the same time a necessary proceeding on the part of the government. The impoverished unions, whose utmost exertions could not raise within themselves sufficient for relieving their own urgent necessities, would of course find it impossible to pay the consolidated annuity for which they were made liable; whilst the continual accumulation of this charge hanging over them would paralyze local effort, and tend to prevent the introduction of capital from other quarters. The accumulation would for the present be put a stop to by this Treasury minute; and if, in consideration of their late sufferings and present difficulties, parliament should confirm the boon, it will it is thought inspire confidence, as well as afford present relief; and it may then be hoped, that at no very distant day the impoverished unions would be able to emerge from their state of depression, and join in the general race of improvement. The requisite confirmation was given in the following year by the 15th and 16th Vict. cap. 16, entitled ' An Act to amend the Acts relating to the Payment of Advances made to Districts in Ireland.' After reciting the 13th and 14th Vict. cap. 14, and the Treasury minute of the 21st October 1851, made " upon representations contained in memorials from many unions in Ireland, of the pressure upon the local resources of several electoral divisions on account of the necessary expenditure for the relief of the poor, and in

The Treasury minute, October 21, 1851.

The 15 and 16 Vict., cap. 16.

anticipation of a measure to be submitted to parliament "
—it is declared to be expedient that the directions contained in the said minute should be confirmed, and it is
accordingly enacted that " the sums payable in the year
1851 in respect of the annuities mentioned in such
minute and directions, shall be remitted and deemed to
be discharged without further payment." The remissions
thus sanctioned amounted altogether to about 75,000*l.*—
that is 48,000*l.* to Munster, 24,000*l.* to Connaught, and
3,000*l.* to Leinster. The remission, it will be observed,
only applied to the annuities due in 1851, and no expectation was held out of similar indulgence in future.

Some account has already been given of the inquiry
The medical into and Report upon the medical charities in
charities. 1842, and of the bill then prepared but not proceeded with, in consequence of the opposition made to
it by the medical profession.° In August 1851 however a bill, founded on that Report, and similar in principle and in its main provisions to the bill of 1842, was
introduced and readily passed, the necessity for such a
measure, and for bringing the rating powers and machinery of the Poor Law in aid of the medical charities,
being then admitted by all parties; and this was the
object of the Act of 1851, as it had been of the bill prepared under the author's direction in 1842.

On the passing of the 14*th and* 15*th Vict. cap.* 68, the
Medical working of the medical charities became so
Charities
Act, 14 *and* closely connected with the operations of the
15 *Vict.,*
cap. 68. Poor Law, that a description of the chief provisions of the Act is here necessary—

Sections 1, 2, 3, 4, 5.—Provide for the appointment of a medical
commissioner, being a physician or surgeon of not less than
thirteen years' standing, to be united with the Poor Law Commissioners in the execution of the Act. The commissioners
may appoint fit persons, being physicians or surgeons of not
less than seven years' standing, to be inspectors, but the

° Ante, pp. 267 and 279.

medical commissioner and the inspectors are restricted from practising professionally.

Sections 6, 7, 8, 9.—The guardians are, whenever required by the commissioners, to divide unions into dispensary districts, having regard to extent and population; and are to appoint a dispensary committee, and provide necessary buildings, and such medicines and appliances as may be required, for the medical relief of the poor. A committee of management consisting of the dispensary committee, the ex-officio guardians, and ratepayers of 30*l.* annual value, are to appoint one or more medical officers, to afford advice and medical aid to such poor persons as may be sent by any member of the dispensary committee, or by the relieving officer or warden.

Sections 10, 11, 12, 13.—On the declaration of a dispensary district, all provisions for affording dispensary relief from the poor-rate or county cess are to cease. Guardians or members of the committee of management, are not to be concerned in furnishing medicines or goods for the use of the dispensary, under penalty of 50*l.* The commissioners are to frame regulations for the government of each dispensary district, and the medical officer is required to vaccinate all persons who may come to him for that purpose.

Sections 14, 15.—Existing medical officers are in the first instance to be the medical officers of the dispensaries. The medical officers of a dispensary district are to attend at the examination of dangerous lunatics, and are also to attend the bridewells within their districts.

Sections 16, 17, 18.—The commissioners and inspectors are empowered to examine on oath, and to summon witnesses. The giving false evidence is declared a misdemeanour, and the refusing to obey summons &c. is subjected to a penalty of 5*l.* Inspectors may visit dispensaries, and attend meetings of guardians. The commissioners are to report upon hospitals and infirmaries. They are also to execute the powers and purposes of the Nuisances Removal and Diseases Prevention Acts, and to report their proceedings annually to the lord-lieutenant.

Such were the chief provisions of this Act, and the powers conferred by it appear sufficient for procuring the establishment of dispensaries in districts where they were much needed, and also for securing better management with regard to medical relief. In their first Report

First report of Medical Charity Commissioners. dated. 15th February 1853, the commissioners remark, that by the Medical Charities Act, a partial and imperfect system of medical relief, unattended with responsibility in its agents, and resting on a financial basis at once uncertain in duration, and unequal in its pressure as a tax, has been exchanged for a system uniform and universal, supported out of the poor-rates, and " influenced in its administration by well-defined responsibilities, under the direction and control of a central authority." The expenditure is estimated at 102,700*l.* per annum. But " having regard to the dimi-

Anticipated expenditure. nution of pauperism, and the improving circumstances of the country," it is thought probable that the cost of dispensary relief under the Medical Charities Act, will not exceed 100,000*l.* in future years.

New electoral divisions. A few more of the electoral divisions were divided, in addition to the subdivisions which had been made the preceding year,[p] and the total number of electoral divisions was now increased to 3,439, that is 1,390 more than what were originally constituted, although still short of the number recommended by the Boundary Commissioners. The permission of out-door relief, and the increase in the number of unions, especially the latter, would no doubt render some increase of electoral divisions necessary; but after the distress out of which these changes had arisen shall have passed away, and when the country has regained its normal state, it is not unlikely that these changes may be found burthensome, and the machinery they have created be beyond what is really necessary for affording relief to the destitute poor. The various changes which had been made in the law, also rendered a new order for regulating the proceedings of boards

New order of proceedings issued. of guardians necessary; and accordingly on the 19th January 1852, the old order was rescinded,

---

[p] Ante, p. 373.

and a new one adapted to the altered circumstances of the unions and the state of the law was issued.

In July 1851, the *14th and 15th Vict. cap.* 35 was passed, to extend the benefits of the General Merchant Seamen's Act relating to apprentices bound to the sea-service by guardians of the poor in Ireland. By this Act, the board of guardians of a union is empowered to apprentice any boy of the age of twelve and upwards being of sufficient health and strength, and who is or whose parents are receiving relief in such union, and who consents to be so bound, into the sea-service for not less than four years, or until he attains the age of twenty-one, or has served seven years, as the case may be. The apprentice is to be furnished with a suitable outfit at the expense of the union, and sent to the seaport where the master or owner of the ship resides ; and it is further provided that any such boys may, if they desire it, be placed out in the naval service. This is a well-devised Act, although it may not be very operative, at least for a time, the Irish generally having little predilection for the sea. The Act however supplies what was certainly an omission in the Act of 1836, and which became more apparent as the number of boys accumulated in the workhouses, without any means for apprenticing or getting them out into service. But the abuses which had resulted from the apprenticeship law in England, prevented its introduction in any shape into the original Irish Poor Relief Act.

Apprenticing boys to the sea-service. 14 and 15 Vict., cap. 35.

Emigration under the provisions of the Poor Law was more active during the year 1850-51 than in any preceding year, although many unions were prevented by their poverty from resorting to it.[q] The commissioners had, as is before stated, applied a portion of the rate-in-aid fund in relieving the overcrowded work-

Emigration.

---

[q] *Ante,* p. 373.

houses in the counties of Clare and Kerry, but the nearly
exhausted state of that fund disabled them from meeting
other urgent applications for similar aid. Indeed the
decrease of the population in the impoverished districts,
as shown in the census returns, together with the smaller
number of applicants for relief, and a greater demand
for labour, would seem to render further aid or stimulus
to emigration both unnecessary and inexpedient. Where
the guardians and ratepayers of a district however were
desirous of raising funds for the purpose, the commissioners did not refuse to give effect to the proposition.
It appears from the Reports of the colonial land and
emigration commissioners, that the total Irish emigra-
Extent of   tion from 1847 to 1850 inclusive, was 833,692,
emigration. nearly all of which was for North America—
the Canada and New Brunswick immigration from all
countries in the same period amounting to 210,904. In
1851, the emigration from Great Britain to the United
States was 267,357, and it was 244,261 in 1852, in
which year the number of Irish emigrants to New York
alone was 118,134. This continuous emigration was
chiefly effected by the aid of remittances from persons
who had previously emigrated, to their friends and relatives at home, to enable them to follow.

The above figures show the extent of the drain upon
Population   the population of Ireland which had been in
census of
1851.   progress during the last six years, and will go
far to account for the startling results of the census
returns of 1851, which exhibit an actual decrease of
considerably over a million and a half in the previous
decennial period, and make the population less than it
was in 1821. The census commissioners,[r] after stating
that the numerical decrease of the inhabitants between
1841 and 1851 amounted to 1,622,739, go on to remark
—"But this being merely the difference between the

---

[r] See 6th part of the Report on the census of Ireland for 1851, published in
1855.

number of people in 1841 and 1851, without making any
allowance for a natural and ordinary increase of population, conveys but very inadequately the effect of the
visitation of famine and pestilence"—" We find that the
population of 30th March 1851, would probably have
numbered 9,018,799, instead of 6,522,385 ; and that consequently the loss of population between 1841 and 1851
may be computed at the enormous amount of 2,496,414
persons." That is to say, the population in 1851
amounted to 6,522,385, whereas under ordinary circumstances, and with the average rate of increase, it would
have amounted to 9,018,799.

It may be convenient in the way of elucidation, to
place the numbers of the four census periods in juxta-
position, thus—

The population of Ireland in 1821 was 6,801,827
        ,,   ,,   in 1831 ,, 7,767,401
        ,,   ,,   in 1841 ,, 8,175,124
        ,,   ,,   in 1851 ,, 6,522,385

How much of the present decrease was owing to emigration, and how much was occasioned by want and
disease, it is impossible to predicate with any degree of
certainty. Both causes were in operation at the same
time, and both were consequent upon the potato failure.
The universal and almost exclusive use of the potato as
an article of subsistence, led to a rapid increase of the
population—its failure led to a still more rapid decrease,
accompanied by an amount of suffering and privation
for which it would be difficult to find a parallel in the
history of any people.

The expenditure from the rates for relief of the poor
in all the 163 unions now established, during Amount of
the year ending on the 29th September 1851, expenditure, and numbers
was as had been expected, considerably less than relieved.
in the preceding year, and amounted to 1,141,647l. The
number relieved in the workhouses on that day was
140,031, and the total number so relieved during the

year was 707,443. The number then receiving out-door relief was 3,160, and the total number who received out-door relief during the year was 47,914. It seems almost superfluous to add, that none of these were relieved under the 2nd section of the Extension Act. The results of the year as regards relief, both numerically and financially, was deemed highly satisfactory, and it was expected that a still further reduction would be effected in the year following.

Before entering on the proceedings of another year (which will moreover be the limit of our inquiry), it may be well to look back for a moment to the disastrous period through which we have latterly passed. Famine and pestilence now happily no longer prevail, and the country has in great measure recovered from the effects of the severe ordeal to which it was subjected. The Poor Law has likewise nearly regained its ordinary state, after passing through the dangers and difficulties of a most calamitous visitation ; and has risen from its trials with an increase of reputation, and also it may be added, with a greatly increased capacity for effecting its objects, through the large additional workhouse accommodation that has been provided. The failure of the potato in 1845 and 1846, the partial failure in 1847, and the more general destruction of the crop in 1848, were followed in each year by the vast efforts made to palliate, and as far as possible to relieve the consequent distress—first by importations of food, and employing the people on public works—next by a partial adoption of the Poor-law principle of relief, as it was administered under the Temporary Relief Act—and lastly by extending the provisions of the Poor Law to meet the emergency, and permitting relief to be afforded out of the workhouse. These circumstances have each occupied our attention in the foregoing pages. They are all exceptional in their nature, but are at the same time most instructive in their results, whether viewed locally or generally—as affecting the empire at large, or Ireland in particular.

The character of the period—the waxings and wanings of distress—the variations in its extent, and the phases of its intensity, are all unmistakeably indicated in the weekly returns from the several unions, of the numbers and mortality in the respective workhouses from the commencement of 1846, and the numbers on the out-relief lists from the passing of the Extension Act in 1847. These weekly returns are given at length in the commissioners' Reports, and from them I have compiled two tables, which will be found at the end,* showing the dates in each year when the most marked changes occurred in the numbers relieved both in and out of the workhouses, and the extent of mortality which took place; but always giving the maximum and minimum numbers in each case. The cost of out-door relief in the respective weeks is also inserted, so that the state of the country at the several periods is as it were mapped out before the reader, and can be taken in at a glance, requiring nothing further in the way of explanation; and to this table the reader's attention is requested.

Tables of numbers relieved and extent of mortality. See p. 404.

The commissioners' sixth Report is dated 2nd May 1853. After the usual weekly summary of the in-door and out-door recipients of relief, it is remarked that the number of out-door poor is so inconsiderable, and liable to so little fluctuation, that " the comparative extent of pauperism in successive years is now almost wholly dependent on the number receiving relief in the workhouses." This number, it is added, " continues to fluctuate almost in the same degree as formerly, notwithstanding the absolute decrease which has taken place; the number in autumn not usually much exceeding one-half the number at another period of the year."

1853. Sixth annual report of the Poor Law Commissioners for Ireland.

* See p. 404.

The satisfactory progress made by the province of Connaught in surmounting the effects of the famine years has already been noticed.[t] Although some of the Connaught unions were still in a state of financial embarrassment, and subject to payment of heavy rates, the reduction of relief in the last three years had been remarkable, the number in the workhouses having decreased from 42,286 in April 1851, to 17,389 in April 1853. In Munster on the contrary improvement continued to be comparatively backward, that province still containing more than half the pauperism of Ireland.

State of Connaught and Munster.

A large number of the children and young persons who had been admitted during the prevalence of the famine, were discharged from the workhouses in the course of the last two years. These must be regarded with satisfaction as the fruits of the Poor Law, but for which, they would in all probability have fallen victims to want and disease. The children still remaining in the workhouses, a great proportion of whom were likewise rescued at the time of the famine, were chiefly orphans, or illegitimate or deserted, and without friends able or willing to take charge of them. The number of these children in the workhouses on the 2nd April 1853 under the age of fifteen, was 82,434, of whom 5,710 were illegitimate; and looking at the large proportion who were. returned as being orphans or deserted, the commissioners say they "cannot but feel that the prospect of enabling a large number of them to leave the workhouses and obtain a permanent position in society, must depend in a great degree upon the exertion made to educate and train them in such a manner as to enable them to do this at an early age." A child of twelve or thirteen is, it is observed, " more easily grafted into society, than if he resides in a public establishment till eighteen or nineteen, when he becomes

The workhouse children.

----

[t] Ante, pp. 373 and 378.

too much accustomed to its routine to exert himself in a
new position, where more labour and individual efforts
have to be exacted, and greater hardships and privations
endured."

The literary education in the workhouse schools was
considered to be on the whole satisfactory. But Their
letters alone, without industrial training, will education and indus-
not, it is truly said, help a boy or girl of fifteen trial train-ing.
to get into employment; and the commissioners there-
fore encouraged the formation of agricultural schools, in
connexion with the national education board. The boys
were moreover in most of the workhouses taught some
kind of trade, such as tailoring, shoemaking, carpentering &c. The girls were taught to wash, and make and
mend their own clothes, and clean their own dormitories
and day-rooms; but there is obviously more difficulty
with them than with the boys, in regard to employment.
As the country improves however, " and when the drain
caused by the continued emigration is more felt," there
can be little doubt, the commissioners say, that in all the
unions where proper attention has been paid to the
education and training of the children, there will be a
demand for those educated in the workhouses as soon as
they are of an age fitted for being useful; and in the
mean time it is satisfactory to learn, that during the year
1852, no less than 5,371 of these children under fifteen
years of age, found employment out of the workhouse.

The drain of emigration just adverted to, must have
given rise to an increased amount of employment for
those who remained, but this was attended with a less
apparent effect upon the rate of wages than Rate of
might have been expected. Another circum- wages and cost of
stance had however occurred closely bearing subsistence.
upon wages which it is necessary to notice, for we find
that the weekly cost of maintenance in the workhouses,
the average of which in 1847, exclusive of clothing, was
as high as 2s. 1½d. per head, had fallen to little more than

1*s.* per head in the years 1850, 1851, and 1852.[u] Comparing the cost of subsistence with the rate of wages, it will therefore appear that there has been relatively a very considerable rise in the latter, although the money-rate in 1852 and 1853 may not appear to differ very materially from what it was in 1845. Employment had likewise become more certain and more steady, so that the labourer's actual earnings during the year were probably greater than before, which coupled with the general reduction in the price of provisions, would enlarge his command of the necessaries and conveniences of life, and tend to improve his condition.

Returns had been obtained from the several unions Remittances showing the extent of remittances from abroad, from emigrants. for enabling certain of the workhouse inmates to emigrate. From these returns it appeared, that in the last year 2,158*l.* was so remitted to enable 877 of such inmates to join their friends in America; 136*l.* to assist 489 to go to England and Scotland; and 221*l.* to enable 31 to proceed to Australia. When the sums remitted were insufficient, assistance was often afforded by the guardians under the provisions of the Poor Law, and 14,041*l.* was so expended for this purpose in the year ending 29th September 1852. In the following year (ending September 1853), 12,865*l.* was so expended by the unions for the emigration of 403 men, 1,202 women, and 996 children, making together 2,601 persons; and including the cost of free passages, about 3,500*l.* is known to have been remitted to enable more than 1,100 inmates of the workhouses to join their friends who had emigrated, or had settled in Great Britain. Others are likewise supposed to have left the workhouses in consequence of similar remittances, which were not made through or known to the boards of guardians.

The valuations of rateable property in the several

---

[u] See table at p. 397.

unions had, as was to be expected, varied more or less with the changes which took place from time to time in the circumstances of the country. In 1845 they appear to have amounted to 13,404,403*l.*, and to 13,187,421*l.* in 1847; but in 1851 the entire valuation of Ireland for the purposes of the poor-rate was only 11,500,000*l.*, so great had been the change caused by the severe ordeal through which the country had passed. Although the principle on which the valuation of property in the several unions was originally founded, namely, what it would let for, was undoubtedly correct, there were counteracting influences at work, and the valuations made under it were rarely altogether satisfactory. Some persons denounced them as being too high, some as being too low, and others as being unequal or partial. *The valuations.*

In order to remedy these asserted defects, and place the valuations on what was expected to be a better footing, the *15th and 16th Vict. cap.* 63 was passed in 1852, ' to amend the Laws relating to the Valuation of Rateable Property in Ireland.' The Act declares it to be expedient to make one uniform valuation of lands and tenements, which may be used for all public and local assessments and other rating. The lord-lieutenant is empowered to appoint a commissioner of valuation " who shall make or cause to be made a valuation of the tenements and hereditaments within every barony, parish, or other division when directed so to do." But further legislation was still necessary, and in the following year the *16th and 17th Vict. cap.* 7, was passed to amend the above, and directing the clerks of unions to prepare lists of tenements proposed for revision by the collectors, and to transmit the same to the commissioner of valuation, together with the opinion of the guardians whether a revision is necessary, and the name of a person whom the guardians recommend as fit to revise the same. The combined *Commissioner of valuations.*

provisions of these Acts are no doubt calculated to effect improvement in the valuations; but the principle of fair letting value as originally prescribed, must still be adhered to in whatever changes are made.

The expenditure for relief of the poor during the

1852.
Amount of expenditure and numbers relieved.

year ending on the 29th September 1852, was 883,267l., being 258,380l. less than in the preceding year,[x] and fully realizing the expectations then held out. The number relieved in the workhouses at the above date was 111,515 and the total number so relieved during the year was 504,864. The number then receiving out-door relief was 2,528, and the total number who received out-door relief during the year was 14,911. A further reduction was likewise still expected. " But the reduction must not, it is said, be expected to go so far as it would have gone if 32 new unions had not been formed, inasmuch as a certain amount of establishment charges must be incurred to maintain the new workhouses, and the necessary staff of officers, in whatever degree the pauperism of the districts in which they are built may hereafter be found diminished."

The expected further reduction was again confirmed,

1853.
Amount of expenditure, and numbers relieved.

the expenditure on relief of the poor during the year ending on the 29th September 1853, being 785,718l., or nearly 100,000l. less than in the previous year. The number relieved in the 163 workhouses was 79,600, and the total number so relieved during the year was 396,436. The number receiving out-door relief was 2,245, and the total number who received out-door relief during the year was 13,232— and now also, important as the reductions which have latterly taken place assuredly are, we are again told that still further reductions may be looked for.[y]

---

[x] Ante, p. 387.

[y] Such in fact took place, the expenditure on relief of the poor for the year 1854 being 760,152l., and for 1855 being still further reduced to 685,259l.

A tabular statement[z] has been given of the annual expenditure and the numbers relieved, down to the end of 1846, after which time the date of the returns was altered to correspond with the half-yearly audits in April and September. The following is a continuation of the statement before given, but also including the number of persons who were relieved out of the workhouse in the successive years under the provisions of the Extension Act—

The year ending Sept. 29.	No. of unions in operation.	Expenditure during the year.	No. in the workhouses on the 29th Sept.	Total no. relieved in the workhouses during the year.	No. receiving out-relief on the 29th Sept.	Total no. who received out-relief during the year.
1847	130	£ 803,684	86,376	417,139	—	—
1848	131	1,732,597	124,003	610,463	207,683	1,433,042
1849	..	2,177,651	141,030	932,284	135,019	1,210,482
1850	163	1,430,108	155,173	805,702	2,938	368,565
1851	..	1,141,647	140,031	707,443	3,160	47,914
1852	..	883,267	111,515	504,864	2,528	14,911
1853	..	785,718	79,600[a]	396,436	2,245[a]	13,232

This table speaks at once to the eye, and by its ascending and its descending numbers indicates the circumstances of the period to which they severally refer. But in addition to the expenditure in the third column, it must not be overlooked that since the passing of the Consolidated Debts Act[b] in 1850, a considerably larger amount of rates has been collected than was required for the immediate relief of the poor. Thus the amount collected in the year ending in September 1853 was 1,000,312*l.*, whereas the expenditure on relief was only 781,523*l.*, the remainder being applied in payment of the consolidated annuities, and in defraying expenses incurred under the Medical Charities Act. At present, it is said, out of 357,858*l.* the entire amount of the two

---

[z] Ante, p. 323.
[a] The number in the workhouses on the 29th September 1854 was 66,506, and at the same date in 1855 it was 56,546.—The number receiving out-door relief on these days respectively was 926 and 655.
[b] Ante, p. 374.

annuities payable in 1852 and 1853, only 28,768*l.* remains unpaid; and the advances made on security of the Rate-in-aid have been wholly repaid, with the exception of a trifling sum due on certain newly arranged townlands.   But it is expected that in a short time "all the exceptional charges on the poor-rates will cease, and that thenceforward the rates will be exclusively applied to the relief of the poor, and the support of the medical charities."

Notwithstanding the general improvement, and the reduction of expenditure which has been shown to have taken place, assistance was still required by some of the western unions, and the government consented to an advance of 30,000*l.* being made to eleven of them,[c] to pay their debts and relieve them from financial embarrassments; but this was done however, on the express condition that they "should not expect further assistance, and should make rates to the satisfaction of the Poor Law Commissioners, to meet their immediate and future wants."   The condition and the assistance were alike well timed and judicious, and secured the objects for which they were intended.

Further advance to the impoverished unions.

The cost of subsistence in the workhouse, may be considered to afford a fair criterion for judging of what is required for the subsistence of the labouring classes generally, there being in fact little difference between the food usually consumed by the peasantry, and that supplied to the inmates of the workhouses.   The average weekly cost per head is ascertained half-yearly, when the union accounts are audited in March and September, and the following table shows the results on these occasions from 1847 downwards [d]—

Average cost of maintenance.

---

[c] These were Cahirciveen, Dingle, Kenmare, Kilrush, Killadysert, Ennistymon, Scariff, Tulla, Clifden, Newport, and Oughterard.

[d] The returns for 1850 were not completed, in consequence of the alterations which were then being made in the number and the boundaries of the unions.

Half-year ending	Average weekly cost of provisions and necessaries.	Average weekly cost of clothing.	Total.
	s. d.	d.	s. d.
1847. 25th March	2 1	3½	2 4½
29th September	2 1½	3	2 4½
1848. 25th March	1 7	3¼	1 10¼
29th September	1 5	3¼	1 8¼
1849. 25th March	1 4½	3¼	1 7½
29th September	1 2¾	3	1 5¾
1851. 25th March	1 0½	2½	1 3
29th September	1 0	2¼	1 2½
1852. 25th March	1 0½	2	1 2½
29th September	1 0½	1½	1 2
1853. 25th March	1 1¾	1¾	1 3½
29th September	1 2½	1½	1 4
1854. Week ended 22nd April[e]	1 9	..	..

In April 1854, we see there was a large increase in the cost of workhouse maintenance, arising no doubt from the increase which had taken place in the prices of provisions. This increase would bear hard upon the labouring classes, unless there were a somewhat proportionate increase in wages. To obtain information on this point, the Poor Law Commissioners caused inquiry to be made by the inspectors in their several districts; and we find it stated as the combined result of their Reports—"that there is now[f] observable a material increase in the money value of agricultural labour, to the extent of about 1*s.* per week on the average throughout Ireland." It appears also, that agricultural employment was more continuous than formerly, and that in most parts of the country the wages of artizans had improved in a still greater ratio than those of common labourers. Unless there were some advance in the price of labour, it is probable that the great increase in the price of provisions would cause an increase in the numbers applying for relief, which

Cost of subsistence and rate of wages.

[e] The average for the half-year ending 25th March 1854, was 1*s.* 7½*d.*, and for the half-year ending 29th September it was 1*s.* 8½*d.* per head. For each of the corresponding periods in 1855, the average was 1*s.* 10¼*d.*

[f] That is on the 1st May 1854.

does not appear to have occurred; and this may be regarded as a further proof, that on the whole the rate of
wages had about kept pace with the increased cost of
subsistence.

Certain changes took place in the Poor Law execu-

Changes in tive in 1852, which it is necessary to notice.
the poor-
law execu- Mr. Ball resigned the office of Poor Law Com-
tive.
missioner, and was succeeded by Mr. Senior.
The temporary inspectors were all discontinued. The
number of these officers in 1847, on the passing of
the Extension Act, was 48; but they had been subsequently reduced to 11, and of these 4 were now
discontinued, and the remaining 7 were placed on the
permanent staff, making the number of inspectors 16,
each having the charge of a larger or smaller number of
unions according to the circumstances of the district.

A new order of accounts adapted to the alterations

New order made in the law had been completed, and was
of accounts. issued in April of the present year; and the
commissioners remark in their Report that "the administration of relief to the destitute poor in Ireland, may
be now looked upon as nearly identical with its normal
state, as originally contemplated on the passing of the
Act 1st and 2nd Vict. cap. 56. Such a result could
hardly have been expected after the severe trials to
which the country had so recently been exposed, but it
was most satisfactory, and must be regarded as a proof
of the enduring soundness of the principle on which
that measure was founded.

I have now brought the narrative of the Irish Poor
Law, down to a period coincident with my histories of
the English and the Scottish Poor Laws; and here, as
originally intended, I should conclude. But in the
autumn of 1853 I again visited Ireland, and examined
many of the unions, chiefly in the south and the west,
in order to see and form my own judgment as to the
working of the law, and the condition of the people.
The results of what came under my own observation,

and of the inquiries which I was enabled to make, were embodied at the time in a letter to Lord John Russell, by whom the measure of Irish Poor Law had been originally introduced and carried through parliament, and who always took a lively interest in everything connected with it; and it now appears to me that I cannot do better than give the substance of that letter, written with all the facts and incidents fresh before me, as a fitting close to the statements contained in the present work. The letter is dated Dublin 16th September 1853, and omitting a short introduction is substantially as follows—

"Eleven years have passed since I quitted Ireland. In the interim the country has suffered from famine and pestilence, and the Poor Law has been subjected to a most severe trial. An examination of the present condition of the country and state of the law cannot therefore fail of being deeply interesting, and I should have been glad to have given more time to it, if other claims had permitted.

The author's letter to Lord John Russell, September 1853.

"The circumstance that now first arrests attention in passing through the country, is the comparatively small number of beggars. Formerly the roads were lined with them, and the traveller wherever he stopped was surrounded by clamorous miserable-looking solicitors of charity. This is now changed. Beggars are rarely seen on the roads, less frequently in the towns; and are not I think on the whole, more numerous than in England. The famine may have been partly the cause of this change, but another if not the chief cause is the workhouses, where the old the feeble the sick and infirm poor are now supported, as the law designed, and as sound policy required that they should be. The workhouses are entirely occupied by this description of paupers, and the very young—there are no able-bodied. The total number of inmates of all classes is now 84,000, which is about the number I estimated at the outset as requiring to be provided for. The cost of relief is moreover about the same as I then estimated that it would probably amount to; and it is not a little gratifying to find that our calculations in these respects are so far verified.

" The Poor Law appears to be now thoroughly naturalized in Ireland. Your lordship would have been delighted to have heard it spoken of as I have done, and that by persons who did not know me, and who praised it as having been the salvation of the country, exclaiming " what should we have done without it!"—Complaints of the expense are it is true sometimes heard, but these are directed rather against the inequality of the charge than against the general amount, some electoral divisions paying heavily, whilst others pay little or nothing, as is sometimes the case with English parishes.

" The changes which have been made, are not I think all of them improvements. Although the subdivision of a few of the unions might have been necessary, this as well as the subdivision of the districts of chargeability, has I fear been carried too far—it has added to the working friction, and swelled the aggregate charge.

" When settlement shall be abolished in England, and union rating established instead of parochial, as I trust will ere long be the case, we may hope to see a similar reform extended to Ireland, which would bring the law back nearly to what your lordship first proposed and carried through the house of commons; and most of the changes which were subsequently made, as well as some of those since added, have in my judgment served to detract from its simplicity, and tended to impede its effective operation.

" All the workhouses which I have seen are in good order and the buildings in perfect condition, and such also I am informed is the case with the others. It is not a little satisfactory to find this the case, after the complaints that were made of these buildings, which are now as much praised as they were at one time decried.

" The most pleasing circumstance connected with the workhouse is the state of the pauper children, who are there educated and trained up in habits of order cleanliness and industry, instead of being left as outcasts, with every likelihood of their becoming a burthen, and possibly a bane to the community. I wish you could have seen with me some of these workhouse schools, and witnessed the benefits they are conferring upon the country. In the rural districts there is little difficulty in getting the boys out to service as soon as they are of an age fit for it, and the girls likewise now generally obtain places, although not so readily; but in the large towns there is still a difficulty with these last, there being proportionally less employment for females in Ireland than in England. A considerable number of girls and young women have been assisted to emigrate within the last three years, and it is very desirable that others should be so assisted and sent out from such of the workhouses as are overstocked with this class of inmates.

" With respect to emigration, I think that it has been already carried farther than was desirable. There appears to be no excess of labourers anywhere, and now in the harvest season there is evidently a want of hands to do the work, and high wages are paid, as much in some instances as 2s. and 2s. 6d. a day; but this is only during the period of urgency. There is still a want of certain and continuous employment in Ireland, and the people do not rely upon regular daily labour as a means of support, although they are I think approximating to it; and the extensive emigration which has taken place, will no doubt help forward the change. The rage for emigrating however continues, although the occasion for it has ceased. It pervades every class, and is strongest with the best educated and most intelligent. I found this to be the case among the boys in the workhouse schools. The sharp active intelligent lads were all eager to emigrate. It was only the more dull feeble and inert who appeared content to remain at home. Yet I know of no country where labour can be applied with the certainty of a better return. Labour is here in fact the thing chiefly needed. It is impossible to pass through Ireland without seeing this, and lamenting the omission.

" It is encouraging to reflect however, that were there less room for improvement in this and other respects, there would be less incentive to exertion ; and when the rage for emigration which still prevails shall have subsided, as subside it will, we may with greater confidence expect that the energies and increased intelligence of the people will be turned to the improvement of their own country, in which they will assuredly find a rich reward, and in furtherance of which they will, in the Poor Law, have a valuable auxiliary."

Such were the impressions derived from what came within the limit of my own observation and inquiry, on again visiting Ireland in the autumn of 1853. That these impressions were not more favourable than the circumstances warranted, is proved by the progressive ameliorations which have since taken place, of the extent of which generally, the proceedings under the Poor Law may be regarded as an index ; and these have shown a continual reduction, both in expenditure and in the numbers relieved. The total cost of relief in the year ending 29th September 1855, including every item of charge, was no more than 685,259*l.* ; and the total number of persons relieved on that day was 57,201, of whom 655 (being exceptional cases) were relieved out of the workhouse.[g] This reduction in expenditure has moreover taken place, notwithstanding the greatly increased cost of maintenance in the workhouses as compared with what it was in 1850 and 1851,[h] making a dif-

---

[g] The weekly cost of the out-relief so given was 40*l.* 4*s.* 4*d.*
[h] Ante, p. 397.

ference on the whole of probably not less than 150,000*l.* ; so that but for this increase, the entire cost of relieving the poor in 1855 might perhaps not have exceeded half a million, and in the event of prices falling to their former level, and other circumstances proving favourable, it may hereafter possibly range at about that amount.

At present however the expenditure under the Irish Poor Law contrasts favourably with what is taking place under the English and Scottish laws—in Ireland it averages 2*s.* per head on the population, whilst in Scotland the average amounts to 4*s.*,[i] and in England to 5*s.* 6*d.* per head—or if we take the valuations in the three countries as a standard of comparison, it will appear that the expenditure on relief of the poor in Ireland amounts to 1*s.* 2½*d.*, in Scotland to 1*s.* 4*d.*, and in England to 1*s.* 5½*d.* in the pound. These comparisons are I think satisfactory, and it is encouraging also to find the commissioners declaring in their last Report,[k] that— " a material diminution of pauperism in Ireland is still going on "—and that—" the improvement in the rate of wages and the increased constancy of employment have not only been sustained, but have further advanced and acquired a still more permanent and healthy aspect." Emigration likewise, both spontaneous and that conducted at the expense of the poor-rates,[m] is considerably lessened, and seems likely ere long to be reduced within its natural limits.   The future therefore appears in every way hopeful for Ireland—may the Irish people on their part, not be wanting in due effort for securing the benefits of which there is at present so fair a promise !

---

[i] See the tenth Report of the board of supervision.

[k] The ninth, dated May 1st 1856.

[m] The amount expended from the poor-rates in 1855, to assist in the emigration of 830 poor persons from different unions, was 6,859*l.* In the previous year the amount had been 22,651*l.*, including 10,000*l.* from the rate in aid, to assist in the emigration of 1,500 young females from the workhouses in the south and west of Ireland.

TABLES OF THE NUMBERS RELIEVED IN AND OUT OF THE WORKHOUSE, WITH
THE EXTENT OF MORTALITY, ETC., REFERRED TO AT PAGE 389.

Numbers relieved in the work-houses in each of the weeks ending on the dates in the first column respectively; together with the number and the rate per 1,000 of the deaths.

Number of destitute persons relieved out of the workhouses under the 1st and 2nd sections of the Extension Act (10th and 11th Vict., cap. 31) respectively, in each of the weeks ending on the dates in the first column; together with the weekly cost of such relief.

Weeks ending	Total number in the workhouses.	Deaths in the week.	Rate per 1,000.	Weeks ending	Numbers relieved under Section 1 of Extension Act.	Numbers relieved under Section 2 of Extension Act.	Total.	Weekly cost of relief.
1846.								
4 April	50,861	159	3·0					
4 July	50,693	146	2·9					
7 Nov.	74,175	312	4·2					
1847.								
2 Jan.	98,762	1,206	12·2					
6 Mar.	115,645	2,590	22·0					
3 July	101,439	1,239	12·2					
4 Sept.	75,376	589	7·8					
13 Nov.	102,776	523	5·1					
1848.				**1848.**				£. s. d.
1 Jan.	117,568	1,362	11·6	5 Feb.	337,665	107,811	445,476	12,788 9 0
12 Feb.	135,467	1,316	9·7	4 Mar.	425,949	228,763	654,712	17,564 18 2
1 July	139,397	620	4·5	1 April	408,923	235,076	643,999	17,092 6 6
9 Sept.	107,320	350	3·3	6 May	485,364	266,430	751,794	18,786 18 5
2 Dec.	172,980	787	4·5	1 July	490,902	342,987	833,889	21,800 14 10
				2 Sept.	279,567	96,523	376,090	10,335 14 5
				7 Oct.	192,401	7,202	199,603	5,925 4 2
				2 Dec.	246,125	31,859	277,984	7,845 12 10
1849.				**1849.**				
13 Jan.	191,445	1,477	7·7	6 Jan.	327,733	75,622	423,355	11,170 7 5
3 Mar.	196,523	1,846	9·4	3 Mar.	422,693	170,012	592,705	15,051 14 3
5 May	220,401	2,730	12·4	2 June	402,184	239,229	642,413	19,263 7 1
16 June	227,329	2,009	8·8	7 July	492,503	291,864	784,367	21,757 8 3
6 Oct.	140,266	488	3·5	1 Sept.	425,197	50,796	276,793	6,493 13 11
1 Dec.	180,641	471	2·7	13 Oct.	114,316	1,647	115,963	2,653 7 2
				3 Nov	102,247	13	102,260	2,336 11 11
1850.				**1850.**				
5 Jan.	203,320	792	3·9	5 Jan.	104,305	345	104,650	2,159 0 3
2 Feb.	230,348	994	4·3	23 Feb.	148,909	..	148,909	3,216 8 8
2 Mar.	237,939	1,150	4·8	1 June	127,727	128	127,855	2,805 9 2
4 May	243,224	1,247	5·1	3 Aug	73,129	40	73,169	1,617 7 5
22 June	264,048	1,126	4·3	14 Sept.	3,794	..	3,794	96 14 2
3 Aug.	219,231	808	3·7	19 Oct.	2,249	..	2,249	63 13 6
28 Sept.	155,173	526	3·4					
7 Dec.	191,341	501	2·6					
1851.				**1851.**				
4 Jan.	206,468	654	3·2	4 Jan.	2,713	6	2,719	76 14 0
22 Feb.	251,836	1,201	4·8	22 Feb.	9,103	20	9,123	229 4 6
22 Mar.	248,501	1,512	6·1	3 May	11,145	7	11,152	268 17 4
7 June	263,397	1,264	4·8	5 July	19,454	28	19,482	486 4 11
2 Aug.	222,038	789	3·6	4 Oct.	3,084	..	3,084	75 10 4
27 Sept.	140,458	386	2·8					
1852.				**1852.**				
3 Jan.	168,248	407	2·4	3 Jan.	3,170	..	3,170	88 6 3
21 Feb.	196,966	594	3·0	6 Mar.	3,396	..	3,396	100 0 10
5 June	187,003	541	2·9	3 July	3,579	..	3,579	102 19 0
18 Sept.	111,117	261	2·3	9 Oct.	2,491	1	2,492	74 1 3
25 Dec.	134,476	281	2·1	25 Dec.	2,998	..	2,998	87 12 10
1853.				**1853.**				
19 Feb.	160,774	627	3·9	26 Feb.	4,152	..	4,152	116 16 10
30 July	113,099	272	2·4	30 July	3,092	..	3,092	96 5 2
1 Oct.	79,410	202	2·5	8 Oct.	1,977	..	1,977	61 16 10

INDEX.